Exploring Rome: Piranesi and His Contemporaries

Exploring Rome: Piranesi and His Contemporaries

CATALOGUE BY CARA D. DENISON,
MYRA NAN ROSENFELD, AND STEPHANIE WILES

THE PIERPONT MORGAN LIBRARY
NEW YORK

CENTRE CANADIEN D'ARCHITECTURE/
CANADIAN CENTRE FOR ARCHITECTURE
MONTRÉAL

Distributed by The MIT Press, Cambridge, Massachusetts, and London, England

This catalogue accompanies an exhibition held at the Centre Canadien d'Architecture / Canadian Centre for Architecture, Montréal
17 August 1993–2 January 1994

Insurance for this exhibition has been provided by
the Department of Communications of Canada

Photography of the Morgan Library material is by David A. Loggie
Photography of the CCA material is by Alain Laforest, Michel Boulet, and François Bastien

Front cover illustration:
Piranesi, *Santa Maria del Priorato: Design for a Vertical Wall Panel* (Cat. no. 35)

Back cover illustration:
Piranesi, *Imaginary Tombs on the Via Appia* (Cat. no. 57)

Frontispiece:
Hubert Robert, *The South Façade of the Palazzo Poli with the Trevi Fountain under Construction* (Cat. no. 97).

© 1993 The Pierpont Morgan Library, New York
© 1993 Centre Canadien d'Architecture / Canadian Centre for Architecture, Montréal

Printed in the United States of America

Library of Congress Catalogue Card Number 93–084265
ISBN 0–262–54071-1 (MIT Press)
ISBN 0–87598–097–X (Morgan Library)

Contents

Foreword

The exhibition *Exploring Rome: Piranesi and His Contemporaries* is concerned with those eighteenth-century artists, architects, collectors, patrons, and antiquarians, who through their studies and investigations in Rome created and spread a new vision of antiquity that led to the establishment of neoclassicism. The critical figure in this activity was the Venetian-born draughtsman and printmaker Giovanni Battista Piranesi, who settled in Rome in 1740. The purpose of this exhibition is to explore the close associations Piranesi developed with contemporary Italian, French, and English artists, architects, and patrons. On the one hand these visitors had come to study the recent excavations at Herculaneum (1738) and Pompeii (1748), and on the other hand they became fascinated by the monuments of modern Rome.

The Morgan Library is fortunate in possessing the largest and most important group of Piranesi drawings in the world. The present exhibition of artists in Rome in the eighteenth century brings together many Piranesi drawings, books, and autographs. The exhibition centers around his drawing of the *Ruins at Pozzuoli*, two splendid renderings of the Temple of Isis at Pompeii, and the very dramatic *Architectural Fantasy*, showing a colossal, arcaded facade fronting a piazza with the Horse Tamers and other antique monuments. His inventiveness as a designer is brilliantly displayed in the series of drawings for mantelpieces, tables, candelabra, sconces, a clock, sedan chairs, a coach, and a gondola. Along with Piranesi's work is an important and fine group of French, Italian, and British drawings. The largest group of drawings shown by a French artist—those of Hubert Robert—includes depictions of ancient ruins and Renaissance monuments, as well as contemporary views of Rome, such as his splendid chalk drawing of the Trevi Fountain. Piranesi's influence is perhaps most apparent in Robert's brilliant pen and wash drawings in a sketchbook dating from his student days in Rome. Works by other artists associated with the French Academy in Rome, such as Jean-Honoré Fragonard, Charles Michel-Ange Challe, Louis-Jean Desprez, and Charles-Joseph Natoire, are also included. Drawings by British artists who spent time in Rome include works of Robert Adam and an Italian sketchbook by Richard Wilson.

Exploring Rome: Piranesi and His Contemporaries was originally presented at the Pierpont Morgan Library in New York from September 12 to November 6, 1989. Curated by Cara D. Denison, curator of drawings and prints, and Stephanie Wiles, associate curator of drawings and prints, it received critical acclaim from visitors, scholars, and the press. Nicholas Olsberg, chief curator of the CCA, and Myra Nan Rosenfeld, research curator, shared the public's enthusiasm and suggested that the CCA present a second showing in Montréal with the addition of works from the CCA's collection. We both eagerly accepted their proposal, and since no catalogue accompanied the New York showing, agreed to jointly produce this catalogue. The exhibition reflects the CCA's interest in the movement of ideas between architecture and other fields, between theoretical explorations and practical applications, and between different countries and cultures. Besides works from the collections of our two institutions, drawings have been borrowed from Trustees and Fellows of the Pierpont Morgan Library and a member of the Founder's Circle of the CCA. In this instance, the Library's own holdings have been enriched by generous loans from The Phillips Family Collection, Alice Steiner, Mr. and Mrs. Henry S. Tang, Mr. and Mrs. Eugene Victor Thaw, and two anonymous private collectors.

Because the CCA's collection complements that of the Pierpont Morgan Library so well, many key works not shown in New York have been added to the Montréal exhibition. The CCA has contributed several early etchings Piranesi executed when he first came to Rome: the views of Rome that he etched for the publications of Giuseppe Vasi and Giovanni Lorenzo Barbiellini; the small map of Rome designed by Giovanni Battista Nolli to which he added a border with *vedute*; and his second independently published work, *Le Antichità Romane de' Tempi della Repubblica*. From the CCA library comes a series of albums in their original eighteenth-century bindings that were owned by several contemporaries of James Caulfield, first earl of Charlemont, the Irish peer whom Piranesi sought to underwrite the publication of *Le Antichità Romane*. The CCA has also contributed works by artists and architects who influenced Piranesi or who were his contemporaries. Among these are Johann Fischer von Erlach's treatise on architecture, the illustrations of which Piranesi copied in several drawings now in the Pierpont Morgan Library; a stage set designed by Filippo Juvarra for the Teatro Capranica, Rome; etched views of St. Peter's designed by Giuseppe Vasi; and a view of Rome designed by Francesco Pannini and etched by Giovanni Volpato. The CCA's collection is particularly rich in works by the French artists and architects who studied at the French Academy in Rome. Included in the exhibition are drawings and etchings by Jean-Laurent Legeay, Louis-Joseph Le Lorrain, Charles De Wailly, Jean-Charles Delafosse, Gabriel-Pierre-Martin Dumont, Ennemond-Alexandre Petitot, and Thomas de Thomon.

The presentation of *Exploring Rome: Piranesi and His Contemporaries* in Montréal has been a very rewarding collaboration by our two institutions. Myra Nan Rosenfeld, the CCA's research curator, worked closely with Cara Denison and Stephanie Wiles on all phases of the preparation and presentation of the exhibition at the CCA. The original research that the three curators have undertaken for the catalogue will add new insights to the consideration of Piranesi's contribution and the role of Rome in the development of neoclassicism.

Phyllis Lambert
Director, Centre Canadien d'Architecture/
Canadian Centre for Architecture

Charles E. Pierce, Jr.
Director, The Pierpont Morgan Library

Acknowledgments

This exhibition has been a collaborative effort between the CCA and the Pierpont Morgan Library. We would like to thank the director of the CCA, Phyllis Lambert, for supporting the presentation of this exhibition at the CCA and providing the opportunity to discover many unexpected treasures in its collections. Charles E. Pierce, Jr., the director of the Morgan Library, was equally enthusiastic about the project and supported the request to lend the splendid drawings, books, and manuscripts from the Library's collections.

We are grateful to Elisabeth Kieven for her essay on Rome as well as the entries on the CCA's two drawings by Pietro Bracci. We wish to thank John Wilton-Ely for contributing the introductory essay on Piranesi. We also wish to thank Henry Millon, Christine Challingsworth, and Jean de Cayeux for writing the entries on the drawings by Filippo Juvarra and Charles-Louis Clérisseau in the CCA's collection as well as on the drawing by Hubert Robert in a private collection in Toronto. At the Morgan Library, Ruth S. Kraemer contributed several entries for the drawings and books in the Library's collection, and Felice Stampfle, the Library's curator emeritus of drawings and prints, generously read through the Piranesi entries, all of which owe a great debt to her scholarship.

The conservation departments in both institutions have been especially helpful. Thea Burns of Queen's University carried out the conservation of the CCA's drawings and prints. Marie Trottier shared her knowledge of eighteenth-century paper and bindings. Douwe Ernsting contributed bibliographic research. Patricia Reyes, Timothy Herstein, and Monica Lenci at the Morgan Library were responsible for the drawings from the Library and worked with the CCA to facilitate their transport. At the CCA, Nicholas Olsberg, chief curator, Gwendolyn Owens, assistant director, and the staffs of the following departments lent their assistance: the Library, Photographic Services, Prints and Drawings, Communications, Exhibitions, Technical Services and Design, the Registrar's Office, and Publications. Andrea Arthurs devotedly and unstintingly helped in every phase of this project, particularly with the preparation and editing of Myra Nan Rosenfeld's essay and entries.

Stephanie Wiles undertook the organization of the project in New York, coordinating efforts with the CCA. Peter Dreyer, curator in the Department of Drawings and Prints, was of invaluable assistance in deciphering inscriptions and reading through entries. Evelyn Phimister, assistant curator, willingly oversaw general departmental tasks while the catalogue was being written. Interns in the Department of Drawings and Prints helped with many aspects of the preparations: Michael Addiego, Charlotte Hayman, Elizabeth Horwitz, Patricia Meilman, Kathleen Stuart (who also assisted in the editorial process), and Peter Wojcik. Elizabeth Gemming translated Elisabeth Kieven's essay from the German. Jean de Cayeux's entries were translated from the French by Dr. Rosenfeld. Kathy Talalay was responsible for copy editing and proofreading a difficult and constantly changing manuscript, which she did with much intelligence and good humor. She was assisted by Moira Duggan. Elizabeth O'Keefe, head of cataloguing at the Morgan Library, organized and edited the bibliography. Other curators of the Library were generous with their time and expertise, including: Anna Lou Ashby, H. George Fletcher, Christine Nelson, Robert Parks, and William Voelkle. Kathleen Luhrs, Mimi Hollanda, and later Julianne Griffin of the Publications Department handled the production of the catalogue. The work of the Library's photographer David A. Loggie is evident throughout the catalogue, and Marilyn Palmeri, Nancy Schmugge, and Edward Sowinski of Photographic Services were extremely helpful with the preparation of the photographs. Inge Dupont, Stacey Berkheimer, and the staff of the Reading Room were cooperative in our research. D. W. Wright oversaw arrangements for insurance and transportation.

Scholars outside of the two institutions have been of great help with the catalogue. Pierre Rosenberg answered inquiries about the career of Louis-Joseph Le Lorrain. Marianne Roland Michel graciously read several of the entries and gave pertinent suggestions. Dr. Rosenfeld's research would not have been possible without the copy of Maurizio Calvesi's edition of Henri Focillon's catalogue of Piranesi that was provided by Caroline Backlund. Ulf Cederlöf kindly provided a photograph of the preparatory drawing for the CCA's gouache by Louis-Jean Desprez that he discovered in a private Swedish collection. Robert Little, besides providing moral support, put Dr. Rosenfeld in touch with David W. Howard, whose genealogical research on the owners of the CCA's albums was fundamental. Other colleagues who were generous with their expertise include E. Peters Bowron, Gail Davidson, Elaine Evans Dee, Eva Karlsson, Emmanuelle de Koenigswarter, George Knox, Hope Mayo, Thomas McCormick, Mary Myers, Allan Morrison, Monique Mosser, Helen B. Mules, Gabriel Naughton, Sheila O'Connell, John Pinto, Paul Quarrie, Andrew Robison, Alistair Rowen, Eliot W. Rowlands, Arlette Sérullaz, Marilyn Sims, Wilma Slaight, Regina Slatkin, Kim Sloan, Megan Smith, and Roberta Waddell.

Exploring Rome: An Introduction

CARA D. DENISON AND STEPHANIE WILES

A voyage to Italy has always been considered essential to the development of an artist. Rome in particular has often been the focus of an artist's study abroad and an important center for the exchange of creative ideas. Throughout the eighteenth century, Rome drew artists, collectors, connoisseurs, and tourists from all over Europe to study antique architecture and statuary, highly acclaimed masterpieces of the sixteenth century, as well as the city's contemporary art. The close associations formed among these travelers often led to extensive patronage of the arts, including excavations, negotiations concerning the purchase of antiquities, and commissioning of art works. It is these associations and interrelationships that this exhibition aims to illuminate and develop. The exhibition is not comprehensive but, rather, limited to the collections at the Morgan Library and the Canadian Centre for Architecture, with a few loans from collectors closely associated with both institutions. It originated and was first shown, without a catalogue, at the Morgan Library in 1989, where it was, as it still is, structured around the Library's strong holdings from the eighteenth century.

The important collection of drawings by the draughtsman and etcher Giovanni Battista Piranesi provided a natural framework for the scope of the exhibition. The Morgan Library owns a large group of Piranesi drawings from the collection of Mrs. J. P. Morgan, who died in 1925; this was presented to the Library in 1966 as the bequest of the late Junius S. Morgan and gift of Henry S. Morgan, her sons. Mrs. Morgan's collection of Piranesi material was first published in 1948 by Felice Stampfle, the Library's first curator of drawings and prints. The drawings range from early architectural fantasies and designs for decoration to those for architectural commissions. The inclusion of several Venetian period drawings was made not only to suggest the range of Piranesi's draughtsmanship but also to demonstrate how he drew on his early work after his arrival in Rome. Piranesi's archaeological activities, which can be studied in large-scale drawings of excavations such as the *Temple of Isis at Pompeii*, given to the Library by Mr. and Mrs. Eugene Victor Thaw, and the *Ruins at Pozzuoli*, reflected, and in turn promoted, the interest in careful firsthand investigation of ancient monuments—an important trend during the eighteenth century. This tendency is particularly evident in Piranesi's printed works; his novel approach can be appreciated in his *Antichità Romane* (see Cat. no. 57), where Piranesi included a greater spectrum of buildings than his predecessors, and placed them within landscape settings, often with the addition of figures. Although Piranesi trained as an architect he constructed almost nothing. Included in the exhibition, however, are drawings connected with two architectural commissions: four for the renovation of Santa Maria del Priorato, and three for the alteration of San Giovanni in Laterano.

Piranesi and other Italian artists, such as Giovanni Paolo Pannini, were closely associated with the French colony in Rome. The French drawings exhibited here demonstrate some of their numerous connections. The French Academy in Rome was founded in 1666 to offer young artists the opportunity to study abroad and to familiarize themselves with the monuments of Rome, classical sculpture, and the paintings of such masters as Raphael, Michelangelo, Carracci, and Domenichino. In the 1720s and 1730s—under the directorate of the Flemish-born painter Nicolas Vleughels—the painters Charles-Joseph Natoire, Louis-Gabriel Blanchet, and the sculptor Edme Bouchardon were students in Rome. In Piranesi's time, the Academy was directed first by Jean-François de Troy, from 1738 to 1751, and then by Natoire, from 1751 to 1775. Before the period of Natoire's directorate, Piranesi had known French artists, including Charles Michel-Ange Challe, who studied at the Academy between 1742 and 1749, and the architect Charles-Louis Clérisseau.

Natoire reported to the marquis de Marigny, director of the king's buildings in Paris, who was responsible to the king for the academies in both Paris and Rome. Like Vleughels before him, Natoire encouraged the study of landscape draughtsmanship, and often led sketching parties to the beautiful villas and parks outside the city. During this period the Academy was located in the Palazzo Mancini (now the Banco di Sicilia) just across the Corso from Piranesi's studio, affording the *pensionnaires* an excellent opportunity to associate with him. The great baroque view painter Pannini, who taught perspective at the French Academy, also influenced Piranesi, as well as other *pensionnaires*. Pannini had an especially great impact on the youthful Hubert Robert, whose watercolors occasionally resemble his. Robert had a lifelong fascination with Roman antiquities, and was sometimes referred to as *Robert des Ruines*. In fact, he was one of the first trained draughtsmen to record accurately the appearance of the newly excavated ruins at Paestum and near Pozzuoli in 1760. The French, who were in the vanguard of appreciating and studying the Greek ruins in Italy, were probably to a degree an influence on Piranesi. Although Piranesi's antiquarian interests are well known—it is reported that he visited the excavations at Herculaneum in the early 1740s—he seems not to have described them until the late 1770s.

Cultivated Englishmen and artists also participated in the tour of Italy that culminated in Rome. Only a small group of British drawings and books are exhibited here but they are a good indicator for the multifaceted role played by the British colony in Rome, as well as the connections that developed among the British, the Italians, and the French. While in Italy, the Scottish architect Robert Adam met Charles-Louis Clérisseau, who became his teacher and companion. Adam described expeditions made in the company of Piranesi, Clérisseau, and Laurent Pécheux (who instructed Adam in figure drawing), referring to them as his "three friends cronys and Instructors." Piranesi and Clérisseau became particularly close to Robert Adam, Piranesi dedicating the *Campus Martius* to Adam and Clérisseau working with him on the *Ruins of the Palace of the Emperor Diocletian at Spalatro in Dalmatia.* Piranesi's application of antique motifs to contemporary design had a profound effect on Adam's later neoclassical works. The influence that French art exerted on British painters who visited Rome at this time is an interesting question, and it has been suggested that Richard Wilson's sensitive use of black and white chalk on gray-green or gray-blue paper may have been the result of his contact with French artists such as Louis-Gabriel Blanchet (see Cat. no. 81) who worked in Rome during the 1750s. Blanchet in particular employed this technique to great effect. Wilson's pupil Thomas Jones saw the Italian landscape through his master's eyes, but his use of watercolor places his work in the mainstream of English landscape drawings of the period.

The significance attached to the study of antiquity was common to nearly all of the artists included in the exhibition. Although interest in the antique increased and developed in different ways during the second half of the eighteenth century—primarily because of the excavations at Herculaneum (begun in 1737) and at Pompeii (begun in 1748)—its importance as a source of inspiration for artists had been established early in the seventeenth century by Poussin, and the study of antiquities was subsequently adopted in the program of the Académie Royale. In 1722, the Richardsons produced the first modern work to emphasize the significance of antique sculpture that was no longer extant. Their book discussed the problems of authenticity in relation to surviving antique versions of the same sculpture, concluding that all surviving versions were probably copies of lost originals (see Cat. no. 75). The publications and autograph material included in the exhibition not only provide some indication of the role played by artists in the connoisseurship, excavation, and sale of antiquities, but they also shed light on other topics predominant throughout the eighteenth century. The artist and dealer Thomas Jenkins, for example, portrayed in a drawing by his friend Wilson (Cat. no. 68), collaborated with Piranesi and Gavin Hamilton in the restoration and sale of antiquities. In Rome, Jenkins was closely associated with Pope Clement XIV, and his knowledge of antique sculpture, coins, and gems was said to be respected by Cardinal Albani and Johann Joachim Winckelmann. The celebrated Warwick Vase is drawn at the top of a letter Piranesi wrote to Charles Townley, who had embarked on his Grand Tour in 1767 (Cat. no. 65). Townley went into partnership with Thomas Jenkins, and supported the excavations undertaken by Gavin Hamilton, who excavated the Warwick Vase at Patanello near Hadrian's Villa in 1771.

Piranesi was the leading advocate for Roman architecture, while the German theorist Johann Joachim Winckelmann championed Greek art. The French too were intensely involved in the Graeco-Roman debate. A letter from Piranesi to the marquis de Marigny explains why he felt compelled to write *Della Magnificenza* as a defense of Roman architecture (Cat. no. 59). At the top of the first page of Piranesi's letter, Marigny has added a note on the artist's championing the Romans, observing that Piranesi could hardly persuade him that the Romans had not borrowed anything from Greek architecture. Similarly, the comte de Caylus, in his *Recueil d'antiquités égyptiennes, étrusques, grecques et romaines*, published between 1752 and 1767 (Cat. no. 116), describes Greek art as perfection and Roman antiquities as derivative. In the *Recueil*, Caylus came close to establishing the basic principles of a history of art and was perhaps the most important forerunner of Winckelmann.

The lavishly illustrated and beautifully printed books produced during the second half of the century set these works apart from those produced by an earlier generation of connoisseurs and antiquarians. Sir William Hamilton's *Collection of Etruscan, Greek, and Roman Antiquities* (Cat. no. 78), for example, was an elaborate compilation. Following the preface by D'Hancarville, the plate section maintained the same layout throughout: an etching of a vase in perspective, its elevation with measurements, all interleaved with colored antique figural scenes etched in two plates. This type of two-plate process using terracotta and black ink to depict the vases also appears in vignettes in volume II of the Abbé de Saint-Non's *Voyage pittoresque* (Cat. no. 124). Indeed, the abbé refers to Hamilton's prospectus in the avant-propos to this volume, although he does not specifically mention the complete Hamilton publication. Books like these were often beautifully bound, further indication that careful planning and presentation of their outward appearance was integral to the conception of the book as a whole. Another outstanding example of this is the neoclassical binding on the Library's copy of Robert Adam's *Ruins of the Palace of the Emperor Diocletian at Spalatro in Dalmatia* (Cat. no. 77). The labor-intensive production of books like these, including the work of an illustrator, papermaker, engraver, printer, and binder, contributed to the enormous cost of production, and both Hamilton and the abbé frequently commented on the heavy financial burden placed on them.

Books from the mid- to late-eighteenth century also emphasized careful, firsthand investigation and measurement of ancient monuments. This was combined with a new movement that extended the field of study to include southern Italy, Greece, and Asia Minor. As Fritz Saxl has pointed out, these later archaeological studies differed from the earlier ones that had used Desgodetz's *Edifices antiques de Rome* (1682) as the authority on accurate ancient detail. Desgodetz's text had consulted classical ones for the reconstruction of ancient buildings. One notable publication of this type was Robert Adam's *Ruins of the Palace of the Emperor Diocletian at Spalatro in Dalmatia* of 1764 (Cat. no. 77). Adam and his entourage spent five weeks drawing and measuring the ruins at Spalato (Split). His work was meant to rival James Stuart's and Nicholas Revett's *The Antiquities of Athens*. The interest in Greek culture in southern Italy was stimulated by publications such as Thomas Major's *The Ruins of Paestum*, published in London in 1767, and culminated with Piranesi's work on Paestum, which appeared in 1778 (Cat. no. 66). Sir William Hamilton's *Antiquities* was also influential in stimulating an interest in Greek culture in southern Italy. His work is dedicated as much to connoisseurship of antiquities as it is to describing and reproducing them in as much detail as possible for artists to copy them accurately. Like Piranesi in his *Diverse maniere*, Hamilton intended the book to serve both as an inspiration and influence to artists. He made particular reference to Wedgwood to whom proofs of some of the plates were sent.

The present exhibition could never have been mounted at the Library and the CCA without the strong concentration of the Library's eighteenth-century Roman holdings, the breadth and depth of which can be seen only in small measure here. All members of the Morgan family were fascinated by Rome, and collected drawings, books, and autograph materials connected with that city. In terms of this exhibition, the collections of Mrs. J. P. Morgan (d. 1925) are most important. Her knowledge and keen interest in architecture and gardens resulted not only in great holdings of Piranesi but also in the acquisition of works by the neoclassical architect Robert Adam. This strong nucleus was built on by other donors, notably Paul Mellon, who gave his collection of travel books to the Library, and the late Gordon N. Ray, whose collection is particularly well known for its lavishly illustrated books. The Giannalisa Feltrinelli collection, on deposit at the Library since 1979, is another extremely important source for Roman publications from the eighteenth century. In addition, the drawing section of the exhibition was enriched by works borrowed from a small group of lenders closely associated with the Library.

Roman Architecture in the Time of Piranesi, 1740–1776

ELISABETH KIEVEN

When Piranesi saw Rome for the first time, in 1740, he was in a city whose face had greatly changed over the past ten years. During the pontificate of Pope Clement XII Corsini (1730–40), Rome had undergone a remarkably active period of urban development, in artistic as well as in economic terms.[1]

Between 1730 and 1737 the Quirinal underwent municipal reorganization, including the building of the papal stables, the enlargement of the Quirinal Palace, and the erection of the Palazzo della Consulta opposite the palace. The great competition for the facade of San Giovanni in Laterano had been held in 1732; the facade was built between 1733 and 1737. That same year the competition for the Trevi Fountain was held, the architecture for which was completed in 1740. During the same period, numerous new churches or church facades were erected, including Santa Maria dell'Orazione e Morte (Ferdinando Fuga, 1732–37), and San Giovanni dei Fiorentini (Alessandro Galilei, 1733–35) in the Via Giulia, SS. Celso e Giuliano (Carlo de Dominicis, 1732–36), and SS. Nome di Maria by Trajan's Forum (Carlo Antonio Derizet), which, in 1740, was still under construction.[2] Piranesi thus had the opportunity to experience firsthand many examples of modern architecture that would soon become the subjects of his *vedute*, and the young architect must have felt hopeful surrounded by so much building activity.

But his expectations were not to be fulfilled. The great plans of the Corsini pontificate had already been abandoned, scuttled in the economic and political aftermath of the War of the Polish Succession, which had broken out in 1733. During this period of turmoil, Don Carlos, the new grand duke of Parma and son of the king of Spain, marched through the papal states on his way to reclaim from the Hapsburgs the Kingdom of Naples, which the Spanish crown had lost in the War of the Spanish Succession. The papacy was ruined financially. His treasury empty, Pope Benedict XIV Lambertini, who was elected in 1740, could no longer finance the grand plans projected by his predecessors. Although the Trevi Fountain was completed to the point where it was functioning by 1743, the execution of its marble statuary was left until 1762.[3] A plan for the piazza of San Giovanni in Laterano that had been developed under Clement XII was not realized; only the old triclinium of the Lateran Palace—meant to be incorporated in an arcade surrounding the piazza in front of the basilica—was erected as a separate structure between 1741 and 1743.[4]

During the first decade of the pontificate of Benedict XIV, the focus of building activities was on restoration and projects that were absolutely necessary, for example, the expansion of the Ospedale Santo Spirito under Ferdinando Fuga (1742–44).[5] After 1750, construction sponsored by the papacy almost came to a standstill. Again, the reason was largely financial—a great number of papal building commissions had been made possible only through donations by the Portuguese king[6]—but the pope

The facade of Santa Maria Maggiore, constructed from 1741 to 1743 under Benedict XIV. Photograph by Wayne Anderson, courtesy of Alinari.

also seems to have lacked artistic vision. Benedict XIV's interests lay more in literature, church history, and the enlargement of the Capitoline collections.[7] In his eighteen-year pontificate, there was no artist that he especially favored or patronized. He did not insist on hiring artists of his choice for his commissions, nor did he attempt to force any of his wishes on the opposition within his entourage.

The first great building commission of his pontificate, the facade of Santa Maria Maggiore (1741–43), was awarded to the papal court architect, simply because he was also the architect of the chapter of the basilica, not because of any papal directive. Fuga, a Florentine by birth, had been appointed to the office of papal architect in 1730 by his compatriot Clement XII, against opposition. Similarly, the decision in 1732 to award the Lateran facade to the architect of the Corsini family, Alessandro Galilei, was made in the face of bitter opposition from the Roman architectural establishment. The situation was entirely different under Benedict XIV. In both the construction of the facade of his former titular church, Santa Croce in Gerusalemme (1743), by the architect Domenico Gregorini[8] and of the Jesuit church San Apollinare (1742–47) by Ferdinando Fuga, the pope provided the money but left the selection of the architect to those in charge of the building. This naturally led to rivalries. The San Apollinare commission, full of intrigue, is a textbook case of the Roman system of patronage.[9] Cardinal Acquaviva, who was for Fuga, and Alessandro Albani, who favored his architect, Carlo Marchionni, engaged in bitter disputes over the head of the church's rector, with Acquaviva the eventual victor.

The young Venetian Piranesi had absolutely no chance to work as an architect in this milieu without the patronage of an influential cardinal. Significantly, only after the death of Benedict XIV and the election of the Venetian Pope Clement XIII Rezzonico was Piranesi able to receive architectural commissions.[10]

The facade of Santa Croce constructed between 1742 and 1744. Photograph by Wayne Anderson, courtesy of Alinari.

In the foreword to the *Prima parte* of 1743, Piranesi mentioned that it was through the building contractor Nicola Giobbe that he made the acquaintance of the Roman architects Nicola Salvi (1697–1751)[11] and Luigi Vanvitelli (1700–76),[12] "due chiarissimi Architetti dell'eta nostra (two most excellent architects of our time)." Both men belonged to that group of young architects sponsored by Clement XII, though neither was part of the Florentine clique. Piranesi's reference to the "insigni opere" of the two, the Trevi Fountain and the military hospital in Ancona, begun by Vanvitelli in 1733, gives an indication of his own taste in contemporary architecture. Interestingly, he makes no mention of Ferdinando Fuga, the busiest Roman architect of the time. Salvi and Vanvitelli, longtime friends who became business partners in 1744, advocated in their designs the *gusto antico*–that is, the deliberate borrowing of elements from the Renaissance and High Baroque. Elegance and restraint in overall form are as characteristic as the retention of hierarchical articulation. The achievements of the sixteenth and seventeenth centuries are carefully integrated, though not to the point of eclecticism. Firm, clear contours dominate; meticulously harmonized decoration is coordinated with the basic underlying principles of construction. The buildings have an air of serene grandeur. In addition to the Trevi Fountain, Vanvitelli's headquarters of the Augustinians at San Agostino (erected 1746–51) embodies the same approach. Both Salvi and Vanvitelli followed the formula proposed by Filippo Juvarra in 1725: to combine the "sodezza dell'arte secondo l'insegnamento di Vitruvio e Palladio (the firmess according to what Vitruvio and Palladio taught)" and the "ornati (ornament)," that is, however, to be installed "con sobrieta (with modesty)," and "ho procurate a tutto mio potere d'imitare in questo lo stile de cavaliere Borromini (I have tried as far as I could to imitate in this the style of the cavalier Borromini)."[13]

This grand style was in direct contrast to the *Barochetto*, the rococo building style favored by the

Vanvitelli, San Agostino (1746–51). Photograph courtesy of the Conway Library, Courtauld Institute of Art, London.

nobility and the upper-middle class.[14] This contrast became especially pronounced during the pontificate of Clement XII. His nephew, Cardinal Neri Corsini, then responsible for major papal commissions, attempted to initiate a more enlightened artistic reform in the spirit of a "new Renaissance," exemplified in the Cappella Corsini in the Lateran (1732) and the facade of the Lateran basilica.[15] Neri Corsini carried out Salvi's monumental Trevi project and forced Ferdinando Fuga to maintain stylistic restraint.[16]

The pope's lack of artistic direction in the 1740s led to the coexistence of divergent architectural tendencies. In Rome every approach was represented. In the construction of new apartment houses, rococo motifs, influenced by Borromini's ornamentation, prevailed.[17] The most prominent example of this was the 1741 addition to the Palazzo Doria Pamphili by Paulo Amelj.[18] The same tendency appears in the churches built for the religious congregations (SS. Trinità degli Spagnoli in the Via Condotti [1741–44] by Emanuele Rodriguez Dos Santos;[19] SS. Quaranta [1744–47] by Giuseppe Sardi;[20] and SS. Bonificio ed Alessio [1746–50] by Tomasso De Marchis).[21] The papal basilicas of Santa Maria Maggiore and Santa Croce, however, are based on models of the High Baroque. Traditional architectural forms prevail in buildings such as the small coffeehouse in the garden of the Quirinal designed for Benedict XIV by Ferdinando Fuga (1741–43)[22] and in the Palazzo Corsini, also by Fuga (1737–56).[23]

Significantly, a return to the High Baroque is evident in the first two monumental buildings erected under Benedict XIV, the facades of Santa Maria Maggiore (1741–43) and Santa Croce (1742–44). Both designs draw inspiration from Andrea Pozzo's *Prospettiva*, published in 1702. In the case of Santa Maria Maggiore there are strong light-and-dark effects and loose contours. In Santa Croce, the facade has the convex-concave movement that was strongly disapproved of under the Corsini pope. The energetic debate over "true architecture" brought about by the Lateran competition of 1732,[24] with its demand for straight lines, right angles, and subordinated, subdued ornamentation, seems to have had no impact. The major restoration work on Santa Maria Maggiore (1746–50) and Santa Maria degli Angeli (1748–50), undertaken for the jubilee year 1750, is undistinguished. Ferdinando Fuga adjusted the columns of the central aisle of Santa Maria Maggiore, made the walls of the side aisles symmetrical, and designed a new high altar.[25] His pragmatic restraint was apparently requested, but the result is uninteresting. Vanvitelli too was busy with the alteration of Santa Maria degli Angeli, working toward a symmetrical regularizing of the interior.[26] Michelangelo, in his restoration of the Baths of Diocletian (1561),[27] had left the essential form of the building exactly as he had found it. Vanvitelli had in mind greater coherence for the interior. He backed the monumental, freestanding columns with pilasters, installed additional columns, and added a unifying entablature. In this way Vanvitelli tried to alleviate the isolation of the columns, in contrast to Michelangelo, and to come to a balance between the vertical and horizontal elements of the structure. This sense for systematic order and organization, typical of the settecento, diminishes the impression of monumental space to some extent. The interior of Santa Maria degli Angeli would have created a much more theatrical effect had Vanvitelli been permitted (as he actually wished) to open up the walls to the adjacent rooms. The charming possibility of changing vistas through these alternately opening and closing *Anraeume* would surely have interested Piranesi as well.[28]

Interior of Santa Maria degli Angeli. Photography by Wayne Anderson, courtesy of Alinari.

Vanvitelli's remodeling of Santa Maria degli Angeli represents, along with the facades of the two papal basilicas of Santa Maria Maggiore and Santa Croce, the most striking addition to public architecture in Rome during the 1740s. Its anti-progressive character stands in conspicuous contrast to the contemporary plans of young architects of the French Academy in Rome for the annual celebration of the investiture of the Kingdom of Naples by the pope, the so-called *Chinea* (in which John Harris identified the first manifestations of neoclassicism).[29]

While Vanvitelli's influence on Piranesi has been investigated,[30] the role of Nicola Salvi, the most important and influential architect in Rome in the 1740s, has not yet received sufficient attention. Salvi can be called the great theoretician of the Roman architectural scene. He left a decisive mark on Vanvitelli.[31] Salvi's achievement influenced not only his Italian colleagues but also, decisively, Soufflot, William Chambers, and Robert Adam.[32] Only the Trevi Fountain and the small Capella Ruffo in San Lorenzo in Damaso remain of Salvi's work in Rome.[33] His career was overshadowed by a serious illness that made it impossible for him to work after 1746. His achievement presents a fusion of cinquecento elements, from Michelangelo and Vignola, with the legacy of Bernini. It is architecture in the spirit of the *Arcadia*, pervaded by reminders of the greatness of Roman tradition and the myth of *Roma aeterna*. Salvi's extraordinary knowledge and comprehension of the buildings and theories of the Roman past never entered his own works as a mere collection of "quotations" but provided an organic, harmonious, and new interpretation of an old tradition. This creative interaction with a great cultural heritage was always appropriate in its expression, logical in its execution, and functional. "Serietà, proprietà, profondità" are key concepts in the inception of his theoretical principles. At the start of the 1740s, Salvi was intensely interested in the architecture of the Renaissance: influences drawn from buildings by Vignola appear in his small church for the Villa Bolognetti on the Via Nomentana.[34] Through Salvi's designs and architecture, Piranesi was able to sharpen his awareness of what was noble and magnificent and gain a sense for the sublime in the architectural tradition of Rome. As in Piranesi's later Lateran designs, there is postulated in Salvi's plans and works the whole of Roman history, the consonance of antiquity, the Renaissance, and the baroque.

The death of Salvi in 1751 and the departure for Naples in 1750 of Fuga and Vanvitelli (who saw no professional future for themselves in Rome) impoverished the architectural scene in the city. It is noteworthy that buildings erected beginning in the 1740s, with the exception of Salvi's, were scarcely recorded in the drawings of foreign architects visiting Rome. Modern Roman architecture had lost its role as a model. Then, the architects Paolo Posi (1708–76) and Carlo Marchionni (1702–86)[35] assumed leading positions. Posi, known mainly for his *Chinea* and other sketches for festival decoration,[36] was called "talento grande senza buona Architettura" by Milizia,[37] who did not even mention Marchionni.

Posi's name is associated primarily with the restoration of the Pantheon,[38] carried out from 1756 to 1758, which "systematized" in the modern sense the ancient upper story by means of a regular series of niches.[39] This so-called beautification, carried out against bitter opposition from scholars such as Monsignore Giovanni Gaetano Battari, seems almost incredible in view of the then growing appreciation for antique buildings. In fact it indicates the lack of vision and the absence of an influential

Piranesi sketch for the alteration of the upper story of the Pantheon. Vatican Library, 3439, 179r.

or leading personality within the arts. Interestingly, a hitherto unknown sketch by Piranesi also takes for its subject the alteration of the upper story.[40] Piranesi's point of departure is the same as that in Posi's plan: to regularize the irregular attic level so that the niches of that level would always be articulated in relation to the aedicule and/or the central columniation of the grand order below. Contrary to Posi, however, Piranesi focused more keenly on the relationship between the upper and lower levels. In Piranesi's drawing there appears over the three-bay intercolumniations, which screen the lower chapel, a section divided into three parts, while a gabled niche corresponds to the lower aedicular bay. This rhythmic but not schematic pattern is executed through complex ornamental surfaces. What Piranesi had in mind here is *imitazione*—a creative association with the legacy of the past, not a copy in the sense of a mere mechanical borrowing. Whether Piranesi's design actually presents an alternative to Posi's plan is questionable. The importance of this drawing, which relates to an existing structure, is that it exemplifies the kind of creative imagination advocated by Monsignore Bottari, Piranesi's patron, as the antidote to the barrenness in contemporary art.[41]

Such complex systems of ornamentation are found in Carlo Marchionni's work too, though applied in a more superficial sense and therefore criticized by younger contemporaries.[42] Marchionni, however, was the architect of the only building from the period after 1750 that was regarded as exceptional even outside the city of Rome, the Villa Albani at the Porta Salaria. Its grounds had been enlarged in 1746 with land purchased by the art enthusiast Cardinal Alessandro Albani,[43] one of the greatest patrons of the eighteenth century. Marchionni had been in his employ since 1728. Construction

Villa Albani by Marchionni, photograph courtesy of Alinari.

began with an open semi-circular arcade of pillars. From 1755, the construction of the casino opposite was undertaken. Cardinal Albani seems to have given precise pointers to Marchionni, for the design plans are recorded in contemporary sources as being the cardinal's own. Marchionni's charming casino–a narrow, elongated building with an open loggia on the ground floor, accented by regularly spaced pilasters–is entirely traditional in style. The Villa Albani derives its significance not from any innovative force of its architectural vocabulary but as a whole in which an evocation of an ancient villa is offered to the settecento. Embedded in the landscape, the villa melds nature, antique statuary, and architecture into a whole, and its magic and refinement are reflected in the comments of visitors and the enchanting drawings of Carlo Marchionni.[44]

How far Piranesi may have been involved in the decoration of the interior is not certain.[45] The relationship between Marchionni, a brilliant draughtsman, and Piranesi still needs investigation. There were no obvious stylistic ties between the two men in their permanent buildings, but there are similarities in examples of their ephemeral festival designs. Marchionni's decorations for the vault of Santa Maria sopra Minerva, which he prepared for the occasion of the canonization of Santa Caterina de Ricci in November 1746, exhibit a similar intertwining of tendrils, shells, and rosettes–ornamental motifs that Piranesi was later to employ in his Lateran designs.[46] Above all, it should not be forgotten that, even though the architecture of the time seemed uninspired, in the area of festival decoration an inexhaustible inventiveness still prevailed. As fewer buildings were actually constructed, a greater emphasis was placed on refacing facades, decorating churches and palaces, and creating designs for great processions–the only public forum where an architect could still be innovative. Marchionni assumes a special position in this area with such exciting decorations as those for the obsequies of the Polish

Marchionni's sacristy of St. Peter's, begun in 1778. Photograph by Wayne Anderson, courtesy of Alinari.

king and the Elector of Saxony in San Salvatore in Lauro in 1764 and of King Carlo Emanuele of Savoy in 1773.[47] In their wealth of eccentric ideas they are closer to Piranesi than previously believed.

Marchionni was also the architect of one of the few major buildings to be realized after 1750. In 1776, as architect at St. Peter's, he planned the new sacristy of the basilica begun in 1778.[48] He was able, even in the face of the gigantic scale of St. Peter's, to design a building that, in its small proportions and high quality, makes a decided impact. But in its references to the old masters from Michelangelo to Bernini,[49] this respectable structure seems light years away from contemporary architectural trends. Roman creativity had exhausted itself.

Against this background of ever more obvious artistic stagnation, in the presence of a heritage that was becoming more of a burden and less of an inspiration, Piranesi's works endure as an earnest attempt to engage in a spirited dialogue with a great past.

1 Pastor 1928–39, vol. XV; Venturi "Gli anni trenta del Settecento," in Maturi 1966, pp. 89–153; Giuntella 1971; Wittkower 1973; Elling 1975.

2 Gaddi 1736; Campiglia 1739.

3 Pinto 1986, pp. 172–219.

4 Bianchi 1955, p. 11; Pane 1956, p. 100; For the project of the square, which is based on a design by Alessandro Galilei (1735–37), see Kieven.

5 Bianchi 1955, pp. 68–73; Pane 1956, pp. 100–104; Kieven 1986, pp 66–69.

6 For the extent that the pope was dependent on Portuguese donations, see Samoggia 1977, which Jennifer Montagu kindly pointed out to me.

7 For Benedict XIV, see Pastor 1928–39, vol. 16; also Rosa 1966, pp. 393–408. Cecchelli 1981–82.

8 Cardinal Aldrovandi, who was in charge of the building, gave the commission to Domenico Gregorini, who had previously worked with him. Varagnoli 1988, pp. 21–65.

9 Bösel and Garms 1981, pp. 335–84.

10 For a discussion of the architectural profession between 1680 and 1750, see Rome 1991.

11 Schiavo 1956; Pinto 1986; Rome 1991, pp. 65–87.

12 De Fusco 1973; Garms 1974.

13 Rovere, Viale, Brinckmann 1937, p. 81.

14 Mallory 1977.

15 Kieven 1989, pp. 69–91.

16 Kieven in Rome 1988, pp. 23–29.

17 The building of private residences in Rome in the eighteenth century had a greater impact on the appearance of the city than the public buildings; see Curcio 1989; Bevilacqua 1989; Mallory 1977.

18 Carandente 1975.

19 Tafuri 1964; Donò and Marino 1989.

20 Mallory 1977, pp. 53–75.

21 Bösel and Garms 1981, p. 355.

22 Matthiae 1952, pp. 39–40; Pane 1956, p. 94.

23 Kieven in Rome 1988, pp. 51–55; Borsellino 1988.

24 For a summary of the competition, see Rome 1991, pp. 78–123.

25 Matthiae 1952, pp. 29–38; Pane 1956, p. 92–94; Kieven in Rome 1988, p. 28, figs. 14–16.

26 De Fusco 1973, pp. 71–76; Bozzoni in Vanvitelli 1979, vol. 1, pp. 301–18.

27 Ackerman 1970, pp. 269–78: Santa Maria degli Angeli.

28 Giovanni Gaetano Bottari criticized Vanvitelli's remodeling sharply in his "*Dialoghi sopra i tre arti del disegno,*" Lucca, 1754. Vanvitelli's defense of his project is published in Vanvitelli 1976–77, vol. I, no. 298. See also Garms 1974. According to Vanvitelli the closing of the adjacent rooms had been decided upon before he started work.

29 Harris in Wittkower 1967, vol. II, pp. 189–91; Eriksen 1974.

30 Wilton-Ely in Vanvitelli 1979, vol. II, pp. 83–100; Cesare de Seta in Bettagno 1983.

31 For Salvi, see Schiavo 1956; Garms 1974; Pinto 1986; Rome 1991, pp. 65–87.

32 Harris 1970, p. 100.

33 For a survey of Salvi's buildings, see Schiavo 1956. Salvi's second masterpiece, the monumental Dominican church of Santa Maria dei Gradi in Viterbo (1737–47) was destroyed in 1944.

34 Schiavo 1956, pp. 233–37; Rome 1991, pp. 75–78.

35 Gaus 1967.

36 Kelly in Wisch and Munshower 1990, vol. VI, part I, pp. 581–620.

37 Milizia 1785, vol. II, p. 281.

38 Somewhat later, Posi's renovation served as an example for architects of how something should not be done (*Osservazioni di Antonio Visentini, Architetto Veneto che servono di continuazione as Trattato di teofilo Gallacini sopra gli Errori degle Architetti*, Venice, 1777).

39 For the precise dates and background information on the renovation, see Pasquali 1991.

40 Bibliotheca Apostolica Vaticana, Codex Ursinianus, vat. lat. 3429 f. 179. Black chalk, pen and brown ink, gray wash (340 x 256 mm). The sheet, inscribed *Autographum Balthassaris Petrucci ob ristaurationem Scenographiae Panthei apud Sebastianum Serlium,* was obviously pasted into the volume with drawings after the *Forma Urbis* by chance, because it was meant to date from the sixteenth century. See De Fine Licht 1968, fig. 134, where it is published without further comment.

41 Monferini in *Piranesi* 1979.

42 "*Marchionni…è di quelli del taglio di Pietro da Cortona, pieno do libertà e capricci, in somma é uno di quelli del vero gusto presente,*" argued the young Giacomo Quarenghi in 1776, Quarenghi 1988, p. 34.

43 For Albani, see Röttgen in Beck and Bol 1982.

44 Berliner 1958–59, pp. 267–396.

45 Gasparri 1985–86, pp. 211–24.

46 A sketch by Marchionni in the collection of the Fondazione Giorgio Cini in Venice is reproduced in Johnston 1971, fig. 28 (who attributed it to V. M. Bigari). Mary L. Myers (in New York 1975, no. 38) identified the drawing. Another unpublished drawing by Marchionni for the same occasion is in the Cooper-Hewitt Museum, New York 1938–88–7241. For a detailed description of the decoration, see "Distinta relazione della solenne processione seguit per il trasporto dello standardo di S. Caterini de Ricci …" in Rome, nella stamperia del Chracas, November 1748.

47 Marchionni's designs for this decoration were published by Berliner 1958–59, pp. 331–41.

48 See Gaus 1967, pp. 67–110.

49 Ibid., Kap VII, "Zur Ornamentik Marchionnis."

Giovanni Battista Piranesi

JOHN WILTON-ELY

Although Piranesi is widely recognized as the supreme exponent of topographical engraving, his life-long preoccupation with the discipline of architecture—past and present—was fundamental to his protean genius. Despite his few design works, he exercised a highly seminal influence on European neo-classicism through his personal contact with visiting artists, architects, and patrons in Rome over the course of nearly four decades. His prolific output of etched plates, which on occasion combined remarkable flights of imagination with a strongly practical understanding of ancient technology, generated a perception of antiquity lasting to our own time. Not only a *vedutista* and archaeologist, Piranesi was also a designer of festival structures and stage sets, interior schemes and furniture, as well as a vigorous polemicist and an imaginative restorer of classical antiquities. The interaction of these rarely combined activities led him to highly original concepts of design that were advocated in a considerable body of theoretical writings and developed further by more singleminded practitioners, several of them represented in this exhibition. The ultimate legacy of Piranesi's unique vision of Roman civilization was an emotional projection of the past which has continued to inspire writers and poets as much as artists and designers.

Piranesi's origins in Venice, where he spent his first twenty years, were to prove of lasting significance for his later career. He was born on 4 October 1720 at Mogliano, near Mestre, the son of Angelo Piranesi, stonemason and master builder. Evidently destined for an architectural career, Giambattista was apprenticed to his maternal uncle, Matteo Lucchesi, a leading designer and hydraulic engineer in the *Magistrato delle Acque*, the organization responsible for the republic's elaborate harbors and sea defenses. After quarreling with Lucchesi, Piranesi continued his studies in the deeply rooted idiom of Palladian design in Venice under Giovanni Scalfurotto. He may well have been involved in the final stages of his new master's principal commission, the church of SS. Simeone e Giuda, built overlooking the Grand Canal between 1718 and 1738.

He acquired an early taste for controversy combined with archaeological inquiry in the Lucchesi circle with its vigorous debates over the Etruscans as the supposed founders of classical architecture. Equally stimulating were the provocative teachings of the Dominican priest Carlo Lodoli who challenged the entire validity of classical canons of architectural design. Furthermore, Piranesi may also have assisted Scalfurotto's nephew, the architect and theorist Tommaso Temanza, in a survey of the Roman arch and bridge at Rimini in 1735 for his book, *Antichità di Rimini*. This may have given the young Piranesi the sense of a future vocation.

In marked contrast to these utilitarian and theoretical exercises, Piranesi's remarkable imaginative faculties were also encouraged over these years. He was instructed in the science of stage design, then dominated by the Bibiena family and their followers in northern Italy, and mastered the elaborate systems of perspective composition under the engraver Carlo Zucchi. Moreover, the intensely urban nature of Venice itself provided a vital theater of architectural experiences which Piranesi was later to exploit in the topographical view, or *veduta*, an art form then being developed in the city by Heinz, Van Wittel, Carlevaris, and, above all, Canaletto. Certainly the most potent of these Venetian influences was the combination of baroque stage design and the elements of the topographical view within the architectural fantasy, or *capriccio*, perfected earlier in the century by Marco Ricci and soon to be developed stylistically in Canaletto's *vedute ideate*. The visual potential of the *capriccio*, however, was to realize its full impact on Piranesi's imagination when he first entered Rome in 1740, employed as a draughtsman in the retinue of the Venetian ambassador, Marco Foscarini.

Rome, already the goal of the "grand tourist," was then swiftly becoming the intellectual capital of Europe, and Piranesi was to encounter there the ferment of new ideas and the radical questioning of the past that characterized the Enlightenment. For an imaginative designer, however, these early experiences were as frustrating as they were exhilarating, since opportunities for new commissions in 1740 were at a particularly low ebb in Rome after a recent building boom, which had involved such leading architects as Fuga, Galilei, Salvi, and Vanvitelli. Since the general character of contemporary Roman architecture appears to have offered him little inspiration in any case, Piranesi chose for his means of livelihood the production of souvenir views for a market already being served by the painter Pannini and the Sicilian engraver Giuseppe Vasi. After acquiring the rudiments of etching under the latter, Piranesi, in collaboration with some young French artists, struck out on his own with a series of small *vedute* used for a succession of guidebooks over several decades, such as Ridolfo Venuti's *Accurata, e succinta descrizione topografica delle antichità di Roma* (1763). He eventually produced some fifty of these plates (the earliest brought together in 1743 under the title *Varie Vedute di Roma Antica e Moderna*). They range from his first tentative efforts to considerably sophisticated compositions.

Piranesi's principal creative energies, however, were concentrated on developing the architectural *capriccio*, both as a vehicle for formal experiment as well as a means of artistic release. He derived much inspiration from early attempts to reconstruct the monuments of antiquity by Ligorio, Montano, and Athanasius Kircher, as well as from Fisher von Erlach's more recent *Entwurff einer historischen Architectur* of 1721. In 1743 Piranesi published a selection of these visionary compositions in the thirteen etched plates of the *Prima Parte di architettura e prospettive*. As a clearly stated reproof to the mediocrity of the contemporary architectural profession, Piranesi already showed in these views of monumental structures and awesome ruins the chief ingredients of his own art—an unorthodox combination of superhuman scale, powerfully receding perspectives upon a diagonal axis, and the modulation of space by skilled lighting. This speculative activity soon brought him into contact with the circle of art and architectural students at the French Academy in Rome, then one of the liveliest centers of research in Europe, under the direction of Jean-François de Troy from 1738 to 1751 and, subsequently, Charles-Joseph Natoire, who was director from 1751 to 1775. Initially the influences were reciprocal, but soon Piranesi's bold conceptions, which put columnar forms and austere surfaces to powerful effect, began to stimulate the imagination of the *pensionnaires*. This is strikingly evident in the festival designs and fantasy compositions of Challe, Clérisseau, Legeay, and Le Lorrain. With the subsequent dispersal of these young designers, Piranesi's innovative conceptions gradually entered the mainstream of European neoclassical architecture during the 1750s.

Sometime in the mid-1740s Piranesi traveled south to Naples, attracted by the exciting discoveries being gradually revealed at Herculaneum. These experiences, by establishing new horizons in the knowledge and interpretation of antiquity, seem to have prompted him to consider ways of presenting archaeological material in visually compelling ways. During the mid-1740s, however, financial difficulties had brought him back to Venice, where he is recorded as having produced interior designs for certain palaces. Some evidence of this activity may be represented within the unique group of exquisite rococo drawings in the Morgan Library, which also includes a scintillating study for a *bissona*, or festival gondola. Paralleling these drawings, a dramatic transformation in his etching style at this time clearly reflects the dominant influence of Tiepolo, especially in four arcane fantasies, the *Grotteschi*. Of far greater significance, however, were the unprecedented imaginative breadth and fluent technique of the fourteen unsigned plates of the *Prisons* (*Invenzioni Capric di Carceri*) that appeared after Piranesi returned to Rome around 1747 as agent for the Venetian printseller Joseph Wagner. These arcane and highly personal works—part Venetian, part Roman—provide a sequence of brilliant improvisations on a popular theme in contemporary theater design. They already show an extremely controlled discipline at work, exploiting the mechanics of the baroque stage design to open up new dimensions of architectural expression.

Now permanently established in his adopted city, Piranesi embarked on a lifelong mission to explore and record the Roman achievement in all its manifold aspects. By 1748 he had issued his first set of independent *vedute*, later entitled *Archi Trionfali*, in which he deployed within the compass of quite small plates the full dramatic range of perspective, lighting, and tone, in conjunction with an unrivaled understanding of ancient building science. Profiting from the dowry of his marriage in 1753 to Angela Pasquini, daughter of Prince Corsini's gardener, he now changed over completely to the larger format of plates, which he had already begun to use for his celebrated series, the *Vedute di Roma*. These 135 plates, issued individually or in groups throughout the rest of his career, were to reflect almost every phase in his stylistic evolution and intellectual progress.

Meanwhile, in fresh acts of speculative composition based on a detailed study of antique remains, Piranesi pioneered new approaches to design in a further series of etched fantasies. Among those collected together in the *Opere varie* of 1750, the *Monumental Roman Harbor* and *Plan for a Magnificent College* had an exceptionally powerful impression on the new generation of *pensionnaires*, which included De Wailly and Peyre, and may also have contributed to the education of the future marquis de Marigny, then on a study tour of Italy with Cochin and Soufflot.

Archaeology was becoming increasingly important to Piranesi by the early 1750s, a period in which he gradually relinquished his French contacts in favor of visiting British architects, such as William Chambers, Robert Adam, Robert Mylne, and George Dance, all of whom in varying degrees benefited from his stimulating interpretations of Roman antiquity. In due course the results of Piranesi's comprehensive antiquarian researches were presented in the four volumes of the *Antichità Romane* (1756), rapidly earning him an international reputation that was marked by his election to an Honorary Fellowship of the Society of Antiquaries of London a year later. This magisterial publication set out to provide an innovative system of archaeological inquiry for the education of contemporary designers and their patrons, as much as for conventional scholarship. Over two hundred and fifty images featured highly original methods of illustration, frequently combining a formidable quantity of data within a single plate with considerable visual impact. Piranesi showed a new concern with constructional techniques and the physical properties of materials, as well as the originality of planning forms and the sheer range of the Roman ornamental vocabulary. As never before, his intimate topographical knowledge (helped by his earlier collaboration with Giambattista Nolli on a reduction of the latter's *Pianta di Roma* of 1748) enabled him to coordinate many diverse and isolated remains within the broader context of Rome as an urban phenomenon with its interrelated defensive and hydraulic systems, using plans and cross-references to the substantial text.

Controversy began to dominate these activities increasingly over the decade. In 1757 Piranesi issued a witheringly critical pamphlet, *Lettere di giustificazione*, directed against the erring Irish patron of the *Antichità*, Lord Charlemont, who had failed to honor his promised financial support. Far more significantly, however, he was soon caught up in the opening exchanges of a fierce debate provoked by mounting claims for the superiority and originality of Greek art and architecture by Laugier, Le Roy, and, preeminently, Winckelmann. The latter had arrived in Rome in 1755 to act as librarian to the great collector and patron, Cardinal Alessandro Albani, in his villa outside the Porta Salaria. Not unsurprisingly, with this new stimulus the latest plates of the *Vedute di Roma* assumed a visual rhetoric as well as an increasing wealth of information that pushed Piranesi's techniques of etching and composition to new heights of expression. Preparatory figure studies from this time onward show Piranesi's humanity increasingly transformed into ciphers of dramatic energy within these heroic compositions.

After years of assiduous investigation supported by scholarly advice, Piranesi delivered his opening salvo in the Graeco-Roman controversy in 1761 with *Della Magnificenza ed architettura de' Romani*. This handsome folio, dedicated to the newly elected Venetian pope, Clement XIII, involved a particularly ingenious sequence of illustrations, backed up by a ponderously erudite text. Piranesi's principal thesis rested on the functional achievements of the Etruscans as a highly inventive race and as the original mentors of the Romans. This rationalistic defense, specifically aimed at Laugier and Le Roy, was uneasily combined with a celebration of the sheer decorative exuberance of late Roman imperial ornament, displayed on large foldout plates of architectural fragments.

This was followed during the 1760s by a sequence of equally lavish folios with a strongly polemical bias and largely sponsored by the pope and members of his family, the Rezzonicos. The *Lapides Capitolini* (1761) traced the extent and complexity of Rome's early history through inscriptions and sculptural remains. The hydraulic science behind the city's aqueducts was reconstructed with ingenious technical diagrams in the *Rovine del Castello dell'Acqua Giulia* (1761), and a similar approach, based on particularly exhaustive fieldwork, was applied to a surviving fourth-century B.C. drainage outlet in the *Descrizione e disegno dell'Emissario del Lago Albano* (1762). Other Roman as well as Etruscan remains in the Campagna were considered in two further works, *Antichità di Albano e di Castel Gandolfo* (1762) and *Antichità di Cora* (1764). But above all, it was the *Campo Marzio dell'Antica Roma* (1762) which most clearly reflected the evolution of Piranesi's theoretical ideas at this climactic point in his career. Exceptionally dedicated to a fellow architect, Robert Adam (who had been closely involved in its preparation when they were together in Rome during the later 1750s), this work demonstrated the Roman genius for monumental urban design and was based on an analysis of the surviving remains of the Campus Martius area, supported by documents and the fragmentary "Several Marble Plan." Many of the plates in the book visually stripped away medieval accretions to reveal the evolution of a complex civilization, reaching a climax in an extravagantly elaborate planning fantasy of six contiguous plates—the *Ichnographia*: yet another exhortation to modern designers to adopt a bold originality.

The reappearance in 1760 of the *Invenzioni capric di Carceri* now entitled *Carceri d'invenzione*, with two further plates, significantly marked another phase of creative tension in Piranesi's architectural career. This definitive version, which was destined to achieve major European significance, involved a substantial reworking of the earlier plates with far stronger tonal contrasts and more specific details of sinister import. Architectural immensity and spatial ambiguity were amplified still further by additional structures receding into infinity, epitomizing the philosopher Edmund Burke's contemporary writings on the Sublime. A new generation of artists and architects studying in Rome, notably represented by Hubert Robert and Desprez, were to be profoundly affected by this highly charged language as it contributed to the early stages of Romanticism.

Impelled by his continuing polemical activity, Piranesi began to formulate a theoretical standpoint that was to govern his work as a designer for the remainder of his life. In 1765, sharply responding to an attack on *Della Magnificenza* by the French critic Mariette, he issued a three-part publication having as its main element the *Parere su l'architettura*—a brisk debate between two opposing architects on the fundamental nature of design. On the one hand was Protopiro, a rigorist disciple of Laugier, and on the other, Didascolo, who voiced Piranesi's own belief in the importance of free experiment, formal variety, and richness in ornament. Inevitably the latter won the argument, and Piranesi's supporting illustrations of imaginary architectural compositions demonstrated an extremely bizarre and eclectic use of motifs, now culled from Egyptian and Greek as well as Roman and Etruscan sources.

Within the context of this theoretical ferment, the 1760s were to prove a highly productive period for Piranesi as a practicing designer, invaluably documented by a range of drawings in the Morgan Library. As a leading *vedutista* in Rome with a growing clientele of foreign patrons, he set up his own printmaking business and showrooms in Palazzo Tomati on Via Sistina in 1760. The following year he was elected to the Accademia di San Luca and six years later was made *Cavaliere di Sperone d'Oro* by the pope. The enlightened patronage of Clement XIII and the Rezzonicos meanwhile provided him with a number of important opportunities to apply his novel principles of design in a variety of projects.

When in 1763 the pope commissioned from Piranesi a new pontifical altar for San Giovanni in Laterano, this developed into an extremely ambitious scheme to replace the entire structure to the liturgical east of the transepts with a monumental tribune and altar. At least five distinct schemes are represented by preliminary studies in the Morgan Library and in a set of twenty-three highly finished presentation drawings, now in the Avery Architectural Library of Columbia University. The most ambitious version of this unrealized commission involved an apsidal screen of giant columns with a hidden light source in the manner of Venetian church designs by Palladio and Longhena. This is represented in the Morgan collection by an exceptionally large study incorporating virtually the entire longitudinal section of the basilica, including the sixteenth- and seventeenth-century alterations. Despite its neoclassical fidelity to antique ornamental sources, the total cohesion of this ornate composition is unquestionably baroque in character with Piranesi as the conscious heir to Borromini's earlier modernization of the nave.

During the same period, between 1765 and 1766, Piranesi renovated the church and headquarters of the Knights of Malta for their grand prior, Cardinal Giovambattista Rezzonico. The Morgan Library possesses a unique group of designs for this work, ranging from a rapid preliminary sketch to meticulous presentation and working drawings. In imaginatively applying his novel mode of design throughout this commission, Piranesi devised a ceremonial piazza with heroic stelae and an entrance screen, richly embellished with ornamental reliefs which involved a complex interplay of Maltese, Rezzonico, and antique symbols reflecting his current polemical and aesthetic concerns. The modest pedimented facade of Santa Maria del Priorato was transformed with equally rich encrustations and the nave interior was amplified by further passages of elaborate ornament, including a large relief panel on the main vault. Undoubtedly inspired by his more ambitious projects for the Lateran, Piranesi created a highly sculptural altar featuring the *Apotheosis of St. Basil* raised on interlocking sarcophagus forms and accentuated by concealed lighting.

As a designer of interiors and furniture, Piranesi's contemporary works included schemes for Clement XIII at Castel Gandolfo, for the cardinal at the Quirinal Palace, and for Senator Abbondio Rezzonico on the Campidoglio. Sadly, no traces of these commissions survive, apart from a pair of elegant side tables for the Quirinal interiors, now in the Minneapolis Institute of Arts and the Rijksmuseum, Amsterdam, respectively. Nothing remains either of the first major contribution in Europe to the Egyptian revival represented by Piranesi's painted interior of the Caffè degli Inglesi in Piazza di Spagna, carried out in the early 1760s.

The sole record of the Caffè walls are two plates among the illustrations to Piranesi's final polemical and theoretical publication, *Diverse maniere d'adornare i cammini*, issued in 1769. Dedicated to Cardinal Rezzonico and addressed to an international audience of designers and patrons, with parallel texts in Italian, French, and English, this work was to prove Piranesi's most influential contribution to the decorative arts. In the lengthy preface he continued to defend the creative originality of the

Etruscans, as well as to discuss the ornamental vocabulary of the Egyptians, but his main theme was the need for creative license in order to fashion a radically modern style based on a broad eclectic study of all forms of antiquity. This was demonstrated by the copious quantity of Piranesi's etched designs produced in little more than a decade. His main subject was the ornamental chimneypiece (sixty-one are represented, including eleven in the Egyptian taste, ranging from the relatively simple to the extravagant), but Piranesi also included well over a hundred separate items of furniture and decorative elements from commodes, clocks, and sconces to coaches and sedan chairs; all are well represented among the Morgan Library's outstanding collection of preparatory studies.

With the death of Clement XIII in 1769 and the inevitable waning of Rezzonico patronage, Piranesi was now to find a ready market for his energies among the host of foreign clients in Rome, especially British collectors such as Charles Townley. He had already enlarged his printmaking business, now aided by his son Francesco (born in 1758) and a group of skilled assistants, to include the actual manufacture of ornamental chimneypieces incorporating classical fragments. Several were exported to Britain and elsewhere, including two illustrated in the *Diverse maniere*, and a thriving industry was to develop in Rome around this original idea. During the 1770s, in collaboration with dealers and entrepreneurs such as the Britons Thomas Jenkins, Gavin Hamilton, and James Byres, Piranesi extended this imaginative approach to the ambitious restoration and virtual fabrication of ornamental antiquities, profiting from the wealth of fragments recovered by Hamilton's scavenging excavations at Hadrian's Villa, Tivoli. This considerable output and ingenuity were effectively advertised and documented by means of Piranesi's issue of 118 separate etchings of antiquities, later collected together in the publication *Vasi, candelabri, cippi, sarcofagi* (1778). These included works not only displayed for sale in his *museo* or showrooms, but also found in other Italian collections as well as in some twenty-five British houses. They ranged from modest cinerary urns to the spectacular Warwick Vase, initially acquired from Piranesi by the eminent collector and envoy at Naples, Sir William Hamilton, and now in the Burrell Collection, Glasgow. Piranesi's skill in decorative synthesis, aided by outstanding restorers such as Cavaceppi, prompted him to take increasing liberties, especially in the reconstruction of large marble candelabra which were to have a considerable impact on the designers of the British Regency and French Empire styles.

Despite these competing interests, Piranesi's concerns with archaeology and the production of the *Vedute di Roma* were to continue undiminished. During the 1770s he produced a number of drawings recording sites south of Rome, such as Pozzuoli and especially Tivoli, where he produced a site plan of Hadrian's Villa. This latter was to be published posthumously in 1781 by Francesco. Within Rome itself a truly monumental record was published of Trajan's Column around 1774, later combined with other plates of the other giant relief columns of Marcus Aurelius, as well as of Antoninus and Faustina.

By now attention was shifting from the difficult, tunneled site of Herculaneum to the more accessible location of Pompeii. From 1770 onward, Piranesi made several expeditions there to prepare a plan and views such as those represented by the sketches of the Temple of Isis in the Morgan collection. In contrast to his vigorous and broadly handled records of this arid setting is the set of highly finished drawings (Sir John Soane's Museum, London) of the three Greek Doric temples at Paestum, which Piranesi surveyed with his son during 1777 and 1778. The gradual acceptance of these gaunt and awe-inspiring structures by the architectural world plots the evolution of neoclassical taste toward the expressive language of primitive forms. Piranesi's twenty plates, when they appeared shortly after his death in 1778 as *Differentes vues . . . de Pesto*, with Francesco's substantial intervention, were to prove a decisive act in transforming an archaeological interest into an emotional understanding.

While at Paestum, Piranesi was already suffering from a malignant bladder complaint, which his strenuous activities aggravated. Shortly after returning to Rome, he died on November 9, 1778, and was eventually buried at his request under the most ambitious and complex of his fabricated candelabrum in Santa Maria del Priorato. This highly appropriate if unconventional creation (now in the Louvre) was to be subsequently replaced at his family's direction by Angelini's somewhat prosaic statue of the architect, dressed *all'antica*, ironically more in keeping with the prevailing climate of neoclassical taste from which he had increasingly distanced himself. His epitaph might well have been the assertion he once made to the French architect Legrand: "I need to produce great ideas and believe that were I given the planning of a new universe, I would be mad enough to undertake it."

Rome Transformed: A Painterly Vision of Architecture

MYRA NAN ROSENFELD

The French drawings in this exhibition from the Canadian Centre for Architecture and a private collection in Toronto reveal how the evocation of ancient and modern Rome was an important point of departure in the creative process not only for the artists and architects who had studied at the French Academy in Rome, but also for those who knew the Roman monuments indirectly through books, prints, paintings, and drawings. All but two of the drawings present us with scenes in which subjects drawn from ancient Rome are transposed to imaginary locations, often alongside buildings from other cultures. The two exceptions, *The Fountain of Pomona at the Villa d'Este* (about 1760) (Cat. no. 91) by Jean-Honoré Fragonard (1732–1806) and *The Piazza del Popolo* (1759) (Cat. no. 89) by Charles De Wailly (1730–98), attest to the theme of the modern buildings of Rome as an equally important source of inspiration.[1]

There were limited opportunities for major architectural and painting commissions during the last half of the eighteenth century in France. When the former *pensionnaires* of the French Academy in Rome returned to Paris, many took work as designers—of stage sets, temporary architecture for festivities, illustrated books, or items of decorative art; others turned to the profession of teaching.[2] Some architects, like Charles De Wailly and Charles-Louis Clérisseau (1721–1820), obtained the *grand prix* of the Académie Royale de Peinture so that they might exhibit paintings and drawings at the Paris Salons, Clérisseau in 1769 and De Wailly in 1771. This situation may account in part for the proliferation of painted and drawn imaginary *vedute* by these architects and artists.[3] When Clérisseau could not obtain clients for architectural commissions, he began selling his drawings. Over one thousand were acquired by Catherine II of Russia (1729–96) in 1779.[4] After Jean-Laurent Legeay (about 1710–after 1788) lost his position as architect to Frederick II of Prussia (1712–86), he spent the rest of his life producing etchings and drawings of fictive ruins. Two of his drawings, *An Arch with Chinese Figures and Ruins* (Cat. no. 82) and *Figures Embarking and Disembarking from the Prow of a Ship in Front of a Tomb* (Cat. no. 83), executed while he was in England between 1765 and 1766, were offered for sale with their mounts in 1766 to baron de Driberg, a member of the court of the duke of Mecklenburg-Schwerin. Gabriel-Pierre-Martin Dumont (1720–91) never practiced as an architect, but spent his entire career publishing suites of etchings and books on ancient and modern architecture, from *Détails des plus intéressantes parties d'architecture de la Basilique de Saint-Pierre* (Paris, 1763) (Cat. no. 118) to others on the Temples of Paestum and modern theater design.[5] The best-known contributions of Louis-Joseph Le Lorrain (1715–59) were in the areas of furniture and interior design. His lack of success as a painter, in contrast to that of Joseph-Marie Vien (1716–1809), a fellow *pensionnaire* in Rome in the 1740s, was one of the reasons he left Paris for St. Petersburg in 1758 to become director of the Imperial Academy of Painting and Sculpture.[6] Ennemond-Alexandre Petitot (1727–1801) also left Paris to find patronage elsewhere. He went in 1753 to Parma, the most francophile court in northern Italy. There he was architect, stage designer, designer of court festivities, and urban planner to duke Filippo of Bourbon (1720–65). The duke–married to Princess Louise-Elisabeth, one of Louis XV's daughters–had a French minister of state, Guillaume Du Tillot (1710–74), who helped him model his court on that of Versailles. Petitot's *Suite de Vases* (Cat. no. 119) (1771) is dedicated to Du Tillot.[7]

Of the *architectes-peintres* whose drawings are represented in Canadian collections, Charles De Wailly, Louis-Jean Desprez (1743–1804), and Thomas de Thomon (1759–1813) had the most successful architectural careers. De Wailly was appointed in 1769 *contrôleur adjoint* of royal buildings and at first worked under Ange-Jacques Gabriel (1698–1782) on the construction of the Opéra at Versailles. Two of his most important projects, the Comédie Française (Théâtre de l'Odéon, 1769–82), designed with Marie-Joseph Peyre (1730–85), and the interior decoration of the salon of the Palazzo Spinola in Genoa (1772–73), were illustrated in the *Supplément* to Diderot's and d'Alembert's *Encyclopédie ou Dictionnaire raisonné des sciences, des arts et des métiers*, published in 1777.[8] Desprez became stage designer to Gustavus III of Sweden (1746–92) in 1784 and architect in charge of the royal castles at Haga and Drottningholm in 1788.[9] After an unofficial stay at the French Academy in Rome and travels through northern Italy, Austria, and Poland, from 1785 to 1799, Thomas de Thomon was appointed architect to Emperor Alexander I of Russia (1777–85) in 1802. His Stock Exchange, located on Vasilievsky Island opposite the Admiralty and the Winter Palace, dominates the city of St. Petersburg.[10]

In the dedication of his *Voyage d'Italie* (Paris, 1758) (Cat. no. 121), written in the 1780s, Charles-Nicolas Cochin (1715–90) characterized the trip he made to Italy between 1749 and 1751 with Abel-François de Vandières (1725–81), the future marquis de Marigny, the writer Jean-Bernard Le Blanc (1706–81), and the architects Jacques-Germain Soufflot (1713–80) and Jérôme-Charles Bellicard (1726–86) as a turning point in the establishment of *le bon goût*, or what we consider neoclassicism, in France.[11] Marigny did encourage the development of neoclassicism in architecture during his tenure as *directeur général des bâtiments, jardins, arts, académies, et manufactures royales* (1751–73) by awarding major commissions to Ange-Jacques Gabriel, Jacques-Germain Soufflot, and Charles De Wailly: to Gabriel, the Place Royale (Place de la Concorde) in 1753 and the Ecole Militaire in 1755; to Soufflot, the Church of Sainte-Geneviève in 1755, and to De Wailly, the Comédie Française (Théâtre de l'Odéon) in 1769.[12] In his *Mémoires*, written between 1780 and 1790, Charles-Nicolas Cochin also cited Jean-Laurent Legeay and Louis-Joseph Le Lorrain as key figures along with Marigny in the establishment of neoclassicism in France.[13] Both John Harris and Svend Eriksen have observed that Legeay's and Le Lorrain's imaginary architectural designs had the most profound influence–Legeay, in his etched and drawn *vedute* of ruins, Le Lorrain, in the temporary buildings he designed between 1745 and 1748 for the festivals of the *Chinea* in Rome.[14] In the *Chinea*, Le Lorrain had already begun to employ the massive, severe classical ornament that he would use later in the painted, illusionistic decoration of the dining room of Count C. G. Tessin's castle of Åkearö in Sweden (1754) and in the suite of furniture (1756–57) he designed for Ange-Laurent de Lalive de Jully (1725–79).[15]

Hubert Burda and André Corboz have pointed out that these imaginary *vedute* contributed to the development of neoclassical architecture by providing architects with visual images that they could use to translate the ideas of theoreticians into concrete form. Imaginary *vedute* were particularly valuable when certain structures such as barrel vaults and cupolas on freestanding columns, praised by Abbé Marc-Antoine Laugier (1713–69) in his *Essai sur l'architecture* (Paris, 1753), could not be found in ancient architecture. *A Vaulted Chamber with the Statue of Menander* (about 1775–80) (Cat. no. 105) by Hubert Robert (1733–1808) is one such drawing. Its barrel vault supported by two rows of freestanding Doric columns, an invention of Robert's, according to Jean de Cayeux, probably was influenced by Laugier's ideas.[16]

The architectural *veduta* was recognized as an independent genre by the Académie Royale de Peinture in France in the eighteenth century. The architects Giovanni Niccolo Servandoni (1695–1766) and Charles-Louis Clérisseau and the painters Pierre-Antoine De Machy (1723–1807) and Hubert Robert were all accepted into the Académie Royale de Peinture as *peintres d'architecture*, Servandoni in 1731, De Machy in 1758, and Robert and Clérisseau in 1769. The *veduta* of ruins had its origins in the etchings of Jacques Androuet Du Cerceau (about 1520–86) and in the paintings of Claude Lorrain (1600–1682), Jean Lemaire (1598–1659), and Pierre Patel the Elder (1620–76). According to Marianne Roland Michel, this genre survived in the rococo in the picturesque and often bizarre fantasies of Juste-Aurèle Meissonnier (1695–1750), Gilles-Marie Oppenord (1672–1742), and Jacques de Lajoüe (1686–1761). In the middle of the eighteenth century, the *veduta* of ruins was infused with new connotations of magnificence and of the sublime as a result of the influence of Giovanni Battista Piranesi. Only Fragonard, according to Roland Michel, was unaffected by Piranesi's influence.[17] Fragonard's red chalk drawing of *The Fountain of Pomona at the Villa d'Este, Tivoli* (about 1760) (Cat. no. 91) displays an independence from Piranesi's interpretation of the *veduta* in spite of the fact that it was drawn during the summer of 1760 when the two artists both visited the Villa d'Este.

There is a complex and seemingly contradictory interrelationship in Piranesi's oeuvre between the scientific investigation he undertook to depict the ruins in his later archaeological works and the imaginary structures that these ruins evoked in his mind in his early visionary works, the *Prima parte* (1743), the *Grotteschi* (1747–50) (Cat. no. 54), the *Opere varie* (1750), and the *Carceri* (1749–61). Piranesi's visionary works have been a catalyst for artistic creativity from the eighteenth century until our times.[18] In the dedication of the *Prima parte* to Nicola Giobbe, a building contractor to the papal court, Piranesi affirmed:

> . . . I will tell you only those living, speaking ruins filled my spirit with images such as even the masterfully wrought drawings of the immortal Palladio, which I kept before me at all times, could not rouse in me. It is thus that the idea has come to me to tell the world of some of these buildings: since there is no hope that an Architect of our times can successfully execute anything similar.[19]

The *Prima parte* was used as a starting point for the compositions of almost all the *vedute* by French artists in the CCA's collection. Not only did Piranesi's early works influence the *pensionnaires* at the French Academy in Rome, but the *Carceri*, the *Prima parte*, the *Varie Vedute* (1745), and the *Anti-*

chità Romane de' Tempi della Repubblica (1748) (Cat. no. 53) were much more popular among French artists and collectors in Paris than were his later publications on archaeology.[20] John Wilton-Ely has perceptively observed that even in the archaeological works such as the *Antichità Romane* (1756–57) (Cat. no. 57), the *Rovine del' Castello dell'Acqua Giulia* (1761), and the *Descrizione e disegno dell' Emissario del Lago Albano* (1762), Piranesi's creative interpretation of Roman architecture was translated into images of a visionary nature. In spite of the rational explanations of the Romans' expertise in engineering in the texts, the images in these works were composed in a superhuman scale according to the principles of baroque illusionism and theater design.[21] According to Rudolf Wittkower, Piranesi's affirmation of the freedom of the artist with respect to the past in the *Diverse maniere* (1769) (Cat. no. 64), as in the *Prima parte*, made it possible for artists and architects, regardless of their national origins, to transform the Roman ruins and to transpose them to other real and imaginary settings.[22]

Piranesi stated in his preface to the *Diverse maniere*:

> An artist, who would do himself honour, and acquire a name, must not content himself with copying faithfully the ancients, but studying their works he ought to show himself of an inventive, and, I myself had almost said, of a creating Genius.[23]

This imaginative juxtaposition of diverse elements is found also in the capricci of Roman ruins painted by Giovanni Paolo Pannini (1691–1765). Pannini placed real and fictive ruins side by side under the guise of biblical, historical, and mythological themes.[24] The theme of Roman antiquity as a source of renewal and progress in the present relates Pannini's capricci to his topographical views. This theme is expressed in Pannini's two paintings *Gallery with Views of Ancient Rome* and *Gallery with Views of Modern Rome* (1758–59) in the Louvre.[25] This same theme was taken up without allegorical overtures by his students at the French Academy in Rome, especially by Hubert Robert. Robert's extensive collection of Pannini's paintings and drawings included versions of the above two paintings of fictitious picture galleries. They were a source of inspiration for Robert when he was planning the transformation of the Grande Galerie of the Palais du Louvre into a museum between 1784 and 1802.[26]

In *Vaulted Passageway with a View of the Pyramid of Cestius through a Doric Portico* (Cat. no. 101), drawn while he was in Rome between 1760 and 1765, Hubert Robert has incorporated Piranesi's *Atrio Dorico* from the *Prima parte* into a composition derived from Pannini's *Alexander Visiting the Tomb of Achilles* (1730–40) in the Musée des Beaux-Arts de Narbonne. The small scale of the figures in relation to the massive barrel vault and Doric columns imparts to Robert's drawing an expression of the enduring magnificence of ancient Rome that is found in Piranesi's etchings in the *Prima parte*. At the same time, however, Robert gives this scene a picturesque quality, a heritage of the rococo, that contrasts with the solemnity of Pannini's painting, an allegory of death.[27]

Jean-Laurent Legeay was one of the most inventive creators of the *vedute* of ruins in the eighteenth century. He brought a new depth of meaning to the Piranesian conception of the ruin in the *vedute* he executed in Germany and England in the 1750s and 1760s.[28] Legeay's *vedute*, with their juxtaposition of disparate elements and disjunction of time and place, are characterized by the quality of "papillotage," a word used by the architect Nicolas Le Camus de Mezières (1721–89) in *Le génie de l'ar-*

chitecture ou l'analogie des arts avec nos sensations (Paris, 1780) to describe the exotic, so-called Chinese elements and discordant harmony found in the paintings of Antoine Watteau (1684–1721), in the *Roman Comique* of Paul Scarron (1610–60), and in the etchings of Jacques Callot (1592–1635). Legeay's *vedute*, like the above works, arouse in the viewer a response of surprise and astonishment.[29] Like Watteau's *Embarquement pour l'Ile de Cythère* (1718–19), on which it is modeled, Legeay's *Figures Embarking and Disembarking from the Prow of a Ship* (1765–66) (Cat. no. 83) invites the viewer to take a metaphysical journey through time, since the location and action of the scene are not precisely defined. In *Arch with Chinese Figures and Ruins* (1765–66) (Cat. no. 82), the ruins of Rome have been depicted next to those of Egypt. A globe next to the Chinese figures on the top of the arch alludes to other distant civilizations. Unlike the revival of Roman antiquity in the Renaissance, the notion of antiquity in the eighteenth century was enlarged and expanded to include other cultures. Johann Bernhard Fischer von Erlach's (1656–1723) treatise, *Entwurff einer historischen Architectur* (Vienna, 1721) (Cat. no. 48), in which European buildings are illustrated along with those from Greece, Egypt, Syria, Persia, Turkey, China, and Japan, is a witness to this new conception of history. The mania for all aspects of Chinese culture, from the philosophy of Confucius and the manufacture of porcelain to the drinking of tea, swept Europe from the end of the seventeenth to the end of the eighteenth century.[30]

The Chinese figures in Legeay's drawing *An Arch with Chinese Figures and Ruins* (Cat. no. 82), executed in England between 1765 and 1766, reveal the influence not only of François Boucher, but also of Sir William Chambers (1723–96). Chambers was one of the major protagonists in the development of *chinoiserie* in architecture in the eighteenth century. He had been to China three times with Swedish trade missions between 1743 to 1749. Just before Legeay arrived in England in 1765, Chambers had completed the garden buildings at Kew, which included a Chinese Pagoda, the House of Confucius, and the Alhambra, a pavilion in the Islamic style. In addition to *Plans, Elevations, Sections, and Perspective Views of the Gardens and Buildings at Kew, Surrey* (London, 1763), Chambers published *Designs of Chinese Buildings, Furniture, Dress, Machines, and Utensils* (1757) and *Dissertation on Oriental Gardening* (1772).[31] Legeay was in close contact with Chambers during his stay in England. There are three drawings in an album in the Victoria and Albert Museum in which Chambers copied tombs and a ground plan by Legeay.[32] In addition, Legeay made a red chalk drawing of the Palladian-Piranesian Casino at Marino near Dublin, which Chambers had built between 1756 and the 1770s for James Caulfield (1728–99), first earl of Charlemont, the Irish peer whom Piranesi had sought to subsidize the publication of his *Antichità Romane* (1756–57) (Cat. nos. 57 and 58).[33] It is quite probable that Legeay's eclecticism was derived not only from his contact with Chambers, and his reading of Fischer von Erlach's treatise, but also from a renewed contact with Piranesi's works, in particular with the *Parere su l'architettura* (1765), in which Egyptian decorative motifs first appeared alongside Greek and Roman ones.

Lord Charlemont's patronage of Sir William Chambers raises the question of Piranesi's influence in Ireland. David S. Howard's research on the owners of several of the albums in the CCA's collection has revealed that in addition to Lord Charlemont there were other readers of Piranesi in Ireland. It would be intriguing to discover if Charles Agar (1736–1809), archbishop of Dublin and the earl of Normanton, the owner of the CCA's albums of the *Vedute di Roma* (1778–84) (Cat. no. 55) and the *Views of the Temples of Paestum* (1778–80) (Cat. no. 66), was in contact with Lord Charlemont. Further research should be undertaken to find out if Agar commissioned any significant buildings as did Lord Charlemont or Dr. Richard Robinson, archbishop of Armagh (1709–94), who may have owned the CCA's copy of *Della Magnificenza ed architettura de' Romani* (Cat. no. 59).[34]

The *vedute* by Louis-Joseph Le Lorrain, Jean-Charles Delafosse (1734–91), and Louis-Jean Desprez, in contrast to those by Hubert Robert and Jean-Laurent Legeay discussed above, all have allusions to eighteenth-century buildings. In Le Lorrain's *Imaginary Buildings Along the Seine* (about 1756) (Cat. no. 84), an equestrian statue, reminiscent of Edme Bouchardon's (1698–1762) *Statue of Louis XV* (1748–62), alludes to the two competitions held in 1748 and 1753 to design the Place Louis XV around this monument. Le Lorrain has focused the spectator's attention on a U-shaped building to the right, whose neoclassical Doric colonnade contrasts with the rococo-style fountains under the Egyptian obelisks and the baroque style of the Corinthian applied columns in the building to the extreme left. In this *veduta*, Le Lorrain may have attempted to express his criticism of Ange-Jacques Gabriel's winning 1753 project for the Place Louis XV (Place de la Concorde). The U-shaped building can be considered more progressive in style than the one to the left, which resembles the two buildings that Gabriel erected on the Place Louis XV (Place de la Concorde).[35] The sobriety and severity of the facade decoration and massive scale of the U-shaped building is similar to an almost contemporary project by Etienne-Louis Boullée (1728–99) for the Hôtel des Monnaies in Paris, known through an etching, dated 1750–60, by Charles Poulleau that was dedicated to the marquis de Marigny.[36]

Jean-Charles Delafosse's *Masquerade in a Vauxhall* (about 1770–80) (Cat. no. 106) transposes Piranesi's world to Paris. Piranesi's *Vestibolo d'antico Tempio* from the *Prima parte* (1743) has been transformed into a temporary entertainment hall in which figures dressed in costumes of La Comédie Italienne party alongside others in carnival outfits and ordinary clothes, oblivious to the antique setting in which they are placed. The monumentality and majesty of this vauxhall, reminiscent of the crossing of Soufflot's Sainte-Geneviève, contrasts with the levity of the atmosphere of the scene.[37]

Louis-Jean Desprez depicted in *The Triumph of Hannibal* (about 1780–90) (Cat. no. 109) an imaginary city that contains allusions to Greek and Roman buildings inspired by his trip to Naples and Sicily in 1777 and 1778 as well as those he designed for Gustavus III of Sweden. A Greek Doric temple resembling those at Agrigento and Segesta has been placed above a structure derived from the stables at Haga (1788) and a tomb similar to the one that appears in the stage set Desprez designed for the opera *Frigga* (1787). The subject of Hannibal's triumph bears a reference to early Roman history, the First and Second Punic Wars (264–41, 218–201 B.C.).[38] In addition, *The Triumph of Hannibal* takes place in the Roman theater at Herculaneum. Desprez's placement of a Greek Doric temple on the hill above a Roman theater may show the influence of the doctrine of superiority of Greek over Roman architecture, espoused by Abbé Marc-Antoine Laugier in his *Essai sur l'architecture* (Paris, 1753) and by the comte de Caylus in *Recueil d'antiquités égyptiennes, étrusques, grecques, et romaines* (Paris,

1752–67) (Cat. no. 116).[39] In addition, Desprez introduced an allusion to a medieval fortified castle. The massive round towers just below the Greek Doric temple are derived from Emperor Frederick II of Sicily's thirteenth-century castle at Lucera in Apulia. Fischer von Erlach had not included any medieval monuments in his treatise.[40] Desprez's eclecticism and his openness to medieval architecture may be the result not only of his Swedish environment (as suggested by Per Bjurström)[41] but also of his French heritage. Earlier in France, Juste-Aurèle Meissonnier, perhaps in a critique of Fischer von Erlach's treatise, had included the gothic cathedrals of Strassburg and Rouen in one of his two etchings, *Parallèle générale des édifices les plus considérables depuis les Egyptiens, les Grecs jusqu'à nos derniers modernes*, published by Gabriel Huquier between 1745 and 1750.[42] In this *veduta* of an imaginary city, Desprez's reference to the Middle Ages reveals how the sources of romanticism can be found in neo-classicism.

Charles De Wailly's *The Piazza del Popolo, Rome* (1759) (Cat. no. 89) and Hubert Robert's *A Vaulted Chamber with the Statue of Menander* (about 1775–1780) (Cat. no. 105) demonstrate how these real and imaginary *vedute* of Rome had an influence on actual building design. *The Piazza del Popolo, Rome* reveals the connections between the *veduta* and city planning observed by Marianne Roland Michel.[43] De Wailly learned from studying the Piazza del Popolo the principles of radial city planning, which he later applied to several projects formulated in Paris: the Opera designed between 1781 and 1798 for the Jardin des Tuileries, and the new harbor at Port-Vendres, built between 1779 and 1783. Jean de Cayeux notes how Hubert Robert's red chalk drawing *A Vaulted Chamber with the Statue of Menander* was a source of inspiration for his project to transform the Grande Galerie of the Louvre into a public museum. One of Robert's proposals, illustrated in the painting *Project for the Renovation of the Grande Galerie of the Louvre* (p. XL), exhibited at the Salon of 1796, reflects ideas he had developed in the mid-1780s when he was first entrusted with that project by the comte d'Angiviller (1730–1809).[44] The broken barrel vault in the drawing has now been transformed into a ceiling spanned by diaphragm arches that support skylights. Hubert Robert's drawings and paintings of ruined vaulted chambers had an influence on two projects Etienne-Louis Boullée designed to be illustrated in his unpublished treatise *Architecture, essai sur l'art*, written in the late 1780s and early 1790s: the design for a Metropolitan Church and that for a Bibliothèque Nationale. Both structures are composed of long barrel vaults supported by colonnades.[45]

Finally, Thomas de Thomon's *Sixteen Sketches of Real and Imaginary Sites in Italy* (about 1785–91) (Cat. no. 114) bear witness to the important role these painterly evocations of architecture played in the training of an eighteenth-century architect. The small sketches were probably part of a pattern book that Thomas de Thomon kept as a source for future designs. Views that he composed himself, like those of the *Church of St. Peter's* (no. 2 in the series of sketches by Thomon), find their place along with a scene adapted from Piranesi's *Carceri* (no. 17 in the series). Thomas de Thomon went on to look at the world of Rome through the eyes of a French painter, Hubert Robert. *A Palace above the Arch of a Bridge* (no. 7 in the series) is based on Robert's painting *Bridge with a Monumental Building* of about 1768, which was itself inspired by Piranesi's *Ponte Magnifico* from the *Prima parte* (1743). Thomon was

Hubert Robert. *Project for the Renovation of the Grande Galerie of the Louvre*, oil on canvas, 1796, Musée du Louvre, Paris.

evolving—in a way parallel to Etienne-Louis Boullée, and from the same visual sources—the seeds of a new revolutionary architecture. The massive scale and severity of the Egyptian pyramid surrounded by four rostral columns (no. 12 in the series by Thomon) is close to Boullée's contemporary project, the *Cenotaph for Turenne*, which was to be illustrated in his *Architecture, essai sur l'art*.[46] Boullée wished to elevate architecture from a trade to an art by infusing it with the emotive powers of poetry and painting. The presumed motto of Correggio, *Ed io anche son pittore*, appears several times in his treatise; Boullée considered the architect to be a kind of painter who invokes the sublime in architecture.[47] Thomas de Thomon was to bring to fruition some of the same ideas as Boullée in the buildings he constructed in St. Petersburg at the beginning of the nineteenth century.

These imaginary *vedute*, painterly visions of architecture, played a major role in the creation and dissemination of a new approach to classical antiquity among artists, architects, and patrons. From Piranesi to Thomas de Thomon, Rome was the starting point for a journey into the past and a flight into the future.

1 Both are versions of earlier drawings; Fragonard's was executed at Tivoli, while De Wailly's was drawn in Paris. Throughout his career in Paris, Fragonard made counter-proofs, etchings, and fanciful versions of subjects he had drawn earlier in Italy. See Cat. no. 91.

2 Oechslin 1972, p. 366.

3 This dual training of Giovanni Battista Piranesi as well as of French eighteenth-century artists and architects has been discussed by Marianne Roland Michel in Brunel 1978, pp. 476–81.

4 McCormick 1990, p. 4, and Hautecoeur 1912, pp. 40–48.

5 The CCA's copy of Dumont's suite of etchings on St. Peter's has on folio 96 an undated engraved broadsheet. Entitled *Catalogue de l'oeuvre complet de M*ʳ *Dumont*, it lists a total of twelve publications and suites of etchings for sale. It must be dated by 1774 since it includes Dumont's *Parallèle de plans des plus belles salles de spectacles d'Italie et de la France . . .*, published in Paris in that year.

6 Cat. no. 84. Rosenberg 1978, p. 194.

7 Cipriani in Brunel 1978, p. 149, pp. 151–53.

8 See Cat. no. 89, and Mosser and Rabreau in Paris 1979.

9 See Cat. no. 109.

10 See Cat. no. 114.

11 See Cat. no. 121.

12 Christian Michel 1991 (Cochin 1758), introduction, pp. 61–64. The question of Marigny's patronage is being investigated by Alden Rand Gordon in a book in progress, *Royal Art Patronage in the Ancien régime: The Role of the Marquis de Marigny* (based on his Harvard Ph.D. dissertation). See also Eriksen 1962, pp. 96–101.

13 Eriksen 1974, note 5, p. 30.

14 Eriksen 1974, pp. 30–36, and Wittkower 1967, pp. 189–96, figs. 1–2, 6, 10–11, 21–25; see also Rome and elsewhere 1976, nos. 106–7, p. 207, p. 210, repr. p. 204 and p. 208 for Le Lorrain's 1748 *Chinea* designs.

15 See Cat. no. 84, and Eriksen 1962, pp. 340–47.

16 Burda 1967, pp. 54–55, fig. 28, p. 134, fig. 30, p. 135; Corboz 1978, pp. 27–38, p. 47, p. 51, fig. 5, p. 9, fig. 6, p. 12, figs. 10–13, pp. 18–19.

17 Roland Michel in Brunel 1978, pp. 477–78, 481–82, 486–87.

18 Tafuri 1987, pp. 28–29, p. 35.

19 Quoted in English in ibid., pp. 340–47.

20 Barbin in Brunel 1978, p. 46.

21 Wilton-Ely 1978, pp. 533–34, 536–39.

22 Wittkower 1982, p. 244.

23 Quoted in English in Wilton-Ely 1978, p. 544.

24 Kiene in Paris and elsewhere 1992–93, pp. 63–68. The concept of the capriccio goes back to definitions given by Vasari in his *Vite* (1568) and Baldinucci in his *Vocabulario* (1681) as an idea or image which has its origin in the artist's imagination.

25 Kiene in Paris and elsewhere 1992–93, pp. 75–89, nos. 40a and 40b, pp. 141–47, repr. 142–43, and pp. 144–45.

26 Roland Michel in Brunel 1978, p. 481; Cayeux 1989, pp. 38–39; Kiene in Paris and elsewhere 1992–93.

27 Roland Michel in Brunel 1978, pp. 483–86, has already noted these characteristics in Robert's ruin *vedute*.

28 Erouart 1982, pp. 168–80.

29 Hobson 1982, p. 52, p. 298.

30 Honour 1961, pp. 17–24.

31 Harris 1970, pp. 4–5, 32–39, 144–62, pls. 23–40.

32 Wittkower 1967, p. 191, figs. 3–5; Harris 1970, Appendix XII, p. 191. Harris dated these drawings between 1749 and 1755 when Chambers was in Paris and Rome. Erouart 1982, pp. 52–53, fig. 70, p. 81, fig. 73, p. 83, fig. c, p. 220; Erouart has convincingly shown by documentary evidence that Chambers executed these drawings in England, not in Paris or Rome, because Legeay was in Germany by 1748 and in England in 1765. Legeay did not return to Paris until 1780 or to Rome until 1786.

33 Wittkower 1967, p. 191, fig. 39; Harris 1970, pp. 42–45, fig. 2, p. 44, pls. 50–54; Erouart 1982, p. 74, fig. 69, p. 79, no. 59, pp. 218–19. The Casino of Marino reveals the influence of many of the palladian pavilions illustrated in Piranesi's *Prima parte* as well as the *Atrio Dorico*. See Robison 1986, no. 8, p. 82, repr. p. 82, no. 13, p. 94, repr. p. 94.

34 According to McCarthy 1986, pp. 161–62, Dr. Richard Robinson fostered the career of Thomas Cooley who was the architect of the Dublin Stock Exchange, one of the first neoclassical buildings in Ireland. Cooley had studied with Robert Mylne.

35 See Cat. no. 84; Eriksen 1974, pp. 41–48, has distinguished two stylistic phases in the early development of neoclassicism between 1750 and 1760: a more conservative style called "measured modernism," used by artists and architects like Gabriel who had not been to Rome, and a more

radical style called "outright modernism," formulated by artists and architects like Le Lorrain who had studied in Rome at the French Academy.

36 Pérouse de Montclos 1969, p. 59, note 1, fig. 20. The engraving in the Musée Carnavalet is inscribed, *L'Hôtel des Monnaies projeté sur le terrain de l'Hôtel de Conty dédié à Monsieur le Marquis de Marigny, conseiller du Roy en ses conseils . . . par son très humble et très obéissant serviteur Boulée fils et architecte.*

37 Middleton 1963, p. 106, pls. 16c and 16d, has observed that Soufflot was also influenced by the same etching from the *Prima parte.*

38 See the *New Encyclopaedia Britannica*, Chicago, 15th edition, 1989, vol. 20, pp. 317–21. It was actually Hamilcar Barca, Hannibal's father, who defended Sicily against the Romans. Hannibal invaded Italy from Spain and France.

39 See Cat. no. 59.

40 See Cat. no. 48; Rykwert 1980, pp. 69–70.

41 Bjurström 1990, pp. 61–78.

42 Nyberg in Meissonnier 1969, pp. 29–30. The CCA owns the preparatory drawing for this etching (DR1986:0747 and DR1986:0746). Meissonnier has depicted (from Fischer von Erlach's treatise) Hagia Sophia, Istanbul (no. 18), the

Karlskirke, Vienna (no. 31), and the Tower of Porcelain at Nanking (no. 22).

43 Roland Michel 1978, p.476.

44 Burda 1967, pp. 89, 105; Corboz 1978, pp. 45–47; Sahut in Paris 1979a, pp. 6–10, no. 58, Musée du Louvre, RF 1975–10, pp. 28–30, repr. p. 29. Robert was first appointed *Garde du Museum* by the comte d'Angiviller in 1784 and held that title until 1792. In 1795, he was appointed member of the *Conservatoire* with Fragonard, De Wailly, the restorer Picault, and the sculptor Pajou. He occupied that position until 1802.

45 Burda 1967, p. 54, p. 89, pp. 95–97, p. 105, fig. 130, p. 181. Burda also noted connections between Robert's *vedute* and the architecture of Ledoux. Corboz 1978, pp. 6–8, pp. 51–53, pp. 31–32, figs. 1–3, pp. 6–7, fig. 21, p. 23.

46 See Cat. no. 114.

47 See Boullée 1968, p. 45. note 1, p. 44, p. 55, and p. 73; quoted in Burda 1967, p. 97, note 448: "Les tableaux du ressort de l'architecture ne peuvent être faits sans la plus profonde connaissance de la nature . . . de la nature : c'est de ses effets que naît la poésie de l'architecture. C'est là vraiment ce qui constitue l'architecture un art, et c'est aussi ce qui porte cet art à la sublimité."

deliziosa

Filippo Juvarra. *Design for Act II, Scene XI, of Tito e Berenice* [CAT. NO. 1].

Giovanni Paolo Pannini. *Classical Ruins with Twelve Figures* [CAT. NO. 3].

Pietro Bracci. *Alternate Ground Plan and Elevation of a Monument for James III, the Old Pretender, in St. Peter's, Rome* [CAT. NO. 8].

Giovanni Battista Piranesi. *Fantastic Monuments* [CAT. NO. 17].

Giovanni Battista Piranesi. *Architectural Fantasy* [CAT. NO. 25].

Giovanni Battista Piranesi. *San Giovanni in Laterano: Longitudinal Section* [CAT. NO. 31].

Thomas Jones. *View of the Villa of Maecenas and the Villa d'Este at Tivoli* [CAT. NO. 72].

Charles-Louis Clérisseau. *The Triumphal Arch and Mausoleum of the Julii at Saint-Rémy, Provence* [CAT. NO. 88].

Louis-Jean Desprez. *The Triumph of Hannibal* [CAT. NO. 109].

Exploring Rome: Piranesi and His Contemporaries

deliziosa

FILIPPO JUVARRA
Messina 1678–Madrid 1736

1. *Design for Act II, Scene XI, of Tito e Berenice*

Presented at the Teatro Capranica, Rome 1714, *Deliziosa*.

Pen and brown ink, gray wash, over graphite on laid paper; brown ink border. 7⅞ x 7⁹⁄₁₆ inches (200 x 192 mm). Watermark: none visible.
Inscribed on the recto in brown ink to the left of lower center, *deliziosa*.

DATE: 1713.

PROVENANCE: sale, London, Christie's, 13 December 1984, lot 205; Count Luigi Cibrario, Turin.

BIBLIOGRAPHY: Viale Ferrero 1968, pp. 11, 17–18 and fig. 3; Viale Ferrero 1970, pp. 59, 61 nos. 11, 12 and pl. 154.

Montréal, Centre Canadien d'Architecture/Canadian Centre for Architecture DR1985:0009

A view through a garden allée lined at either side with fountains on monumental pedestals topped by urns on consoles. The allée, terminated by pairs of standing figures on tall pedestals, opens onto a flight of steps rising to an elevated terrace that, at left and right, returns to enclose the lower level. At the terrace level at left and right, arches supported on column clusters are oriented diagonally toward the center of the composition. The focus of both the allée and diagonal axes is a two-story palace with wings that recede to left and right. In the center, at the junction of the two wings, there is an arched entrance in a convex bay, crowned by a third concave level. Two-story rectangular buttresses alternate with arched bays in the two wings of the lower level of the palace. The arched central entrance reveals a courtyard with an axial arched opening in the distance. In the foreground, drapery and branches with leaves frame the darker upper portion of the composition. Additional trees are indicated behind and to the left and right of the palatial structure at the terrace level.

Mercedes Viale Ferrero first identified, published,

and reproduced the drawing. She confirmed an earlier attribution to Juvarra, associating the subject with the set design for Scene VI of the opera *Tito e Berenice*. The opera, written by Carlo Sigismondo Capece (1652–1728), with music by Antonio Caldara (1670?–1736), was performed at the Teatro Capranica in Rome on 7 January 1714 (Viale Ferrero 1968, pp. 15–18; Viale Ferrero 1985, p. 131).

The drawing, inscribed *deliziosa* (no. 3 in the Cibrario group), is on one of ten sheets by Juvarra formerly owned by Luigi Cibrario. The attribution of the group to Juvarra was first noted by L. Rovere, V. Viale, and A. E. Brinckmann (Rovere, Viale, Brinckmann 1937, p. 159), but the drawings in the group were neither listed or reproduced. The group was again noted by V. Viale in the catalogue of an exhibition held in Messina in 1966 (Messina 1966, p. 111). Only in 1968 were the ten sheets discussed and reproduced by Viale Ferrero in *Antichità viva*. She associated a number of the sheets with specific scenes in the opera written for the Teatro Capranica. Viale Ferrero's observation (Viale Ferrero 1968, p. 15) that some of the sheets were also related to drawings for the opera found in an album by Juvarra in the Biblioteca Nazionale in Turin (BNT, Riserva 59.4) was developed further in her *Filippo Juvarra, scenografo e architetto teatrale* (Viale Ferrero 1970, pp. 58–61). While a number of the drawings in BNT, Riserva 59.4 were able to be associated with drawings from the Cibrario Collection for the opera, none was for a garden setting.

A second drawing, no. 4 in the Cibrario Collection, shows a palace garden with a pair of square, arched, domed pavilions marking flights of steps between the upper level of the palace terrace in the background and a garden toward the proscenium. In 1968 and 1970, Viale Ferrero suggested this garden scene might be an alternative design for the sheet inscribed *deliziosa* (Viale Ferrero 1968, p. 18; Viale Ferrero 1970, p. 61, note 11). However, in her 1981 study of the opera *Lucio Papirio* by Francesco Gasparini, Viale Ferrero identified the drawing as a design for a "Gabinetto nell'appartamento di Emilia" from Act I, Scene II of that opera (Viale Ferrero 1981, p. 248).

Viale Ferrero discovered the libretto of *Tito e Berenice* in the library of the Conservatorio di Santa Cecilia in Rome. The libretto, published in 1714, includes the author and composer but not the designer. The opera consists of three acts with ten scene changes. Viale Ferrero (1970, p. 61) associates six related drawings from the Cibrario Collection (C) and nine scene designs from the Biblioteca Nazionale, Turin, Riserva 59.4 (BNT, Riserva 59.4) with the scene changes as follows:

I: Campagna con tende militari di Tito (C1)
II: Camere imperiali (BNT, Riserva 59.4, 57[3])
III: Terme suburbane di Claudio (BNT, Riserva 59.4, 76[4]; with preparatory drawing on 54[2])
IV: Parte del Tempio di Giove Capitolino (BNT, Riserva 59.4, 68[3]; with possible preparatory drawings on 36[1] and 119[1])
V: Galleria
VI: Deliziosa (CCA DR1985:0009 [formerly, C3] and C4) (Viale Ferrero 1981, p. 248, subsequently linked C4 to the opera *Lucio Papirio*, also performed at the Capranica the same season in 1714)
VII: Gabinetto imperiale (C2)
VIII: Veduta del Tevere (perhaps BNT, Riserva 59.4, 85[3])
IX: Appartamenti terreni (BNT, Riserva 59.4, 87[2])
X: Grande anfiteatro (C5 and 6; with preparatory drawing on BNT, Riserva 59.4, 54[1] verso)

Drawings are lacking only for scene changes V and VIII. Two additional scene designs in the Cibrario Collection, *Cortile* (acquired by the J. Paul Getty Museum, 88.GA.1) and *Atrio o Piazza*, have not found precise correspondence among the scenes of the opera. (The two remaining drawings by Juvarra in the Cibrario group are projects for a palace salon interior and an elaborate setting for a painting. Both were also acquired by the Canadian Centre for Architecture.)

A scene entitled *Deliziosa* is the sixth among the ten scene changes listed at the beginning of the libretto of *Tito e Berenice*. A scene change with this title, however, is absent in the libretto. The titles of all but one of the scene changes for *Deliziosa* are found in the libretto. The anomaly corresponds with a scene change in Act II, Scene XI, entitled *Giardini*. In this, the final scene in Act II, the libretto includes a *Ballo di giardinieri*. It seems likely, therefore, that the scene design in the Canadian Centre for Architecture is that for Act II, Scene XI.

Viale Ferrero (1970) associates twelve additional drawings in BNT, Riserva 59.4 with scenes prepared for the Teatro Capranica (22[1], 31[3], 43[1], 56[2], 59[5], 61[1], 79[2], 105[2], 113[2], 115[2], 125[1], 125[2]). Juvarra made at least twenty-seven designs for the Capranica for the 1714 opera season.

The story of Titus and Berenice, though found in Dio's *Roman History* (LXVI, 15.4) and Suetonius's *Lives* (VII), probably owed more to Racine's *Bérénice* and Corneille's *Tite et Bérénice*, both known to Capece (Viale Ferrero 1981, p. 249, note 10). The story of the opera, a tragedy in which Titus's reason overcomes his passion for Berenice, inspired a number of composers and librettists. Other productions in Italy during the eighteenth century were staged at the Teatro Grimani, Venice, 1725; Teatro Reggio, Turin, 1771; Teatro Prini, Pisa, 1776; and Teatro La Fenice, Venice, 1793 (Sartori 1990, vol. I, pp. 419, 421; Stieger 1975, part I, vol. III, p. 1205).

Viale Ferrero notes that Juvarra had worked before with both Capece and Caldara (Viale Ferrero 1968, p. 17). Capece wrote operas for the theater of the Queen of Poland in the Palazzo Zuccari, for which Juvarra had prepared a number of scene designs. Caldara wrote music for one of the acts of the opera *Giunio Bruto*, with scene designs by Juvarra, which was sent in 1711 to Joseph I of Austria.

The Teatro Capranica was remodeled between 1694 and 1695 by Carlo Buratti. It was worked on again in the summer and fall of 1713 following a design of Tommaso Mattei (Ruggiero 1989, p. 526). The proprietor of the theater commissioned an appraisal from Mattei in October of 1713, perhaps in anticipation of further work or perhaps to evaluate the completed renovations (Rovere, Viale, Brinckmann 1937, p. 143).

Juvarra may also have been involved in renovations of the stage. In November 1713 he prepared two drawings for the stage and possibly considered a new design for a proscenium arch (Viale Ferrero 1981, pp. 254–55). One of the two drawings in the Biblioteca Nazionale Turin (Riserva 59.1, 12) for the stage, showing tracks for flats, was first reproduced in 1937 (Rovere, Viale, Brinckmann 1937, pl. 196). Both drawings were reproduced by Viale Ferrero in 1970 (p. 331, pl. 187 and fig. 12) as was a drawing of a proscenium arch which she associated with the Teatro Capranica (p. 366, fig. 128[2]).

The several drawings from the Cibrario Collection reveal a similar lightness of touch, depth of field, and openness that identify them as a group different from most of Juvarra's bolder, firmer drawings of scene designs executed earlier for the Teatro Ottoboni and the theater of the Queen of Poland in the Palazzo Zuccari (see Viale Ferrero 1970, p. 59, and pls. 8–149). Similar atmospheric effects appear, however, in a number of the preparatory sketches for scenes for the Teatro Capranica in Riserva 59.4 in the Biblioteca Nazionale in Turin.

Within the Cibrario group, the *Deliziosa* scene has closer conceptual affinities to the *Sala Imperiale* and the *Cortile* designs (Viale Ferrero 1970, p. 373, figs. 2 and 7) than to the military camp, the second garden scene, and the amphitheater (Viale Ferrero 1970, figs. 1, 4, and 5). In the *Deliziosa* scene, heavy brown ink lines describe the foliage and garden furniture in the foreground while lighter ink lines, with relatively light gray wash depict the remainder of the scene. In the shaded allée of the foreground, a more intense gray wash enframes and gives substance to the scene, silhouettes the pairs of standing gesturing figures as well as the arches of the terrace level, and then reveals the garden palace in full light.

The garden palace appears to be largely open at the lower level with tall arched bays leading to the inner court. Residential spaces seem confined to the second level with perhaps a suite of spaces in the central third level. The buttresses that flank the arched openings of the lower level imply lofty vaulted spaces at both the lower and second levels otherwise not indicated. The buttresses may have been intended as rectangular salient bays to unify the levels of the palace. The receding wings, responding as they do to the di-

rection of the arches of the middle ground, suggest strong diagonal avenues that meet at the terrace before the entry to the palace.

A palace with a central focus and receding wings is unusual in scene designs by Juvarra, occurring, though, in two scenes for the Teatro Ottoboni from an album in the Victoria and Albert Museum (Viale Ferrero 1970, p. 321, pl. 118 and fig. 52 recto). Pairs of arches or column pairs with lintels leading diagonally to the center of the scene are used in several designs by Juvarra. Two examples are also on sheets from the album in the Victoria and Albert Museum (Viale Ferrero 1970, pls. 107 and 116). Another occurs in the *Cortile* from the Cibrario group (Viale Ferrero 1970, p. 373, fig. 7).

The spatial layering characteristic of much early eighteenth-century scene design is dramatized in the *Deliziosa* scene through the contrast between the shaded allée with its silhouetted figures and the brilliantly lighted palace. The use of four layers or flats to show spatial depth was already well developed in the earliest-known scene designs by Juvarra of 1706 for the Teatro San Bartolomeo in Naples, for example, the *Sala Reggia* scene (Viale Ferrero 1970, pl. 4; Millon 1984, T 085). The *Gabinetto* for *Costantino Pio* in 1710 (Viale Ferrero 1970, pl. 10), though tighter and more enclosed than the *Deliziosa*, depicts several distinct layers as do his designs for an atrium in an unidentified opera for the Teatro Ottoboni (Viale Ferrero 1970, pl. 127), for the *Terme suburbane* (Cibrario Collection) for *Tito e Berenice* at the Teatro Capranica, and a grand gallery, probably also designed for an opera at the Teatro Capranica (Viale Ferrero 1970, p. 343, fig. 43[1]).

Viale Ferrero, in an article on Francesco Gasparini, notes that in early eighteenth-century operas having nine or ten scene changes, six or seven generic scenes regularly recurred. The remainder of the scenes would be related to specific aspects of the libretto (Viale Ferrero 1981, p. 246). Within the suite of designs, a garden or *Deliziosa* scene, a palace together with a garden, often occurred. In fact, there are over a dozen palace garden scene designs by Juvarra (Viale Ferrero 1970, pls. 13, 25, 26, 33, 38, 46, 48, 75, 82, 108,

NO. 2

144, 147, 167; and Millon 1984, drawing in Bellinga, p. 166).

Juvarra's mastery of the innovations in scene design that flowed from Ferdinando and Francesco Galli da Bibiena, perhaps reinforced by his early study of the perspective publications of Andrea Pozzo, was manifest by 1706 in his designs for the Teatro San Bartolomeo. By 1713, the date of *Deliziosa*, Juvarra was among the most appreciated and accomplished scene designers in Europe. He was unequaled as a draughtsman.

GIOVANNI PAOLO PANNINI

Piacenza 1691–Rome 1765

2. *Classical Ruins, with Antique Statues and Eight Figures*

Pen and black ink, watercolor, over black chalk. 14 x 9⅜ inches (356 x 238 mm). Watermark: none visible through lining.

Signed with initials at lower left, in pen and black ink, *I P P*.

PROVENANCE: Pierre-Jean Mariette (Lugt 1852); Sir Geoffrey Harmsworth; sale, London, Sotheby's, 25 March 1982, one of two in lot 79.

BIBLIOGRAPHY: Sotheby's *Preview*, London 1982, no. 16, p. 3, repr. color, cover; Morgan Library *FR* XX, 1984, p. 286, repr. no. 24.

EXHIBITION: New York 1989.

The Pierpont Morgan Library. Purchased on the von Bulow Fund, Acc. no. 1982.18:1

Giovanni Paolo Pannini, who came to Rome about 1711, played a central role in the artistic life of the city at mid-century. Pannini taught at the Accademia di San Luca and was professor of perspective at the French Academy, a post he held for more than thirty years until his death in 1765. He exerted a considerable influence on younger artists, particularly the French, including Hubert Robert whose work sometimes resembles that of Pannini (see Cat. no. 96).

Pannini was frequently cited in the *Correspondance des directeurs de l'Académie de France à Rome* as an example of an artist for the *pensionnaires* to follow or imitate. As Michael Kiene points out, Pannini's early works are executed in darker, more somber tonalities than his later ones, which are characterized by clarity and precision, and a preference for blues and grays. The use of these colors stems from theoretical considerations, his patrons, and his French friends, particularly Nicolas Vleughels (Paris and elsewhere 1992–93, pp. 27–28).

Pannini's talent lay in his skill as a perspective draughtsman and in his seemingly limitless ability to arrange and rearrange Roman monuments into pictures of great charm. Although many similar compositional elements appear in Pannini's paintings, this drawing and Cat. no. 3 do not seem to be connected with any of his known pictures. It is apparent from their comparable size and the mount and mark of Pierre-Jean Mariette (1694–1774) that they were made as a pair, probably at Mariette's request. Mariette's mount is recognized by its blue color, gold borders, and ruled black lines embellished with an open cartouche in which the collector inscribed the artist's name. Mariette was a connoisseur of the first rank, and according to Chennevières he owned at least twenty-six drawings by Pannini (Mariette 1851–60, vol. IV, p. 79, note 1). References to Pannini drawings intended for Mariette occur in the *Correspondance des directeurs* of the 1760s. There Natoire refers to drawings by Pannini that he is sending to Mariette in care of Marigny. On 8 July 1761, for example, Natoire states that he has taken the opportunity of enclosing several colored drawings by Pannini and Robert, and on 14 October of that year he included a package of two drawings by Pannini for Mariette.

In the present drawing, Pannini places within the ruins of an antique palace or basilica two well-known antique statues, *Silenus with the Infant Bacchus*, now in the Louvre, and *The Nile*, in the Vatican Museum. Two drawings in the Graphische Sammlung Albertina, Vienna, are virtual replicas of the Morgan drawings (fig. 1) (Inv. nos. 2941, 2942). There are, however, slight differences in the coloration of the sheets.

FIGURE 1 G. P. Pannini, *Antique Hall in Ruins.* Graphische Sammlung Albertina, Vienna, Inv. 2942.

Moreover, the Albertina drawings are signed *Pannini*. Since the quality of all four drawings is equally high, it must be assumed that Pannini sometimes repeated his most successful compositions.

GIOVANNI PAOLO PANNINI

Piacenza 1691–Rome 1765

3. *Classical Ruins with Twelve Figures*

Pen and black ink, watercolor, over black chalk. 13⅞ x 9⅜ inches (352 x 238 mm). Watermark: none visible through lining.

Signed with initials at lower left, in pen and black ink, *I P P*.

PROVENANCE: Pierre-Jean Mariette (Lugt 1852); Sir Geoffrey Harmsworth; sale, London, Sotheby's, 25 March 1982, one of two in lot 79.

BIBLIOGRAPHY: Sotheby's *Preview*, London 1982, p. 3, repr. color, back cover; Morgan Library FR XX, 1984, p. 286.

EXHIBITION: New York 1989.

The Pierpont Morgan Library. Purchased on the von Bulow Fund, Acc. no. 1982.18:2

See Cat. no. 2. The motif of figures standing behind a cloth and looking over a balustrade appears in several paintings by Pannini, such as *Alexander Cutting the Gordian Knot* (Collection Lord Iliffe, Basildon Park). The statue of *Apollo Citharoedos* also appears in a Pannini drawing in the Département des Arts Graphiques in the Louvre (Inv. no. 6724; Paris and elsewhere 1992–93, no. 48).

NO. 3

GIOVANNI PAOLO PANNINI
Piacenza 1691–Rome 1765

4. *View of the Great Vaulted Portico of the Villa Albani, Rome*

Pen and black ink, watercolor, and some graphite, including perspective points, some rendered by compass. 19 x 27⅝ inches (483 x 701 mm). Watermark: none visible through lining.

PROVENANCE: Kate de Rothschild and Yvonne Tan Bunzl, London.

BIBLIOGRAPHY: Vici 1976, p. 45, fig. 39; Morgan Library *FR* XVIII, 1978, pp. 242, 281, repr. no 15.

EXHIBITIONS: New York 1981, no. 90; New York 1989.

The Pierpont Morgan Library. Purchased on the Fellows Fund, with the special assistance of Mr. Rowland Burdon-Muller, Mrs. W. Rodman Fay, Mrs. Enid A. Haupt, Mrs. Gerard B. Lambert, Mr. Robert B. O'Connor, and Mr. John S. Thacher, Acc. no. 1977.43

From 1746, Carlo Marchionni (1702–86) began constructing a large villa for Cardinal Alessandro Albani on the Via Salaria (see Wilton-Ely in London 1972, pp. 593–94). Marchionni's design was for a two-story building with the ground-floor loggia opening onto a garden. The villa housed the cardinal's important collection of antiquities which had been assembled with the help of his curator and librarian, the classical scholar and theorist Johann Joachim Winckelmann. Numerous artists were involved in the decoration of the villa, including Anton Raphael Mengs who, in 1761, painted his *Parnassus* for the main salon of the villa, a work conceived under the influence of Winckelmann. Piranesi was also active in the decoration of the Villa Albani, although the extent to which he was involved remains uncertain. The Library's drawing, after an antique relief now used as an overdoor ornament in the Galleria del Parnaso, led Carlo Gasparri to suggest that the reliefs might have been acquired by Cardinal Albani through Piranesi (see Cat. no. 28).

Pannini's highly finished drawing captures the

grandeur of the elegant portico. As is characteristic of many of his architectural interiors, the scale is slightly exaggerated, and the portico appears larger and longer than it actually is. Michael Kiene has pointed out that Pannini's earliest known work dates from 1708. It is a copy of a treatise by Giulio Troili, first published in Italian in 1672 and reissued in 1683. Among the perspective illustrations are those re-garding the rotation of sculpture in space and the gradation of depth–both techniques in which Pan-nini became so skilled (Paris and elsewhere 1992–93, pp. 23–26). Although the subject and disposition of the Library's drawing is typical of Pannini's work, the rendering of the architecture is somewhat more la-bored, and the depiction of figures less spontaneous than those in other drawings by him.

GIOVANNI PAOLO PANNINI
Piacenza 1691–Rome 1765

5. *A Picture Gallery*

Pen and brown ink, gray and brown wash, and graphite. 13⅛ x 16³/₁₆ inches (333 x 411 mm). Watermark: not available.

Signed on the back of *fauteuil* at the lower left, *Pannini.*

PROVENANCE: Jean Groult; given by him to François Max-Kann (according to inscription on verso); Didier Aaron Inc., New York.

BIBLIOGRAPHY: Paris and elsewhere 1992–93, pp. 77–78, fig. 58, under no. 39.

EXHIBITIONS: New York 1988, no. 27, repr. on front and back cover; New York 1989.

Private Collection, New York

The drawing can be compared to Pannini's pictures of ancient and modern Rome in which baroque interiors were filled with sculpture and paintings depicting ancient and modern views of the city. Two such paintings were commissioned by Etienne François, duc de Choiseul, who was the French ambassador to Rome from 1754 to 1757 (see Arisi 1986, nos. 470 and 471). It was through Pannini's friend and future brother-in-law Nicolas Vleughels that the artist was introduced to many of the great French patrons in Rome, including Cardinal de Polignac and Cardinal de La Rochefoucauld. Pannini's *Gallery of Cardinal Silvio Valenti Gonzaga*, painted for that patron, is close in spirit to the exhibited sheet. Both depict old master paintings hung from ceiling to floor (Arisi 1986, nos. 397, 398, and 400). Pannini's typically dramatic theatrical space in these works is enhanced by the addition of curtains, drawn back as if revealing the scene.

When compared to the deep recession of space so characteristic of Pannini's paintings of interiors, the space in this drawing is much more intimate and finite. Here a gentleman sits in the center of the room, a draughtsman copies paintings, and other figures walk about, animatedly studying the pictures. The traditional identification of the seated figure as Cardinal Bernis is problematic because Bernis was only made ambassador to Rome in 1769, four years after Pannini's death. Recently, Michael Kiene has connected the sheet with Pannini's *Gallery of Cardinal Silvio Valenti Gonzaga* and related it to a drawing in Pannini's sketchbook in the British Museum as well (Paris and elsewhere 1992–93, pp. 77–78). Although this drawing is clearly not preparatory for the painting, the depiction of a more intimate, relaxed setting may well have been one of the artist's early ideas for the commission. Certainly the two central figures in both the painting and the drawing bear a close physical resemblance.

NO. 5

GIUSEPPE GALLI BIBIENA
Parma 1696–Berlin 1757

6. *A Large Funeral Hall in Ruins*

Pen and brown ink, brown and gray wash; framing line in brown ink. 16⅞ x 22⅜ inches (428 x 567 mm). Watermark: none visible through lining.

PROVENANCE: Mayr-Fájt (no mark; see Lugt S. 1804a); Janos Scholz (no mark; see Lugt S. 2933b); Donald M. Oenslager, New York.

BIBLIOGRAPHY: Mayor 1945, no. 39, repr.; Scholz 1962, no. 32, repr.; Oenslager 1975, p. 66, fig. 36.

EXHIBITIONS: Northampton 1961, no. 17; Philadelphia 1968, no. 35, repr.; St. Petersburg, Florida 1971, no. 17.

The Pierpont Morgan Library. Gift of Mrs. Donald M. Oenslager, Acc. no. 1982.75:114

Giuseppe Galli Bibiena belonged to a family of theater architects who served the princes of Europe for three generations, building opera houses and churches, decorating palaces, and producing temporary decorations for court fêtes. Their ability to achieve a new monumentality and to create an illusion of dramatic movement into space in their work was largely based on Ferdinando Bibiena's innovation of the *scena per angolo*, a technique adopted by set designers and artists. By the time Piranesi produced his *Prima Parte di Architetture, e Prospettive,* he must have known Ferdinando's *L'Architettura Civile,* published in 1711, and Giuseppe's *Architettura e Prospettive* that appeared in 1740, the year Piranesi arrived in Rome. It is clear from Piranesi's dedication letter in the *Prima parte* to Nicola Giobbe that his designs were inspired by similar principles that informed the work of the Bibienas: "In all these drawings you will see the great contribution of Perspective.... I would add that if a man cannot recognise its use and importance in Architecture he cannot appreciate the source from which it draws its most considerable beauty" (Scott 1975, pp. 45–46).

The attribution of drawings to the Bibiena family is extremely complicated given that they worked in similar styles and their drawings were seldom signed.

However, over two hundred of them reproduced in contemporary etchings and engravings are marked with Ferdinando's or Giuseppe's name, providing at least a hint of individual styles. Moreover, some drawings in a sketchbook in Vienna are stylistically close to this sheet, which supports the attribution to Giuseppe (see Philadelphia 1968, no. 35). The ruins depicted here, reminiscent of the Colosseum in Rome, belong to a group of designs that combine classical ruins with baroque monuments.

NO. 6

PIETRO BRACCI

Rome 1700–Rome 1773

7. *Ground Plan and Elevation of a Monument for James III, the Old Pretender, in St. Peter's, Rome*

Graphite underdrawing, pen and brown ink, brush and brown wash and white gouache with a brown ink border on prepared brown laid paper. 14⁹/₁₆ x 9⅝ inches (372 x 245 mm). Watermark: none.
Signed in brown ink in the lower left corner, *Petrus Bracci Inv. et. delin.*

DATE: 1766.

PROVENANCE: Bracci Archive, Rome; Duke Arturo Pini di San Miniato, New York, and Montréal.

BIBLIOGRAPHY: Lambert 1988, p. 52, fig. 22.

Montréal, Centre Canadien d'Architecture/Canadian Centre for Architecture DR1966:0001:018

8. *Alternate Ground Plan and Elevation of a Monument for James III, the Old Pretender, in St. Peter's, Rome*

Graphite underdrawing, pen and brown ink, gray and beige wash and white gesso, goldish-brown wash, and black chalk with two brown ink borders on prepared brown laid paper; sarcophagus on a flap. 16¼ x 9⅞ inches (412 x 251 mm). Watermark: fleur-de-lis in a circle (unidentified).
Inscribed in brown ink on the base of the statue on the tomb, *Jacobus III.* Inscribed in brown ink, left, adjacent to the base of the tomb, *Petrus Bracci Rom. F.* Scale lower edge of drawing, inscribed *Scala di... 30 Palmi Romani.*

DATE: 1766.

PROVENANCE: Bracci Archive, Rome; Duke Arturo Pini di San Miniato, New York, and Montréal.

Montréal, Centre Canadien d'Architecture/Canadian Centre for Architecture DR1966:0001:033

Pietro Bracci was trained as an architect, painter, and sculptor, and is considered one of the most proficient sculptors in eighteenth-century Rome. His most prominent works are the statue of *Oceanus* in the central niche of the Trevi Fountain (1762) and the monument to Pope Benedict XIV in St. Peter's (1764–68). In St. Peter's, monuments were originally reserved for saints and popes, witnesses of the tradition and history of the church. Pope Urban VIII extended the privilege of interment to Catholic sovereigns in 1633, in the full tide of the counter-reformation during the Thirty Years War, when he had the body of Countess Matilde of Tuscany transferred from Mantua. He commissioned Bernini to design her tomb. Queen Christina of Sweden, who had converted to Catholicism, was the next to be honored, though she had come to Rome in 1656 as a powerless monarch.

The continuous loss of political power and influence suffered by the papacy during the eighteenth century is visibly expressed in the Stuart monuments, the last royal tombs to be erected in St. Peter's. They no longer represented an alliance of strength, but an alliance in defeat. James III, king of Great Britain and Ireland, and his consort, Queen Maria Clementina Sobieska, in fact never reigned as legitimate royalty except in their own minds and those of the popes. James Francis Edward Stuart, Prince of Wales (1688–1766), only son of James II, was born at St. James's Palace in London, but the Glorious Revolution of 1688 deprived the Catholic James II of his throne, and his son grew up in exile at the court of Louis XIV. Furthermore, the Act of Settlement of 1701 excluded the male line of the Stuarts from the succession. After the failure of the rise of his Scottish supporters in 1715, James "III" had to leave France. From 1719 onward, he established, with papal money, a shadow court in Rome, officially recognized by the pope as that of England. In 1745 the last Jacobite uprising failed, and the merciless revenge of the English troops extinguished all further actions. James III was no longer a threat to the British government and the House of Hanover but became as the Old Pretender more and more an object of curiosity and pity. The hopes of the papacy to regain influence in the British Isles by supporting the claims of a Catholic monarch had proved a failure as well. But as one cannot admit defeat in St. Peter's, Pietro Bracci was called in 1766 not to depict reality in the Stuart monument, but a two-fold illusion – not the portrait of a sad and bitter man but the image of a king.

To create a monument in St. Peter's was the greatest challenge for every architect and sculptor. The royal tombs occupied the narrow bays of the side aisles, thus differing in width from the wider *aediculae* of the papal tombs. The narrowness of these bays stood in marked contrast to their height, which was predetermined by the giant columns that flanked the bays and formed the given framework for every design. The tomb for James III was to be erected in the south aisle across from that of his wife Maria Clementina Sobieska. Pietro Bracci had executed her tomb in 1739, after a design of Filippo Barigioni (*Venuti*, 1766, p. 477).

It is not known whether Bracci's designs were commissioned by the king's second son, Cardinal Henry, duke of York, archpriest of St. Peter's, or whether Bracci presented his drawings without request. The two drawings in this entry are part of a set of four presentation drawings, formerly in the Bracci Archive in Rome (Domarus 1915, pp. 62–63; Gradara 1920, pp. 87–88), all drawn to scale and obviously intended as alternative solutions. The third (fig. 1) is in the Musée des Beaux-Arts de Montréal (Dr. 1985.86) and the fourth (fig. 2) is in the Art Institute of Chicago (Joachim and McCullagh 1979, p. 83, no. 129; 1966.353). A possible fifth project, mentioned by Domarus and Gradara (pl. XXXVI), now in the CCA (DR1966:0001:019), should be omitted from this group.

When Bracci chose to represent the king in full size as a standing figure, he adhered to a new type of Roman tomb that had only two precedents: the statue of Cardinal Neri Corsini, executed in 1734 by Giuseppe Maini in the Corsini Chapel of the Lateran Basilica, and his own statue for the tomb of Pope Benedict XIV, which was in progress in 1766. For the royal monument, Bracci used the scheme of the "honorary statues"– similar to the one of Henri IV of France in the Lateran or to the one of Philip IV of Spain in Santa Maria Maggiore which depicts the kings in the guise of a Roman emperor. By introducing this different typology, Bracci found a way to distinguish the royal monuments from those of popes, princes, and cardinals, clearly marking the difference in hierarchy but in keeping with the style and appearance of the other monuments in St. Peter's. Another innovation in the first scheme (DR1966:0001:018) was the asymmetrical arrangement of only one allegory (Constancy) seated below the statue of the king and accompanied by a putto. This enhanced the concave movement of the base, giving the impression of more depth while also enlarging the narrow space between the columns. The allegory and the king's statue are not linked but stand isolated, framed by and set against the background of the niche. The important idea was to make use of the full height of the wall by eliminating the sheltering niche which had been used for all other royal tombs. Bracci had tried this traditional scheme in the second alternative design in the CCA (DR1966:0001:033) and in the third drawing in the Musée des Beaux-Arts de Montréal (fig. 1). In the former, Bracci returns to the conventional symmetrical arrangement – two allegories, Strength and Faith, flanking a sarcophagus. The bay, however, was too narrow and the arrangement looks a bit overcrowded. In a first version, which is preserved under the flap, the sarcophagus has been omitted and instead a putto and a lion had been part of the sculptural ensemble, which presented a more asymmetrical arrangement. In the first design in the CCA, the statue of the king, in full armor *all'antica* on a high pedestal in the attitude of a victorious warrior, is no longer twisted to fit the narrowness of the niche, as in the two alternative projects, but stands straight and erect. The asymmetrical arrangement of the allegory of Constancy is bound within one great movement. Her reclining and relaxed figure responds to the commanding, forceful, and spacious movements of the king, who seems to march out of the dark background into the light coming from one

FIGURE 1 Pietro Bracci, *Unexecuted Project for a Monument to James III in St. Peter's Rome.* Musée des Beaux-Arts de Montréal, Dr. 1985.86.

FIGURE 2 Pietro Bracci, *Project for the Tomb of James III, the Old Pretender.* Art Institute of Chicago, 1966.353.

of the smaller domes of the side aisle. The dark beige tinted paper, the brown wash, and the strong heightening with white gouache are characteristic of Bracci's drawing technique. They demonstrate his ability to create volume and three-dimensionality. The contrast of strong shadows and bright light enhances the impression of a truly baroque movement in the drawing. The details look rather coarse, but this kind of drawing was not made for the beauty of the line but to suggest the sculptural quality of the design, the effect of shining white marble emerging from a shadowy background. In the fourth drawing (fig. 2), Bracci presented another more conservative version of this project, again introducing the central sarcophagus and two symmetrically arranged allegories. In this design, Bracci not only depicted an illusion but also conveyed a vision of monarchy. There he is, the king–gracious and noble, swift but composed, commanding but serene, forceful but dignified. The forceful appearance may have been a reason why the project was never executed. Though Pope Clement XIII supported the interment of James III in St. Peter's, he was not favorable to the political ambitions of the king's sons. A triumphant monument to James III would have caused diplomatic repercussions with the British government.

The two drawings in the CCA not only demonstrate Bracci's superb sense of elegance and controlled movement but also sum up the qualities of late Roman baroque art. Later in 1819, Canova executed his monument to the last Stuarts in St. Peter's, paid for by the prince regent, future George IV, undisputed king of Great Britain. It is less successful than Bracci's project but perhaps the more appropriate memorial to the House of Stuart.

PAOLO POSI

Siena 1708–Rome 1776

9. *Design for the Chinea of 1760: The Temple of Neptune*

Pen and brown ink, gray wash and watercolor, over traces of graphite. 15⅞ x 22 inches (403 x 558 mm). Watermark: none visible through lining.

Signed at lower right of border in pen and brown ink, *Paolo Posi Architetto.* Inscribed on ruin in center foreground, in pen and brown ink, *Crede di Priapo il Tempio Elian divoto,/Ma Nettuno vi trova; onde di rabbia/Và sul solito Altar' á sciorre il voto.;* inscribed in border, *Disegno della Prima Machina rappresentante il Tempio di Nettuno. Incendiata per commando di Sua Eccellenza il Sig. DON LORENZO COLONNA Gran Contestabile/del Regno di Napoli &.&. come Ambasciatore straordinario di S.M. il RE' delle due Sicilie &.&.&. in congiuntura della presentazione della Chinea alla Santitá di Nostro/Signore PAPA CLEMENTE XIII. nella Vigilia de Gloriosi Santi APOSTOLI PIETRO, e PAOLO l'Anno MDCCLX.*

PROVENANCE: H. M. Calmann, Ltd., London.

BIBLIOGRAPHY: Morgan Library *FR* XII, 1963, pp. 88–89, repr.; Morgan Library *Review*, p. 161; New York 1971, under no. 180; London 1990a, p. 20.

EXHIBITION: New York 1989.

The Pierpont Morgan Library. Purchased as the gift of the Fellows, Acc. no. 1962.7

Paolo Posi came to Rome from Siena about 1725 or 1726. He enrolled in the Accademia di San Luca and studied with Filippo Barigioni. Between 1751 and 1775, as architect for the Colonna family, Posi designed the firework machines for the festivals of the *Chinea.* The festival was celebrated each year in Rome on 29 June, the feast day of St. Peter and St. Paul. During the ceremony, a member of the Colonna family presented to the pope in the name of the king of Naples a white mule bearing a coffer of gold. The festival originated in the thirteenth century, when Charles of Anjou accepted the Kingdom of the Two Sicilies as a fief of the Church. To mark the occasion, a great pyrotechnical machine was set up in the Piazza dei SS. Apostoli in front of the Palazzo Colonna. Sometimes another apparatus for fireworks was erected in the Piazza Farnese. After the fireworks, the machine–an elaborate construction of wood, canvas, and stucco–was burned to the accompaniment of recitations and music.

From 1723, it became customary to hold fireworks

displays on two successive evenings outside the Palazza Colonna in Piazza dei SS. Apostoli. Two structures were now required for the festival. This drawing and the following one record Posi's designs for the *prima machina* and *seconda machina* of the celebration on 29 June 1760 when Don Lorenzo Colonna presented his tribute to Pope Clement XIII. The presence of an elaborate foreground tableau is a characteristic shared by all of these drawings. A study for the *seconda machina* for the *Chinea* festival of 1769 shows that the foreground figures and landscape elements were, at least in this case, drawn first

as a kind of base over which the fireworks machine would be added (see London 1990a, no. 23, repr.).

Both of the Morgan drawings were later engraved by Giuseppe Vasi after perspective drawings by Giuseppe Palazzi, Posi's pupil and assistant. This is confirmed by the inscription on the print, *Paolo Posi Architetto, Giuseppe Palazzi disegno, Giuseppe Vasi incise.* From 1757, Giuseppe Palazzi's name was included on these prints. During the last years of Posi's life, Palazzi played a major role in designing the machines for the festival, eventually taking over his mentor's role as architect of the *Chinea*.

Disegno della Prima Machina rappresentante il Tempio di Nettuno Incendiata per commando di Sua Eccellenza il Sig. DON LORENZO COLONNA Gran Contestabile del Regno di Napoli &&. come Ambasciatore straordinario di S.M. il RE delle due Sicilie &&& in congiuntura della presentazione della Chinea alla Santità di Nostro Signore PAPA CLEMENTE XIII. nella Vigilia de Gloriosi Santi APOSTOLI PIETRO, e PAOLO l'Anno MDCCLX.

Paolo Posi Architetto.

PAOLO POSI

Siena 1708–Rome 1776

10. *Design for the Chinea of 1760: Chinoiserie*

Pen and brown ink, brown, gray, and pinkish-brown wash, over traces of graphite. 16⅛ x 22¼ inches (409 x 565 mm). Watermark: none visible through lining.

Signed at lower right of border in pen and brown ink, *Paolo Posi Architetto*; inscribed in border, *Prospetto della Seconda Machina rappresentante una Deliziosa all'uso cinese. Eretta per commando di Sua Eccellenza il Sig. DON LORENZO COLONNA Gran/Contestabile del Regno di Napoli & &. come Ambasciatore straordinario di S.M il RE' delle due Sicilie &.&.&. la Sera delli 29. Giugno 1760. Festa di Gloriosi Santi/Apostoli PIETRO, e PAOLO in occasione d'aver presentata la Chinea alla Santitá di Nostro Signore PAPA CLEMENTE XIII.*

PROVENANCE: H. M. Calmann, Ltd., London.

BIBLIOGRAPHY: Morgan Library *FR* XII, 1963, pp. 88–89; Morgan Library *Review*, p. 161; London 1990a, p. 20.

EXHIBITIONS: San Francisco 1966, no. 16, pl. IV; New York 1971, no. 180, repr.; Storrs 1973, no. 75; New York 1989.

The Pierpont Morgan Library. Purchased as the gift of the Fellows, Acc. no. 1962.8

See Cat. no. 9. This design represents the *seconda machina* erected for the 1760 celebration. The fashion for *chinoiserie* was popular in Europe during the second half of the century.

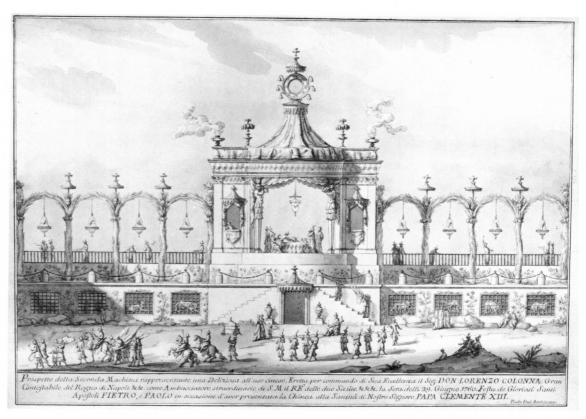

Disegno della Prima Machina rappresentante il Tempio di Nettuno. Incendiata per commando di Sua Eccellenza il Sig.º DON LORENZO COLONNA Gran Contestabile del Regno di Napoli &.&. come Ambasciatore straordinario di S. M. il RE delle due Sicilie &.&.&. in congiuntura della presentazione della Chinea alla Santità di Nostro Signore PAPA CLEMENTE XIII. nella Vigilia de Gloriosi Santi APOSTOLI PIETRO, e PAOLO l' Anno MDCCLX.

Paolo Posi Architetto *Giuseppe Palazzi disegno* *Giuseppe Vasi incise*

PAOLO POSI, architect

Siena 1708–Rome 1776

GIUSEPPE VASI, etcher

Corleone 1710–Rome 1782

GIUSEPPE PALAZZI, delineator

Rome 1740?–Rome 1810

11. *The Prima Machina of the Chinea of 1760: The Temple of Neptune*

Etching on laid paper. Platemark: 15³/₁₆ x 20¹⁵/₁₆ inches (386 x 532 mm); page: 17¾ x 26⁵/₁₆ inches (451 x 668 mm). Watermark: fleur-de-lis inside two circles with a *V* on the top (not identified).

Inscribed below image, *Disegno della Prima Machina rappresentante il Tempio di Nettuno. Incendiata per commando di Sua Eccellenza il Sig.ⁿ DON LORENZO COLONNA Gran Contestabile del Regno/di Napoli &.&. come Ambasciatore straordinario di S.M. il RE' delle due Sicilie &.&.&. in con-giuntura della presentazione della Chinea alla Santitá di Nostro Signore/PAPA CLEMENTE XIII. nella Vigilia de Glo-riosi Santi APOSTOLI PIETRO, e PAOLO l'Anno MDCCLX./*; lower left, *Paolo Posi Architetto*; center, *Giuseppe Palazzi disegno*; lower right, *Giuseppe Vasi incise.*

COLLECTORS' MARK: recto, lower right, letters *G* and *V* surrounding an oval stamped in purple ink with the num-ber *162* in graphite. Verso, lower right, two *C*s intertwined and surmounted by a crown in a circle stamped in brown ink (both unidentified).

DATE: 1760.

PROVENANCE: Robin Halwas Ltd., London.

BIBLIOGRAPHY (for the etching but not for the CCA's ver-sion): Scalabroni 1981, p. 101, no. 336, repr.

Montréal, Centre Canadien d'Architecture/Canadian Centre for Architecture DR1988:0437:028

See Cat no. 9. This and the following etching are part of a set of 56 in the CCA's collection. A total of 106 were executed in 1722, 1768, 1777, from 1779 to 1781, and from 1783 to 1784.

Prospetto della Seconda Machina rappresentante una Deliziosa all'uso cinese. Eretta per commando di Sua Eccellenza il Sig. Principe Don LORENZO COLONNA Gran Contestabile del Regno di Napoli ¿.¿. come Ambasciatore Straordinario di SUA MAESTA il RE' delle due Sicilie ¿.¿.¿. la 'Sera delli 29. Giugno 1760. Festa de Gloriosi SS. Apostoli PIETRO, e PAOLO in occasione d'aver presentata la Chinea alla Santita' di Nostro Signore PAPA CLEMENTE XIII.

Paolo Posi Architetto.   *Giuseppe Palazzi disegnò.*   *Giuseppe Vasi incise.*

PAOLO POSI, architect

Siena 1708–Rome 1776

GIUSEPPE VASI, etcher

Corleone 1710–Rome 1782

GIUSEPPE PALAZZI, delineator

Rome 1740?–Rome 1810

12. *The Seconda Machina of the Chinea of 1760: A Pavilion in the Chinese Style*

Etching on laid paper. Platemark: 15 x 21 inches (381 x 534); page: 17⅞ x 26¼ inches (453 x 665 mm). Watermark: none. Inscribed below image, *Prospetto della Seconda Machina rappresentante una Deliziosa all'uso cinese. Eretta per commando di Sua Eccellenza il Sig. Principe Don LORENZO COLONNA Gran Contestabile del/Regno di Napoli &.&. come Ambasciatore Straordinario di SUA MAESTA il RE' delle due Sicilie &.&.&. la 'Sera delli 29. Giugno 1760. Festa de Gloriosi SS. Apostoli PIETRO, e/PAOLO in occasione d'aver presentata la Chinea alla Santitá di Nostro Signore PAPA CLEMENTE XIII./*; lower left, *Paolo Posi Architetto*; center, *Giuseppe Palazzi disegno*; lower right, *Giuseppe Vasi incise.*

COLLECTOR'S MARK: verso, lower right corner, two Cs intertwined surmounted by a crown in a circle, stamped in brown ink (unidentified).

DATE: 1760.

PROVENANCE: Robin Halwas Ltd., London.

BIBLIOGRAPHY (for the etching but not for the CCA's version): Scalabroni 1981, p. 101, no. 337, repr.

Montréal, Centre Canadien d'Architecture/Canadian Centre for Architecture DR1988:0437:029

UNKNOWN ARTIST, member of the workshop of
Giuseppe Vasi

13. *A Procession in the Church of St. Peter's, Rome*

in Honor of the Saint's Day of Pope Pius VI
(1717–99) during the Jubilee Year 1775

Etching on laid paper. Two etchings: platemark (left):
27¹¹⁄₁₆ x 19³⁄₁₆ inches (703 x 488 mm), platemark (right):
27¾ x 19³⁄₁₆ inches (705 x 488 mm); left sheet: 32 x 22¹⁄₁₆
inches (813 x 561 mm); right sheet: 31¾ x 21⅝ inches (807 x
550 mm). Watermark: left sheet, left of center (illegible)
and *FABRIANO*; right sheet, right of center (illegible) and
FABRIANO (unidentified).

Inscribed across both sheets, lower edge below first border,
*Alla Santità del Sommo Pontefice/Papa PIO VI, Felicemente
Regante/L'Interno della Basilica Vaticana colla rappresen-
tanza dell'Ordine, con cui l'Ecclesistica Gerarchia de' Cardi-
nali/Arcivescovi, Vescovi, Prelati, ed altri Personaggi, proces-
sionalmente colla Santità Sua si iporta per celebrare le Sagre
Solenni Funzioni,/prostrato à Suoi SS. Piedi Giuseppe Vasi
Conte Palatino, e Cavaliere dell'Aula Lateranense, da se/dis-
egnato, ed inciso in rame l'Anno del Giubbileo 1775. umil-
mente Da, Dona, e Dedica*; below, a list of twenty sculptures
and monuments in St. Peter's preceded by arabic numerals.

DATE: 1775–90.

PROVENANCE: sale, Bern, Galerie Kornfeld, 21 June 1985,
lot 74.

BIBLIOGRAPHY (for these plates but not for the CCA's versions): Scalabroni 1981, p. 32, no. 434, p. 124, fig. 434; Rome
and Mogliano Veneto 1989, p. 29, no. 8, repr. p. 21.

*Montréal, Centre Canadien d'Architecture/Canadian
Centre for Architecture* DR1985:0662-0663

A Procession in Front of the Apse of the Church of St. Peter's, Rome

Dedicated to Cardinal Leonardo Antonelli
(1730–1811)

Etching on laid paper. Two etchings: platemark (left): 27⅝
x 19⅜ inches (702 x 493 mm), platemark (right): 27¹¹⁄₁₆ x

19⅜ inches (704 x 492 mm); left sheet: 31⁹⁄₁₆ x 22¹⁄₁₆ inches
(802 x 561 mm); right sheet: 31¹³⁄₁₆ x 22 inches (808 x 558
mm). Watermark: left sheet, left of center (partially illegible) and *FABRIANO*; right sheet, center *FORNARI*(?) and
FABRIANO (unidentified).

Inscribed across both sheets, center, lower edge below first
border, *All'Eminentissimo e Reverendissimo Principe/il
Cardinal Leonardo Antonelli del Titolo di S. Sabbina/La
Veduta del Fianco destro della Basilica Vaticana con l'Ordi-
nanza della Solenne Cavalcata del Somo Pontefice da sè di-
segnata/e medesimamente incisa in rame l'anno.1778. Giuseppe Vasi Conte Palatino, e Cavalier dell'Aula Lateranense
umte D.D.D.*, with a list of the participants in arabic numerals from 1 to 15.

DATE: 1778–90.

PROVENANCE: sale, Bern, Galerie Kornfeld, 21 June 1985,
lot 74.

BIBLIOGRAPHY (for these plates but not for the CCA's versions): Scalabroni 1981, p. 32, no. 435, p. 124.

*Montréal, Centre Canadien d'Architecture/Canadian
Centre for Architecture* DR1985:0664-0665

The Piazza and Church of St. Peter's, Rome

Dedicated to Cardinal Henry Benedict Maria, duke
of York (1725–1807)

Etching on laid paper. Two etchings: platemark (left): 28 x
19⁵⁄₁₆ inches (711 x 491 mm), platemark (right): 27⅞ x 19⁵⁄₁₆
inches (708 x 491 mm); left sheet: 31⅞ x 22¹⁄₁₆ inches (810 x
561 mm); right sheet: 31¹¹⁄₁₆ x 22 inches (806 x 557 mm).
Watermark: left sheet, upper left of center (illegible) and
FABRIANO; right sheet, lower left of center (illegible) and
FABRIANO.

Inscribed across both sheets, center, lower edge below first
border, *All'Altezza Reale Eminentissima di Errigo Benedetto
Maria Vescovo di Frascati/Cardinal Duca d'Yorck Vice-Can-
celliere della S. Rom.^{na} Chiesa, Sotto Decano del Sagro Col-
legio/ed Arciprete della Sagrosanta/Basilica Vaticana &c.&c.
/Il Prospetto principale del Tempio e Piazza di S. Pietro/in
Vaticano, e Palazzo Pontificio, Presenta, e Dedica/l'Umilis-
simo Devotissimo Obbligatissimo Servo Giuseppe Vasi Conte
Palatino e/Cavaliere dell'Aula Lateranense, dal medesimo*

disegnato ed inciso l'anno 1774., with a list of the other buildings depicted following arabic numerals 1 to 13.

DATE: 1774–90.

PROVENANCE: sale, Bern, Galerie Kornfeld, 21 June 1985, lot 74.

BIBLIOGRAPHY (for these plates but not for the CCA's versions): Rome and Mogliano Veneto 1989, p. 28, no. 7, repr. p. 21.

Montréal, Centre Canadien d'Architecture/Canadian Centre for Architecture DR1985:0666-0667

These six etchings of St. Peter's illustrate the differences in technique and content between Vasi's large-scale *vedute* of Rome and those of Piranesi. In *Delle Magnificenze di Roma Antica e Moderna*, Vasi depicted the buildings as backdrops for important events, whereas Piranesi concentrated on the buildings themselves (Sassoli 1992, p. 19). Piranesi also used single copper plates of a horizontal format for the large-sized illustrations of the *Vedute di Roma*. Vasi had used plates of a horizontal format for the medium-sized illustrations in the volumes of *Delle Magnificenze*. When he turned to large-scale etchings, however, he employed a vertical format. This practice necessitated the use of more than one plate in order to show a panoramic view. Each scene here is shown in two plates. The resulting paper sheets would have to have been placed next to each other since the inscriptions run from one plate to the other. For his *Panorama of Rome from the Janiculum* (1765), announced in the preface to volume I of *Delle Magnificenze*, Vasi used twelve copper plates of the same vertical format and size as these illustrations of St. Peter's (Scalabroni 1981, p. 30, no. 313, p. 91, repr. in Sassoli 1992, vol. I, p. 27, fig. 9, 2560 x 10000 mm).

The first pair of etchings, which depict a papal procession in St. Peter's, is based on a painting signed by Giovanni Paolo Pannini (1691–1765) in 1730, *The Interior of Saint Peter's on the Occasion of the Visit of Cardinal Melchior di Polignac September 4, 1729*, now in the Louvre. Vasi and Pannini knew each other extremely well, and Vasi based several other etchings on Pannini's paintings (Arisi 1986, p. 331, no. 200, repr.

pp. 331, 171, 462). In the two etchings exhibited here, Vasi has placed the viewer in the same position as Pannini did in the aforementioned painting, inside St. Peter's at the entrance to the nave. As in Pannini's painting, the spectator witnesses the procession from a bird's-eye viewpoint in the center.

In one of his earliest plates of the *Vedute di Roma*, the *Interior of the Basilica of St. Peter's*, dated by Robison between 1748 and 1749, Piranesi has placed the spectator at an angle slightly to the left, in the middle of the nave, thus focusing the viewer's attention on Bernini's baldachin at the crossing (Robison in Bettagno 1983, p. 21; Hind 1922, p. 39, no. 4; Focillon 1964, p. 54, no. 788; Wilton-Ely 1978 [1988], pl. 4). Piranesi emphasized the structure of the Church of St. Peter's and reduced to a minimum both the number of spectators and the sculptural decoration. Vasi, on the other hand, makes the spectator a witness to all the pomp and circumstance of the papal procession, much in the same way Pannini did in his 1754 painting *The Exit of the duc de Choiseul from the Piazza of St. Peter's*, now in the Gëmaldegalerie, Berlin (Arisi 1986, pp. 450–51, no. 445, repr. pp. 450–51, and pls. 154, 155, pp. 166–67). The pope in Vasi's pair of etchings, carried aloft in a litter under a baldachin, is as lost amid the priests, bishops, and cardinals, as is the duc de Choiseul, seated in his carriage in the piazza surrounded by the members of his suite on foot.

The second pair of etchings shows a procession moving from the apse of St. Peter's through one of Bernini's colonnades to the Piazza. It is dedicated to Cardinal Leonardo Antonelli (1730–1811). Vasi shows the apse and dome of St. Peter's in the foreground, with one wing of Bernini's colonnade receding to the right toward a panoramic view of the Castel Sant'Angelo and the city of Rome in the distance. Here again, Pope Pius VI (1775–99) is barely visible. He appears on a horse under an umbrella next to the number 7 in the center of the second etching. It would be impossible to have such an extensive view of St. Peter's and the Castel Sant'Angelo from a position so close to the apse, where Vasi has placed the spectator. A similar view of the side of St. Peter's showing the apse, dome, and one arm of the colon-

A Procession in the Church of St. Peter's, Rome.

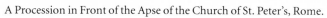

A Procession in Front of the Apse of the Church of St. Peter's, Rome.

The Piazza and Church of St. Peter's, Rome.

nade of the Piazza occurs in the left corner of Vasi's aforementioned *Panorama of Rome from the Janiculum* (1765). In this view of a papal procession, the spectator is obliged to change his viewpoint as the participants in the procession move along. This type of *veduta* of St. Peter's has no equivalent in either Piranesi's or Pannini's oeuvre. Piranesi represented only the apse of St. Peter's from a similar viewpoint in a plate of the *Vedute di Roma* dated by Robison between 1750 and 1751 (Hind 1922, p. 39, no. 5; Focillon 1964, p. 54, no. 789; Robison in Bettagno 1983, pp. 23–24; Wilton-Ely 1978 [1988], pl. 20).

The last two etchings of this set, *The Piazza and Church of St. Peter's, Rome,* are not listed by Scalabroni in her *catalogue raisonné* of Vasi's etchings. They reveal the influence of Piranesi's third *View of the Basilica and Piazza of St. Peter's* in his *Vedute di Roma,* which must have been issued by 1763 (Hind 1922, p. 70, no. 120; Focillon 1964, p. 51, no. 720; Wilton-Ely 1978 [1988], pl. 120; see Cat. no. 118). The cardinal to whom these two etchings are dedicated, Henry Benedict Maria, duke of York (1725–1807), the second son of James III, the Old Pretender, may have been responsible for the commission of his father's tomb, which was designed by Pietro Bracci in St. Peter's (Cat. nos. 7 and 8). Book VI of Vasi's *Delle Magnificenze,* entitled *Le Chiese parrocchiali,* was dedicated to Cardinal Henry Benedict Maria.

Although the inscription states that these last two etchings were executed by Giuseppe Vasi in 1774, this view of the Piazza and Church of St. Peter's is a larger version of a plate often inserted, according to Scalabroni, in posthumous editions of Book III of *Delle Magnificenze,* originally published in 1753. Scalabroni attributed this later plate to Vasi's son Mariano, because it has, on the facade of St. Peter's, the two clocks that were installed by Giuseppe Valadier (1762–1839) after he was appointed *architetto camerale* to Pope Pius VI in 1786 (Scalabroni 1981, p. 67, no. 114bis, 195 x 321 mm). It is quite possible that Mariano, who continued his father's workshop after his death, updated an etching that Vasi had designed but not completed in his lifetime. The six etchings forming this set of views of St. Peter's must have all been issued posthumously, because each was executed on the same paper. They all have a partially illegible watermark of paper made in Fabriano similar to one in the paper used by Francesco Piranesi for his *Raccolta de' Tempi Antichi,* published in 1790 (Robison 1986, p. 232, no. 76).

GIOVANNI VOLPATO, etcher and engraver

Angarano di Bassano 1735–Rome 1803

FRANCESCO PANNINI, delineator

Rome about 1725–Rome about 1794

14. *Panorama of Rome from Monte Mario*

Etching and stipple engraving on laid paper. Three sheets joined; total of three platemarks: 18⅞ x 82 inches (480 x 2084 mm); sheet: 19¾ x 84 inches (492 x 2132 mm). Watermark: right center of first sheet on left, on no. 11, fleur-de-lis in a double circle with *CB* below; left of center of second sheet, on no. 18, fleur-de-lis in a double circle with *CB* below (Robison 1986, p. 223, no. 39).

Inscribed lower left, *Francesco Panini delin.*; center, *VEDUTA IN PROFILO DELLA CITTÀ DI ROMA DALLA PARTE DI MONTE MARIO PRESA NELLA SUA ESTENSIONE DALLA PIAZZA DEL POPOLO SINO ALLA BASILICA DI S.PIETRO IN VATICANO*; below, a list of monuments numbered in arabic numerals from 1 to 39; below, in center, *In Roma nella Calcografia della Reverendia Camera Apostolica appresso la Curia Innocenziana l'Anno 1779*; lower right, *Giovanni Volpato sculp.*

DATE: 1779.

PROVENANCE: sale, Bern, Galerie Kornfeld, 21 June 1985, lot 79.

BIBLIOGRAPHY (for this plate but not for the CCA's version): Petrucci 1934, no. 1232 (copper plate); Bassano del Grappa and Rome 1988, p. 32 (copper plate), p. 132, no. 206, repr. pp. 136–37; Rome and Mogliano Veneto 1989, pp. 95, 99, under no. 65.

Montréal, Centre Canadien d'Architecture/Canadian Centre for Architecture DR1985:0673

Giovanni Volpato came to Rome in 1771 after having been active in Venice as an etcher specializing in the reproduction of paintings. While in Venice he was a member of the workshops of Francesco Bartolozzi, Joseph Wagner, and the painter Francesco Maggiotto. After having been made a member of the Academies of Painting and Sculpture of Parma and Verona in 1769, he was called to Rome to complete the etchings of Raphael's *Loggie* in the Vatican palace, begun by Giovanni Ottaviani and published by the *Calcografia Camerale Apostolica*. Volpato's colored etchings of the pilasters and the illusionistic paintings in the vaults were published between 1772 and 1776. Before he left Venice, Volpato etched several of the illustrations of Paolo Antonio Paoli's book on Paestum, *Rovine della Città di Pesto detto Ancora Posidonia*, published later in Rome in 1784.

In Rome, Volpato set up a large workshop that produced etchings of *vedute* of Rome, as well as etchings of important paintings by artists such as Annibale Carracci, Gaspard Dughet, and Claude Lorrain. At the same time his activities diversified. He established a factory that produced unglazed porcelain figurines after ancient statues; he became a dealer in antiquities, selling a group of statues of the *Muses* to

NO. 14

Gustavus III of Sweden in 1784. He also took part in excavations at the Piazza San Marco, the Baths of Caracalla, and at Palestrina. He was particularly involved with the English and German communities in Rome. He befriended the Scottish painter and antiquarian Gavin Hamilton, and etched the paintings published in Hamilton's *Schola Italica Picturae* (1773). He was friendly with Angelica Kauffmann, to whom he dedicated a series of etchings of Guercino's paintings in the Palazzo Ludovisi. He also knew Goethe and the English artist Thomas Jenkins. He was a close friend of Antonio Canova for whom he arranged the commission of the *Tomb of Pope Clement XIV* (pope 1769–74). Canova reciprocated by sculpting Volpato's tombstone in the portico of the Basilica of SS. Apostoli. In 1826, 186 of his copper plates were acquired by the *Calcografia Camerale Apostolica* (now the *Calcografia di Roma*). Volpato's workshop was continued by his descendants until 1831.

Volpato's most influential work was the series of colored etchings of Raphael's *Loggie.* They had an influence on the copy of the *Loggie* commissioned by Catherine the Great for the Winter Palace in St. Petersburg, the interior of Gustavus III's pavilion in the park of Haga near Stockholm, Karl Friedrich Schinkel's design for a pavilion at Charlottenburg, and Marie Antoinette's *Grand Cabinet* by Pierre Rousseau at Fontainebleau (Giorgio Marini in Bassano del Grappa and Rome 1988, pp. 13–20).

There is only fragmented information about Francesco Pannini's life. He was trained in the workshop of his father, Giovanni Paolo Pannini (1691– 1765). Francesco Pannini specialized in executing preparatory drawings for etchings of architectural subjects. He also worked in collaboration with other engravers, such as Domenico Montagù, Giuseppe Vasi, Francesco Polanzani, Domenico Cigni, and Giovanni Ottaviani, whose prints were published by the *Calcografia Camerale Apostolica* (Margiotta in Rome and Mogliano Veneto 1989, pp. 94–95, nos. 61– 80, pp. 96–113). According to a letter from Gavin Hamilton to Lord Shelburne, 9 February 1775, Francesco Pannini did the coloring for Giovanni Volpato's etchings of Raphael's *Loggie* (Grazia Bernini Pezzini in Bassano del Grappa and Rome 1988, p. 23, nos. 187–98, pp. 124–27, repr. pp. 42, 45, 46). Francesco Pannini also collaborated with Volpato on the frontispiece of Paolo Antonio Paoli's book on Paestum (Bassano del Grappa and Rome 1988, p. 112, no. 145, repr. 114), the etchings of the Galleria Farnese published in 1777 (Bassano del Grappa and Rome 1988, pp. 132–39, nos. 207–12, repr. pp. 138–39), and a series of *Vedute di Roma* published by the *Calcografia Camerale Apostolica* between 1773 and 1780 (Bassano del Grappa and Rome 1988, pp. 127–32, nos. 199–205, repr. pp. 134–35).

The watermarks found on this etching of Volpato's *Panorama of Rome* show that it was executed on the same type of paper used by Giovanni Battista and Francesco Piranesi between the late 1760s and the early 1790s. Since the quality of the etching is brilliant, the CCA's version must be an early impression. Pannini has depicted a panorama of Rome from Monte Mario, extending from the Church of Santa Maria del Popolo at the left, to the Church of St. Peter's at the right. This panorama is based on a painting of the same subject by Francesco's father, Giovanni Paolo Pannini, that was executed in 1749 and is now in the Gemäldegalerie in Berlin. In turn, Giovanni Paolo Pannini's painting was based on a similar view executed by the Dutch artist Jan Frans von Bloemen in 1735 (Arisi 1986, p. 428, no. 395, repr. p. 428, pl. 165, p. 157). Here in the etching, Francesco Pannini has decreased the space occupied by the hill itself to show more detail of the thirty-nine monuments in the distance. In Giovanni Paolo Pannini's painting, the viewer sees merely the domes and spires of the churches. Anita Margiotta noted that Volpato increased the contrast between light and shadow when he made etchings after Francesco Pannini's drawings. There is a more even distribution of light in both Francesco's drawings and his father's paintings (Margiotta in Rome and Mogliano Veneto 1989, p. 99, under no. 65, p. 108, no. 75, repr. p. 108, p. 111, no. 78, repr. p. 111).

If we compare this etched panorama with Giovanni Battista and Carlo Nolli's 1748 *Map of Rome*

(Cat no. 52), we see that Francesco Pannini increased the distances between the Piazza del Popolo, at the left, and the Church of St. Peter's, at the right, in order to include the largest number of monuments. Most buildings shown in this etched panorama are churches, although one finds palaces, such as the Palazzo Borghese at no. 12, ancient monuments, such as the Mausoleum of Hadrian, now the Castel Sant'Angelo at no. 28, or squares, such as the Piazza of St. Peter's just below no. 38. Some of the most important churches of Rome are shown in this panorama, including Santa Trinità dei Monti at no. 6, SS. Carlo e Ambrogio al Corso at no. 8, Santa Maria Maggiore at no. 11, Sant' Agnese in Agone on the Piazza Navona at no. 13, and the Gesù at no. 20. Francesco Pannini and Giovanni Volpato's panorama of Rome is quite different in character from the huge *Panorama of Rome from the Janiculum* (1765) that Giuseppe Vasi etched in twelve plates (Scalabroni 1981, p. 91, no. 313, repr. in Sassoli 1992, vol. 1, p. 27, fig. 9, 2560 x 10000 mm). Giovanni Paolo and Francesco Pannini give the spectator only a selected group of thirty-nine major monuments. In contrast, Vasi shows the viewer the streets of Rome cluttered with smaller buildings alongside the important ones. Giuseppe Vasi shows a more realistic view of the fabric of the actual modern city, whereas Francesco Pannini presents a more idealized panorama in a pastoral setting, indicated by the peasants with cows in the foreground.

VICENZO BRENNA

Florence 1747–Dresden 1820

15. *Design for a Painted Cupola with "Venus at her Toilet"*

Gouache. 21⅝ x 23¾ inches (550 x 603 mm). Watermark: none visible through lining.

PROVENANCE: Edmond Fatio (his mark at lower right; not in Lugt); Stephen Spector.

EXHIBITION: New York 1989.

The Pierpont Morgan Library. Gift of Stephen Spector, Acc. no. 1962.22

Little is known about Brenna's early artistic training. He and the architect Giacomo Quarenghi (1744–1817) were mentioned as fellow students with Stefano Pozzi (ca. 1707–68) in Rome during the years 1766 to 1768. Brenna became well known, however, when he collaborated with the Polish painter Franciszek Smugliewicz (1745–1807) on the *Vestigia delle terme di Tito e loro interne pitture*, published by a Roman art dealer, Ludovico Mirri, in 1776. The folio volume has also been referred to as *Le Antiche camere delle terme di Tito e le loro interne pitture* by Giuseppe Carletti because Carletti wrote the descriptive text to the sixty engravings by Marco Carloni (or Carlone, 1742–96). The engravings, made after Brenna and Smugliewicz's drawings, depicted recently discovered paintings in the rooms then believed to be the Baths of Titus, but which present-day scholarship recognizes as the chambers of Nero's Golden House or *Domus Aurea*.

The Morgan Library's spectacular sheet of a semicircular cupola has a bright red background with various friezes of animals and fantastic creatures. *Venus at her Toilet* is in the center of the cupola: she is shown half nude, holding a mirror and adjusting her hair, flanked by two winged Erotes holding platters (*phiale*). Two similar fresco fragments with Erotes have been found in a house at Boscoreale; one is now at the Louvre, the other in the Pierson Museum, Amsterdam.

The Morgan drawing is preparatory for plate 10 of the *Vestigia delle terme di Tito* (fig. 1), engraved by Marco Carloni and inscribed *Vinc. Brenna disegnò Carloni Romano incise*. Plate 8 is an engraving of the entire wall with niche, cupola, statues of Juno, Minerva, Venus, and Cupid, and a bathtub. According to the inscription, Smugliewicz and Brenna collaborated here. Plate 11 (fig. 2), an engraving of *Venus at her Toilet*, is inscribed *Franc. Smugliewicz's Pit. designò*. Since the Venus is identical to the one in the Library's drawing and the print after it, Smugliewicz may have added this vignette to Brenna's design. As

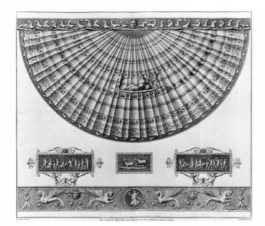

FIGURE 1 Marco Carloni, *Cupola Design with "Venus at Her Toilet."* Avery Architectural Library, Columbia University, New York.

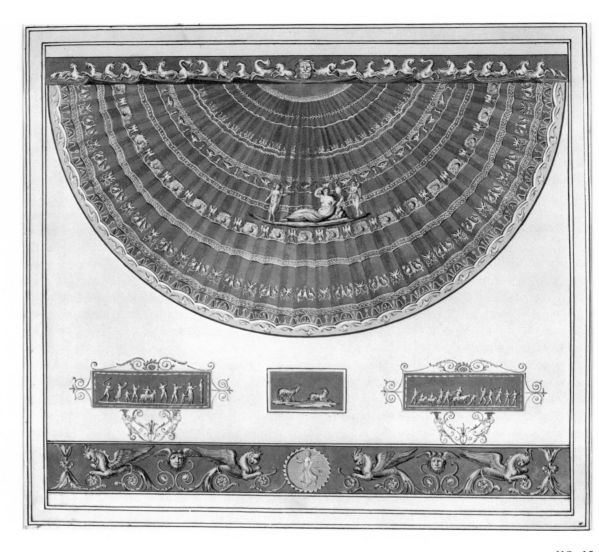

FIGURE 2 Franciszek Smugliewicz, *Venus at Her Toilet.* Avery Architectural Library, Columbia University, New York.

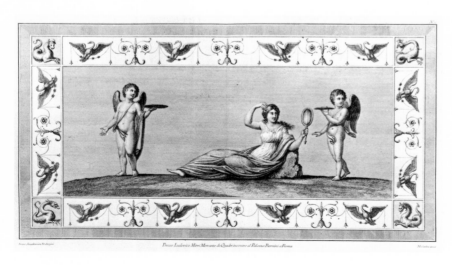

an architect, Brenna was probably more interested in the structural and decorative elements of this room, whose decoration is pictured in the engravings on plates 8, 10, and 11 of the *Vestigia*. The room also appears as camera 25 in the *Indice della Pianta del Sotterraneo* on plate 3 where it is described as *Camera in fondo rosso con arabeschi, e quadri di figure lumeggiate ad oro, e basamento di marmi. Vi è un nicchione semicircolare, e si veggono le vestigia del Labro, e delle statue* (Chamber with red background and arabesques as well as figure paintings lit up with gold and a base of marble. There is a large semicircular niche where traces of the basin and the statues are visible).

In her study *La Découverte de la Domus Aurea et la formation des grotesques à la Renaissance,* Nicole Dacos mentions the grafitti on the vault of room 34 in the *Domus Aurea: BRENNA DELINEA [VIT] ET APERUIT* (Dacos 1969, p. 142). This clearly proves that Brenna was one of the artists who took part in the excavations of these rooms, under the direction of Ludovico Mirri. Dacos further states that when strong light is projected on its walls, camera 34 still reveals those well-known motifs of the Pompeian style—putti, garlands, and masks standing out on a red background.

At the present stage of the excavations of Nero's *Domus Aurea,* it is not possible to determine the exact use of any of the rooms of the palace, except the library. Suetonius in his *Lives of the Caesars* mentions two baths (*balineae*) and a circular dining hall. One of the baths was for salt and the other for sulphurous water (see Boëthius 1960, p. 117). The style of the *Domus Aurea* wall paintings is the so-called fourth Pompeian style, which is also found in the frescoes of many villas at Stabiae, Boscoreale, and Boscotrecase: they show a delicate framework of architectural elements in perspective view, enshrining figures and mythological scenes, as well as purely decorative components such as *grotteschi* and fantastic human and animal forms.

There is a related drawing of a lunette from the Baths of Titus (London 1972, no. 1586) and a preparatory drawing for plate 7 in the *Vestigia* at the Cooper-Hewitt Museum in New York (1961–176–1). Executed in the same bright red gouache, the drawing at the Cooper-Hewitt possibly illustrates the decoration of another wall of the same room that appears in the Morgan drawing. There is also an engraving of a ceiling design identical with plate 26 in the *Vestigia* at the Cooper-Hewitt (1989–112–7). As recently as 1990, a folio volume of thirty-three drawings in gouache and watercolor after Roman wall paintings appeared on the art market (London, Sotheby's, 11 July 1990, lot 15). Three are signed by Smugliewicz, two by Vicenzo Brenna, five by both, and all ten are inscribed: *Presso Ludovico Mirri Mercante de Quadri incontro al Palazzo Bernini a Roma/Carloni incise e dipinse.* This connects them with the publisher of the *Vestigia.* As the compiler of the sale catalogue suggests, they may have been purchased from Ludovico Mirri in the early nineteenth century.

Shortly after or during the time of his collaboration with Smugliewicz on the *Vestigia,* Brenna must have made the acquaintance of the Polish art patron and future translator of Winckelmann, Stanislas Kosta Potocki (1755–1821). Potocki translated Winckelmann's *Geschichte der Kunst des Alterthums* into Polish; it was published in three volumes in 1815. Between 1777 and 1778, Potocki initiated the project of reconstructing Pliny the Younger's villa, the *Laurentinum,* located near Ostia. Brenna is named as the artist of some of the drawings connected with this project; they are still preserved in two albums at the National Library in Warsaw. The inscription on the second album reads: *Interieurs de la Villa de Pline le jeune par Brenna*; it contains eight designs and, on a piece of paper glued to the inside cover, an interesting notation in Potocki's hand, referring to Brenna's successful career in Russia: "Vincent Brenna, aujourd'hui Architecte de l'Empereur de Russie milionaire a ce que l'on dit, . . . volé plusieurs de ces dessins en quittant la Pologne, ainsi que d'autres objets de l'art." Brenna, who had worked in Poland for some years, left in 1783 for Russia and became imperial court architect to Czar Paul I in 1796. His fame there primarily rests on his activity in the palaces of Pavlovsk and Gatchina (summer palace). After Paul's assassination in 1801, Brenna left for Germany, where he is documented in Dresden in 1818, and where he probably died before or during 1820.

Both Smugliewicz and Brenna left Rome around 1780. The Polish artist, who had been studying painting in Rome on a stipend given him by King Stanislaus II Augustus (Poniatowski), was recalled by him, and returned to his native country in 1785. He settled in Warsaw, where he founded an art school. In 1797 he moved to Vilna (now Vilnius, Lithuania) where he taught at the university. Around 1800 or 1801, he was in St. Petersburg working also for Paul I. He is considered the chief representative of neoclassicism in Poland.

GIOVANNI BATTISTA PIRANESI
Mogliano Veneto 1720–Rome 1778

16. *Architectural Complex*

Pen and brown ink, brown wash, over black chalk. Verso: Black chalk sketch of colonnade. 10⅟₁₆ x 7⅟₁₆ inches (255 x 181 mm). Watermark: none.

PROVENANCE: Mrs. J. P. Morgan, New York; her sons, Junius S. Morgan and Henry S. Morgan, New York.

BIBLIOGRAPHY: Stampfle 1948, pp. 123–24, no. 4; Mayor 1952, fig. 40; Thomas 1954, no. 42, repr.; Morgan Library *FR* XV, 1969, pp. 118–19; Morgan Library *Review*, 1969, p. 160; Stampfle 1978, no. 4, repr.; Pane 1980, pp. 108ff., fig. 34.

EXHIBITIONS: New York 1949, p. 7, no. 4, fig. 2; Waterville 1956, no. 12; Newark 1960, no. 51, repr.; New York 1971, no. 225, repr.; New York 1989.

The Pierpont Morgan Library. Bequest of the late Junius S. Morgan and gift of Henry S. Morgan, Acc. no. 1966.11:4

This drawing probably dates to around 1750, a period when Piranesi began synthesizing the Venetian freedom of touch with Roman solidity and grandeur of form. He has applied the wash expressively in the drawing, freely brushing it on in some areas to suggest light and shade, and in others, using it to produce a convincing sense of depth or three-dimensionality, particularly noticeable in the shorthand notations that describe the sculptural ornament.

This kind of grand architectural complex is related in spirit to Piranesi's *Prima Parte di Architetture, e Prospettive,* a collection of twelve etchings of imaginary temples, palaces, ruins, and a prison, published in July 1743. These etchings were later included in his *Opere varie,* first published in 1750. In his introduction to the *Prima parte,* Piranesi explained why he considered this kind of architectural drawing so important in his oeuvre. Lamenting that it was impossible for an architect of his time to execute any grand buildings, he wrote, "there is no course open to me or to any other modern architect but to set out in drawings our ideas and thus regain from Sculpture and Painting the advantage which, as the great Juvarra says, they have gained over Architecture" (Scott 1975, p. 13).

GIOVANNI BATTISTA PIRANESI

Mogliano Veneto 1720–Rome 1778

17. *Fantastic Monuments*

Pen, brown ink, brown wash over graphite underdrawing on cream laid paper. 7¾ x 10⅞ inches (198 x 277 mm). Watermark: none.

Inscribed at lower right, in brown ink in a later hand, *Piranesi.*

DATE: 1747–50.

PROVENANCE: A. Rateau, Paris; F. Stonor, London; W. R. Jeudwine, Old Master Drawings, London; Charles E. Slatkin Galleries, New York; Phyllis Lambert, New Haven, Chicago, and Montréal.

BIBLIOGRAPHY: Lambert 1988, p. 47, fig. 16.

EXHIBITIONS: New York 1967, p. 4, pl. 18; Venice 1978, p. 43, no. 34, p. 43, repr.; Vancouver and elsewhere 1989–90, p. 80, no. 67, repr. p. 82.

Montréal, Centre Canadien d'Architecture/Canadian Centre for Architecture DR1967:0003

This drawing was first attributed to Piranesi and dated between 1745 and 1750 by Hylton Thomas in the Slatkin Galleries exhibition catalogue. Jörg Garms has already noted (letter of 14 February 1984, CCA Prints and Drawings, Research Files) that the inscription is not in the artist's hand, an observation supported by comparing this inscription with Piranesi's handwriting on a letter exhibited here (3 August 1772, Cat. no. 65). Thomas found a similarity between this drawing and the *Fantastic Monument* in the Museum of Fine Arts, Boston, particularly in the limpid, transparent washes, lines drawn freely in pen, and silhouetted architectural elements in the foreground that were applied in dark brown ink with a brush (fig. 1) (Thomas 1954, pp. 42–43, no. 23, repr.). In the CCA's drawing, Piranesi represents a courtyard in the middle ground, viewed from an oblique angle. Above, several other architectural elements

FIGURE 1 G. B. Piranesi, *Fantastic Monument*. Museum of Fine Arts, Boston, 26.426.

FIGURE 2 G. B. Piranesi, *The Fantastic Port Monument* (left pl.). National Gallery of Art, Washington, 1979.32.1.

FIGURE 3 G. B. Piranesi, *Foro antico Romano*, in *Prima parte* (first edition, first issue), pl. 11. National Gallery of Art, Washington, 1976.2.1.

FIGURE 4 G. B. Piranesi, *Gruppo di Scale*, in *Prima parte* (first edition, first issue), pl. 8. National Gallery of Art, Washington, 1976.2.1.

loom in the distance: to the left, a round building with porticos surmounted by triangular pediments, and to the right, two three-tiered towers placed in front of the triple-storied frontispiece of a facade.

Andrew Robison's very careful dating of Piranesi's early etchings–the *Prima parte* (1743), the *Grotteschi* (1747–49), the *Carceri* (1749–50), and several individual plates executed after his return in September 1747 to Rome from his second trip to Venice (Moretti in Bettagno 1983, pp. 132–33)–permits us to date the CCA's drawing precisely. In conception and technique, it is closest to the etching *The Fantastic Port Monument* or *Fall of Phaeton* (fig. 2). In 1965, Maurizio Calvesi discovered a proof of this etching on the back of two early etchings of the *Vedute di Roma* (1745–49): the *Vedute di Santa Maria Maggiore* and the *Vedute di Piazza di Monte Cavallo*. In *The Fantastic Port Monument*, there are several areas where ink has been applied to the plate after it was etched and then been blotted out. This technique simulates the effect of the washes in drawings and creates an impression of shifting light and shadows caused by the moving clouds.

Robison suggested that the drawing in Boston, and the Louvre's *Fantastic Monuments in a Palatial Interior* were both executed by Piranesi in preparation for *The Fantastic Port Monument* (Robison 1986, pp. 33–34, no. 27, repr. pp. 132–33 and p. 34, fig. 37, p. 35, fig. 39). In *The Fantastic Port Monument* (fig. 2), a domed structure surrounded by four spiral columns, reminiscent of Fischer von Erlach's reconstruction of the *Mausoleum of Artemisia at Halicarnassus* (Cat. no. 23), is set on concave supports in a courtyard (Patella in Rome and Cori 1979, pp. 18–19, figs. G, H).

Most of the architectural elements in the CCA's drawing can be traced to the first issue of the first edition of *Prima parte*, published by Piranesi in 1743, before his trip back to Venice from Rome in 1744 (Moretti in Bettagno 1983, pp. 137–38). However, his freedom with the pen and brush here is quite different from the hesitant and more carefully delineated drawings in the Morgan Library and in the National Gallery of Scotland, which Piranesi executed between 1740 and 1742 in preparation for two plates of the first

issue of the *Prima parte*–the *Prospetto d'un regio Cortile*, and the *Mausoleo antico* (Robison 1986, pp. 17–19, and p. 18, fig. 17, p. 19, fig. 19, p. 86, no. 10, p. 75, no. 5). The CCA's drawing and the preparatory drawings in Boston and in Paris for *The Fantastic Port Monument* reveal the fruits of Piranesi's two trips to Venice and his renewed exposure to Tiepolo's drawings, especially in the use of limpid, transparent washes. The courtyard in the CCA's drawing, shown in three-point perspective according to Ferdinando Galli Bibiena's precepts for the *scena per angolo*, is very similar in composition to the *Foro antico Romano*, one of the plates included by Piranesi in the first issue of the *Prima parte* (fig. 3) (Robison 1986, pp. 12–14, and p. 91, no. 12, p. 14, fig. 5, *Direzioni a' Giovani Studenti nel Disegno dell'Architettura Civile*, 1731–32, pl. 48). The articulation of the colonnade in the CCA's drawing, which has piers composed of four doubled columns supporting segmental pediments, is also found in the *Gruppo di Scale* of the *Prima parte* (fig. 4) (Robison 1986, p. 84, no. 9). The round pavilion in the upper lefthand corner was influenced by the *Mausoleo antico* also from the *Prima parte* (Robison 1986, p. 75, no. 5). There is a variant of the CCA's drawing in the British Museum dated between 1747 and 1748, showing a courtyard in the middle ground surmounted by a round domed building in the distance (Thomas 1954, p. 42, no. 21, repr.; see Cat. no. 48, fig. 2). The two drawings by Piranesi in the CCA and the British Museum clearly reveal his debt to the early architectural fantasies that Juvarra executed in Rome between 1704 and 1714 (Millon in Brunel 1978, p. 354, figs. 22, 23, p. 361, figs 24, 25, p. 362).

John Harris has suggested that the etching of *The Fantastic Port Monument*, as well as the *Parte di ampio magnifico porto* and the *Pianta di ampio magnifico collegio*, both published in the 1750 *Opere varie*, represent Piranesi's response to the imaginary monuments designed by the *pensionnaires* of the French Academy in Rome, in particular Louis-Joseph Le Lorrain, for the *Feste della Chinea* in the 1740s. At that time, Piranesi lived across the street from the French Academy on the Via del Corso (Harris in Wittkower 1967).

NO. 18

NO. 18 verso.

GIOVANNI BATTISTA PIRANESI

Mogliano Veneto 1720–Rome 1778

18. *Design for a Title Page*

Pen and brown ink, brown wash, over black chalk; smudges of red chalk. Verso: Study of standing male nude in black chalk. 15½ x 20⁷⁄₁₆ inches (395 x 519 mm). Watermark: fleur-de-lis in circle with letters $C^{A}C$ above and letter *F* below.

PROVENANCE: Mrs. J. P. Morgan, New York; her sons, Junius S. Morgan and Henry S. Morgan, New York.

BIBLIOGRAPHY: Stampfle 1948, pp. 124, 129, no. 7; Thomas 1954, p. 17, no. 14, repr.; Morgan Library *FR* XV, 1969, pp. 118–19; Morgan Library *Review* 1969, p. 160; Bacou 1974, p. 30; Bacou in Brunel 1978, p. 39, fig. 4; Robison 1977, pp. 387, 400, note 5; Stampfle 1978, no. 7, repr.; Wilton-Ely 1978, under no. 9; Cavicchi and Zamboni in Bettagno 1983, fig. 82; Robison 1986, p. 27, fig. 29.

EXHIBITIONS: New York 1949, p. 7, no. 7, figs. 4, 8 (verso); Northampton 1961, no. 22, pl. 47; New York 1971, no. 220, repr.; London 1978, under no. 9; Washington 1978, p. 31, no. 1; New York 1989.

The Pierpont Morgan Library. Bequest of the late Junius S. Morgan and gift of Henry S. Morgan, Acc. no. 1966.11:7

Following his return to Venice in 1744, Piranesi came under the influence of such artists as Canaletto, Marco Ricci, and most importantly, Tiepolo. In this drawing, the sarcophagus, elaborate feather, wing, and medaillons to the left, and the fasces and banner are all set against the backdrop of a great scroll. Above the sarcophagus is a hanging lamp; two sistra are placed beneath the crown. The drawing was presumably executed sometime after 1744, placing it close to the time when Piranesi began producing elaborate title pages and frontispieces for his series of etchings. The drawing may not have been made in Venice, however, for as Andrew Robison has proposed, its execution on what appears to be central Italian paper would suggest a date after Piranesi's return to Rome (Robison 1986, p. 27).

The combined influences of Venice and Rome are evident not only in individual motifs but in the handling and technique of the drawing. The sarcophagus firmly anchors the composition, giving it a Roman solidity of form, further strengthened by the energetic black chalk underdrawing. The lightness of touch and rococo quality evident in the feathers, the wing, and the medallion, display the Venetian influence, which can be more clearly seen in the Library's *Design for a Title Page with a Pulpit* (Cat. no. 19). While the large size, elaborate composition, and style of these drawings relate them to Piranesi's etchings of the period, neither design seems to have been carried any further. There is a very loose relationship between the present drawing and the four etchings from the *Grotteschi*, particularly *The Monumental Tablet*.

The black chalk nude on the vertically oriented verso is a large-scale counterpart of the *ignudi* of the *Gondola* (Cat. no. 21), where other similar motifs, such as the outspread wing and crown, also appear. The top of the head, hands, and feet of the nude are missing; so it is possible the sheet was cut down at some point. This seems to be confirmed by certain details of the recto, particularly the wing, which has been cut off at the left, and the crown at the top of the sheet, which may have once included an orb and cross such as those on the crown of the gondola.

GIOVANNI BATTISTA PIRANESI
Mogliano Veneto 1720–Rome 1778

19. *Design for a Title Page with a Pulpit*

Pen and brown ink, brown wash, over black chalk; some red watercolor; compass marks for the construction of the pulpit. 20 x 29½ inches (508 x 750 mm). Watermark: bow and arrow (Robison 1986, watermark 50).

PROVENANCE: Mrs. J. P. Morgan, New York; her sons, Junius S. Morgan and Henry S. Morgan, New York.

BIBLIOGRAPHY: Stampfle 1948, pp. 123, 124, no. 8, fig. 4; Thomas 1954, under no. 14; Morgan Library *FR* XV, 1969, pp. 118–19; Morgan Library *Review* 1969, p. 160; Scott 1975, p. 12, fig. 7; Robison 1977, pp. 387, 400, note 5; Stampfle 1978, no. 8, repr.; Robison 1986, p. 26, fig. 28.

EXHIBITIONS: New York 1949, pp. 6, 7, no. 8; New York 1971, no. 221, repr.; London 1978, no. 9; New York 1989.

The Pierpont Morgan Library. Bequest of the late Junius S. Morgan and gift of Henry S. Morgan, Acc. no. 1966.11:8

Like the previous sheet, this one probably dates sometime after Piranesi's second return trip to Venice, from 1745 to 1747. It is executed on Venetian paper with a watermark that corresponds to those in the first edition of the *Prima parte* (fifth through sixth issues), the first edition of the *Grotteschi*, and in a proof of a *veduta* at Chatsworth, all of which date to about 1747 to 1749. In view of these dates, it is particularly interesting to note that the same kind of tablet in the Library's drawing is also found on the etched title pages and index of Piranesi's *Antichità Romane de' Tempi della Repubblica, e de' primi Imperatori*, first published in 1748. Another similarity between this drawing and that series of etchings is found on the title page introducing the second group of etchings depicting ruins outside of Rome, *Antichi Romane fuori di Roma*. There a chain of medallions attached to a dramatically large feather and quill is placed above a sarcophagus on which the inscription appears. The same elements are incorporated at the top center in the Library's drawing.

The influence of Tiepolo in the fluid application of a golden-brown wash is even more apparent than in Cat. no. 18. The rococo lightness of the composition is enhanced by the exuberantly decorated pulpit, which has been carefully constructed with a compass and ruler. Although the inclusion of the pulpit seems incongruous in this context, it does not appear to have been added later because the feathers and quill above it are clearly drawn over the uppermost pen lines of the pulpit. The ground plan, on the other hand, is drawn free hand. It may have been added later, for it does not overlap the preexisting frame of the tablet. It is tempting to suggest that the ground plan may be an afterthought since the composition is more evenly balanced without it. Elisabeth Kieven speculates that the drawing may be a kind of elaborate presentation drawing and suggests that this type of pulpit is north Italian in style.

NO. 19

GIOVANNI BATTISTA PIRANESI

Mogliano Veneto 1720–Rome 1778

20. *Capriccio*

Pen and brown ink, brown wash, over black chalk. 14^{7}/$_{16}$ x 20^{1}/$_{8}$ inches (367 x 511 mm). Watermark: bow and arrow (Robison 1986, watermark 50).

Inscribed at lower left, *tronco/grande/per terra/ò sia terreno*; at lower center, two illegible words.

PROVENANCE: Mrs. J. P. Morgan, New York; her sons, Junius S. Morgan and Henry S. Morgan, New York.

BIBLIOGRAPHY: Stampfle 1948, p. 124, no. 9, fig. 2; Thomas 1954, under no. 14; Morgan Library *FR* XV, 1969, pp. 118–19; Morgan Library *Review* 1969, p. 160; Scott 1975, p. 51, fig. 59; Robison 1977, pp. 387, 400, note 5; Stampfle 1978, no. 9, repr.; Robison 1986, p. 30, fig. 33, under no. 21.

EXHIBITIONS: New York 1949, p. 8, no. 9, fig. 5; Oberlin 1951, no. 17; Stockholm 1970, no. 46, repr.; New York 1971, no. 222, repr.; Washington 1978, p. 38, no. 15; New York 1989.

The Pierpont Morgan Library. Bequest of the late Junius S. Morgan and gift of Henry S. Morgan, Acc. no. 1966.11:9

NO. 20

Tiepolo's *Vari capricci, scherzi*, and his ten *Capricci*, the prints published by Zanetti in 1743 and again in 1749, were certainly a source of inspiration for Piranesi's four impressive fantasies, the etched *Grotteschi*, which date from 1747 to 1749. Like Cat. nos. 18 and 19, the Library's *Capriccio*–ruins with fountain, fallen columns, and satyrs–is related in mood and even space to the *Grotteschi*. The drawing does not relate specifically to any one print, but it is important to point out that the size of the drawing and these prints are almost identical.

Individual motifs–the water pouring from a vase to the right of center, the fallen columns, and the crouching animal-like forms–appear in somewhat different form in the etching *The Skeletons*. The lower part of the Library's drawing has been cut off, possibly eliminating the bones that appear in the foreground of the print. The way in which Piranesi has carefully worked out the light and shade in the background by creating irregularly shaped areas is also close to the print. In both the drawing and print, the light areas are generally left untouched allowing the brightness of the paper to come through. In the drawing, light areas are contrasted with areas of rapidly applied wash and loosely scribbled hatching in pen similar to the graphic vocabularly in the print. Andrew Robison has pointed out that although these foreground elements are reminiscent of the *Grotteschi*, the background buildings and encircling arcade can be related to Piranesi's more strictly architectural fantasies, the earlier *Tempio antico*, for instance, in the *Prima parte*, and his later *Ponte Magnifico* which was included in the *Opere varie*. Indeed, the watermark on this drawing is the same as that in Cat. nos. 19, 21, and 22, dating from about 1747 to 1749.

GIOVANNI BATTISTA PIRANESI

Mogliano Veneto 1720–Rome 1778

21. *Gondola*

Pen and brown ink, brown wash, over black chalk. Verso: Ornament with sun and star motifs in black chalk; design for decorative frame in pen and brown ink; similar sketch in red chalk. 11⅝ x 26⅞ inches (296 x 683 mm). Watermark: bow and arrow (Robison 1986, watermark 50).

PROVENANCE: Mrs. J. P. Morgan, New York; her sons, Junius S. Morgan and Henry S. Morgan, New York.

BIBLIOGRAPHY: Stampfle 1948, pp. 123–24, 129, no. 10, fig. 3; Mayor 1952, pp. 6, 33, fig. 2; Thomas 1954, pp. 16–17, no. 16; Morgan Library *FR* XV, 1969, pp. 118–19; Morgan Library *Review* 1969, p. 160; Robison 1973, pp. 389–92, pl. 47, fig. 1; Scott 1975, p. 13, fig. 8; Pane 1978, p. 164; Penny 1978, p. 7, pl. 10; Stampfle 1978, no. 10, repr.; Wilton-Ely 1978, pp. 18, 30, 106, fig. 14.

EXHIBITIONS: New York 1949, pp. 6–8, 13, no. 10, figs. 6, 7 (detail); Oberlin 1951, no. 16, repr.; New York and elsewhere 1957, no. 102, pl. 67; New York 1971, no. 219, repr.; New York 1974, no. 24, repr.; London 1978, no. 11, repr.; Venice 1978, p. 30, under no. 8bis; New York 1981, no. 95, repr.; New York 1989.

The Pierpont Morgan Library. Bequest of the late Junius S. Morgan and gift of Henry S. Morgan, Acc. no. 1966.11:10

NO. 21 verso.

The Library's *Gondola* is a magnificent example of Piranesi's early rococo style. Artists such as Tiepolo and Guardi also drew these ceremonial gondolas, or *bissone,* which were designed by architects and theatrical craftsmen for Venetian water festivals. This drawing was probably executed about 1744–45. The watermark, a bow and arrow, is Venetian and what is particularly interesting is that an identical watermark appears in a proof of the *Veduta Piazza Navona with S. Agnese on the Right* (Hind 16) at Chatsworth (Robison 1986, watermark 50).

Andrew Robison has shown that in one of Piranesi's earliest views in his *Veduta di Roma, The Basilica and Piazza of Saint Peter's* (Cat. no. 55), the artist recast the central section of the gondola for use as the body of a carriage. Certain details, like the nude hanging over the shield, the large wing surmounting the gondola, and the general form of the carriage as well as the general similarity of the ornament, reappear in the carriage. The most striking difference between the drawing and the print, however, is the substitution of a shield for a crown. The inclusion of this fantastic carriage within the larger context of the great ceremonial space of St. Peter's is intriguing–a statement on Piranesi's imaginative skills as a designer combined with his talent as an engraver of *vedute.*

GIOVANNI BATTISTA PIRANESI

Mogliano Veneto 1720–Rome 1778

22. *Design for Wall Panel*

Pen and brown ink, brown wash, over black chalk. Verso: Sketch for a table support, in pen and brown ink. $12^{13}/_{16}$ x $14^3/_4$ inches (325 x 375 mm). Watermark: bow and arrow (Robison 1986, watermark 50).

PROVENANCE: Mrs. J. P. Morgan, New York; her sons, Junius S. Morgan and Henry S. Morgan, New York.

BIBLIOGRAPHY: Stampfle 1948, p. 124, no. 12, fig. 7; Mayor 1952, pp. 6, 33, fig. 3; Thomas 1954, pp. 16–17, no. 15, repr.; Morgan Library *FR* XV, 1969, pp. 118–19; Morgan Library *Review* 1969, p. 160; Stampfle 1978, no. 12, repr.

EXHIBITIONS: New York 1949, pp. 6–8, no. 12; Kansas City 1956, p. 37, no. 163; New York 1971, no. 223, repr.; Washington and elsewhere 1974–75, p. 46, no. 93, repr.; London 1978, no. 10; New York 1989.

The Pierpont Morgan Library. Bequest of the late Junius S. Morgan and gift of Henry S. Morgan, Acc. no. 1966.11:12

Piranesi's biographer J.-G. Legrand commented in his manuscript on the life of the artist that "le jeune artiste avait commencé differens travaux d'architecture et de décoration dans l'intérieur des palais de quelques sénateurs et nobles vénetiens" (Wilton-Ely 1978, p. 14). No works of this type by Piranesi are known, but the suggestion that this sheet should be connected with such Venetian decorations can be supported by the rococo style of the drawing. Two other designs for wall panels in the Library's collection exhibit a similar lightness of composition and delicate touch in the application of pen and wash (Stampfle 1978, nos. 11, 13). The watermark on the present drawing is typically Venetian and is identical to one found on the Library's drawing depicting a wall panel with a rococo shield and sconces. These correspond with watermarks Andrew Robison found in Piranesi's etchings dating from 1747 to 1749.

The sketch on the verso is difficult to decipher and has been described as a table or table support.

NO. 22

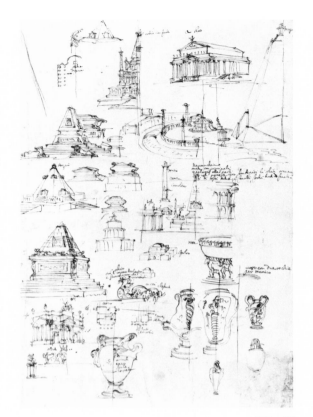

NO. 23

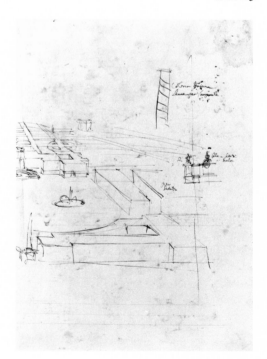

NO. 23 verso.

GIOVANNI BATTISTA PIRANESI

Mogliano Veneto 1720–Rome 1778

23. *Sheet of Sketches after Fischer von Erlach*

Pen and brown ink. 16⅜ x 11⅛ inches (418 x 283 mm). Watermark: fragment of a fleur-de-lis in double circle. Inscribed at upper left, *statua di giove*; at upper center above Mausoleum of Artemisia (Fischer, Book I, pl. VI), *cochio con Cavali* and above Temple of Diana (Fischer, Book I, pl. VII), *a buo*(?); at upper right above Mausoleum of Moeris (Fischer, Book I, pl. XI), *tempio*; at left center above Egyptian pyramid (Fischer, Book I, pl. XIII), *tempio*; at center to right of column, *dorico/senza/involtar/lita* (?); below the Temple of Nineveh (Fischer, Book I, pl. X), *nau-machia/naumachia/ovata con principali/palazzi alle parti/e nel mezo e sopra frontispici li soliti ornamen/ti di trofei Statue, e Cavali, Cochi tirati da Cavali*; at center above the View of Obelisk of Marcus Aurelius and Lucius Verus (Fischer, Book I, pl. XX), *trofei*; to the right of the structure with a dome (Fischer, Book II, pl. II), *Apoleo*; to the left of the vase supported by bulls (Fischer *Vases*, no. 1), *rose*; above the coach drawn by elephants (probably Fischer, Book II, pl. III), *cochio/con l'/imperator dentro/e fama sopra che l'/incorona/a sei elefanti*; to the right, *vaso con due rechie/per manico*; at the lower left to the left of arch, *trofei*; on the ground plan of arch, *arco/arco* and to the right, *arco e pure/nella fronte/arco/elefanti/con cochio*; below triumphal arch, *soldato*; on vase (Fischer, *Vases*, no. 3), *animal /egizio/virile/ alla meta*.

PROVENANCE: Mrs. J. P. Morgan, New York; her sons, Junius S. Morgan and Henry S. Morgan, New York.

BIBLIOGRAPHY: Stampfle 1948, no. 17, fig. 5; Corfiato 1951, pl. 56; Mayor 1952, pp. 3–4; Thomas 1954, p. 16, no. 3; Morgan Library *FR* XV, 1969, pp. 118–19; Morgan Library *Review* 1969, p. 160; Scott 1975, p. 305, under note 5; Wittkower 1975, p. 265, no. 347, repr.; Wilton-Ely 1976, p. 531, note 6; Stampfle 1978, no. 17, repr.; Wilton-Ely 1978, p. 15, no. 12, repr.; Bjurström 1979, under no. 205; Pane 1980, p. 29, fig. 6; Robison 1986, p. 14, fig. 8.

EXHIBITIONS: New York 1949, p. 8, no. 17, fig. 3; Northampton 1961, p. 100, no. 22, pl. 47; New York 1971, no. 216, repr.; Rome and elsewhere 1976, pp. 272–73, no. 143 (recto), repr.; London 1978, no. 25; Venice 1978, no. 4, repr.; New York 1989.

This drawing and the following one are copies Piranesi made after details of the Austrian architect Fischer von Erlach's *Entwurff einer historischen Architectur* published in Vienna in 1721. Fischer's pictorial history, which included oriental as well as ancient buildings, was one of the first surveys of world architecture (Cat. no. 48). Piranesi may have encountered the book in the library of his first patron, the Venetian builder Nicola Giobbe, who opened his library to the young artist and introduced him to leading architects, among them Luigi Vanvitelli (London 1978, p. 20). Fischer's attempt to imaginatively reconstruct antique buildings clearly had a formative influence on Piranesi who likewise became fascinated with publishing reconstructions of ancient buildings as well as modern ones.

In copying Fischer's designs Piranesi worked his way through the book systematically, beginning at the upper lefthand side of the sheet and working down the page in an organized way. He reproduces fairly accurately the central motif of each plate that interested him. Piranesi included such monuments as the Mausoleum of Artemisia at Halicarnassus (Book I, pl. VI), the Temple of Diana at Ephesus (Book I, pl. VII), the Temple of Nineveh (Book I, pl. X), the Pyramids of the Tomb of Sotis (fig. 1) (Book I, pl. XIV), and the Egyptian Tombs near Cairo (Book I, pl. XV). In some cases, because he copied only the main forms of the building, he included an inscription to describe an aspect of its decoration in more detail. Plate XIV of Fischer's first book, the Pyramids of the Tomb of Sotis, is particularly interesting because of the larger, more dramatically posed figures. The theatrical gesture of the figure to the right of the tomb is similar to the type Piranesi used in his later depictions of ruins.

As Piranesi moved toward the bottom of the sheet, he began to copy more freely. Plate XX from Fischer's first book, the Obelisk of Marcus Aurelius and Lucius Verus at Corinth, is partially copied in the center of the sheet. Piranesi has drawn the triumphal column and a domed temple to the left of the obelisk rather than to the right as it appears in Fischer's depiction. The Triumphal Arch at the lower left seems to be the one in honor of Catulus and Marius at Orange, but if so Piranesi has taken liberties with the decoration, which more closely resembles the trophies and chariot from the Arch of Drusus (Book II, pl. V). He has also excerpted amusing details such as the chariot being drawn by elephants, evidently taken from the top of the Triumphal Arch on Augustus's Bridge (fig. 2) (Book II, pl. III).

Much of the lower section of the sheet shows the artist's interest in the fifth book, Fischer's *Divers Vases Antiques, Aegyptiens, Grecs, Romains, & Modernes: avec Quelques uns de l'invention de l'Auteur.* In a few of these sketches, Piranesi divides the vase in half lengthwise, depicting one vase on the left half and another on the right (see Fischer, nos. 3 and 4). In some areas, Piranesi has described what he saw in Fischer's book but has not drawn it. For example, the inscriptions *vaso con due rechie/per manico* and *animal/egizio/virile/alla meta* presumably refer to no. 4 which depicts a vase with ears as handles (in the background to the right) and an Egyptian relief (in the foreground). Fischer's *Divers Vases Antiques* may also have served as an inspiration for Piranesi's *Vasi, candelabri, cippi*, published in two volumes between 1770 and 1778.

The verso shows a rough copy of the right side of the garden and buildings of Schönbrunn, a summer residence near Vienna that Fischer constructed for the emperor (Book IV, pl. III). The upper section of the verso sketch depicts part of Trajan's column, which Fischer incorporated in his church, the Karlskirche, in Vienna.

FIGURE 1 Fischer von Erlach, *The Pyramids of the Tomb of Sotis*. Canadian Centre for Architecture, Montréal, WM 671 CAGE.

FIGURE 2 Fischer von Erlach, *The Bridge of Augustus*. Canadian Centre for Architecture, Montréal, WM 671 CAGE.

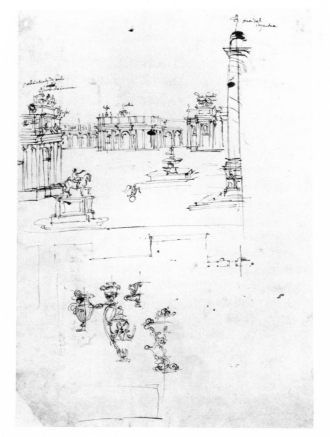

NO. 24

NO. 24 verso.

GIOVANNI BATTISTA PIRANESI

Mogliano Veneto 1720–Rome 1778

24. *Sheet of Sketches after Fischer von Erlach*

Pen and brown ink. Verso: Villa and garden. 16⁵⁄₁₆ x 11¹⁄₁₆ inches (415 x 282 mm). Watermark: none.

Inscribed at the right above Trajan's column (Fischer C), *stua* [statua] *del imperatore*; at the left above the triumphal arch (Fischer D), *cochio tirato da cavali/trofei* [crossed out] */et fama che incorona/trofei/[v]ari rilevi*; above the building in the center of the sheet (Fischer B), *trofei cochio*; above the basilica (Fischer A), *due Cavali/tenuti da un/soldato/sopra*; to the right of the ground plan, *arco*.

PROVENANCE: Mrs. J. P. Morgan, New York; her sons, Junius S. Morgan and Henry S. Morgan, New York.

BIBLIOGRAPHY: Stampfle 1948, no. 18; Mayor 1952, pp. 3–4; Thomas 1954, under no. 3; Wittkower 1975, p. 265; Wilton-Ely 1976, p. 531, note 6; Stampfle 1978, no. 18, repr.; Wilton-Ely 1978, p. 15, fig. 12.

EXHIBITIONS: London 1978, under no. 25; Venice 1978, no. 4, repr.; Oechslin in Brunel 1978, p. 404, fig. 5c; New York 1989.

The Pierpont Morgan Library. Bequest of the late Junius S. Morgan and gift of Henry S. Morgan, Acc. no. 1966.11:18

Like Cat. no. 23, this sheet contains sketches copied from Fischer von Erlach's *Entwurff einer historischen Architectur.* The upper half of the sheet depicts the left half of Fischer's Forum of Trajan (Book II, pl. VII) showing from left to right the Triumphal Arch (Fischer D), part of the architectural complex near the basilica and the basilica itself (Fischer B and A), Trajan's column (Fischer C), a fountain, and in the foreground, an equestrian statue (Fischer F). In the lower half of the sheet, beneath the view of the forum, Piranesi has drawn a rough ground plan of the forum and a number of partially sketched vases, including three that appear in plates 10, 11, and 12 of Fischer's *Divers Vases Antiques.*

GIOVANNI BATTISTA PIRANESI

Mogliano Veneto 1720–Rome 1778

25. *Architectural Fantasy*

Pen and brown ink, brown wash. 12¹⁵⁄₁₆ x 9⁵⁄₁₆ inches (329 x 491 mm). Watermark: fragment of the letter *P*.

PROVENANCE: Spencer, London; Janos Scholz (Lugt S. 2933b).

BIBLIOGRAPHY: Freedley 1940, pl. 9; Tolnay 1943, no. 142, repr.; Tietze 1947, p. 202, pl. 101; Mayor 1952, p. 38, fig. 24; Scholz 1962, no. 68; Volkman 1965, pl. 7; Scholz 1976, no. 144, repr.; Morgan Library *FR* XVII, 1976, p. 176, pl. 17; Stampfle 1978, p. xxxii, no. A-4, repr.

EXHIBITIONS: Venice 1957, no. 98; Oakland 1960, no. 62; Northampton 1961, no. 24, pl. 98; Hamburg and Cologne 1963–64, no. 118; New Haven 1964, no. 82, repr.; London 1968a, no. 71, pl. 24; New York 1971, no. 226, repr.; Los Angeles 1976, no. 72, repr.; Dallas and Houston 1977–78, no. 144, repr.; London 1978, no. 45; Florence 1980, no. 39; Notre Dame 1980, no. 166, repr.; New York 1981, no. 96, repr.; New York 1989.

The Pierpont Morgan Library. Gift of Mr. Janos Scholz, Acc. no. 1974.27

Piranesi's architectural fantasies are clearly creative visions, drawn without the practical restrictions of a patron or commission. In this boldly executed architectural complex, a triumphal arch is approached by a colossal stairway and set into a great two-story colonnade with circular wings surmounted by obelisks and trophies. The triumphal arch appears frequently in Piranesi's drawings made in Rome during the 1740s and early 1750s. With vigorous strokes, the artist has rapidly sketched figures, fountains, and architectural sculpture. All of these, particularly the colonnade sculpture, work to emphasize the colossal scale and grandeur of the architecture. In execution, there is a strong emphasis placed on both texture and solidity of form, which Piranesi has achieved by reinforcing contours and adding areas of bold hatching. The vigorous application of pen and wash contrasts markedly with the delicate penwork of some of his other architectural fantasies (Cat. no. 26).

NO. 26

GIOVANNI BATTISTA PIRANESI

Mogliano Veneto 1720–Rome 1778

26. *Architectural Fantasy*

Pen and brown ink, brown wash, some graphite; perspective lines and a few details in red chalk. Irregularly trimmed along lower edge and then made up by the artist and worked in a bolder manner. 10⁹⁄16 x 16⅞ inches (270 x 428 mm). Watermark: illegible design (possibly a fleur-de-lis) within double circle.

PROVENANCE: P. & D. Colnaghi and Co., London.

BIBLIOGRAPHY: Morgan Library *FR* XVI, 1973, p. 119; Stampfle 1978, no. A-1, repr.

EXHIBITIONS: London 1966, no. 21, pl. IX; London 1978, no. 41, repr.; New York 1989.

The Pierpont Morgan Library. Purchased as the gift of Miss Alice Tully, Acc. no. 1971.4

The precise penwork and neatly applied wash in this drawing are characteristic of Piranesi's early architectural fantasies. Here, as in many of his etched capricci, the ornament is based on Roman architectural elements, including rostral columns and obelisks. In the left foreground, Piranesi has included such recognizable antique sculptures as the *Horse Tamers* (today in the Piazza del Quirinale), the group which in the drawing is shown flanking the statue *La Dea Roma* (today in front of the Palazzo Senatorio). The drawing was probably executed in the 1740s when the artist was working on etchings for the *Prima parte*.

Areas along the lower edge of the drawing have been cut out by the artist and then made up; the new areas are carefully reworked. In general there are fewer figures in these areas, and the passages that have been reworked around the *Horse Tamers* and *La Dea Roma* seem to have been done specifically to create a greater contrast between these statues and the background. The dramatically oblique perspective and careful delineation of the drawing is similar to Piranesi's *Reconstruction of the Circus Maximus* in Berlin. This and two other drawings—one in the British Museum and the other in a private collection—are preparatory studies for the secondary frontispieces to the *Antichità Romane* (Cat. no. 57).

GIOVANNI BATTISTA PIRANESI

Mogliano Veneto 1720–Rome 1778

27. *View of an Interior*

Pen and brown ink, gray and brown wash, over black chalk, with revisions by the artist in pen and darker brown ink and wash and red chalk; framing line in pen and brown ink. 7⅜ x 9¹¹⁄₁₆ inches (187 x 246 mm). Watermark: none visible through lining.

Inscribed by the artist across the architrave in pen and brown ink, *IMPERATOR/JOANES BTTA PIRANESIS/SEPULCRUM EREXIT* and signed at lower right, *Piranesi;* inscribed on verso, *B.P.L. N⁰ 124* and numbered in pen and black ink, *N27.*

PROVENANCE: Edmond Fatio; his sale, Geneva, Nicolas Rauch, 3–4 June 1959, no. 203.

BIBLIOGRAPHY: Morgan Library *FR* X, 1960, pp. 59–61; Fischer 1968, pp. 222–23, fig. 14; Morgan Library *Review* 1969, p. 160; Erichsen 1976, p. 215, fig. 5; Garms in Brunel 1978, pp. 275–76. fig. 22; Stampfle 1978, no. A-2, repr.; Bjurström 1979, under no. 205; Sobotik 1986, p. 60, fig. 5.

EXHIBITIONS: New York 1971, no. 217, repr.; London 1978, no. 33; New York 1989.

The Pierpont Morgan Library. Purchased as the gift of the Fellows, Acc. no. 1959.14

Manfred Fischer dates this drawing to Piranesi's early years, pointing out the similarity between it and the etching *Vestibolo d'antico Tempio* which appeared in Piranesi's *Prima parte,* 1743 (fig. 1). The drawing is similar stylistically to two other drawings in the British Museum—a *Tempio antico* and a *Doric Atrium*—both preparatory for the *Prima parte* (Ro-

FIGURE 1 G. B. Piranesi, *Vestibolo d'antico Tempio* in *Prima parte.* Miriam and Ira D. Wallach Division of Art, Prints and Photographs, New York Public Library.

NO. 27

bison 1986, figs. 20 and 21). As John Wilton-Ely observed, the composition of the Library's drawing lies somewhere between the unfinished sketch of a colonnaded hall in the British Museum and the etching. In the exhibited sheet, Piranesi has used perspective lines and a ruling pen and compass to lay out the interior. The delicately applied areas of wash and the precise draughtsmanship contrast markedly with the revisions that he made in a darker brown ink with a broader pen. The revised areas include scratching out the decoration on top of the sarcophagi that flank the central stairway. Piranesi reworked the foreground sculpture into a seated figure with outstretched arms, placing it on a circular plinth. He also revised the lines on the floor in front of the sculpture into a semi-circular pattern to correspond with the shape of the plinth. A similar monument, as John Wilton-Ely has pointed out, appears in a summary black chalk sketch on the right side of the British Museum drawing (London 1978, no. 32b).

The revisions Piranesi made behind the central stairway are extremely important in linking this drawing more closely with the *Vestibolo d'antico Tempio*. Originally the entablature was flat and supported a sarcophagus surmounted by a crown. Beneath the sarcophagus was a coat of arms flanked by two angels; the inscription on the architrave read IMPERATOR/JOANES BTTA PIRANESIS/SEPULCRUM EREXIT. The whole was supported by two central columns. The revisions, however, show an entirely different conception of the space. Piranesi drew curved lines over the flat entablature and extended these below the architrave to create a semi-circular group of columns which, as Garms has pointed out, is reminiscent of Palladio's Redentore. The effect achieved by the lines added above the columns is of multiple receding arches and cupolas similar to those in the etching. Additionally, Piranesi reworked the side walls in front of these columns to include two levels of standing figures in niches, similar to those found in the print. Certain details, including the coffering of the side arch, were not reworked but in their original form come close to corresponding details in the print. The area beneath the central arch and behind the screen of columns is difficult to read but is intriguing: three or four different ideas seem to emerge. There is a very light black chalk sketch of an obelisk, and behind this a pedimented facade of a domed building. Piranesi has drawn over this in pen and brown ink connecting the columns with curved lines suggesting an atrium-like effect. Many similar background elements also appear in the two British Museum drawings mentioned above. The nature of Piranesi's revisions, many of which bring the composition closer to the etching, indicate that they were made about the same time as the drawing. As Garms observed, the principal difference between the drawing and print in terms of architectural models is that one moves from Palladio's San Giorgio Maggiore to the Redentore, resulting in a "Redentore" brought back to an antique severity.

In addition to formal connections between the drawing and the print, Garms points out that the funerary theme appears throughout the *Prima parte*. Piranesi's enigmatic inscription on the architrave reveals that the idea of a tomb was crucial to his original conception of the design – an idea entirely consistent with many of the etchings in the series.

GIOVANNI BATTISTA PIRANESI
Mogliano Veneto 1720–Rome 1778

28. *Lunette with Trophies, Winged Serpents, and Dolphins in Spandrels*

Red chalk over black chalk; corrections in helmet in black chalk. 10⁷/₁₆ x 22 inches (266 x 560 mm). Watermark: fleur-de-lis in circle with letter *V* below.

PROVENANCE: Mrs. J. P. Morgan, New York; her sons, Junius S. Morgan and Henry S. Morgan, New York.

BIBLIOGRAPHY: Stampfle 1948, no. 35; Stampfle 1978, no. 35, repr.; Gasparri 1985, p. 216, no. 5; Hannah 1987, pl. 25; Amsterdam 1989, p. 155, under note 18.

EXHIBITION: New York 1989.

This highly finished drawing is a careful copy of one of a pair of Imperial Roman marble reliefs used as overdoors in the Galleria del Parnaso of the Villa Albani in Rome (fig. 1). They are dated to the period of Emperor Trajan (A.D. 98–117) and have been shown to be basically antique in spite of their unusual form and extensive restorations (Gasparri 1985, p. 216). The reliefs must have been in place in the gallery by 1757. Their earliest publication seems to be in 1759 when the comte de Caylus reproduced them in volume III of his *Recueil d'antiquités égyptiennes, étrusques, grecques et romaines* (fig. 2) (Cat. no. 116). At that time they were already restored. He wrote:

> Je dois le dessein de ces deux Bas-reliefs aux soins que M. l'Abbé Barthélemy s'est donnés, dans son voyage d'Italie, pour faire copier les monumens singuliers, dont il ne pouvoit faire l'acquisition. Il m'a donné ces deux Couronnemens de porte, formés en ceintre, & éxécutés en marbre; leur largeur n'est que d'environ *trois pieds & demi*. Les armes, qui composent ces trophées, ne doivent avoir au plus, que la moitié de leur proportion naturelle. Les originaux appartiennent à M. le Cardinal Alexandro Albani, & on les voit dans sa vigne, avec quelques restaurations qu'il y a fait faire, & qui sont ponctuées sur la Planche.

The restorations that Caylus refers to, however, are not marked on the print. In 1766, the reliefs were mentioned by Winckelmann in his *Versuch einer Allegorie*, and in 1785 they were published in Stefano Morcelli's *Indicazione antiquaria per la villa suburbana dell'eccellentissima Casa Albani* (Hannah 1987, p. 272, note 9).

The connection of the drawing with the reliefs seems to have been made independently by Carlo Gasparri and Robert Hannah. The reliefs were rather heavily restored, and some of the details of the restored sections differ from those in the drawing (G. Lippold, *Photographische Einzelaufnahmen antiker Skulpturen*, Munich 1893–1940, no. 4686; as quoted in Hannah, p. 272, note 6). For instance, the handle of the sword at the bottom left of the drawing is ram-

headed, but plain in the relief. The helmet at the lower right also shows differences as do the flaps under the corselet. That the differences appear in the damaged areas suggests to Hannah that the drawing may reflect Piranesi's activity as a restorer. Gasparri points out that the reliefs must have been seen by Piranesi prior to their restoration and their use as overdoor ornaments, which suggests to him that they were acquired by Cardinal Albani through Piranesi. This and other details led Gasparri to surmise that Piranesi was involved in the final decoration of the Galleria del Parnaso.

A drawing of an antique frieze in the Villa Albani, signed by Angelo Piranesi and dated 1776, is found on page 210 of Arnout Vosmaer's *Album Amicorum* in the Rijksprentenkabinet, Amsterdam. The drawing is inscribed *Fregio Antico di Marmo, che si vede nella Villa Albani/Dedicato al Sig^r Vosmaer/In atto d'ossequio da Angelo Piranesi* (Amsterdam 1989, p. 153). The drawing was made when Angelo was twelve, and as the Amsterdam catalogue notes, was possibly reworked by his father.

FIGURE 1 Gallery of Parnassus, Villa Albani, Rome (detail), Alinari.

FIGURE 2 Lunette from Caylus's *Recueil d'antiquités* (vol. VI, pl. XLV). The Pierpont Morgan Library, New York.

NO. 28

GIOVANNI BATTISTA PIRANESI

Mogliano Veneto 1720–Rome 1778

29. *Six Masks*

Pen and brown ink. Verso: Horse and rider with shield and spear; pedimented niche in black chalk. 8 x 13⁷⁄₁₆ inches (203 x 342 mm). Watermark: none.

Inscribed at upper right in pencil, *B.P.*; on verso in niche, *Mezzo*.

PROVENANCE: Mrs. J. P. Morgan, New York; her sons, Junius S. Morgan and Henry S. Morgan, New York.

BIBLIOGRAPHY: Stampfle 1948, no. 43; Morgan Library *FR* XV, 1969, pp. 118–19; Stampfle 1978, no. 43.

EXHIBITION: New York 1989.

The Pierpont Morgan Library. Bequest of the late Junius S. Morgan and gift of Henry S. Morgan, Acc. no. 1966.11:43

This is one of the Library's three boldly executed drawings of antique masks depicting various expressions (see Stampfle 1978, nos. 44 and 45). Such masks appear in many of Piranesi's etchings but are most frequently found decorating chimneypieces throughout his *Diverse maniere.* The mask found at the upper right of this drawing, for example, is extremely close to plate 38 of that book.

At the beginning of the *Diverse maniere,* Piranesi included an etched plate of individual antique ornaments. He commented in the index list to that plate: "Of Etruscan monuments of various kinds, relating to the sacred, public and private uses of the Tuscan nation, and of the ornaments used by them in the

fore-said monuments contained in Plate I." Three masks are depicted there: a mask representing a satyr, a comic mask, and a lion mask. These clearly reveal Piranesi's archaeological interest in ancient masks and his desire to incorporate them into his own works.

GIOVANNI BATTISTA PIRANESI

Mogliano Veneto 1720–Rome 1778

30. *San Giovanni in Laterano*

Longitudinal section through length of nave looking toward the south wall, with proposed scheme for alteration of west end

Pen and brown ink, brown and gray wash, over pencil; on three pieces of paper pasted together; in left half of drawing, moldings marking horizontal divisions of wall in gray-black ink. Verso: Computations and head of a putto, in pen and brown ink. 21 x 58¼ inches (534 x 1,481 mm). Watermark: fleur-de-lis in a double circle with letters *CB* above; occurs three times (Robison 1986, watermark 35; 1761–mid-1760s).

Inscribed lower right, *Originale del Cav.ᵉ Gio. Batta Piranesi;* at upper left in a nineteenth-century hand in pencil, *San Giovanni in Laterano;* also inscribed *B.P.* as on no. 43.

PROVENANCE: Mrs. J. P. Morgan, New York; her sons, Junius S. Morgan and Henry S. Morgan, New York.

BIBLIOGRAPHY: Stampfle 1948, no. 55; Thomas 1954, under no. 50; Fischer 1968, figs. 11–12; Morgan Library *FR* XV, 1969, pp. 118–19; Morgan Library *Review* 1969, p. 160; New York 1971, under no. 231; Stampfle 1978, no. 56, repr.; Barroero in Pietrangeli 1990, p. 174; Rome 1992, under no. 13.

EXHIBITIONS: New York 1949, pp. 10–11, no. 56, fig. 11; Northampton 1961, no. 66; London 1978, no. 220, repr.; New York 1989.

The Pierpont Morgan Library. Bequest of the late Junius S. Morgan and gift of Henry S. Morgan, Acc. no. 1966.11:55

Since its foundation under Constantine in the early fourth century, San Giovanni in Laterano, one of the great basilican churches of Rome, has been closely allied with the papacy. It housed the pope's throne, and in the middle of the transepts, the papal altar where only the pope could say Mass. The Lateran was rebuilt many times, and in 1646 the modernization of the nave was undertaken by Borromini. During the 1730s, the east front of the church was given a new facade based on Alessandro Galilei's designs.

On 20 September 1763, Natoire, director of the French Academy in Rome, wrote to the marquis de Marigny informing him that Clement XIII had commissioned a new pontifical altar for the Lateran from Piranesi. This plan subsequently expanded to include the tribune to the west of the transept (see Fischer 1978, and Wilton-Ely in Rome 1992). The proposed alterations had to be abandoned in 1767, but a number of preparatory drawings for the project are in the Morgan Library's collection, three of which are included in this exhibition. The Avery Architectural Library at Columbia University, owns a set of twenty-three drawings for the tribune, numbering from one to twenty-five (numbers 13 and 24 are missing). The inscription on the first sheet indicates that during 1764 Piranesi made designs for the church at the request of Clement XIII and in 1767 presented the drawings to the pope's nephew, Cardinal Rezzonico.

Five versions for Piranesi's proposed alterations in the Lateran appear in the Avery drawings. Although different in certain respects, the Library's drawing is preparatory for the finished longitudinal section of *Tavola Ottava* from the Avery set. This represents Piranesi's third solution for the project—the main proposal being to raise the roof of the sanctuary in two stages. As John Wilton-Ely observed, the vaulting of the forechoir is here raised above the roof of the nave and transepts. The half-dome of the apse is higher, allowing it to be lit by three clerestory windows as seen in *Tavola Duodecima* of the Avery drawings. The inspiration for the columnar screen below the half-dome derives from Palladio's Venetian church designs, particularly the Redentore. While the spontaneity of execution of the tribune and the crossing are characteristic of Piranesi's work, the rather dry, mechanical transcription of Borromini's nave has led Felice Stampfle to suggest that it may have been drawn by another hand.

NO. 30

NO. 30 verso.

GIOVANNI BATTISTA PIRANESI
Mogliano Veneto 1720–Rome 1778

31. *San Giovanni in Laterano*

Longitudinal section, beginning at transept and showing proposed scheme for alteration of choir

Pen and brown ink, brown wash, over graphite. Verso: Ground plan of an apse in graphite. 12⁹⁄₁₆ x 21⅜ inches (320 x 545 mm). Watermark: none.

Inscribed on verso in pen and brown ink, *Ponte S. Angelo/Teatro di Marcello/Piramide Nuova/Foro di Nerva/Curia Ostilia/Tempio di Cibelle/S. Urbano/Foro di Titto/Portico d'Otavia/Interno.*

PROVENANCE: Mrs. J. P. Morgan, New York; her sons, Junius S. Morgan and Henry S. Morgan, New York.

BIBLIOGRAPHY: Stampfle 1948, no. 56; Corfiato 1951, pl. 62; Thomas 1954, under no. 50; Fischer 1968, pp. 209–11, fig. 5; Morgan Library *FR* XV, 1969, pp. 118–19; Morgan Library *Review* 1969, p. 160; Bacou 1974, p. 124, repr.; Stampfle 1978, no. 56, repr.; Barroero in Pietrangeli 1990, p. 174.

EXHIBITIONS: New York 1949, pp. 10–11, no. 56, fig. 11; Northampton 1961, no. 66; New York 1971, no. 231, repr.; New York 1989; Rome 1992, no. 7, repr.

The Pierpont Morgan Library. Bequest of the late Junius S. Morgan and gift of Henry S. Morgan, Acc. no. 1966.11:56

This longitudinal section is a preparatory drawing for *Tavola Terza* of the Avery set. It depicts the southern end of the transept and includes Cavaliere d'Arpino's fresco of *The Ascension,* which dates from the time of Clement VIII. In this drawing, Piranesi explores the possibility of introducing an ambulatory around the presbytery, included in the section of it beyond the apse. The decorative system of stars and medallions connected with swags in the apse demonstrates Piranesi's desire to harmonize his design with Borromini's nave.

GIOVANNI BATTISTA PIRANESI

Mogliano Veneto 1720–Rome 1778

32. *San Giovanni in Laterano*

Section through choir showing proposed alteration; at right, ground plan of a section of Borromini's side nave

Pen and dark brown ink, gray wash, over pencil; brush and pen trials at right; compass marks in lower right niche. 13⅝ x 15¼ inches (247 x 388 mm). Watermark: fleur-de-lis in double circle with letters *CB* above (Robison 1986, watermark 35).

Ground plan inscribed in graphite with measurements in *palmi romani.*

PROVENANCE: Mrs. J. P. Morgan, New York; her sons, Junius S. Morgan and Henry S. Morgan, New York.

BIBLIOGRAPHY: Stampfle 1948, no. 57; Mayor 1952, fig. 98; Thomas 1954, under no. 50; Fischer 1968, pp. 209–14, figs. 6, 7; Stampfle 1978, no. 57, repr.; Barroero in Pietrangeli 1990, p. 174.

EXHIBITION: New York 1989.

The Pierpont Morgan Library. Bequest of the late Junius S. Morgan and gift of Henry S. Morgan, Acc. no. 1966.11:57

The ground plan on the right side of this sheet was drawn first and is partially overlapped by the section through the choir. It is oriented in the opposite direction to the section through the choir.

The watermark is the same as the three in Cat. no. 30. Robison also found this watermark in Piranesi's later Roman editions of the *Opere varie* in the British Library; the Kunstbibliothek, Berlin; and the Beinecke Library, Yale University, dating from 1761 to the mid-1760s (Robison 1986, p. 213).

NO. 32

NO. 33

FIGURE 1 Vault, Santa
Maria del Priorato, Rome.

GIOVANNI BATTISTA PIRANESI

Mogliano Veneto 1720–Rome 1778

33. *Santa Maria del Priorato: Design for the Central Panel of the Vault*

Pen and brown ink, brown wash, over black chalk. 20⅞ x 12½ inches (532 x 317 mm). Watermark: none.
Inscribed on plaque beneath the statue of St. John the Baptist in pen and brown ink, *S. IOAÑES/PROTECT*or.

PROVENANCE: Mrs. J. P. Morgan, New York; her sons, Junius S. Morgan and Henry S. Morgan, New York.

BIBLIOGRAPHY: Stampfle 1948, no. 50, fig. 8; Corfiato 1951, pl. 64; Mayor 1952, pp. 18, 33, 40, fig. 94; Thomas 1954, under no. 46; Morgan Library *FR* XV, 1969, pp. 118–19; Morgan Library *Review* 1969, p. 160; Wittkower 1975, p. 251, no. 323, repr.; Pressouyre in Brunel 1978, fig. 17; Wilton-Ely 1976, pp. 220–22, 225, fig. 21, repr.; Bettagno 1978, pp. 84–85, no. 464, repr.; Stampfle 1978, no. 50, repr.; Wilton-Ely, 1978 p. 97, fig. 168.

EXHIBITIONS: New York 1949, p. 9, no. 50; Kansas City 1956, p. 37, no. 164; Northampton 1961, no. 62, pl. 52; New York 1971, no. 227, repr.; London 1978, no. 234, repr.; New York 1989; Rome 1992, no. 34, repr.

The Pierpont Morgan Library. Bequest of the late Junius S. Morgan and gift of Henry S. Morgan, Acc. no. 1966.11:50

In 1764, Cardinal Rezzonico, grand prior of the Order of Malta, commissioned Piranesi to renovate his priory church. The priory, established on the Aventine toward the end of the fourteenth century, suffered various vicissitudes and was rebuilt in 1568 when the adjoining building was enlarged to become the Villa di Malta (see Wilton-Ely 1976, pp. 214–17). During the seventeenth century, the villa was enlarged and the gardens laid out; the priory so appears in G. B. Nolli's 1748 *Map of Rome* (Cat. no. 52).
Piranesi's renovations included extensive work on

the foundations and the roof of the church, as well as on the exterior and interior. To the exterior he added an attic story (destroyed in 1849) and applied ornament. The interior of the building was enhanced by the addition of attached columns and elaborate cartouches, a highly sculptural altar, and a richly decorated stucco vault. Outside the grounds, Piranesi created a rectangular piazza, the Piazza de' Cavalieri di Malta.

Piranesi's work on the church is fully documented by an account book kept by Giuseppe Pelosini, the *capomastro muratore.* The book, now in the Avery Architectural Library at Columbia University, covers the period from 2 November 1764 to 31 October 1766 and was probably submitted by the artist to Cardinal Rezzonico when the work was completed. It was endorsed by Piranesi on 10 April 1767. Santa Maria del Priorato and the piazza constitute Piranesi's only completed architectural project. His tomb was placed in the church at the request of Cardinal Rezzonico.

The Library's six drawings connected with the Aventine commission relate to both the exterior and interior decoration (Stampfle 1978, nos. 50–54, A-5). This drawing for the central panel of the vault emphasizes the naval exploits of the Knights of Malta. In the center, the traditional iconography of the cross appears along with galleys and shields, symbolic of centuries of sea conquests. St. John the Baptist, the patron saint of the order, stands in the lower section. At the top, Piranesi has included the shirt of humility worn by the knights in memory of the Baptist's camel-hair garment, and above that, the papal tiara. The axis of the panel is formed by a large rudder with the image of the Baptist supported at the lower end by juxtaposed warship prows with the triple ram of swords (Rome 1992, p. 62). These swords are also incorporated on the entrance screen in the piazza and repeated on the altar. The sculptor Tommaso Righi carried out the decoration, and the completed relief (fig. 1) follows Piranesi's design very closely. The finished character of the drawing suggests that it may have been a presentation drawing intended for Cardinal Rezzonico's approval.

GIOVANNI BATTISTA PIRANESI
Mogliano Veneto 1720–Rome 1778

34. *Santa Maria del Priorato: Design for the Lower Part of the High Altar*

Pen and brown ink, gray wash, over black chalk; additions in black chalk and pencil (monogram). 18⁹⁄₁₆ x 14⅜ inches (472 x 365 mm). Watermark: fleur-de-lis in single circle with letter *V* above.

Computations at upper left and right; scale at bottom.

PROVENANCE: Mrs. J. P. Morgan, New York; her sons, Junius S. Morgan and Henry S. Morgan New York.

BIBLIOGRAPHY: Stampfle 1948, no. 51; Mayor 1952, pp. 17–19, 33, fig. 92; Thomas 1954, under no. 46; Morgan Library *Review* 1969, p. 160; Fischer 1968, p. 208; Morgan Library *FR* XV, 1969, pp. 118–19; Scott 1975, p. 218, fig. 249; Wittkower 1975, p. 252, no. 326, repr.; Wilton-Ely 1976, pp. 220, 225, fig. 19; Bettagno 1978, p. 85, no. 477, repr.; Stampfle 1978, no. 51, repr.; Wilton-Ely 1978, pp. 98–99, fig. 173; Pane 1980, pp. 38ff.

EXHIBITIONS: New York 1949, pp. 8–9, 14, 20, no. 51, fig. 10; Kansas City 1956, p. 37, no. 165; Northampton 1961, no. 59, pl. 50; New York 1971, no. 229, repr.; London 1972, no. 1271; Berlin 1975, under no. 858; London 1978, no. 233, repr.; New York 1989; Rome 1992, no. 33, repr.

The Pierpont Morgan Library. Bequest of the late Junius S. Morgan and gift of Henry S. Morgan, Acc. no. 1966.11:51

NO. 34

This finished drawing for the lower part of the high altar is very similar to the completed altar executed in gypsum and stucco by Tommaso Righi (fig. 1). A preliminary sketch also in the Library's collection shows the basic form of the altar, which at this early stage included flanking pairs of candelabra (Stampfle 1978, no. A-5). The candelabra are also common to Piranesi's fourth scheme of the altar for the Lateran tribune (Rome 1992, p. 61).

The definitive form of the Santa Maria del Priorato altar becomes apparent in a more finished pen and chalk study, now in the Kunstbibliothek, Berlin. There, as in this drawing, the candelabra were elimi-

nated. Like the previous sheet, the finished quality of this work and its three-dimensional effect, heightened by Piranesi's reworking in black chalk, suggests that it may have been a presentation drawing for Cardinal Rezzonico.

FIGURE 1 Interior, Santa Maria del Priorato, Rome (detail).

GIOVANNI BATTISTA PIRANESI
Mogliano Veneto 1720–Rome 1778

35. *Santa Maria del Priorato: Design for a Vertical Wall Panel*

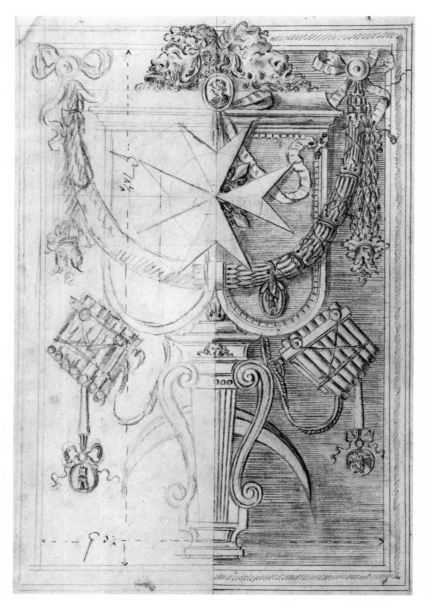

NO. 35

Black chalk and pen and brown ink. 15 13/16 x 10 7/16 inches (403 x 266 mm). Watermark: fleur-de-lis in double circle with *CB* above (Robison 1986, watermark 38).

Measurements of the inner design inscribed in *palmi romani* in pen and brown ink: at lower left, *p 8½* and at upper left, *p 12½*.

PROVENANCE: Mrs. J. P. Morgan, New York; her sons, Junius S. Morgan and Henry S. Morgan, New York.

BIBLIOGRAPHY: Stampfle 1948, no. 53; Mayor 1952, pp. 17–18, fig. 87; Thomas 1954, p. 19, no. 46; Wittkower 1975, pp. 256–58, no. 334, repr.; Wilton-Ely 1976, pp. 218–19, fig. 8; Bettagno 1978, p. 80, no. 452, repr.; Stampfle 1978, no. 53, repr.; Wilton-Ely 1978, p. 95, fig. 164.

EXHIBITIONS: New York 1949, pp. 9–10, no. 53; Northampton 1961, no. 57, pl. 48; New York 1971, no. 230, repr.; London 1978, no. 230, repr.; New York 1989; Rome 1992, no. 31, repr.

The Pierpont Morgan Library. Bequest of the late Junius S. Morgan and gift of Henry S. Morgan, Acc. no. 1966.11:53

In front of the facade of Santa Maria del Priorato, Piranesi designed the Piazza de' Cavalieri di Malta. To the north of the piazza he placed an entrance screen, and along the wall opposite the screen, set a group of stelae, or commemorative pillars, with decorative reliefs. This careful working drawing is preparatory for the vertical panel on the righthand stele of the south wall of the piazza.

John Wilton-Ely has shown that the designs for the stelae reflect Piranesi's concern for an innovative system of design (as expressed in the *Parere*, 1765) as well as his belief in the continuing function of ancient symbolism (Wilton-Ely 1978, p. 95). In this drawing, the iconography of the Order of the Knights of Malta is combined with the tower, the double-headed eagle, and the crescent of the Rezzonico arms—motifs taken from Roman sources, e.g., friezes in the Capitoline Museum, the Trophies of Marius, Trajan's column, and the aquiline relief at SS. Apostoli. There are also Etruscan associations in the images, such as the lyre and shepherd's pipes, reflecting Piranesi's interest in Etruscan motifs. He would use these symbols again in his *Diverse maniere.*

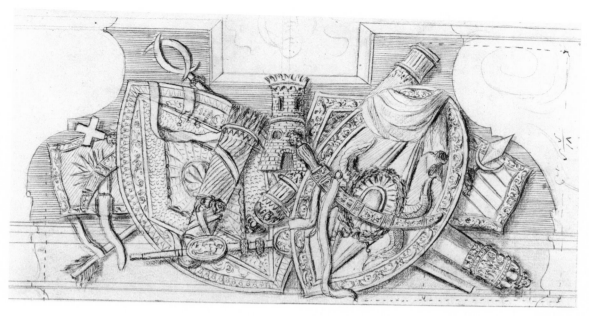

GIOVANNI BATTISTA PIRANESI

Mogliano Veneto 1720–Rome 1778

36. *Santa Maria del Priorato: Design for a Horizontal Panel*

Pen and brown ink with black chalk underdrawing and also overwork. 8⅛ x 14⅞ inches (207 x 379 mm). Watermark: none.

Inscribed with measurements in *palmi romani* in pen and brown ink: at lower center, *p 9¾* and at right edge, *p 5⁵/₁₂*.

PROVENANCE: Mrs. J. P. Morgan, New York; her sons, Junius S. Morgan and Henry S. Morgan, New York.

BIBLIOGRAPHY: Mayor 1952, fig. 89; Thomas 1954, under no. 46; Wilton-Ely 1976, pp. 217–18, fig. 6; Bettagno 1978, p. 80; Stampfle 1978, no. 54, repr.

EXHIBITIONS: London 1978, no. 229; New York 1989; Rome 1992, no. 30, repr.

The Pierpont Morgan Library. Bequest of the late Junius S. Morgan and gift of Henry S. Morgan, Acc. no. 1966.11:54

The drawing is a design for the decorative relief panel below the central stele of the piazza's south wall. Although less complex than the previous design, it also incorporates the Rezzonico castle, here set among battle trophies alluding to the Order of Malta's military history.

GIOVANNI BATTISTA PIRANESI

Mogliano Veneto 1720–Rome 1778

37. *Design for Mantelpiece with Confronted Elephant Heads*

Pen and brown ink, brown wash, over black chalk, smudges of red chalk, on what seems to be a counterproof of a print not yet identified. Verso: Fragment of Ottaviani etching after Guercino. 8⅜ x 12¹¹/₁₆ inches (213 x 322 mm). Watermark: none.

Inscribed in pen and brown ink at lower right, *Rotta de c . . . /Carioni.*

PROVENANCE: Mrs. J. P. Morgan, New York; her sons, Junius S. Morgan and Henry S. Morgan, New York.

BIBLIOGRAPHY: Stampfle 1948, no. 61; Thomas 1954, under no. 48; Morgan Library *FR* XV, 1969, pp. 118–19; Morgan Library *Review* 1969, p. 160; Stampfle 1978, no. 61, repr.

EXHIBITIONS: New York 1949, no. 61, fig. 14; Northampton 1961, no. 68; New York 1971, no. 234, repr.; New York 1978, no. 267; New York 1989.

The Pierpont Morgan Library. Bequest of the late Junius S. Morgan and gift of Henry S. Morgan, Acc. no. 1966.11:61

Designs for decoration constitute the largest single category of drawings in the Library's Piranesi collection; they number about forty. Several are connected

with Piranesi's *Diverse maniere d'adornare i cammini*, a compilation of chimneypieces, furniture, and interior designs published in 1769 and dedicated to the artist's patron Cardinal Rezzonico. We know from extant correspondence with British patrons, however, that many of the plates of the *Diverse maniere* were in circulation well before they were published (see Cat. no. 63). Its text was aimed at an international audience of patrons and practicing designers (Cat. no. 64).

The majority of the designs are the sixty-one chimneypieces appearing in the first part of the book. They are highly complex, demonstrating a balance between innovation and the practical and acceptable. Although there is little doubt that the Morgan drawing was made in connection with the *Diverse maniere*, it does not appear in the publication. The bold penwork, rapid notation of ornament, and areas of wash and parallel hatching to convey the sculptural quality of the mantelpiece are characteristic of this group of drawings.

In 1764, Piranesi published *Raccolta di alcuni disegni del Barbieri da Cento detto il Guercino*. The present drawing was executed on the back of a fragment of an Ottaviani etching after Guercino. The verso print has been largely cut off but carries the partial inscription, *oris Angli*. Based on the inscriptions that appear in the *Raccolta*, the text presumably once read, *Ex Collectione Tomae Ienkins Pictoris Angli*. This plate, however, does not appear in any of the editions of the *Raccolta* that we know of, suggesting that it may be an unused design for the book.

GIOVANNI BATTISTA PIRANESI

Mogliano Veneto 1720–Rome 1778

38. *Design for Mantelpiece*

Red chalk and some black chalk, pen and dark brown ink. Verso: Sketch of wall decoration, in pen and brown ink; two pieces of paper joined. 9⅛ x 14⁵⁄₁₆ inches (232 x 364 mm). Watermark: fragments of circles on the right and left sides.

PROVENANCE: Mrs. J. P. Morgan, New York; her sons, Junius S. Morgan and Henry S. Morgan, New York.

BIBLIOGRAPHY: Stampfle 1948, no. 63; Fischer 1966, p. 23, no. 2, n. 10; Morgan Library *FR* XV, 1969, pp. 118–19; Morgan Library *Review* 1969, p. 160; Rieder 1973, p. 317; Stampfle 1978, no. 63, repr.; Wilton-Ely 1978, p. 104, fig. 188.

EXHIBITIONS: New York 1949, pp. 11–12, no. 63; London 1971, no. 235, repr.; London 1978, no. 255; New York 1989.

NO. 38

FIGURE 1 G. B. Piranesi, *Mantelpiece*, in *Diverse maniere* (Focillon 893). Canadian Centre for Architecture, Montréal.

The Pierpont Morgan Library. Bequest of the late Junius S. Morgan and gift of Henry S. Morgan, Acc. no. 1966.11:63

The drawing, with the wreath in the center of the lintel and lion paws terminating in lions' heads on the jambs, is a study for Piranesi's *Diverse maniere* (fig. 1) (Focillon 893). One of Piranesi's simpler and more practical designs, it appealed to French empire designers. The motif of the lion monopod was used by Percier and Fontaine on the design for a writing desk in their *Recueil de décorations intérieures* of 1801 (London 1978, p. 101).

GIOVANNI BATTISTA PIRANESI

Mogliano Veneto 1720–Rome 1778

39. *Design for Coach*

Pen and brown ink, brown wash; two extraneous cross marks in red chalk. Verso: Fragment of etching from *Diverse maniere* (Focillon 890). 5⅛ x 5⁷⁄₁₆ inches (131 x 138 mm). Watermark: none.

PROVENANCE: Mrs. J. P. Morgan, New York; her sons, Junius S. Morgan and Henry S. Morgan, New York.

BIBLIOGRAPHY: Jesse 1843–44, p. 312; Stampfle 1948, no. 97, fig. 12; Thomas 1954, pp. 19–20, no. 48, repr.; Rieder 1973, pp. 316–17; Stampfle 1978, no. 97, repr.; Wilton-Ely 1978, pp. 106–7, fig. 197.

EXHIBITIONS: Kansas City 1956, no. 168; London 1978, no. 260a; New York 1989.

The Pierpont Morgan Library. Bequest of the late Junius S. Morgan and gift of Henry S. Morgan, Acc. no. 1966.11:97

In the later plates of the *Diverse maniere*, Piranesi experimented with the decoration of such various objects as sedan chairs, coaches, clocks, vases, sconces, and candelabra, many of which are frequently incorporated in complete decorative schemes. There are eighteen designs for coaches and sedan chairs. As

FIGURE 1 G. B. Piranesi, *Designs for Clocks, Tables, and Sedan Chairs* (Focillon 920). Canadian Centre for Architecture, Montréal.

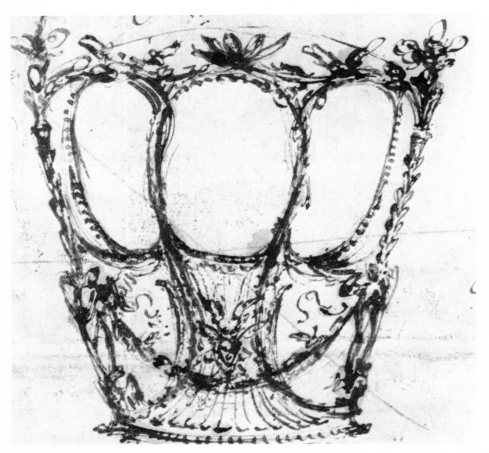

NO. 39

40. *Design for Coach and Sedan Chair*

Pen and brown ink and red chalk. Verso: Fragment of etching from *Diverse maniere* (Focillon 862). 4⅞ x 8⅜ inches (125 x 213 mm). Watermark: none.
Inscribed in red chalk, *farfal*[la?].

PROVENANCE: Mrs. J. P. Morgan, New York; her sons, Junius S. Morgan and Henry S. Morgan, New York.

BIBLIOGRAPHY: Jesse 1843–44, p. 312; Stampfle 1948, no. 98; Thomas 1954, under no. 48, repr.; Rieder 1973, p. 317; Stampfle 1978, no. 98, repr.

EXHIBITIONS: Kansas City 1956, no. 171; New York 1989.

The Pierpont Morgan Library. Bequest of the late Junius S. Morgan and gift of Henry S. Morgan, Acc. no. 1966.11:98

The two studies are preparatory for an etching depicting coaches, sedan chairs, tables, and decorative wall panels in Piranesi's *Diverse maniere* (Focillon 922). The coach, with the triple opening and circular paneling, is preparatory for a coach found on the bottom right of the etching. After roughly sketching out the drawing in red chalk, Piranesi drew over it in pen and brown ink, changing and clarifying the design as he worked. The red chalk drawing of a sedan chair to the right shows a less finished stage of design and accordingly does not correspond as closely to the etching. It is connected with the etched sedan chair found at the upper right of the plate which is in reverse of the drawing; the goat finials and ivy ornament that appear in both the drawing and etching clearly connect the two.

Both this drawing and the previous one are executed on the back of etchings of mantlepieces. Since Piranesi's mantlepieces, which comprise the majority of the designs in the *Diverse maniere*, occur in the first part of the book, these two drawings provide further evidence that the coaches, sedan chairs, and other decorative objects are slightly later in date.

John Wilton-Ely has pointed out, the fact that these were not merely capricci is supported by a letter of January 1768 in which the earl of Carlisle describes his intention of having a coach made to a design recently purchased from Piranesi (London 1978, p. 103). The Library's design for a coach is an earlier idea for the etched design of the coach, with the triple opening and trophy finials, in the *Diverse maniere* (fig. 1) (Focillon 920). Although the drawing and etching do not correspond precisely, the basic design is the same and certain decorative details such as the winged head are repeated in both. Felice Stampfle suggested that the cross marks in red chalk over the coach design may indicate this was a discarded sketch. As Jonathan Scott observed, the coach in the etching appears in Piranesi's view of St. Peter's (Scott 1975, p. 226).

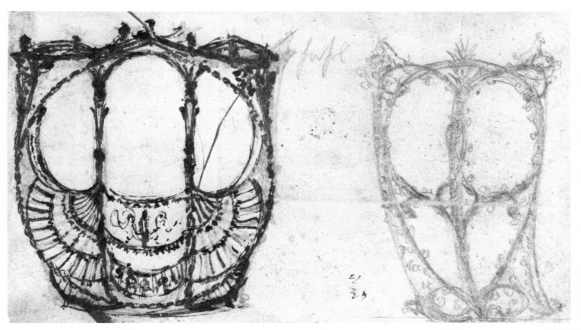

NO. 40

GIOVANNI BATTISTA PIRANESI

Mogliano Veneto 1720–Rome 1778

41. *Design for Clock*

Red chalk over black chalk. 4½ x 2⁷⁄₁₆ inches (115 x 62 mm). Watermark: none.

PROVENANCE: Mrs. J. P. Morgan, New York; her sons, Junius S. Morgan and Henry S. Morgan, New York.

BIBLIOGRAPHY: Stampfle 1948, no. 103; Rieder 1973, p. 317; Stampfle 1978, no. 103, repr.; Wilton-Ely 1990, fig. 7.

EXHIBITIONS: Kansas City 1956, no. 169; London 1978, no. 265a; New York 1989.

The Pierpont Morgan Library. Bequest of the late Junius S. Morgan and gift of Henry S. Morgan, Acc. no. 1966.11:103

This drawing is preparatory for the clock found on the lefthand side of the pier table in a plate of the *Diverse maniere* (fig. 1) (Focillon 924). In the clock the dial is incorporated into a pineapple. The inscription on the plate makes it clear that the center clock and other objects in the book were made for Senator Rezzonico's palace on the Campidoglio. It reads: *Quest' orologio A e stato eseguito in metallo/dorato per ordine di Sua Eccza il Sig.ʳ/D.Abondio Rezzonico Senatore di Roma,/come ancora alcuni altri orna'mti chesi/vedono*

NO. 41

sparsi nelle altre tavole di questa/raccolta quali sono stati messi in opera/nel suo Palazzo sul Campidoglio.

FIGURE 1 G. B. Piranesi, *Designs for Clocks, Urns, and a Side Table* (Focillon 924). Canadian Centre for Architecture, Montréal.

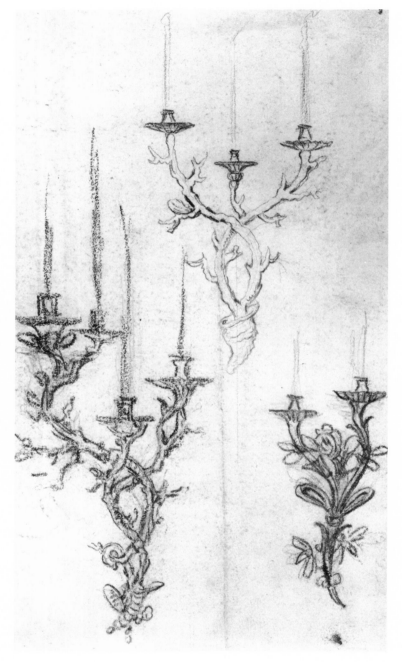

GIOVANNI BATTISTA PIRANESI

Mogliano Veneto 1720–Rome 1778

42. *Three Sconces*

Red chalk over black chalk. Verso: Lid and handles of a vessel, in black chalk. 9³⁄₁₆ x 5³⁄₁₆ inches (234 x 132 mm). Watermark: none.

PROVENANCE: Mrs. J. P. Morgan, New York; her sons, Junius S. Morgan and Henry S. Morgan, New York.

BIBLIOGRAPHY: Stampfle 1948, no. 106; Thomas 1954, pp. 19–20, no. 49, also under no. 48; Rieder 1973, p. 317; Bacou 1974, p. 132; Stampfle 1978, no. 106, repr.; Wilton-Ely 1978, p. 103, fig. 185; Wilton-Ely 1990, fig. 6.

EXHIBITIONS: London 1978, no. 265b, repr.; New York 1989.

The Pierpont Morgan Library. Bequest of the late Junius S. Morgan and gift of Henry S. Morgan, Acc. no. 1966.11:106

Here Piranesi experiments with various designs for sconces, moving from two naturalistic and organic inventions at the left and upper center to the more stylized sconce on the right. The latter design is preparatory for an etching in the *Diverse maniere* (Focillon 923) (see Cat. no 64). The lid of the vessel drawn on the verso shares some characteristics with a vase in the etching, notably the knob constructed out of four leaves, and the decoration of the upper rim in a Lesbian leaf pattern.

Inscriptions found on some of the plates of the *Diverse maniere* confirm that Piranesi was designing furniture for Cardinal Rezzonico's apartments at the Quirinal and Senator Rezzonico's in the Palazzo Senatorio. The etching (Focillon 923), for example, which includes a side table and a clock flanked by two vases and sconces, is inscribed: *Questo tavolino ed alcuni altri ornamenti che sono sparsi in quest'opera,/ si vedono nell'appartamento di Sua Eccza Monsig^r D.Gio: Batta Rezzonico/Nipote e Maggiorduomo di N.S. PP. Clemente XIII.* The existence of the side table has been verified by the discovery of two executed versions of the work, one now at the Minneapolis Institute of Art and the other at the Rijksmuseum in Amsterdam.

GIOVANNI BATTISTA PIRANESI
Mogliano Veneto 1720–Rome 1778

43. *Figure Studies*

Pen and brown ink. 9¹⁄₁₆ x 5½ inches (230 x 140 mm). Watermark: fragment of a circle.

PROVENANCE: J. A. Duval le Camus, Paris (Lugt 1441); Wertheimer, Paris 1947; Janos Scholz (no mark; see Lugt S. 2933b).

BIBLIOGRAPHY: Mayor 1952, p. 39, fig. 41; Thomas 1954, p. 60, no. 70, repr.; Stampfle 1978, no. A-9, repr.; Morgan Library *FR* XVIII, 1978, p. 283.

EXHIBITIONS: Venice 1957, no. 97, repr.; Oakland 1960, no. 63; New York 1965, p. 343, repr.; London 1968a, no. 72; Middletown, Connecticut 1969, no. 40; New York 1971, no. 237, repr.; Washington and elsewhere 1974–75, no. 94; Los Angeles 1976, no. 69, repr.; Montgomery 1976, no. 72; London 1978, no. 108; New York 1989.

The Pierpont Morgan Library. Gift of Mr. Janos Scholz, Acc. no. 1976.34

Piranesi's figure studies are difficult to place chronologically within the artist's oeuvre. On the basis of style and execution, Hylton Thomas has dated this sheet and several others like it from around 1760 to 1765 (Thomas 1954, p. 26). Piranesi's figures possess a startling vivacity and animation, often expressed through their gesticulating poses. When more than one figure appears on a sheet, they are unrelated and their size often varies widely. In the Library's drawing as in many others, Piranesi has not indicated any setting but simply used parallel hatching around the figures to provide a background and ground line, implying that drawings of this kind were primarily studies of pose and movement. Accordingly, Piranesi is not interested in carefully delineating the form of the human body, evidenced in the way the extremities are schematically indicated; the hands, for example, terminate in extended multiple penstrokes. Academy studies are rare in Piranesi's oeuvre, although one of these, a standing man, appears on the verso of the Library's *Design for a Title Page* (Cat. no. 18). Here the man's anatomy and pose is carefully

NO. 43

studied in black chalk. The range of Piranesi's figure drawings shows that while some, mainly the pen and ink sketches, were probably done from memory, others were drawn in his studio using assistants as models.

For the most part, Piranesi's figures represent types. They function as figural models for his prints rather than direct studies. Thomas compared Piranesi's compilation of figure studies to Watteau's building up of figural motifs, which he could then use later or borrow at will. Indeed, according to Janos Scholz's records, this drawing was originally part of an album of figure studies, broken up in 1946. While it is evident that human figures are not the focal point of Piranesi's etchings, as John Wilton-Ely has observed, they play an important role in conveying emotional tone, introducing dynamic values into the design, and emphasizing the grandeur of the architectural setting.

GIOVANNI BATTISTA PIRANESI

Mogliano Veneto 1720–Rome 1778

44. *Temple of Isis at Pompeii*

Reed and quill pens and brown-black ink over black chalk;
framing line in pen and brown ink, over black chalk. 20½
x 30¾ inches (520 x 780 mm). Watermark: shield with
bend, sword and fleur-de-lis between letters *F* and *M* (Robison 1986, watermark 61).

Numbered by Piranesi in pen and brown ink from 1 to 20
and inscribed at lower right in pen and gray-black ink, *Veduta di due ale dell'atrio del Tenysio* [sic] *d'Iside (on the
back)*; on verso at lower right in pen and brown ink, *Veduta
di due ale dell'atrio del/Tempio dIside* and at lower left, *Part.
2.ᵃ/Tav. 20*; numbered at center, *19*.

PROVENANCE: H. M. Calmann, Ltd., London; sale, London, Christie's, 29 June 1962, lot 41, repr.; Marvin L. Levy,
New York.

BIBLIOGRAPHY: Hawley 1964, p. 318, repr.; Morgan Library *FR* XIII, 1964, pp. 103–5; Morgan Library *Review*
1969, p. 160, pl. 42; Stampfle 1978, no. A-7, repr.

EXHIBITIONS: Cleveland 1964, no. 13, repr.; London 1972,
no. 729; Ann Arbor 1977, no. 35, repr.; Detroit and Chicago
1981, vol. II, no. 89a, repr.; New York 1989.

The Pierpont Morgan Library. Gift of Mr. Marvin L.
Levy, Acc. no. 1963.12

At mid-century, the ruins around Naples began to assume a new importance. The first significant excavations at Herculaneum commenced in 1738, while
those at Pompeii began about ten years later. In the
1770s, further progress was made at these excavations, and Piranesi undertook a number of trips to
the sites in order to study and record their remains
with a view toward publishing a series of etchings. We
know from a drawing in Amsterdam dated 1776 that
by this time Piranesi had completed some of his work
on the drawings of Pompeii. The Library's drawing
and another of the Temple of Isis (Cat. no. 45) were
executed during this period, shortly before the
artist's death in 1778. Most of his drawings were eventually used, either directly or indirectly, by his son
Francesco, who published the three-volume series of
elephant folios, *Les Antiquités de la Grande Grèce*, in
Paris between 1804 and 1807. During this time, Francesco also collaborated with Louis-Jean Desprez,
producing etchings from Desprez's drawings of
Pompeii. Wilton-Ely proposes that Desprez and Giovanni Battista Piranesi may have worked together at
Pompeii in the 1770s (London 1978, p. 128).

Many of Piranesi's drawings of Pompeii represent
the Temple of Isis which he studied from almost
every point of view. In this sheet, which was not used
directly for any of the etchings, he depicts the temple
from the northeast corner. The temple proper, which
rests on a high podium, is only partly visible at the
rear center of the drawing, which includes a full view
of the sacred enclosure with its colonnade and two
tall pylons, along with altars and pedestals. Other
drawings of the Temple of Isis from the same group
are in the Kunstbibliothek, Berlin, and the British
Museum. The British Museum drawing shows a rear
view of the Temple, and the four drawings in Berlin
depict the pronaos, including an interior view of the
pronaos and cella, the right flank of the temple, the
Egyptian temple in the courtyard, and a view into a
priestly dependency (Thomas 1952–55, p. 23). A
small-scale drawing of the temple appears on page 97

of the *Album Amicorum* that belonged to the Dutch collector Arnout Vosmaer (now in the Rijksprentenkabinet, Amsterdam; see Amsterdam 1989, p. 169). The drawing is inscribed by Piranesi: *Veduta del Tempio d'Iside a Pompei/Il Cavalier Piranesi da in atto/d'amicizia al Sg^r Vosmaere*. Below the inscription is a note by Vosmaer which states that the drawing was made in Rome on 10 January 1776 by Giovanni Battista, clearly placing it as a recollection of Piranesi's work in Pompeii. *The Temple of Isis* is illustrated in plates LIX through LXXII of the *Antiquités de la Grande Grèce.*

The attribution of the large Pompeii drawings to Giovanni Battista has been doubted by some scholars. Arthur Hind discussed the problem, pointing out that the architecture in both the drawings and etchings is worthy of Giovanni Battista, but the staffage has none of his characteristic style (Hind 1914, pp. 187–88; Hind 1922, pp. 19–20). The figures are coarsely drawn, and, as Hind stated, they share similarities with figures found in plate 1 of the *Raccolta de' Tempi Antichi* signed by Francesco. Although disturbed by the evidence of the title page, which states that the etchings are based on drawings by Giovanni Battista, he tentatively concluded that the Pompeii and Paestum drawings are by Francesco. Hylton Thomas, however, follows previously expressed opinions of such earlier scholars as Kurt Cassirer, Jakob Rosenberg, Karl Parker, James Byam Shaw, and others that the drawings are most likely by Giovanni Battista (Thomas 1952–55, note 14).

While scholarly opinion generally seems to accept the attribution to Giovanni Battista, it is often made with reservations given certain stylistic inconsistencies within the drawings. This holds true for the Morgan sheet where there appear to be two distinct hands. The architectural elements have been painstakingly laid out with a ruler. Andrew Robison suggested recently in conversation that the very precise architectural passages should probably not be attributed to Giovanni Battista but to another hand, and that areas of the drawing, such as the frieze of the temple and the decoration of the Egyptian temple, appear to be retouched by Giovanni Battista. The

foreground figures and objects are much more crudely executed than the architecture, and with a broader pen. That the figures are not an integral part of the composition – in many of these drawings the relationship between figures and setting is out of scale, the figures invariably being somewhat too large for the setting – presumably indicates that they were added later. Since the figures, however, are drawn with the same ink as Giovanni Battista's additions to the architecture, the possibility that they may be by Giovanni Battista himself cannot be ruled out.

GIOVANNI BATTISTA PIRANESI
Mogliano Veneto 1720–Rome 1778

45. *Temple of Isis at Pompeii*

Quill and reed pen in black and some brown ink, black wash, over black chalk; perspective lines and squaring in graphite; several accidental oil stains. 20½ x 30⅛ inches (522 x 764 mm). Watermark: shield with bend, fleur-de-lis and sword between letters *F* and *M* (Robison 1986, watermark 61).

Inscribed along lower right edge in pen and brown ink, *(on back) Veduta in angolo del tempio d'Isibe* [sic] and numbered by Piranesi from 1 through 23, in a different brown ink; on verso at upper center, *Tav. 12*, at lower left, *Part.2./Tav./14*, at lower right, *veduta in angolo del tempio d'Iside.*

PROVENANCE: sale, London, Christie's, 27 November 1973, lot 314; Mr. and Mrs. Eugene Victor Thaw, New York.

BIBLIOGRAPHY: Scott 1975, p. 249, fig. 295; Stampfle 1978, no. A-11, repr.

EXHIBITIONS: New York and elsewhere 1975–76, no. 56, repr.; Detroit and Chicago 1981, vol. II, no. 89b, repr.; New York 1989.

The Pierpont Morgan Library. Gift of Mr. and Mrs. Eugene Victor Thaw, Acc. no. 1979.41

This view of the Temple of Isis is taken from inside the north colonnade of the sanctuary. The temple and its precincts are seen from an angle that allows for a full view of the temple proper on its high podium as well as the sacred enclosure with its colonnade, the Egyp-

NO. 45

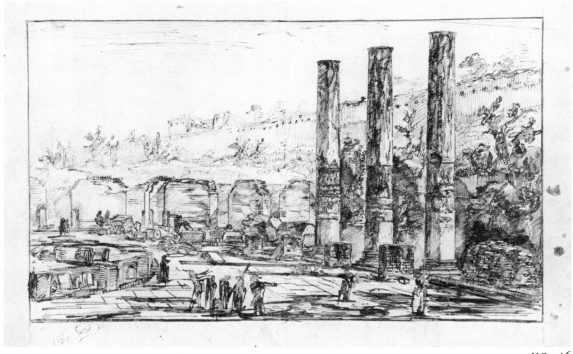

NO. 46

tian temple, and the altars and pedestals. Like Cat. no. 44, this drawing was made for publication in *Les Antiquités de la Grande Grèce*. A plate was engraved after this drawing but never used; it was reduced to approximately half the size of the drawing. The recto of the copper plate (Focillon 1091) depicts the *Dimostrazione dell'impluvio della casa medesima* from *Les Antiquités de la Grande Grèce* (Petrucci 1953, p. 305). On the verso of this plate, Maurizio Calvesi discovered the image that relates to the Library's drawing. Proofs of this etched design and other such *roveschi* were pulled in the 1960s (Rome 1967–68, no. 133; Focillon [Calvesi/Monferini] 1963, pl. 254).

The plate corresponds closely to the Library's drawing. A few minor architectural details were altered, but the figures have been entirely changed. In the drawing, there are two foreground figures, one seated and one standing. These were replaced in the print with two groups of figures in the right and center foreground. Two additional figures appear directly in front of the sanctuary and differ in character from those in the drawings. They are executed with a much closer attention to costume detail and exhibit a more graceful quality.

GIOVANNI BATTISTA PIRANESI
Mogliano Veneto 1720–Rome 1778

46. *Ruins at Pozzuoli*

Pen and brown-black ink, over black chalk, on a heavy, light brown paper. 19⁵⁄₁₆ x 30 inches (490 x 760 mm). Watermark: animal within a circle with letters *RUSS* below. Inscribed at lower left margin in pen and gray-black ink, the letter *P* in a rough cartouche; fragment of a somewhat similar inscription on verso.

PROVENANCE: purchased in London, 1961.

BIBLIOGRAPHY: Morgan Library *FR* XI, 1961, pp. 93–95, repr. (as *Ruins of Pompeii*); Morgan Library *FR* XIII, 1964, p. 103; Morgan Library *Review* 1969, p. 160; Stampfle 1978, no. A-6, repr.

EXHIBITIONS: New York 1971, no. 236, repr.; London 1972, no. 728; London 1978, no. 320, repr.; New York 1989.

The Pierpont Morgan Library. Purchased as the gift of the Fellows, Acc. no. 1961.1

This monumental drawing is also a product of the 1770s, when Piranesi made a number of trips to the south to study the Roman ruins. At first thought to be Pompeii, the site was identified as Pozzuoli by Hylton Thomas on the basis of an engraving of the same subject by Giuseppe Vasi. The three columns are those of the marketplace at Pozzuoli, known in the eighteenth century as the Serapeum or Temple of Serapis. In the Museum of Fine Arts, Boston, there is a Hubert Robert drawing of the Serapeum taken from the opposite side from the present drawing (fig. 1). Characteristically, Piranesi represented a sweeping view of the site and reduced the size of the figures, giving a somewhat exaggerated impression of the grandeur of the ruins. Robert's drawing is a more spontaneous, intimate depiction of figures among the ruins. A number of other views by Robert of the Temple of Serapis, several of which depict the entrance to the temple, are known (Rome 1990–91, no. 47). An aquatint, *Vuë de l'entrée du Temple de Sérapis à Pozzuoli près de Naples*, dated 1762 and signed *Robert del*, was published in Saint-Non's *Recueil de griffonis* (Cat. no. 123).

The Abbé de Saint-Non first visited Pozzuoli in 1759 and returned there with Robert in the spring of 1760. In his diary the abbé records that he traveled to Pozzuoli on 28 November 1759. He describes the ruins of an ancient amphitheater and the temple of the Serapeum. His description of the temple comes very close to Piranesi's and Robert's renderings of it:

> L'on voit près de là les restes d'un Temple dédié à Serapis, qui étoit de la plus grande magnificence; la forme de ce temple est un grand quarré très Régulier autour duquel étoient pratiquées de petites chambres destinées sans doute pour le Service du Temple; de grandes Colones de marbre formoient un grand portique quarré pavé de marbre blanc, de vingt pieds de large environ tout autour du Temple; en dedans et dans le milieu de ce quarré étoit une partie circulaire un peu plus élevée que le reste du Temple, entourée d'une colonnade d'une plus petite proportion avec quatre Escaliers pour y monter (Rosenberg 1986, p. 103).

FIGURE 1 Hubert Robert, *The Serapeum, Pozzuoli*. Forsyth Wickes Collection, Museum of Fine Arts, Boston, 65.2601.

NO. 47

UNKNOWN ARTIST, possibly a member of the workshop of Giovanni Battista Piranesi

47. *A Sheet of Sketches*

Pen, brown ink, brush and brown wash, over black chalk underdrawing on beige laid paper. 11¹¹⁄₁₆ x 8⅞ inches (297 x 225 mm). Recto: Volute, Curved Entablature, and Segmental Pediment; Verso: Tiara, Seated Man Turning to the Viewer, Eye, Horn. Watermark: none
Inscribed on verso, lower left corner in graphite, later hand, illegible *Guidi* or *Guardi*(?).

DATE: 1747–80.

PROVENANCE: Hans Calmann Ltd., London; Charles E. Slatkin Galleries, New York; Phyllis Lambert, New Haven, Chicago, and Montréal.

BIBLIOGRAPHY: *Connoisseur*, advertisement for Hans Calmann, Ltd., February 1955, repr. p. 50; Cavicchi and Zamboni in Bettagno 1983, p. 202, fig. 86 (recto); Bettagno 1983, p. 399, fig. 195 (recto).

EXHIBITIONS: Wellesley and New York 1960, no. 49; Northampton 1961, p. 29, no. 42, p. 6, pl. 6; Poughkeepsie 1961, no. 63, repr.; Venice 1978, p. 30, no. 8bis, repr. (recto and verso); Vancouver and elsewhere 1989–90, pp. 80, 83, no. 68, repr. p. 82 (verso).

Montréal, Centre Canadien d'Architecture/Canadian Centre for Architecture DR1955:0001 r and v

The sheet of paper on which these sketches have been executed has been cut along the edges. The artist who executed these drawings used the recto in a vertical position and the verso in a horizontal one. It is quite obvious from the verso that the sheet was originally much larger. Since this sheet of drawings was first published in 1961, it has been attributed to Piranesi; scholars have observed influences of Tiepolo's style and have used this drawing as evidence that Piranesi worked in Tiepolo's studio during his second trip to Venice, from 1745 to 1747. In his homage to Piranesi, written in 1779 after Piranesi's death, Lodovico Bianconi stated: "In mezzo a queste occupazioni, . . . vennegli improvisa voglia di ritornare a Venezia per mettersi sotto il celebre Tiepoletto, di cui faceva, e giustamente, gran caso" (Bianconi 1802, p. 130; Moretti in Bettagno 1983, pp. 132–33).

The attribution of this sheet of drawings to Piranesi was first doubted by Mimi Cazort, Richard Hemphill, and Myra Nan Rosenfeld in 1986 (CCA Research Files, Richard Hemphill report, 5 May 1986). In December of 1991, the drawing was sent to the Pierpont Morgan Library for examination alongside the three early drawings by Piranesi to which it has always been compared: *Design for a Title Page with a Pulpit* (Cat. no. 19); *Design for a Title Page* (Cat. no. 18); and the *Capriccio* (Cat. no. 20). Robison has noted that these three drawings exhibit an important change in Piranesi's drawing style that can be related to innovations in his etching technique in the *Grotteschi*, published in Rome between 1747 and 1749. In these three drawings, Piranesi used, for the first time, short parallel lines and stipple-like squiggles, elements similar to the hatching and tonal scratching found in the etchings of the *Grotteschi* (Robison 1986, pp. 25–32). Piranesi also left empty white spaces between intermittent areas of wash.

When compared with the Morgan drawings, it was evident that the CCA's sheet was drawn on paper different from all three drawings in the Morgan Library. It also had a different style of draughtsmanship. The parallel lines on the recto of the CCA's drawing are much harsher, as are the areas of wash. The squiggles on the recto of the CCA's drawing are also much more abbreviated than those in the Morgan drawings. On both the recto and verso of the CCA's drawing, there is a lack of definition of form and spatial relationships, indicating a lesser artist, more likely a member of Piranesi's workshop. Robison has also noted that the three drawings in the Morgan Library do not show the influence of Tiepolo's drawing style, but rather that of Canaletto, Franceso Fortebasso, and Pier Antonio Novelli. Robison rightly pointed out that Tiepolo did not use these short parallel lines or rapid squiggles to indicate shadows, as did the above-mentioned artists and Piranesi. The figure of the seated man on the verso of the CCA's drawing has been compared with those by Tiepolo, but when compared with several figures in drawings executed by Tiepolo in the 1740s, now in the Morgan Library, this figure was not found to have been influenced by his drawing technique. Tiepolo did not use such heavy shadows, and his three-dimensional form was articulated more clearly (fig. 1) (New York 1971, pp. 46–47, nos. 79–82, repr.).

The CCA's sheet of sketches is important since it raises the question of Piranesi's workshop, a subject that merits much more study. Cavicchi and Zamboni have published two sketchbooks (now in the Biblioteca Estense in Modena: A, Ms. Campori n. 1523, γy6,33, and B, Ms. Campori n. 1522, γy6,32) that shed light on Piranesi's workshop. Both sketchbooks have a combination of drawings by Piranesi and members of his family–his sons Francesco and Angelo, and daughter Laura. The first sketchbook, A, is undated, whereas the second sketchbook, B, has the signature of Angelo Piranesi as well as several inscribed dates from 1772 to 1777. Francesco's activity in running his father's workshop from 1778 to 1788, before he turned to political activity, is well known. Less is understood about the contributions of Piranesi's other children, Angelo and Laura. Cavicchi and Zamboni believe that the CCA's drawing is similar in style to several in the first sketchbook, A, which they attribute mainly to Piranesi and which they believe were executed in the late 1740s and early 1750s when Piranesi was issuing the editions of the *Prima parte*, the *Grotteschi*, the *Carceri*, and the *Opere varie*. Since the drawings in the first sketchbook (folios 9r and 55v) that Cavicchi and Zamboni compare with this sheet of sketches in the CCA have the same shortcomings, I am inclined to doubt their attribution to Piranesi. At the present time, it is not possible to date precisely the CCA's sheet of sketches because there is not enough evidence to determine whether these drawings were executed after Piranesi's drawings in the late 1740s or later, in the 1760s and 1770s. It would seem unlikely that Piranesi had a workshop before 1743 or before his first trip back to Venice. He must have started his workshop only after returning from his second trip to Venice, in 1747.

NO. 47 verso.

FIGURE 1 G. B. Tiepolo, *Ariadne with a Winged Putto and Two Other Figures.* The Pierpont Morgan Library, New York, IV, 127.

JOHANN BERNHARD FISCHER VON
ERLACH, designer and author
Graz 1656–Vienna 1723

JOHANN ADAM DELSENBACH, etcher
Nuremberg 1687–Nuremberg 1765

48. *The Temple of Nineveh*

in Entwurff/Einer Historischen Architectur,/In Abbildung unterschiedener berühmten Gebäude,/ des Alterthums und fremder Völcker,/Umb aus den Geschicht-büchern, Gedachtmüss-Müntzen, RUINen und/eingeholten wahrhafften Abrissen, vor Augen zu stellen./In dem Ersten Buche./Die von der Zeit vergrabene Bau-arten der alten Jüden, Egyptier, Syrer, Perser, und Griechen./In dem Andren./Alte unbekante Römische./In dem Dritten./ Einige fremde, in-und ausser-Europäische, als der Araber, und Türcken, etc. auch/neue Persianische, Siamitische, Sinesische, und Japonesische Gebäude./In dem Vierten./Einige Gebäude von des AUTORIS Erfindung und Zeichnung./Alles mit grosser Mühe gezeichnet und auf eigene Unkosten herausgegeben, von/ser Kaiser: Maj: Ober Bau Inspectorn Johann Bernhard Fischers, von Erlachen./Auch kurtzen Teutschen und Frantzösischen Beschreibungen. *Leipzig, [The Author], 1725.*

Etching (image) and engraving (inscription) on laid paper (Book I, plate X). Platemark: 11½ x 16⁷⁄₁₆ inches (292 x 418 mm); page: 14 x 18¹¹⁄₁₆ inches (356 x 475 mm). Watermark: fleur-de-lis, right of center (Kunoth 1956, p. 19, no. 3). Inscribed at upper right corner, *TA: X*; lower left, inside platemark, *Der Antiquitaet Kundigen mainung nach, ein Tempel von Ninive,/aus einer Medaille abgenomen, welche man in einer Egyptischen Mumie/gefunden, So bey Hern Joh: Pietro Belori in Rom züsehen war.*; below, to the left, *J.B.F. v.E: del:*; center, *Cum Privil: Sacr: Cæsar: Maje:*; lower right, *Temple tiré d'une medaille trouvée prés d'une Momie d' Egypte/qui Selon l'opinion des Connoisseurs est un temple de Ninive. Cette Médaille/a appartenu à Monsieur Jean Pierre Belori à Rome.*
DATE: execution of this etching, 1725.

PROVENANCE: Ben Weinreb Architectural Books, Ltd., London.

BIBLIOGRAPHY (for this plate but not for the CCA's version): Kunoth 1956, pp. 45–46.

Montréal, Centre Canadien d'Architecture/Canadian Centre for Architecture WM671 CAGE

This copy of the second edition of Fischer von Erlach's treatise is in a modern binding covered with black speckled paper; it has a brown leather spine and corners. Most of the pages are on hinges; others are sewn directly into the spine. The German title page is slightly different from the first 1721 edition. This copy also contains the dedication (one unnumbered folio) to Emperor Charles VI of Austria (reign 1711–40) in German, inscribed *Vienna 1721*, and a preface in French (one unnumbered folio, recto and verso). The five books in this copy have twenty illustrations in Book I, fifteen in Book II, fifteen in Book III, twenty-one in Book IV, and thirteen in Book V, all drawn from the first 1721 edition. All the illustrations have roman numerals except for those of Book V, which have arabic numerals in the upper righthand corners. Each book has a printed title page. Following the title page of Book I is an illustrated one (for the whole treatise) etched by Johann Ulrich Kraus (Augsburg 1655–1719). Following that is a map of the Mediterranean basin. These two illustrations must have been misplaced when the treatise was rebound because they have the numbers *3* and *4* in the upper righthand corner, an indication that they were to follow the printed title page for the whole work and the dedication, numbered pages *1* and *2*, respectively.

The text pages that correspond to the illustrations are in French. Many are missing. Book I has corresponding text pages only for plates I through XII and XVIII through XIX. The plates of Book II have corresponding text pages for plates III through IV, VI through VIII, XI, and XIII only. The plates of Book III have no corresponding text pages; there is one page after plate VII, a key to the illustration of the City of Mecca shown in that plate. Likewise, the plates of Book IV have no corresponding text pages. One page, a list of inscriptions, *Inscriptio obelisci*

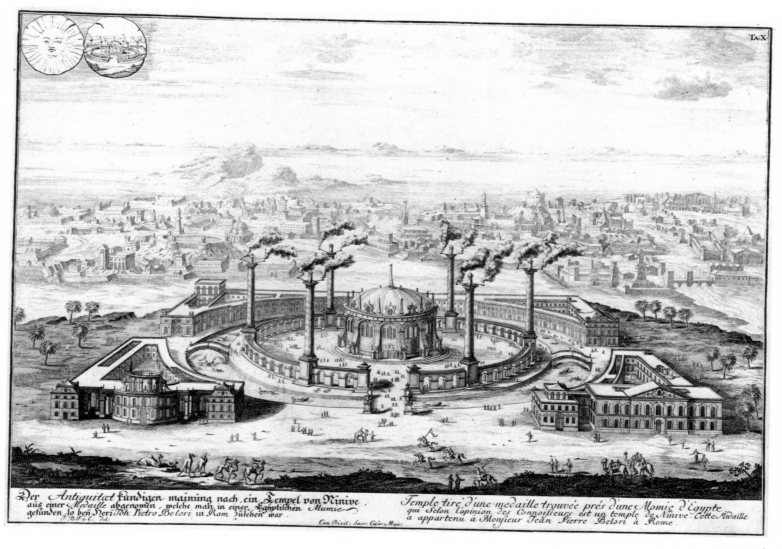

NO. 48

Wratislaviani, follows plate XXI, *The Tomb of Wratislav de Mitrowitz*. The plates of Book V have no corresponding text pages. Plate IX of Book I has two corresponding pages of text, whereas the other plates have only one. There is no text page for the map of the Mediterranean basin.

The Nationalbibliothek in Vienna has a presentation manuscript of Fischer von Erlach's treatise (Cod. miscr. 10791), dated 1712, with thirty-seven handwritten pages of text, and seventy-four proofs for the etched illustrations of the first 1721 edition. The first edition was given its printing privilege by Emperor Charles VI on 18 October 1720 (Kunoth

1956, pp. 17–18). The watermark in the paper exhibited here is the same as one found in a first edition of the treatise, now housed in the library of the University of Zagreb. There was a third edition, published in Leipzig in 1742, and two other editions, published in London in 1730 and 1737, were translated into English by Thomas Lediard (Kunoth 1956, p. 20).

The five books of Fischer von Erlach's treatise are as follows: Book I: *The Ancient Buildings of the Jews, Egyptians, Syrians, Persians, and Greeks*; Book II: *Roman Buildings*; Book III: *Buildings of the Arabs, Turks, Persians, Siamese, Chinese, and Japanese*; Book IV: *Buildings Designed by the Author*; and Book V: *Vases*.

This was the first treatise published in Europe in the eighteenth century that traced the history of architecture in exemplary buildings from both European and non-European cultures (Aurenhammer 1973, p. 153). Aurenhammer believes that Fischer von Erlach began planning his treatise when he went to London in 1704. There he met Sir Christopher Wren who may have encouraged him. Aurenhammer has also suggested that Fischer von Erlach presented his treatise to Emperor Charles VI in 1712, in an attempt to strengthen his position as court architect (Aurenhammer 1973, pp. 29–31). Much of Fischer von Erlach's knowledge of Egyptian, Babylonian, and Roman architecture was acquired during his stay in Rome (1671–87) where he came in contact with a group of antiquarians connected with the courts of the pope and of Queen Christina of Sweden. His knowledge of Egyptian architecture owed much to the publications and collection of the Jesuit papal librarian Athanasius Kircher (1602–80). Fischer von Erlach also met Giovanni Pietro Bellori (1615–96), the custodian of Queen Christina's collection and the secretary of the Accademia di San Luca (Aurenhammer 1973, pp. 18–22; Iversen 1958, pp. 324–25). Aurenhammer has suggested that Fischer von Erlach's knowledge of Oriental and Middle Eastern architecture was also gained through published travel accounts to which he was first exposed during his trip to London. These included Jacques Spon and George Wheler's *Voyage d'Italie, de Dalmatie, de Grèce et du Levant* (Lyons, 1678); G. J. Grelot's *Relation nouvelle d'un voyage de Constantinople* (Paris, 1680); and Johan Nieuhof's *L'Ambassade de la Compagnie orientale des Provinces Unies vers l'Empereur de la Chine, ou Grand Cam de Tartarie* (Leiden, 1655; Aurenhammer 1973, pp. 157–59). Iversen has pointed out that Fischer von Erlach's approach to the history of architecture was more aesthetic than scientific; Iversen also postulated that his treatise was aimed at patrons rather than architects. Fischer's reconstructions of ancient buildings were not based on archaeological research, like Piranesi's, but rather on secondary sources (Iversen 1958, p. 324).

Kunoth has attributed the execution of the plate exhibited here, *The Temple of Nineveh*, to Johann Adam Delsenbach, who signed several other plates in Fischer von Erlach's treatise. The town of Nineveh, the oldest city of the Assyrian Empire (eighth century B.C.), was not excavated until the middle of the nineteenth century. The Palace of Sennacherib was discovered between 1845 and 1851, and the Temple of Nineveh between 1929 and 1932 (*Encyclopaedia Britannica*, 15th ed., Chicago 1989, vol. VIII, pp. 717–18). Kunoth has noted that Fischer used Athanasius Kircher's reconstruction of the city of Nineveh from his *Turris Babel* (Amsterdam, 1679) as a source for plate III of Book I of his treatise, *Spectacula Babylonica* (Kunoth 1956, pp. 28–32, figs. 8, 9). It is thus surprising that Fischer von Erlach identified the Temple of Nineveh in this plate as being in Egypt; he stated in the text page as well as in the inscription that his rendition was based on a medal, owned by Pietro Bellori, found inside an Egyptian mummy. According to Kunoth, no such coins or medals have been found. Rather, Fischer invented a round building surmounted by a dome and surrounded by an arcade and columns resembling the Column of Trajan. A variant of this building appears in the background of plate XI of Book V (Kunoth 1956, fig. 177), behind the *Vases of Galathea and Triton*. A preparatory drawing adapted for plate III of Book I and plate XI of Book V is found in a manuscript in the Albertina that has preparatory sketches for Fischer von Erlach's treatise (Codex Montenuovo, folio 24; Kunoth 1956, p. 46, fig. 176).

Piranesi was influenced by Fischer von Erlach's treatise. The two sheets with sketches of buildings that Piranesi copied from Fischer's treatise were executed between 1741 and 1743 (now in the Morgan Library, Cat. no. 24), when Piranesi was working on the *Prima parte*. Piranesi's depictions of imaginary monuments, for example, *Mausoleo antico* (fig. 1), were directly influenced by illustrations such as Fischer's *Temple of Nineveh* (Robison 1986, p. 14, pl. 5, p. 75; Wilton-Ely 1978 [1988], p. 15, fig. 11, p. 17; Scott 1975, p. 48, figs. 52, 53). One also finds Fischer von Erlach's influence in several of Piranesi's etchings issued in the late 1740s and in 1750,

The *Fantastic Port Monument* and *Magnificent Port* (Robison 1986, pp. 132–33, no. 27, and p. 129, no. 26). There is a further connection between the illustration of *The Temple of Nineveh*, exhibited here, and a drawing by Piranesi of *Forum with Temple* (now in the British Museum) executed between 1747 and 1750 (fig. 2) (Thomas 1954, p. 42, no. 21, pl. 21). The column in the foreground, the domed building in the background, and the semi-circular colonnade in the middle ground all seem to be derived from *The Temple of Nineveh.*

Reudenbach has also suggested that the buildings illustrated in Fischer von Erlach's treatise had an influence on the fantastic monuments depicted in the first frontispiece of volume I of the *Antichità Romane* (1756), and in the second frontispieces of volumes II and III of the same work, both depicting *Imaginary Tombs on the Via Appia* (Reudenbach 1979, pp. 18–21, and p. 20, fig. 11, p. 21, fig. 12, p. 24, figs. 17, 18; Cat no. 57). Later, when Piranesi wrote the *Della Magnificenza ed architettura de' Romani* (1761) and the *Diverse maniere* (1769), he turned again to Fischer von Erlach's treatise for information on Egyptian architecture (Wittkower 1982, pp. 265–66, and p. 265, fig. 345, p. 266, fig. 346; Cat. no. 64).

A letter accompanying fifty-seven proofs of *Diverse maniere*, and written by Piranesi to Thomas Hollis on 18 November 1767, includes what seems to be a critique of information on Egyptian architecture in Fischer von Erlach's treatise. Piranesi writes: "You will see employed in this work something hitherto unknown in the genre. Egyptian architecture appears here for the first time. The first time, because until now the world has always believed that there was nothing in Egypt but pyramids, obelisks, and colossi, and that this system of architecture had insufficient elements to adorn and sustain it" (Pevsner and Lang 1968, pp. 216, 229; Wilton-Ely 1978 [1988], p. 107, note 44, p. 134). It is quite possible that in this letter Piranesi is referring to the illustrations of Fischer von Erlach's treatise, in particular to plates IV, XI, XIII, XIV, and XV of Book I (Kunoth 1956, pp. 32–33, fig. 12, pp. 47–48, fig. 30, pp. 49–50, fig. 30a, pp. 50–51, fig. 31; Cat. no. 64).

FIGURE 1 G. B. Piranesi, *Mausoleo antico*, in *Prima parte*, pl. 3, state I (first edition, first and second issues). National Gallery of Art, Washington, 1976.2.1.

FIGURE 2 G. B. Piranesi, *Forum with Temple.* Trustees of the British Museum, London.

Arco di Tito Vespasiano

Veduta di S. Giovanni in Laterano

Piranesi inc.

JEAN-LAURENT LEGEAY

Paris about 1710–Rome after 1788

49. *The Arch of Titus, Rome*

in ROMA ANTICA/DISTINTA PER REGIONI,/ SECONDO L'ESEMPIO/DI SESTO RUFO, VITTORE E NARDINI;/Ornata di Rami delle più celebri Fabbriche/antiche diligentemente intagliate;/ Coll'aggiunta dello stato di Roma nel secolo XII., e delle/memorie di varie Antichità trovate in diversi luoghi/della Città di Roma scritte da Ulisse Aldovrandi,/ Flaminio Vacca, Francesco de' Ficoroni,/Pietro Santi Bartoli, ed altri fino/all'anno MDCCXLI./TOMO PRIMO. *Rome, Giovanni Lorenzo Barbiellini, 1744*

Etching on laid paper (vol. I, pl. 3, between pp. 30 and 31). Platemark: 5⅛ x 7 inches (130 x 177 mm); page: 6¼ x 7½ inches (160 x 191 mm). Watermark: none.
Inscribed at lower edge below first etched border, *Dessi. et Grav. par J.L. Legeay Archit*; lower edge, just above the second etched border, center, *Arco di Tito Vespasiano*.

DATE: execution of this etching, 1739–41.

BIBLIOGRAPHY (for this plate but not for the CCA's version): Erouart in Brunel 1978, p. 202, note 9, p. 209, fig. 3; Erouart 1982, p. 223, no. 99, p. 224, fig. 241; Wunder in Brunel 1978, p. 559, fig. 10, p. 564.

GIOVANNI BATTISTA PIRANESI

Mogliano Veneto 1720–Rome 1778

The Façade of the Church of San Giovanni in Laterano, Rome

in ROMA MODERNA/DISTINTA PER RIONI,/E CAVATA/DAL PANVINIO, PANCIROLO, NARDINI,/ e altri Autori/Ornata di vari Rami diligentemente intagliati rappresen-/tanti le Basiliche, e altri insigni Fabbriche/fino all'anno MDCCXLI./. . ./TOMO SECONDO. *Rome, Giovanni Lorenzo Barbiellini, 1744*

Etching on laid paper (vol. II, pl. 3, between pp. 38 and 39). Platemark: 4⅞ x 7¾ inches (125 x 197 mm); page: 5⁵⁄₁₆ x 8¹¹⁄₁₆ inches (162 x 223 mm). Watermark: left center, cut off at edge, not decipherable.

Inscribed at lower left, inside platemark, *Piranesi inc.*; center, *Veduta di S. Giovanni in Laterano.*

DATE: execution of this etching, 1740–41.

PROVENANCE: Library of the Cathedral of Fabriano by 1764; Marlborough Rare Books, Ltd., London.

BIBLIOGRAPHY (for this plate but not for the CCA's version): Hind 1922, p. 77, no. 4 (from *Varie Vedute*); Focillon 1964, p. 16, no. 80 (*Varie Vedute*); Focillon (Calvesi/Monferini) 1967, p. 291, no. 80, p. 291 (*Varie Vedute*); Scott 1975, p. 16; Wilton-Ely 1978 (1988), p. 27, fig. 25, p. 26 (*Varie Vedute*); London 1978, p. 35, no. 68; Bettagno 1978, p. 11, fig. 9; Bertelli and Pietrangeli 1985, p. 37, no. IV, pl. IV (*Varie Vedute*); Millon in Brunel 1978, p. 352, note 26; Cavicchi and Zamboni in Bettagno 1983, pp. 203–4, 209, note 24.

Montréal, Centre Canadien d'Architecture/Canadian Centre for Architecture POY16773:1–2

Silla Zamboni discovered in 1964 that Jean-Laurent Legeay and Philothée-François Duflos (1710–46), *pensionnaires* at the French Academy in Rome, as well as Piranesi, had etched a series of views of Rome in small format that were inserted by Giovanni Lorenzo Barbiellini in 1741 into the first edition of *Roma antica distinta per Regioni* and its accompanying volume, *Roma moderna distinta per Rioni*. This publication was unknown to both Hind and Focillon, who only became aware of the plates when they were reissued later in 1745 in the *Varie Vedute* (Zamboni 1964, pp. 66–85). The etchings in the *Roma antica* and *Roma moderna* are some of Piranesi's earliest known works; they must have been executed between 1740, the year of his arrival in Rome, and 1741, the date of the first edition of Barbiellini's publication.

Henry Millon discovered that as many as seven views by Piranesi were included in the 1741 edition of this publication: *The Façade of the Church of San Giovanni in Laterano*, exhibited here; *The Trevi Fountain* (Focillon 1964, p. 16, no. 94; Bettagno 1978, fig. 10); *The Papal Palace on the Piazza del Quirinale* (Focillon 1964, p. 16, no. 95; Wilton-Ely 1978 [1988], p. 26, fig.

23 [*Varie Vedute*]); *The Church of San Sebastiano fuori le Mura* (Focillon 1964, p. 17, no. 106; Bettagno 1978, fig. 12); *The Church of San Paolo fuori le Mura* (Focillon 1964, p. 17, no. 109; Wilton-Ely 1978 [1988], p. 26, fig. 27 [*Varie Vedute*]); *The Castel Sant'Angelo* (Focillon 1964, p. 17, no. 118; Bettagno 1978, fig. 8); *The Baths of Diocletian* (Focillon 1964, p. 16, no. 88; Millon in Brunel 1978, p. 360, fig. 17); and *The Fountain of the Acqua Paola on the Janiculum* (Focillon 1964, p. 17, no. 112; Millon in Brunel 1978, p. 360, fig. 18). Erouart and Millon further noted that the same view of the Trevi Fountain was published with both Legeay's and Piranesi's name (Erouart in Brunel 1978, pp. 204–5, figs. 11, 12, p. 211; Erouart 1982, p. 224, no. 100, p. 24, fig. 16; Millon in Brunel 1978, p. 352, note 26). Other than *The Arch of Titus* exhibited here, Legeay etched the facade of *San Lorenzo fuori le Mura* (Erouart 1982, p. 222, no. 92), *The Arch of Constantine* (Erouart 1982, p. 223, no. 96, fig. 24, p. 24; Cat. no. 50), and *The Papal Palace on the Piazza del Quirinale* (Erouart 1982, p. 223, no. 97, fig. 173, p. 169; Wilton-Ely 1978 [1988], p. 26, fig. 24 [*Varie Vedute*]). Scott has suggested that all these views were designed like modern-day postcards, and were probably kept loose and then added to the volumes at the request of the buyer. No two editions of the work exhibited here have the same number of plates by the different artists (Scott 1975, p. 16). That the paper of the etchings is different from the text pages in the CCA's volumes supports Scott's point of view.

In addition to the plates by Legeay and Piranesi exhibited here, the CCA's two volumes of *Roma antica* and *Roma moderna* contain, in volume I (pl. 4, between pp. 52 and 53), *The Baths of Diocletian* by Piranesi (fig. 1) and, in volume II (pl. 8, between pp. 178 and 179), *The Papal Palace on the Piazza del Quirinale* (fig. 2) by Legeay. Volume II (pl. 9, between pp. 198 and 199), contains two works signed by Piranesi, *The Trevi Fountain* (fig. 3), and *The Acqua Paola* (pl. 15, between pp. 290 and 291). These two volumes in the CCA are bound in an eighteenth-century vellum binding; the spines of both are stamped in gold *ROMA/ANTICA /TO.1* and *ROMA/MODERNA/TO.2.* On the title pages of both is the same inscription in

FIGURE 1 G. B. Piranesi, *The Baths of Diocletian*, in *Roma antica distinta per Regioni* (pl. 4), published by Lorenzo Barbiellini. Canadian Centre for Architecture, Montréal, POY16773:1.

FIGURE 2 Jean-Laurent Legeay, *The Papal Palace on the Piazza del Quirinale*, in *Roma moderna distinta per Rioni* (pl. 8), published by Lorenzo Barbiellini. Canadian Centre for Architecture, Montréal, POY16773:2.

FIGURE 3 G. B. Piranesi, *The Trevi Fountain,* in *Roma moderna distinta per Rioni* (pl. 9), published by Lorenzo Barbiellini. Canadian Centre for Architecture, Montréal, POY16773:2.

brown ink, *Bibliotheca Ecclesia Cathedralis Fabriano per dono/Di Can.^{ci} da Sanctis 1764.*

In 1745, the series of small-format views of Rome was published as *Varie Vedute di Roma antica e moderna disegnate e intagliate da celebri autori in Roma* by Fausto Amidei (active 1731–77) with a frontispiece by Paolo Anesi (Bertelli and Pietrangeli 1985, pp. 18–19; Bettagno 1978, fig. 13). The views by Jean-Laurent Legeay, Duflos, and Piranesi that had appeared in the earlier Barbiellini publication were reissued and other views by Piranesi, Legeay, Jérôme-Charles Bellicard (1726–86), and Paolo Anesi were added. Some volumes of the 1745 edition of the *Varie Vedute* contain only twenty-seven views by Piranesi. However, Andrew Robison has discovered at the Huntington Library in San Marino, California, a 1745 edition with a total of ninety-eight views, of which forty-eight are by Piranesi, nine by Duflos, eight by Jean-Laurent Legeay, two by Anesi, two by Bellicard, and the rest anonymous (Robison 1970 "Prolegomena," p. 178, note 9). A second edition of the *Varie Vedute* was published by Amidei in 1748.

Giovanni Bouchard published the *Varie Vedute* twice – first in 1748, and a second time in 1752, with a new frontispiece that read: *Raccolta di varie vedute di Roma si antica che moderna intagliate in maggior parte dal celebre Giambattista Piranesi* (Erouart 1982, p. 32, fig. 25). Various numbers of these same plates by Legeay, Bellicard, Piranesi, and Duflos were also reissued in the 1750, 1760, 1771, and 1789 editions of *Mercurio Errante,* as well as in the 1763 and 1766 editions of Ridolfino Venuti's *Accurata, e succinta descrizione topografica delle antichità di Roma* (Cat. no. 50) (Hind 1922, pp. 76–78; Focillon 1964, H, pp. 15–16, nos. 72–119, pp. 16–17; Focillon [Calvesi/Monferini] 1967, H, pp. 290–91, nos. 72–119, pp. 291–92; Erouart 1982, pp. 222–24, nos. 92–100; London 1973–74, nos. 1, 2; Millon in Brunel 1978, pp. 352–54; Bertelli and Pietrangli 1985, pp. 19–20, and pls. I–XLVIII, for all 48 views by Piranesi in the *Varie Vedute*; Bettagno 1978, pp. 11–12, pls. 7–21).

Jean-Laurent Legeay had received the *grand prix d'architecture* in 1732. He did not take up his residence in the Palazzo Mancini in Rome until the end of 1737 or the beginning of 1738, when he arrived with the engraver Charles-Nicolas Cochin the Elder (1688–1754), and the painters Noel Hallé (1711–81) and Charles-François Hutin (1715–76). During his stay in Rome, Legeay contributed five etched views of Rome to *Il quinto Libro del Novo teatro delle Fabriche et edifici fatte-fare in Roma e fuori di Roma dalla Santità di nostro Signore Papa Clemente XII,* published by G. G. de Rossi in 1739. He also designed decorations for the *Feste della Chinea* and took part in the *concorso Clementino* before leaving Rome on 9 January 1742 for Paris (Erouart 1982, pp. 222–23, nos. 87–91, p. 23, figs. 14, 15, p. 169, fig. 172).

John Harris had suggested in 1967 that Legeay had a formative influence on Piranesi's early architectural fantasies, particularly on the *Prima parte* of 1743 and the *Opere varie* (1750) (Harris in Wittkower 1967, pp. 191–92). However, most authors now agree that by comparing the etchings of the two artists executed during the 1740s, Piranesi, although younger than Legeay, appears superior to the latter in developing a new approach to the genre of the *veduta* (Erouart 1982, p. 30; Wilton-Ely 1978 [1988], p. 26). When we compare the two views exhibited here, it is obvious that Piranesi was well on his way toward making innovations in both composition and technique. Legeay does not focus the attention of the viewer on the main monument depicted in the *veduta.* Instead he places the Arch of Titus at a distance from the picture plane. He does not differentiate between the Arch of Titus and the surrounding buildings. The viewer's eye moves through the arch and away into the distance. On the other hand, Piranesi is able to focus the viewer's attention on the church facade by positioning the facade of San Giovanni in Laterano close to the picture plane and at an angle diagonally across from the portal of the triclinium, which is radically foreshortened. In addition, by making the impression of the burin lighter in three areas – the facade of the Lateran palace, the ruins of the aqueduct of Nero, and the hospital in the background – Piranesi is able to retain the viewer's gaze on the facade of the church, which is etched in darker lines. Piranesi, much in the style of Jacques Callot, Parmigianino, and Rembrandt, creates a feeling of palpable atmosphere around the buildings by varying the thickness and length of the etched lines, and by eliminating the etched border around the image. Legeay, in contrast, uses regular lines of the same thickness and length, which approximate the effect of intaglio engraving.

Legeay's approach to the *veduta* is much closer to that of Giuseppe Vasi. Twelve years later, in plate 46 of volume III of his *Delle Magnificenze di Roma Antica e Moderna* (Rome, 1753), Giuseppe Vasi presented a view of the Church of San Giovanni in Laterano placed in the same composition devised by Piranesi (Wilton-Ely 1978 [1988], pp. 26–27, fig. 27, p. 27). Because the etched lines are even throughout the plate, the sharp contrasts of light and shade, as in Legeay's

etching, make the composition static. The secondary buildings have the same importance as the main subject of the *veduta*, the facade of San Giovanni in Laterano. Even twelve years later, Vasi, the older artist, was unable to match the achievements of his younger, former assistant. In the opinion of Myra Nan Rosenfeld, Cavicchi and Zamboni have correctly attributed to Piranesi a preparatory drawing (in sepia wash over graphite underdrawing) for the view of the facade of San Giovanni in Laterano, which they discovered in a sketchbook in the Biblioteca Estense, Modena (Cavicchi and Zamboni in Bettagno 1983, p. 184, folios 37v, 38, fig. 99, pp. 203–4, Ms. A Modena, Biblioteca Estense, Ms. Campori n. 1523, γγ 6,33).

NO. 50

JEAN-LAURENT LEGEAY

Paris about 1710–Rome after 1788

50. *The Arch of Constantine, Rome*

Etching (image) and engraving (inscriptions) on laid paper (vol. I, pl. 6, opposite p. 13). Platemark: 5⁵⁄₁₆ x 7¹⁄₁₆ inches (134 x 180 mm); page: 10⅜ x 7⅝ inches (262 x 194 mm). Watermark: none.

Inscribed upper left corner, inside etched border, 6; lower left, below first etched border, *Des. et Grav. par J.L. LeGeay*; lower edge, center, below first etched border, *Arco di Costantino Magno*; lower right corner, above second etched border, *Tom.I.*; upper right corner, inside etched border, *Pag. 13*.

DATE: execution of this etching, 1739–41.

BIBLIOGRAPHY (for this plate but not for the CCA's version): Rome and elsewhere 1976, p. 180, under no. 88, fig. 89bis (without title); Erouart 1982, p. 31, fig. 24 (without title), p. 223, no. 96.

GIOVANNI BATTISTA PIRANESI

Mogliano Veneto 1720–Rome 1778

Pyramid of Caius Cestius, Rome

Etching (image) and engraving (inscriptions) on laid paper (vol. II, pl. 72, opposite p. 19). Platemark: 5⅛ x 7⅝ inches (130 x 193 mm); page: 10⅜ x 7⅝ inches (263 x 194 mm). Watermark: none.

Inscribed lower edge, center, inside platemark, *Piramide di Caio Cestio vicino alla Porta S. Paolo*; left corner, inside platemark, *Piranesi inc.*

DATE: execution of this etching, 1742–45.

BIBLIOGRAPHY (for this plate but not for the CCA's version): Hind 1922, p. 78, no. 34 (*Varie Vedute*); Focillon 1964, p. 17, no. 110, (*Varie Vedute*); Focillon (Calvesi/Monferini) 1967, p. 292, no. 110 (*Varie Vedute*); Bertelli and Pietrangeli 1985, p. 11, no. XXXIV, p. 157, pl. XXIV (*Varie Vedute*); Wilton-Ely 1978 (1988), p. 28, fig. 29 (*Varie Vedute*).

in Ridolfino Venuti,

ACCURATÀ, E SUCCINTA/DESCRIZIONE TOPOGRAFICA/ DELLE/ANTICHITA DI ROMA/DELL'ABATE/RIDOLFINO VE- NUTI CORTONESE/PRESIDENTE ALL'ANTICHITA' ROMANE,/

E Membro Onorario della Regia Società/degli Antiquarj di Londra, Rome, Giovanni Battista Bernabò and Giuseppe Lazzarini, 1763.

PROVENANCE: Ben Weinreb Architectural Books, Ltd., London.

Montréal, Centre Canadien d'Architecture/Canadian Centre for Architecture w213:1–2

The etchings designed by Legeay, Duflos, Bellicard, and Piranesi for the 1741 Barbiellini publication (Cat. no. 49) and for the *Varie Vedute* were also inserted into Ridolfino Venuti's book, *Accuratà, e succinta descrizione topografica delle antichità di Roma*, in both the first and second editions (1763 and 1766). Piranesi's contributions to Venuti's book were mentioned by Legrand in his 1799 *Life of Piranesi* (Erouart and Mosser in Brunel 1978, p. 225, note 25). The CCA's copy is in an eighteenth-century binding with a brown leather spine and pulp covers faced with yellow, orange, and red marbled paper. The abridged title of the book, *ANTICHITA/DI/ROMA/I/ANTICHITA/DI/ROMA/II*, is embossed in gold on a red leather strip placed on the spines of both volumes.

There are ten plates by Piranesi in the first volume of the CCA's copy of Venuti's work (pls. 3, 4, 28, 31, 36, 41, 42, 51, 52, 56: Focillon 1964, pp. 16–17, nos. 102, 103, 89, 88, 85, 84, 83, 81, 82, 78), and eight plates in volume II, in addition to the one exhibited here (pls. 62, 64, 65, 70, 75, 78, 91, 95: Focillon 1964, pp. 16–17, nos. 105, 108, 107, 104, 111, 101, 100, 118). Besides the plate by Legeay exhibited here, volume I has the same illustration of *The Arch of Titus* by Legeay as found in the 1741 and 1744 editions of *Roma antica . . . Roma moderna* (pl. 7, opposite p. 15; see Cat. no. 49). Volume II (pl. 88, opposite p. 80) has only one illustration by Legeay: the *View of the Piazza Navona* (fig. 1) (Erouart 1982, p. 223, no. 95, fig. 238, p. 223 [without title]).

Ridolfino Venuti (1703–65), an advisor to Cardinal Albani, was Winckelmann's predecessor as papal antiquary. He held the post of *commissario delle Antichità della Camera Apostolica* from 1746 until his death in 1765. Like Piranesi, he had been elected a member of the London Society of Antiquarians and

FIGURE 1 Jean-Laurent Legeay, *View of the Piazza Navona*, in Ridolfino Venuti, *Accuratà, e succinta descrizione topografica delle antichità di Roma* (pl. 88). Canadian Centre for Architecture, Montréal, w213:2.

was the author of several books on the antiquities of Rome. Piranesi had to receive Venuti's permission to conduct excavations during the years he was preparing *Antichità Romane* (1756), *Rovine del Castello dell' Acqua Giulia* (1761), *Descrizione e disegno dell'Emissario del Lago Albano* (1762), *Campus Martius* (1762), *Antichità di Cora* (1764), and *Antichità di Albano e di Castel Gandolfo* (1764). Ridolfino Venuti was the brother of Marcello Venuti (1701–55), who had directed the excavations at Herculaneum between 1738 and 1740. Both brothers were members of the Accademia delle Antichità e delle Inscrizioni Etrusche of Cortona, originally called the Accademia degli Occulti. In this context, they had become acquainted with Montesquieu and Voltaire, who were also members (Monferini in Bettagno 1983, pp. 35–44).

Piranesi and Venuti had a stormy relationship, criticizing each other in their books. In 1757, Piranesi added an illustration of a sepulchral urn, plate LVII, *Avanzi di un Collegio di Silvano Aureliano*, to an updated version of volume IV of the first edition of *Antichità Romane* (1756). In that illustration, Piranesi pointed out that Venuti had stated erroneously in his *Spiegazione de' bassorilievi che se osservano nell'urna sepolcrale detta volgarmente d'Alessandro Severo*, published in 1756, that the sepulchral urn in question was discovered on the Aventine Hill. According to Piranesi, this urn had actually been found four miles outside of Rome, beyond the Porta Maggiore (Focillon [Calvesi/Monferini] 1967, p. 300, no. 395, p. 310; Scott 1975, p. 125, note 5, p. 309; Monferini in Bettagno 1978, p. 39, fig. 205). It is thus ironic that

FIGURE 2 G. B. Piranesi, *Pyramid of Caius Cestius*, in *Vedute di Roma*, pl. 13. The British Architectural Library, RIBA, London.

FIGURE 3 G. B. Piranesi, *Pyramid of Caius Cestius*, in *Vedute di Roma*, pl. 57. The British Architectural Library, RIBA, London.

Piranesi's etchings were used to illustrate Venuti's book.

In comparing Legeay's *Arch of Constantine* to Piranesi's *Pyramid of Caius Cestius*, we find the same differences noted earlier in the analysis of the etchings inserted into the 1741 and 1744 editions of *Roma antica . . . Roma moderna*. Most authors date the *Pyramid of Caius Cestius* later than *San Giovanni in Laterano*, which was included in the 1741 and 1744 editions (Cat. no. 49). This view of the *Pyramid of Caius Cestius* was first published in the *Varie Vedute* in 1745. By cutting off the top of the pyramid at the edge of the platemark and overlapping the etched lines in a dense pattern, Piranesi conveys a sense of the great mass of the monument. He also uses cross-hatching in addition to the parallel lines employed in *San Giovanni in Laterano*. One of Piranesi's innovations in the *Pyramid of Caius Cestius* was to depict one of the crenellated towers of the Porta San Paolo by a series of quickly applied sketchy lines. This gives the effect of light shimmering in the atmosphere as well as on the surface of the stone (Scott 1975, p. 16;

Wilton-Ely 1978 [1988], p. 28). These qualities are a witness to the influence of the etching technique of Marco Ricci's *Capricci*, a technique also found in the title page as well as several plates from Piranesi's *Prima parte* (1743) (Robison 1986, p. 17, fig. 15, pls. 1, 3, 4).

Two successive images of the *Pyramid of Caius Cestius* by Piranesi in his *Vedute di Roma* reveal his great progress after returning to Rome in 1747 from his second trip back to Venice. The first of these etchings, which appears in the *Vedute di Roma* (Hind 1922, p. 48, no. 35; Focillon 1964, p. 155, no. 810; Wilton-Ely 1978 [1988], p. 33, fig. 44, p. 34, pl. 13), is found in the two earliest groups of the *Vedute* in Chatsworth and Princeton, believed by Robison to have been etched no later than 1749 (Robison in Bettagno 1983, pp. 18–19). In this first etching in the *Vedute di Roma* (fig. 2), Piranesi sets the *Pyramid of Caius Cestius* back from the picture plane, increasing the space around the monument. No longer is the apex of the monument cut off at the top by the platemark as in the earlier etching of 1742 to 1745 exhibited here. Piranesi places the Porta San Paolo at the same angle to the picture plane as the pyramid, creating a unification of the space. Since Piranesi depicts the Porta San Paolo in much greater detail in the first etching of the *Vedute di Roma* (fig. 2), he is able to give the viewer a more convincing impression of the actual site. There is now a greater density of the etched lines, and an even greater sense of atmosphere than in the earlier view of the *Pyramid of Caius Cestius* exhibited here.

In the second view of the *Pyramid of Caius Cestius* (fig. 3), which Piranesi etched in 1761 for the *Vedute di Roma* (Hind 1922, p. 48, no. 36; Focillon 1964, p. 52, no. 745; Wilton-Ely 1978 [1988], p. 34, fig. 45, pl. 57; Robison in Bettagno 1983, pp. 32–33), he placed the pyramid close to the picture plane as in the earlier small view exhibited here. However, he created a new sense of drama and foreboding by making the tonality of the etching dark, and including barren trees and a ruined portion of the city wall. The gigantic pyramid fills most of the picture plane, imparting a menacing atmosphere to the *veduta* (Wilton-Ely 1978 [1988], p. 33).

GIUSEPPE VASI, author, delineator, and etcher

Corleone 1710–Rome 1782

51. *The Basilica of Santa Maria Maggiore*

in DELLE MAGNIFICENZE DI ROMA ANTICA E MODERNA/LIBRO TERZO/CHE CONTIENE/LE BASILICHE E CHIESE ANTICHE DI ROMA/ DEDICATE/ALLA SANTITÀ/DI NOSTRO SIGNORE/PAPA BENEDETTO XIV.,
Rome, Book III, Heirs of Giovanni Barbiellini, 1753

Etching on laid paper (Book III, pl. 48). Platemark: 8 x 12⁷/₁₆ inches (204 x 316 mm); page: 9¹³/₁₆ x 14¹¹/₁₆ inches (250 x 374 mm). Watermark: in the center, fleur-de-lis in a circle with a *B* above and a *V* below (unidentified).
Inscribed at lower left, *G. Vasi dis. sc.*; lower right, *48*; center, *Basilica di S. Maria Maggiore*; below, a list of monuments preceded by roman numerals.

DATE: execution of this etching, 1752–53.

PROVENANCE: Ben Weinreb Architectural Books, Ltd., London.

BIBLIOGRAPHY (for this plate but not for the CCA's version): Scalabroni 1981, p. 68, no. 122, repr. fig. 122; Sassoli 1992, vol. I, p. 19, vol. II, Book III, pl. 48.

Montréal, Centre Canadien d'Architecture/Canadian Centre for Architecture W7358:3 CAGE

GIUSEPPE VASI, author and delineator

Corleone 1710–Rome 1782

GIOVANNI BATTISTA PIRANESI, etcher

Mogliano Veneto 1720–Rome 1778

The Ponte Milvio, Rome

in DELLE MAGNIFICENZE DI ROMA ANTICA E MODERNA/LIBRO QUINTO/CHE CONTIENE/I PONTI E GLI EDIFIZJ SUL TEVERE/ DEDICATE/ ALLA SERENISSIMA REALE ALTEZZA/DI D. FILIPPO BORBONE/PRINCIPE DELLE DUE SICILIE...,
Rome, Book V, Heirs of Giovanni Barbiellini, 1754

Etching on laid paper with letterpress (Book V, pl. 84). Platemark: 5¹³/₁₆ x 10½ inches (148 x 266 mm); page: 9⅞ x 14¾ inches (251 x 375 mm). Watermark: center, illegible. Inscribed at lower left, *G. Vasi dis. e inc.*; center, *Ponte Milvio detto Ponte Molle.*; lower right, *84*; below, list of monuments preceded by roman numerals.

DATE: execution of this etching, 1740–41.

PROVENANCE: Ben Weinreb Architectural Books, Ltd., London.

BIBLIOGRAPHY (for this plate but not for the CCA's version): Millon in Brunel 1978, p. 348, note 18, p. 351, figs. 12, 14, 15; Scalabroni 1981, pp. 22–24, under no. 35, p. 51, no. 166, p. 73, fig. 166; Sassoli 1992, vol. II, Book V, pl. 84.

Montréal, Centre Canadien d'Architecture/Canadian Centre for Architecture W7358:5 CAGE

Giuseppe Vasi, Piranesi's main competitor in the production of *vedute* of the city of Rome, was only ten years his senior and a native of Sicily. Vasi arrived in Rome in 1736. His earliest known etchings, three depictions of a mausoleum for the king of France, after drawings by Juvarra, are dated 1739 (Millon in Brunel 1978, pp. 346–47, fig. 1; Scalabroni 1981, pp. 16, 37). Pope Clement XII (1730–40) founded in 1738 the *Calcografia Camerale Apostolica*. In 1739, Vasi contributed fifteen plates to *Il secondo libro del Nuovo Teatro delle fabbriche et Edifici fatte fare in Roma dalla Santità di Nostro Signore Clemente XII*, which was published by Domenico Campiglia, superintendant of the *Calcografia Camerale Apostolica* (Scalabroni 1981, pp. 45–48, nos. 11–25). Vasi continued to produce etchings for the *Calcografia* throughout his career. In addition, he did etchings of the temporary buildings erected for the *Feste della Chinea* in Rome between 1745 and 1778 (Cat. nos. 11 and 12) (Scalabroni 1981, pp. 97–108, nos. 323–67). Vasi also made etchings in 1747 of the temporary decorations designed by Vicenzo dal Re for the festivities in Naples commemorating the birth of Prince Filippo, son of King Carlo III of the Two Sicilies. King Carlo III appointed Vasi as chamberlain of the Palazzo Farnese, where Vasi set up his workshop (Scalabroni 1981, pp. 17–18, 29–32, nos. 49–57, pp. 53–55).

Vasi's most important achievement was the series

Basilica di S. Maria Maggiore.
1. Collegio de PP. Benitezieri della Basilica, 2. Campanile di S. Brassede, 3. Monastero delle Monache Filippine, 4. Canonica della Basilica di S. Maria Maggiore.

of ten volumes on the city of Rome entitled *Delle Magnificenze di Roma Antica e Moderna* and published between 1747 and 1761. Books I, II, and V were, according to Scalabroni, designed and etched between 1740 and 1748; the remaining books–III, IV, and VI to X–were designed and executed between 1752 and 1761. Book I, *Le porte e mura*, although published in 1747, was probably in progress between 1741 and 1743, since the dedication to Carlo III, King of the Two Sicilies, is dated 3 November 1744. Book V, *I ponti e gli edifizj sul Tevere*, as we shall see below, was based on an earlier book on the same subject whose illustrations were etched between 1740 and 1743. Book II, *Le Piazze principale*, was ready to be printed in 1748, according to Vasi's letter to Giovanni Gaetano Bottari dated 13 September 1748. It was probably in progress between 1741 and 1744. The authors of the first two books were Padre Giuseppe Bianchini and Cesare Orlandi. Since the use of outside authors for the texts was holding up the production of his books, Vasi decided to write the texts for the remaining eight volumes himself (Scalabroni 1981, pp. 20–27, 57). Scalabroni and Sassoli have noted that Vasi's *Delle Magnificenze* was different in character from Piranesi's publications. Vasi was not particularly interested in the ancient city. Rather, he wished to show the modern city as a backdrop for events related to the daily lives of the ordinary populace or to the great processions organized by the popes and visiting monarchs. For Sassoli, Vasi's books addressed the travelers and pilgrims who came to visit the papal city. In 1763, Vasi published an index to his *Delle Magnificenze*. Entitled *Itinerario istruttivo per ritrovare le antiche e moderne magnificenze di Roma*, it was also published in French and went through nine printings, the last in 1838 (Scalabroni 1981, pp. 28, 30; Sassoli 1992, pp. 11–14, 19, 32).

The ten volumes comprising the CCA's copy of the *Delle Magnificenze* are in a modern binding made of boards covered with blue-gray paper with a white vellum spine and corners. The spine is embossed in gold, *VASI/ROMA/I-[X]*. The copy of Book III exhib-

ited here, *Le basiliche e chiese antiche di Roma*, is the first edition. It has the dedication to Pope Benedict XIV dated 17 August 1753; a preface with the papal *imprimatur*; twenty full-page illustrations numbered from 41 to 60 in arabic numerals; a vignette on the title page; a decorated initial on the first page of the dedication; seven unnumbered three-quarter-page illustrations; and fifty pages of text numbered with roman numerals, including an index (the last page is incorrectly numbered XLII) (Scalabroni 1981, pp. 67–69, nos. 114–39). Book V, also exhibited here, is the second edition, dedicated on 24 November 1754 to Prince Filippo of the Two Sicilies. It contains twenty full-page illustrations numbered from 81 to 100; seven unnumbered three-quarter-page illustrations; a vignette of the Ponte Lucano on the title page; a decorated letter on the dedication; a vignette on the first page of the preface with the papal *imprimatur*; and forty-nine pages of text, including an index (Scalabroni 1981, pp. 72–77, nos. 161–88).

Piranesi's eighteenth-century biographers, Lodo-vico Bianconi and J.-G. Legrand, state that immedi-ately following his arrival in Rome from Venice in 1740, Piranesi spent six months in Giuseppe Vasi's workshop, but he left as a result of Vasi's jealousy. Legrand writes ". . . after six months the student was more gifted than his master. Vasi's patience could not contain his anger; he said constantly [to Piranesi]: You are too much of a painter to ever be a good etcher" (Focillon 1963, pp. 36–39; Millon in Brunel 1978, p. 345, note 1, p. 351; Erouart and Mosser in Brunel 1978, p. 223). Art historians have always won-dered whether Piranesi executed any etchings pub-lished under Vasi's name. Following Focillon's sug-gestion that a technical analysis of the two artists' etching techniques would yield an answer, Henry Millon analyzed the illustrations of Book V, *I ponti e gli edifizj sul Tevere*, in order to find evidence of etchings executed by Piranesi in Vasi's workshop. Millon discovered that the platemarks of twelve three-quarter-page illustrations were close in size (about 150 x 270 mm) to those Piranesi did for one of his first works, the *Antichità Romane de' Tempi della Repubblica* (about 130 x 250 mm; Cat. no. 53). Furthermore, Millon noted that of the fourteen full-page illustrations, six were composed of three plates with the central plate the same size as the twelve three-quarter-page illustrations. He suggested that these eighteen smaller illustrations were originally etched between 1740 and 1743 by Vasi for a lost book on the Tiber River, *Vedute di Roma sul Tevere*. In the introduction to Book I of *Delle Magnificenze* dated 3 November 1744, Vasi stated that he had already etched the illustrations for the book on the Tiber River (Millon in Brunel 1978, pp. 338–49, note 18, pp. 348–49, note 20, p. 349). Since the publication of Millon's article, Scalabroni has discovered a copy of the *Vedute di Roma sul Tevere*, dedicated to Cardinal Aquaviva, ambassador of the king of Naples to the Holy See, with fifteen illustrations approximately the same size as the three-quarter-page illustrations in Book V, and with no text (Scalabroni 1981, pp. 51–52, nos. 34–48). These smaller illustrations were reused (with the addition of text) in the two editions of Book V, the first dedicated to Elisabeth Farnese, dowager queen of Spain, on 3 March 1754. The second edition dedicated to Prince Filippo of Bourbon is exhibited here (Scalabroni 1981, pp. 22–27).

Millon has suggested that the style of several of the etchings from the *Vedute di Roma sul Tevere* is similar to Piranesi's illustrations from the *Antichità Romane de' Tempi della Repubblica*. He has attributed to Piranesi plate 84, the *Ponte Milvio*, exhibited here, and plate 89, the *Ponte Sisto* (Millon in Brunel 1978, pp. 350–51, figs. 12 and 13; Scalabroni 1981, p. 74, no. 174 [*Ponte Sisto*], fig. 174). The Ponte Milvio, or the Pons Milvius, was built in 109 B.C. Millon's point of view has not been accepted by Scalabroni (Scalabroni 1981, p. 26). However, a comparison between the etching of the *Ponte Milvio* and the *Basilica of Santa Maria Maggiore* from Book III of the *Delle Magnificenze*, also exhibited here, supports Millon's hypothesis. In the *Ponte Milvio*, there is a very subtle modulation of the burin, especially when one compares the darker etched lines in the foreground and middle ground with the lighter ones in the background. This modulation of the line of the burin is not found in Vasi's etchings. Vasi does not differentiate between the middle ground and the background in the etching of the *Basilica of Santa Maria Maggiore*. Scalabroni has noted that this even handling of the burin is a hallmark of Vasi's style. She also has noted that Vasi used a solution different from Piranesi's to incise the lines on his copper plates. Vasi employed a mixture of strong Parmesan vinegar, copper sulfate, ammonia salts, and alum. This solution produced evenly modulated lines in the copper. In contrast, Piranesi used nitric acid that penetrated deeper into the copper and produced a more varied modulation of lines, an effect closer to actual pen and ink drawing (Scalabroni 1981, p. 18). Vasi's etching of the *Basilica of Santa Maria Maggiore* is rather schematic and lacks a sense of atmosphere. In contrast, Piranesi's etching of the *Ponte Milvio* is filled with shimmering light and a palpable atmosphere. These same qualities are also found, as Millon has noted, in the other early etchings that Piranesi executed from 1740 to 1748 in Rome (Millon in Brunel 1978, pp. 347–51). We can cite his illustration of the *Façade of the Church of San Giovanni in Laterano* for *Roma moderna distinta per Rioni* (1740–41) (Cat. no. 49); the etching of *The Arch of Constantine* from the *Antichità Romane* (1748) (Cat. no. 53); and the etching of the *Real Villa dell'Ambrogiana* that Piranesi made in Rome, after a drawing by Giuseppe Zocchi for the latter's *Vedute delle Ville e d'altri luoghi della Toscana*, published by Giuseppe Allegrini in Florence in 1744. Zocchi's preparatory drawing for this plate is in the Morgan Library (Millon in Brunel 1978, p. 347, note 17; Bettagno 1978, pp. 12–13, fig. 23; CCA Library M48371, pl. 17). In addition, this same impression of palpable atmosphere impregnated with shimmering light is also found in the small etched *vedute* that Piranesi added to the 1748 *Map of Rome* engraved by Carlo Nolli (Cat. no. 52). These same differences in style are apparent when we compare Piranesi's view of Santa Maria Maggiore, in the lower right corner of Nolli's map, with Vasi's view in Book V of *Delle Magnificenze*.

Further support for Millon's assertation of Piranesi's authorship of the above mentioned etchings in the *Vedute di Roma sul Tevere* can be found in the small *vedute* of the bridges along the Tiber, etched by Piranesi on the borders of a map, *Pianta del Corso del Tevere*, which was engraved in 1744 by Carlo Nolli and dedicated to Pope Benedict XIV. Lamberto Donati discovered two states of this map in the Vatican Library. In the first state, there are several inscriptions and reinforcements of the shadows in ink in Piranesi's hand that were also carried out in the second state. Piranesi's *vedute* of the bridges on the Tiber have the same painterly quality found in the plates of the *Ponte Sisto* and the *Ponte Milvio*, which Henry Millon contends Piranesi, not Vasi, executed for the *Vedute di Roma sul Tevere* (Zamboni in Bettagno 1978, pp. 13–14, fig. 25, *Ponte Milvio* in the upper right corner near the coat of arms of Benedict XIV, the *Ponte Sisto* in the lower left corner).

Thus Legrand was correct in his comment that Vasi found Piranesi's style of etching too painterly. Piranesi probably left Vasi's workshop, not only because he was not given credit for the etchings he did, but also because of his difference in approach to the art of etching, a result of his Venetian training.

GIOVANNI BATTISTA NOLLI, surveyor and draughtsman (map)

Como 1701–Rome 1756

CARLO NOLLI, engraver (map)

Como 1720–Naples after 1770

GIOVANNI BATTISTA PIRANESI, draughtsman and etcher (border)

Mogliano Veneto 1720–Rome 1778

52. *Small Map of Rome Dedicated to Cardinal Alessandro Albani*

in Giovanni Battista Nolli, NUOVA PIANTA/DI/ ROMA/DATA IN LUCE/DA /GIAMBATTISTA NOLLI, *Rome, 1748*

Engraving (map) and etching (illustrated border) on laid paper (folios 33, 34). Platemark: 18⅜ x 26½ inches (467 x 673 mm); page: 19¹⁄₁₆ x 28¾ inches (485 x 730 mm). Watermark: center, fleur-de-lis in a double circle (unidentified).

Inscribed center, inside platemark, along lower border on base of the column of Trajan, *LA TOPOGRAFIA/DI ROMA/ DI GIO. BAT͠TA NOLLI/ DALLA MAGGIORE/IN QUESTA MINOR/TAVOLA DAL MEDESIMO RIDOTTA*; just below, on a fragment of an entablature, *Scala di 2500 Palmi Romani d'Architettura*; on the end of this entablature, *Piranesi/e Nolli /incisero*; in upper left corner, in a cartouche, the dedication to Cardinal Alessandro Albani signed at the bottom, *Roma il di primo del 1748/Uͫo Divotise Oblᵐᵒ servitore/Gio Battista Nolli*; below, in a scroll, a list of monuments represented on the map numbered 1 to 86 in arabic numerals; upper right corner, a list of the monuments numbered from 87 to 170 in arabic numerals; on the edge of a scroll, *si stampa in Roma con Privil; e licenza de'Superiori*.

DATE: execution of this etching, 1748.

PROVENANCE: Graham Foundation, Chicago.

BIBLIOGRAPHY (for this plate but not for the CCA's version): Hind 1922, p. 78; Frutaz 1962, p. 26, vol. I, no. CLXIXb, p. 236, vol. III, fig. 419; Focillon 1964, p. 14, no. 40; Focillon (Calvesi/Monferini) 1967, pp. 286–87, no. 40; Scott 1975, pp. 19–25, fig. 22, p. 21; Wilton-Ely 1978, p. 25, note 1, p. 128, repr., endpaper; Rome and Mogliano Veneto 1989, p. 22, no. 1, repr. p. 22; Philadelphia 1989, pp. 17–21, fig. 13, p. 35.

Montréal, Centre Canadien d'Architecture/Canadian Centre for Architecture M3224 CAGE

This map of Rome is bound in a volume with five other eighteenth-century maps of the city. The binding is modern, made of boards covered with green linen and a black leather spine and corners with the title *NOLLI NUOVA PIANTA DI ROMA* stamped in gold on the spine. There are forty-eight folios in this volume, which has two other maps designed by Giovanni Battista Nolli: folios 1 to 32 comprise his large 1748 *Map of Rome* (Frutaz 1962, vol. I, no. CLXIXa, pp. 234–35, vol. III, figs. 396–418), and folios 35 to 36, just after this one, contain an updated version of Bufalini's 1551 *Map of Rome*, also dated 1748, and dedicated, like the large map, to Pope Benedict XIV (1740–58) (Frutaz 1962, vol. I, no. CLXIXc, pp. 236–

37, vol. III, fig. 420). According to Frutaz, these maps were usually bound together. The CCA volume has on its title page the title of Nolli's large *Map of Rome*: *NUOVA PIANTA/DI/ROMA/DATA IN LUCE/DA/GIAM-BATTISTA NOLLI/L'ANNO/MDCCXLVIII*. All the folios making up the large 1748 *Map of Rome* are present, in addition to the title page, the *Avviso al Lettore* (folio 1), the list of 1,320 monuments (folios 2–5) the last folio of which is inscribed lower left, *Carlo Nolli incise*, the twelve plates bound on hinges (folios 6–29), and finally an alphabetic index of monuments (folios 30–33) whose last folio is inscribed lower right, *Car. Nolli inc.*

Giovanni Battista Nolli, an architect and engraver, arrived in Rome from Como in 1736 and spent eight years surveying the city in preparation for his large *Map of Rome*. There is a preparatory drawing executed by Nolli in pen and ink for the large *Map of Rome* in the Biblioteca dell'Istituto di archeologia e storia dell'arte in Rome (Frutaz 1962, vol. I, no. CLXVII, pp. 231–32, vol. III, pls. 383–94). The large map was engraved by Rocco Pozzi, Pietro Campana da Soriano, and Nolli's son Carlo; the vignettes were designed by the painter Stefano Pozzi. According to Frutaz, the small map exhibited here, a reduced version of the large map, was engraved by Nolli's son Carlo. There were three editions of the small map; the CCA's copy corresponds to the first edition, since 170 monuments are listed. The number of monuments was increased by four in the second 1773 edition by Ignazio Benedetti. A third edition was produced by Giuseppe Vasi in 1781 (Scalabroni 1981, pp. 124–25, no. 436). Piranesi had collaborated in 1744 with Carlo Nolli on a map of the banks of the Tiber that was inserted into Count Bernardino Bernardini's *Descrizione e nuovo ripartimento de' Rioni di Roma fatto per ordine di N.S. Papa Benedetto XIV*, published in Rome in 1744 by Generoso Salomoni and dedicated to Cardinal Annibale Albani (1692–1751), the brother of Cardinal Alessandro Albani (1692–1779) to whom the small *Map of Rome* is dedicated (Frutaz 1962, vol. I, no. CLXVIII, pp. 232–33, and vol. III, fig. 395; Zamboni in Bettagno 1978, pp. 13–14). Cardinal Alessandro Albani, the

of Johann Winckelmann, was a great collector of antiquities.

Frutaz has noted that Nolli's small *Map of Rome* was innovative because he placed the Basilica of St. Peter's and the Piazza del Popolo, which were located at the northwestern extremity of the city, at the top of the map, and the Baths of Caracalla, which were located at the southern extremity of the city, at the bottom. Earlier maps had reversed these positions making it difficult for the viewer to coordinate the actual location of the monuments in the city with the map itself (Frutaz 1962, p. 26). It is interesting that when Nolli republished Bufalini's 1551 *Map of Rome* (folios 35 and 36 in this volume), he placed St. Peter's, the Vatican, the Porta del Popolo, and the Baths of Caracalla in the same locations as in his own map. The orientation Nolli gave the city of Rome in his 1748 map is still used in modern maps of the city. Although Piranesi criticized Nolli's 1748 map of modern Rome, he adapted it in his own 1774 *Map of Rome* and the *Campus Martius* (Hind 1922, p. 87; Focillon 1964, no. 600 J, p. 43; Scott 1975, p. 19; Philadelphia 1989, pp. 17–18). Piranesi's 1774 *Map of Rome* is found on folio 1 of the CCA's version of the *Vedute di Roma* (Cat. no. 55).

Ceen and Scott have noted that Giovanni Battista Nolli's main objective in his 1748 *Map of Rome*, like Vasi's in *Delle Magnificenze*, was to present the fabric of the modern city. In the middle of the eighteenth century Rome had a population of about 150,000 inhabitants. It was not an important commercial center but rather a city of the popes. Its focus was on the activities connected with the papal court and with the court spectacles presented by important royal visitors and members of the Roman nobility. It was also a center for pilgrims who visited the holy sites, and for tourists who came to visit the monuments of classical antiquity (Scott 1975, pp. 19–25).

Piranesi designed and etched the small *vedute* on the bottom of the map, the cartouche with the dedication and coat of arms of Cardinal Alessandro Albani, the two putti, and the borders of the scrolls listing the monuments shown on the map. The *vedute* on the bottom of the map illustrate, reading from left

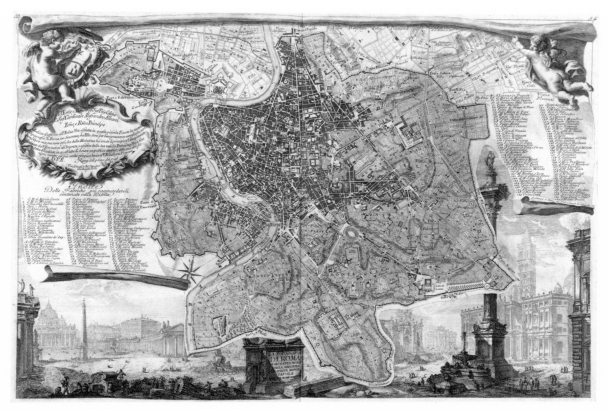

to right, the Piazza of St. Peter's, Bernini's Fountain of the Four Rivers (1648–51) in the Piazza Navona, the base of the Column of Trajan, the facade of the Church of Santa Croce in Gerusalemme (1743) by Domenico Gregorini, the Trevi Fountain (1732–62) by Nicola Salvi and Pietro Bracci, the facade of the Church of Santa Maria Maggiore (1741–43), and the corner of the Palazzo della Consulta (1732–37) on the Piazza del Quirinale, both designed by the papal architect, Ferdinando Fuga (1699–1782). The facade of the Church of Santa Croce in Gerusalemme, the Trevi Fountain, and the facade of the Church of Santa Maria Maggiore were all carried out during the papacy of Benedict XIV (1740–58). His titular church was that of Santa Croce in Gerusalemme (see essay in this volume by Elisabeth Kieven).

Piranesi's *vedute* at the bottom of Nolli's map reveal his mastery of the etching technique. They are typical of his style as it evolved after his return to Rome in 1747 from his second trip to Venice when he absorbed influences from the etchings of G. B. Tiepolo and Marco Ricci. The subtle quality of the lines etched with dark ink in the foreground and light ink in the background, the effect of shimmering light as it falls on the facades of the buildings, almost dissolving their surfaces, and the density of the atmosphere, all reveal Piranesi's greatness as an etcher. When we compare these small *vedute* to Piranesi's earlier etchings of Rome – *The Façade of the Church of San Giovanni in Laterano* (1740–41) inserted into Barbiellini's 1744 *Roma moderna distinta per Rioni* (Cat. no. 49), the *Pyramid of Cestius* etched between 1742 and 1745 and originally published in the *Varie Vedute* (1745), or *The Basilica and Piazza of St. Peter's,* executed between 1745 and 1748 for the *Vedute di Roma* – we can see how much progress Piranesi made in his mastery of the medium. The *vedute* at the bottom of this map exhibit a much greater variety of tone than the above-mentioned etchings. Scott has rightly noted that these small *vedute* are closest in style to *The Arch of Constantine* in the *Antichità Romane de' Tempi della Repubblica* (1748) (Cat. no. 53), and the *Grotteschi* (1747–49) (Cat. no. 54).

Piranesi's view of St. Peter's here is quite different from the one done between 1745 and 1748 for the *Vedute di Roma.* Rather than showing the facade of the church and the piazza from a central point of view, he has placed the spectator at an asymmetrical view-

FIGURE 1 Giuseppe Vasi, *Basilica of St. Peter's*, in *Delle Magnificenze di Roma*, vol. III, pl. 41. Canadian Centre for Architecture, Montréal, W7358 CAGE.

point. There is a much more expansive sense of space and sharper contrast between the dark shadows in the foreground and the brilliant light in the background. Like Giuseppe Vasi in his view of St. Peter's, plate 41 in volume III of *Delle Magnificenze* (1753) (fig. 1), Piranesi was influenced by the composition of Giovanni Paolo Pannini's 1741 painting of the Piazza of St. Peter's (Arisi 1986, p. 385, no. 308). Piranesi reused this same composition for his view of St. Peter's in several editions of the *catalogo inciso* (1761–75) (Mayer-Haunton in Bettagno 1978, pp. 10–11, nos. 1–6, repr. nos. 1–6) and in his second view of the Piazza of St. Peter's in the *Vedute di Roma*, which can be dated with a *terminus ante quem* of 1761, when it appeared for the first time in the first edition of the *catalogo inciso* of that year in the Accademia di San Luca (Hind 1922, p. 66, no. 101; Focillon 1964, p. 51, no. 721; Wilton-Ely 1978 [1988], pl. 101; Mayer-Haunton in Bettagno 1978, p. 10, no. 1, repr. no. 1). The other *vedute*– *Santa Croce in Gerusalemme*, the *Trevi Fountain*, and *Santa Maria Maggiore*– are all very similar to the plates in the *Vedute di Roma*: they are all shown from a similar asymmetrical viewpoint (Hind 1922, p. 40, no. 9, p. 41, no. 11, p. 66, no. 104; Wilton-Ely 1978 [1988], pls. 40, 104, 7). Robison has dated the view of Santa Maria Maggiore between 1745 and 1748. It appears in the earliest volume at Chatsworth of the *Vedute di Roma* and thus must have been designed at the same time as the small view at the bottom of Nolli's 1748 *Map of Rome* (Robison in Bettagno 1983, pp. 18–21). The view of Santa Croce in Gerusalemme has been dated by Robison between 1757 and 1758. It appears in a volume of the *Vedute di Roma* in Geneva dated in those years (Robison in Bettagno 1983, pp. 29–30). The view of the Trevi Fountain, which resembles the one at the bottom of the Nolli map, can be dated to 1761, when it was mentioned for the first time in the *catalogo inciso* of that year in the Accademia di San Luca (Mayer-Haunton in Bettagno 1978, p. 10, no. 1, repr. no. 1). Thus the compositions of the *vedute* etched by Piranesi at the bottom of Nolli's small 1748 *Map of Rome* were reused throughout his career.

GIOVANNI BATTISTA PIRANESI

Mogliano Veneto 1720–Rome 1778

53. *The Arch of Constantine*

in ANTICHITÀ ROMANE DE' TEMPI DELLA REPUBBLICA,/E DE' PRIMI IMPERATORI,/ DISEGNATE, ED INCISE DA GIAMBATTISTA PIRANESI/ ARCHITETTO VENEZIANO:/E DALLO STESSO DEDICATE/ ALL'ILLMO E REVMO SIG. MONSIG. GIOVANNI BOTTARI,/CAPPELLANO SEGRETO DI N.S. BENEDETTO XIV/UNO DE CUSTODI DELLA BIBLIOTECA VATICANA/E CANONICO DI S. MARIA IN TRASTEVERE., *Rome,* [The Author], 1748

[Date of the binding of the etchings in this volume, late 1750s.] Etching on laid paper (pl. 9). Platemark: 5 1/16 x 10 1/8 inches (129 x 258 mm); page: 13 7/16 x 17 7/16 inches (341 x 442 mm). Watermark: left of center, fleur-de-lis in a single circle surmounted by the letters *CB*.

Inscribed inside platemark, upper left, *Tav. 9*; lower left, *PIRANESI F.*; lower right, *ARCO DI COSTANTINO IN ROMA*.

DATE: execution of this etching, 1748.

PROVENANCE: family of the princes of Radali after 1842 (their coat of arms on the bookplate inside the front cover); Artemis Fine Arts, Ltd., London.

BIBLIOGRAPHY (for this plate but not for the CCA's version): Chamberlain 1937, repr. p. 62; Focillon 1964, p. 15, no. 50; Focillon (Calvesi/Monferini) 1967, p. 289, no. 50; Millon in Brunel 1978, p. 350, note 22.

EXHIBITION: London 1982.

Montréal, Centre Canadien d'Architecture/Canadian Centre for Architecture DR1986:0192:009

The CCA's copy of *Antichità Romane de' Tempi della Repubblica* is in an eighteenth-century binding made of pulp boards covered with orange paper stamped in gold. Two pieces of this paper were used to cover each board. There is a vellum spine with *PIRANE/ ANTIC/ ROMAN* embossed in gold, as well as vellum edges on the boards. This type of stamped paper, known as *Doré d'Allemagne*, originated in Augsburg, Germany, but became widely used all over Europe during the eighteenth century; it was imported into

England and France. Several German printers also established presses in Italy–at Bassano, Rome, and Florence. This type of paper is often designed with Chinese motifs as shown here (fig. 1) (Doizy and Ipert 1985, pp. 72–73, repr. p. 74). A set of fifteen early plates of the *Vedute di Roma* executed in the 1740s, bound in paper boards covered with *Doré d'Alle-magne* paper, was sold in London in 1982 (London 1982, pp. 62–63, no. 31, repr.). The watermark in the illustrations and text pages is the same as in the etchings of a dedication copy of this work found by Robison in the Gabinetto Nazionale delle Stampe, Rome, and printed in 1748 (Robison 1986, p. 26, no. 3). An eighteenth-century watermark, a fleur-de-lis in a single circle with an *L* below and *S* above, is also found in the endpapers and plain sheets, which

are interspersed with the etchings in the CCA's copy. It is the same watermark that Robison found in the endpapers of a 1757 dedication copy of the *Antichità Romane* in the Biblioteca Nacional, Madrid (Robison 1986, p. 218, no. 13). The CCA's copy of the *Antichità Romane de' Tempi della Repubblica* has the two frontispieces (Bettagno 1978, the first, fig. 94), the dedication to Giovanni Gaetano Bottari (1689–1775) inscribed lower left, *Roma 20 Luglio 1748* (Bettagno 1978, fig. 96), two plates of inscriptions, and twenty-three of the twenty-five illustrations included in the first edition (Focillon 1964, pp. 14–15, nos. 41–70). Although the 1792 sales catalogue of Piranesi's work lists a date of 1741 for this volume, most scholars accept 1748, on the dedication page, as the correct date for the printing of the first edition of this work (Hind

NO. 53

FIGURE 1 *Chinese Figures*, detail of stamped paper, recto of front cover (detail 2) of *Antichità Romane de' Tempi della Repubblica.* Canadian Centre for Architecture, Montréal, DR1986:0192:001–030.

FIGURE 2 *Bookplate of princes of Radali*, glued on inside cover of *Antichità Romane de' Tempi della Repubblica.* Canadian Centre for Architecture, Montréal, DR1986:001–030.

FIGURE 3 G. B. Piranesi, *The Tomb of Nero*, in *Grotteschi*, second edition, first issue. National Gallery of Art, Washington, 1978.49.3.

1922, p. 75, repr. p. 10; Chamberlain 1937, pp. 63–67; Focillon 1964, p. 14; Focillon [Calvesi/Monferini] 1967, pp. 287–88; Robison 1970 "Prolegomena," pp. 178–79; Scott 1975, p. 17; Wilton-Ely 1978 [1988], p. 28).

The watermarks in the paper used for the illustrations and endpapers, as well as the quality of the etchings, indicate that the CCA's copy is a very early edition printed in 1748 and bound in the late 1750s (CCA Research Files, Mimi Cazort report, 17 April 1986). The bookplate (fig. 2) has the coat of arms of the princes of Radali (Two Sicilies). (In 1842, Wilhelm, count of Saxony was the first member of his family to be given the title of Prince of Radali [Mannucci 1925–33, vol. IV, p. 291; Ruvigny 1914, p. 1561].) The CCA's copy of the *Antichità Romane de' Tempi della Repubblica* is missing the illustrations of plate 4, *Veduta del Arco di Aosta* (Focillon 1964, p. 14, no. 45), and of plate 17, *Arco di Rimini* (Focillon 1964, p. 15, no. 59). This series of etchings was reissued in 1765 with the addition of two plates—the *Arco di Galieno* and the *Tempio di Minerva Medica* (the latter by Francesco Piranesi)—and given a new title, *Alcune vedute di archi triomphali* (Hind 1922, pp. 2, 76; Focillon 1964, p. 15, no. 71; Focillon [Calvesi/Monferini] 1967, pp. 287–88; Scott 1975, p. 18, figs. 18, 19; Wilton-Ely 1978 [1988], p. 29, figs. 33, 34).

Giovanni Gaetano Bottari (1689–1775), an antiquarian to whom this volume is dedicated, was a close friend of Piranesi and lived in the Palazzo Corsini where he was librarian to Cardinal Neri Corsini. At the time, Piranesi lived across from the French Academy on the Via del Corso. The title page of the first edition has the inscription at the lower left, *si vende dall'autore dirimpetto l'accademia di Franzia* (Monferini 1979 [1983], p. 221).

Henry Millon has suggested that Piranesi prepared the plates for the *Antichità Romane* in two phases. He believes that the twelve views of Rome were etched between 1740 and 1741, while Piranesi was working on the small *vedute* printed in both *Roma antica distinta per Regioni* and *Roma moderna distinta per Rioni*, and first published by Giovanni Lorenzo Barbiellini in 1741 (Cat. no. 49).

Millon has suggested that Piranesi drew the views of the cities in northern Italy—the *Ponte* and *Arco di Rimini* (pls. 16–17 [Focillon 1964, p. 15, nos. 58–59]), the *Tempio di Pola in Istria* (pl. 21 [Focillon 1964, p. 15, no. 63]), the *Amphiteatro di Verona* (pl. 25 [Focillon 1964, p. 15, no. 67]), and the *Arco di Trajano in Ancona* (pl. 28 [Focillon 1964, p. 15, no. 70])—while he was back in Venice, either during his first trip in 1744, and/or his second, from 1745 to 1747. Therefore, Piranesi would have etched these views in Rome between 1747 and 1748, when the book finally was published (Millon in Brunel 1978, pp. 352–53). If one compares the plate of *The Arch of Constantine* from the *Antichità Romane* exhibited here, with one of the small early views of Rome, for example, *The Façade of the Church of San Giovanni in Laterano* which was included first in Barbiellini's 1741 publication (Cat. no. 49), it is apparent that the dense overlay of crosshatching in *The Arch of Constantine* is closer to the technique used in the *Grotteschi*, which were printed between 1747 and 1749, after Piranesi's return to Rome from his second trip to Venice in September 1747 (fig. 3) (Robison 1986, p. 25, pp. 29–30, no. 23, pp. 120–21). In *San Giovanni in Laterano*, this crosshatching occurs only in the foreground near the border; the contrast between light and shadow is sharper and less modulated. The shimmering effect of light and shadow in *The Arch of Constantine* shows the influences Piranesi absorbed, during his second trip to Venice, from the works of Tiepolo, Marieschi, and Canaletto (Robison 1986, p. 24). In addition, Piranesi created a greater sense of space by placing the arch at a sharper angle to the picture plane than he had in the facade of San Giovanni in Laterano. Hind found a proof of the *Ponte di Rimini* printed on the back of the second issue of the frontispiece of the *Prima parte* which dates the *Ponte di Rimini* between 1743 and 1744 (Millon in Brunel 1978, p. 352; Hind 1922, p. 75; Robison 1986, p. 67, no. 1, state II). I would suggest that Piranesi worked on the planning and execution of the *Antichità Romane* over a considerable period of time, perhaps starting as early as 1743 or 1744, but not 1740.

GIOVANNI BATTISTA PIRANESI

Mogliano Veneto 1720–Rome 1778

54. *Decorative Capriccio with Triumphal Arch in Background*

Etching, engraving, drypoint, burnishing (Robison 22-III). Platemark: 15½ x 21 inches (393 x 530 mm). Watermarks (throughout volume): fleur-de-lis in a double circle with letters *CB* above (Robison 1986, nos. 36–39). Inscribed at lower left, *Piranesi inv; incise, e vende in Roma/ in faccia all'Accademia di Francia.*

PROVENANCE: J. Pierpont Morgan (his bookplate on inside front cover).

EXHIBITION: New York 1989.

The Pierpont Morgan Library, PML 12610

This volume contains etchings from various works by Piranesi that were combined to form the *Opere varie*. The title page in the Library's edition is the second version that was produced for the book; it is found in issues from 1761 to the late 1790s (Robison 1986, p. 135, fig. 63). The watermarks that appear throughout the *Opere varie* are also characteristic of later editions. Although a number of the plates in the Library's copy are in reverse order, their disposition closely follows Hind's description of what he identified as the later edition B (Hind 1922, p. 79). The principal difference, however, is the addition of several miscellaneous plates at the end. Following the title page there are seventeen plates from the *Prima parte*, including the title plate. Two plates are missing: the *Antico Dorico* and *Rovine d'antichi Edificj*. The *Prima parte* etchings are followed by the *Parte di ampio magnifico*, the reduced version of plates from the *Antichità Romane*, which first appeared in the *Lettere di giustificazione* of 1757, and the four plates of the *Grotteschi*. The *Pianta di ampio magnifico collegio* appears next, followed by the sixteen plates (including the title plate) of the *Carceri*. Toward the end of the book, there are a few plates from the *Antichità Romane de' Tempi della Repubblica*, the *Trofei di Ottaviano Augusto*, and the *Diverse maniere.*

NO. 54

The caption plate for the *Gruppo di Scale* (which reads *Gruppo di Scale ornato di magnifica Architettura, le quali stanno disposte in modo che conducano/a varj piani, e specialmente ad una Rotonda che serve per rappresentanze teatrali.*) was mistakenly printed beneath the *Sala all'uso degli antichi Romani*. The correct caption was subsequently cut out and pasted over it. Andrew Robison has recognized this as a characteristic feature of what he catalogues as the second edition, fifth issue of the *Prima parte*. He dates these volumes to the "late 1760s?–early 1770s?" (Robison 1986, p. 81).

The plate shown here is one of the four from the *Grotteschi*. These were not incorporated in the combination volume *Opere varie* until 1750, but they were almost certainly published shortly after Piranesi's return to Rome from Venice in September of 1747 since the artist's new address opposite the French Academy in Rome is inscribed on the prints (Robison 1986, p. 25). The prints relate in style and content to three large drawings in the Library's collection (Cat. nos. 18, 19, and 20).

GIOVANNI BATTISTA PIRANESI

Mogliano Veneto 1720–Rome 1778

55. *Vedute di Roma disegnate ed incise da Giambattista Piranesi Architetto V[enez]iano*

Rome [Giovanni Bouchard, Bouchard and Gravier, and later The Author], about 1745/48–1778

DATE: printing and binding of these volumes, 1778–84.

PROVENANCE: W. Olliff of Ireland by 1784 (his bookplate); Charles Agar (1736–1809), archbishop of Dublin, earl of Normanton after 1806 (his coat of arms on a bookplate); Urban Huttleston Rogers Broughton (1896–1966), Lord Fairhaven after 1930 (his coat of arms on a bookplate); all these found inside the front cover of volume I; only the first and third found inside the front cover of volume II; Ben Weinreb Architectural Books, Ltd., London.

Montréal, Centre Canadien d'Architecture/Canadian Centre for Architecture IDM85–B15668:1–2 CAGE

The Basilica and Piazza of St. Peter's

Etching on laid paper (vol. I, folio 4). Platemark: 15¾ x 21³⁄₁₆ inches (401 x 539 mm); page: 21⅛ x 30⅝ inches (538 x 777 mm). Watermark: none.

Inscribed in brown ink in upper right corner on platemark, 3; etched inside platemark, below lower etched border, center, *Veduta della Basilica, e Piazza di S. Pietro in Vaticano* with list of the monuments preceded by arabic numerals; below, to the right, *Presso l'Autore a Strada Felice nel Palazzo Tomati vicino alla Trinità de' monti. A paoli due e mezzo. Piranesi del. Scol.*

BIBLIOGRAPHY (for this plate but not for the CCA's version): Hind 1913–14, p. 263; Hind 1922, pp. 38–39, no. 3, state IV; Focillon 1964, p. 54, no. 787; Focillon (Calvesi/Monferini) 1967, p. 344, no. 787; Robison 1970 "Vedute," variant of Hind, state IV, no. 3, D, p. 185; Robison 1973, p. 389, fig. 2 (detail), p. 391, fig. 3, p. 392; Robison in Bettagno 1983, p. 21; Wilton-Ely 1978 (1988), p. 30, pl. 3, fig. 35.

The Aqueduct of Nero

Etching on laid paper (vol. II, folio 100). Platemark: 19⅝ x 27⅞ inches (499 x 708 mm); page: 21⅛ x 30⅝ inches (538 x 777 mm). Watermark: right of center, fleur-de-lis in a double circle surmounted by the letters *CB* (Robison 1986, p. 223, no. 39).

Inscribed in brown ink in upper right corner on platemark, *99*; etched above lower etched border, center, on a stone, *Avanzi degl'Aquedotti Neroniani che/si volevano distruggere per la loro/vecchiezza, ma per ordine di Nro. Sig.^{re}/Papa Clemente XIV. sono restati in piedi./2. Scala Santa*; lower left, inside platemark below the etched border, *Cavalier Piranesi F.*

BIBLIOGRAPHY (for this plate but not for the CCA's version): Hind 1913–14, p. 264; Hind 1922, p. 69, no. 118, state I; Focillon 1964, p. 57, no. 850; Focillon (Calvesi/Monferini) 1967, p. 352, no. 850; Murray 1971, p. 39, fig. 42, p. 40, details: p. 41, fig. 43, p. 42, fig. 44; Wilton-Ely 1978 (1988), pl. 118.

The bindings of these two volumes can be dated to the eighteenth century and were probably executed in England. Both are made of pulp boards; each is covered with two pieces of marbled paper glued onto the boards. The pebble pattern of the marbled paper in gray, powder blue, yellow, and pink (fig. 1) corresponds to a pattern found frequently in marbled papers manufactured in England after 1655. This type of paper was popular on bindings (Doizy and Ipert 1985, pp. 51, 61–62, fig. 2, p. 53). Both volumes have vellum spines and edges; the spine of the first volume is embossed in gold with *PIRANE/VEDUTE/DI/ROMA/TOM I*; that of the second volume is embossed in gold with the same title but *TOM II*. Inside the front cover of the first volume, along the lower edge, a torn vellum flap has been glued in and is inscribed in brown ink, *dute di Roma/N.16.* The two endpapers of the first volume and the front endpaper of the second volume all have the same watermark—a fleur-de-lis in a shield surmounted by a crown with the letters *LVG* below. This is a variant of several watermarks identified by Heawood (Heawood 1950 [1981], p. 106, no. 1843, pl. 261, p. 106, no. 1844, pl. 260, p. 106, no. 1847, pl. 262, p. 107, no. 1852, pl. 263). These watermarks are found in papers used in England from the

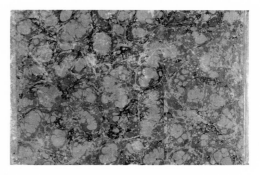

FIGURE 1 Detail of marbled paper on recto of front cover of G. B. Piranesi, *Vedute di Roma*, vol. 2. Canadian Centre for Architecture, Montréal, IDM85–B15668:2 CAGE.

The Aqueduct of Nero.

FIGURE 2 Bookplate of William Olliff, glued on inside cover of G. B. Piranesi, *Vedute di Roma*, vol. 1. Canadian Centre for Architecture, Montréal, IDM85–B15668:1 CAGE.

1760s through the 1780s. The back endpaper of the second volume is made of two sheets of eighteenth-century paper that are glued together; the watermarks here are illegible.

The history of the owners of these two volumes of the *Vedute di Roma* can be traced from the end of the eighteenth well into the twentieth century. The first owner was William Olliff of County Cork, Ireland. According to David S. Howard, Olliff had a standard type of bookplate engraved by A. Buck (also of County Cork) with his coat of arms and other figures. But for his *Vedute di Roma*, Olliff had a special bookplate (fig. 2) made in the style of Piranesi: a gigantic entablature on which is placed Olliff's name, a Corinthian capital, and several small figures in the foreground. The designer and etcher's name, *Nathaniel Grogan*, and the date, *1784*, are inscribed in the lower right corner of the bookplate. According to Howard, Grogan was an Irish artist who fought in the American Revolution and died in 1807. Olliff may have been an ancestor of Sir Joseph Francis Olliffe, physician to the British Embassy in Paris, who was knighted in 1852 (Burke 1884 [1969], p. 756). The CCA's copy of the *Vedute di Roma* must have been acquired by Charles Agar (1736–1809), archbishop of Dublin, from William Olliff some time after 1806, when he was made an earl. Agar's bookplate, the same as in the CCA's volume of Piranesi's *Différentes vues de quelques restes de trois grands édifices . . . de Pesto* (Cat. no. 66, fig. 2), is pasted on the inside of the front cover of the first volume next to Olliff's. The name *Normanton* is also inscribed in the upper left-hand corner of the inside covers of both volumes. That both William Olliff and Charles Agar, earl of Normanton, were Irish raises the possibility of some connections with the Irish peer James Caulfield, first earl of Charlemont (1728–99), to whom the first edition of the *Antichità di Roma* was dedicated. The whereabouts of these two volumes of the *Vedute di Roma* was unknown until about 1930. Some time after that date, they were acquired by Urban Huttleston Rogers Broughton (1896–1966), the eldest son of Urban Hanlon Broughton. His bookplate (fig. 3)

is found on the back of the front cover of both volumes. Urban Huttleston Rogers Broughton, a member of Parliament and the president and director of several engineering companies, lived at Grovesnor Square, London, and Anglesey Abbey, Cambridgeshire. He served in the Lifeguards during the first World War and was made Lord Fairhaven in 1929 for his valor (Burke 1970, vol. I, pp. 978–79). This bookplate, according to David S. Howard, was engraved by J. F. Badeley in 1930 shortly after Fairhaven was ennobled, and shows his baron's coronet.

Piranesi executed the large-format etched plates of the *Vedute di Roma* in serial fashion beginning, according to Robison, as early as 1745, before his second trip to Venice from 1745 to 1747, and continuing until his death on 9 November 1778 (Robison in Bettagno 1983, p. 21). An early publication, which contained thirty-four etchings of the *Vedute di Roma* and had the title page *Le Magnificenza di Roma*, was published by Giovanni Bouchard and printed in 1751. Other series of etchings were published by Bouchard and Gravier, and finally by Piranesi himself when he moved from the Via del Corso to his quarters at the Palazzo Tomati on the Strada Felice in 1761. Both the title page and the frontispiece in the CCA's copy are variants of Hind's state III, with Piranesi's Palazzo Tomati address (Hind 1922, p. 38, nos. 1, 2). The complex chronology of the early series of the *Vedute di Roma* has been discussed by Robison in four major articles published between 1970 and 1983. Robison has refined the chronology proposed earlier by Hind, showing that many of Hind's mistakes were a result of his acceptance of the chronology established by Piranesi's sons in the 1792 catalogue of their father's work (Hind 1922, pp. 38–73; Robison 1970 "Vedute," pp. 181–82; Robison in Bettagno 1983, pp. 11–14). Only one plate of the *Vedute di Roma* was dated by Piranesi on the etching itself. This is the *View of the Waterfall at Tivoli*, which is inscribed below the title, *Eqvues Piranesius del sculp 1766* (Hind 1922, pp. 59–60, no. 75; Focillon 1964, p. 53, no. 779; Focillon [Calvesi/Monferini] 1967, p. 343, no. 779). Thus, the date of 1765 for this etching given in the 1792 catalogue of Piranesi's work cannot be accepted, which both Hind and Focillon did (Robison in Bettagno 1983, p. 13).

In his 1983 article, Robison established, on the basis of an analysis of several early datable volumes of Piranesi's works, the sequence of execution for the first fifty-nine etchings of the *Vedute di Roma* listed in the first broadsheet of Piranesi's works for sale in 1761 (Mayer-Haunton in Bettagno 1978, pp. 9–10, no. 1, fig. 1; Accademia di San Luca, Rome). Two of the earliest of these volumes are at Chatsworth and the Princeton University Library. The first volume, at Chatsworth, was probably printed between 1745–46 and 1748, and contains the title page and frontispiece, as well as twelve views (Robison in Bettagno 1983, pp. 18–21). The second, at Princeton, was most likely printed between 1748 and 1749, and has the title page and frontispiece, as well as seventeen views (Robison in Bettagno 1983, pp. 21–22).

More research is still needed on the chronology of the last seventy-six plates of the *Vedute di Roma*. According to Hind, Focillon, Monferini, Mayer-Haunton, and Robison, a total of 134 etchings, including the title page and frontispiece, were executed by the time of Piranesi's death in 1778. One hundred and thirty-four etchings are listed in the twenty-sixth broadsheet of Piranesi's oeuvre. A copy of the broadsheet dated to November of 1778 is now in the Sir John Soane's Museum (Hind 1922, p. 73; Focillon 1964, p. 50; Focillon [Calvesi/Monferini] 1967, pp. 333–36, Mayer-Haunton in Bettagno 1978, p. 10, no. 6, repr.). The one-hundred-thirty-fifth etching of the *Vedute di Roma*, the *Arch of Benevento*, was announced in a broadsheet, now in the Gough Collection of the Bodleian Library, Oxford. Hind dated the Bodleian broadsheet around 1773. The *Arch of Benevento* was eliminated from the broadsheets that are now in the Museo Civico, Bassano del Grappa, and the Sir John Soane's Museum, published in 1775 and 1778, respectively, because the *Arch of Benevento* was probably designed before 1778 but was not printed until after Piranesi's death. The first state was inscribed *C.* [cavaliere] *Piranesi ??.* (Hind 1922, p. 73,

no. 135; Focillon 1964, p. 55, no. 107, under no. 823; Focillon [Calvesi/Monferini] 1967, p. 349, no. 107, under no. 823; Mayer-Haunton in Bettagno 1978, p. 10, nos. 5, 6, figs. 5, 6).

The CCA's copy of the *Vedute di Roma* can be clearly established as a posthumous Roman edition. Folio numbers were added in brown ink in the upper right corners of the sheets, beginning with the first folio, the *Map of Rome and the Campus Martius*, dedicated to Pope Clement XIV. Some time later, the title page was erroneously given a number *1* in black ink. The CCA's copy of the *Vedute di Roma* has the title page and the frontispiece separated between the two volumes (vol. I, folio 2: Hind 1922, p. 38, no. 1; Focillon 1964, p. 50, no. 719; vol. II, folio 68: Hind 1922, p. 38, no. 2; Focillon 1964, p. 54, no. 786). This altered order, as well as the illustrations of the *Map of Rome and the Campus Martius* (vol. I, folio 1: Hind 1922, p. 87; Focillon 1964, p. 43, no. 600, J) and the illustration of the *Arch of Benevento* (vol. II, folio 102), were also found by Hind and Focillon in two other posthumous Roman editions, one in the British Museum, and the other in the Bibliothèque Nationale (Hind 1922, C, pp. 32, 78; Focillon 1964, p. 50; Focillon [Calvesi/Monferini]) 1967, p. 333). The CCA's copy does not contain the two views of the interiors of the Pantheon and Colosseum that were also added by Francesco Piranesi to several posthumous Roman editions of the *Vedute di Roma*. These views are not listed in the last broadsheet produced in November of 1778 in the Sir John Soane's Museum (Hind 1922, p. 73, no. 136; Focillon 1964, p. 55, no. 106, under no. 822; Focillon [Calvesi/Monferini] 1967, p. 348, no. 106, under no. 822; Hind 1922, p. 73, no. 137; Focillon 1964, p. 55, no. 108, under no. 823; Focillon [Calvesi/Monferini] 1967, p. 349, no. 108, under no. 823). Hind and Focillon believed that the *Map of Rome and the Campus Martius* was issued on 15 September 1778 as stated by Francesco Piranesi in the catalogue of his father's works. Monferini rightly suggested that it must have been etched by 1774, since Clement XIV died in that year, and Piranesi clearly indicates in the inscription that he had already received the papal *ap-*

FIGURE 3 Bookplate of Urban Huttleston Rogers Broughton, Lord Fairhaven, inside cover of G. B. Piranesi, *Vedute di Roma*, vol. 1. Canadian Centre for Architecture, Montréal, IDM85– B15668:1 CAGE

probatio. In addition, this map is listed in the twenty-first broadsheet issued in 1775, and now in Bassano del Grappa (Focillon [Calvesi/Monferini] 1967, p. 324; Mayer-Haunton in Bettagno 1978, p. 10, no. 5, fig. 5). The inclusion of the *Arch of Benevento* establishes a *terminus post quem* of 1778, and the bookplate of William Olliff, a *terminus ante quem* of 1784 for the printing and binding of the CCA's edition of the *Vedute di Roma.*

The watermarks also indicate that the CCA's copy of the *Vedute di Roma* was issued in Rome posthumously. The paper of all the etchings including that of the *Map of Rome* is uniform. It is heavy paper with a watermark similar to that found by Robison in paper from the late 1760s until the early 1790s, in particular in a copy of Francesco Piranesi's *Raccolta de' Tempi Antichi*, published in 1790, now in the John Work Garrett Library, Johns Hopkins University, Baltimore (Robison 1986, p. 223, no. 39). The etchings of the CCA's copy of the *Vedute di Roma* were executed in a variety of states I–IV. However, they all have been reworked so heavily, particularly in the shadows, that large deposits of ink have rubbed off on the versos of the folios.

The two views exhibited here, *The Basilica and Piazza of St. Peter's* and *The Aqueduct of Nero*, illustrate, as Peter Murray noted in 1971, the changes in style that occurred between Piranesi's earlier and latest etchings. Robison has suggested that this view of *The Basilica and Piazza of St. Peter's* was originally designed and etched between 1745–46 and 1748 because it appears in the early Chatsworth and Princeton volumes discussed above (Robison in Bettagno 1983, pp. 18–22). The original first state of *The Aqueduct of Nero* was dated by Hind and Focillon as 1775, according to the 1792 catalogue of Piranesi's work. This etching must have been originally designed and etched between 1775 and 1778. It was not listed in the Bassano del Grappa broadsheet of 1775 but was in the last broadsheet as *Archi Neroniani Vicino alla Scala Santa* issued in November of 1778 and now in the Sir John Soane's Museum (Mayer-Haunton in Bettagno 1978, p. 10, no. 6, fig. 6).

In the earlier *veduta* of the Basilica and Piazza of St. Peter's, the focus of the composition – the facade – is placed in the background far from the picture plane. The high point of view of the spectator lies just to the left of the center, indicated by the obelisk. The space flows without interruption from the *repoussoir* figures and carriages, in the foreground, to the Church of St. Peter's, in the background. The dark shadows are kept in the foreground, while most of the scene is shown in brilliant light. Since the CCA's version of this etching is posthumous, there is a much greater contrast between the shadows in the foreground and the lighted areas in the background than is usually found in earlier impressions. This plate has been heavily reworked and reinked. Piranesi has adapted the rococo, Venetian gondola in the drawing in the Morgan Library, executed between 1744 and 1745 either during or just after his first trip to Venice, for the design of the third carriage in the foreground (Cat. no. 21). Likewise, the uniform, brilliant light which pervades the atmosphere in this *veduta* is typical of Piranesi's style after he returned to Rome from his first trip to Venice. It supports Robison's opinion that Piranesi was working on the earliest plates of the *Vedute di Roma* before and during his second trip back to Venice between 1745 and 1747.

In the *veduta* of *The Aqueduct of Nero*, executed between 1775 and 1778, the spectator is placed at a very low point of view close to the picture plane and at an asymmetrical position to the extreme right. This aqueduct was located near the Porta Maggiore and was an extension of the Acqua Claudia. It was probably completed by Domitian between A.D. 81 and 96. Now the aqueduct is placed at a sharp angle with respect to the picture plane. The space in which the aqueduct and the small figures are placed is much more restricted than in the earlier *veduta*. There is also a much sharper contrast of light and shadow caused by a greater inking of the entire plate. Shadows now pervade the scene from foreground to background. The artist has created in the later illustration a more expressive image, with a foreboding atmosphere.

GIOVANNI BATTISTA PIRANESI

Mogliano Veneto 1720–Rome 1778

56. *The Villa d'Este at Tivoli*

Etching on laid paper. Platemark: 18½ x 31¼ inches (470 x 709 mm); sheet: 21¼ x 28½ inches (536 x 729 mm). Watermark: none visible.

Inscribed left of center, on a stone plaque, *VEDUTA. DELLA/ VILLA . ESTNSE/IN TIVOLI*; lower right corner, inside second etched border, *C. Piranesi inc.*

DATE: execution of this etching, 1766–75.

PROVENANCE: William H. Schab Gallery, New York.

BIBLIOGRAPHY (for this plate but not for the CCA's version): Hind 1922, p. 36, no. 105, p. 66; Coffin 1960, pp. 132–33, fig. 135; Focillon 1964, p. 55, no. 826; Focillon (Calvesi/ Monferini) 1967, p. 349, no. 826; Scott 1975, pp. 25, 247, *passim*, fig. 237; New York 1984b, no. 47, repr.; Preston Thayer in Philadelphia 1989, p. 113, no. 105, repr. p. 185.

Montréal, Centre Canadien d'Architecture/Canadian Centre for Architecture DR1985:0272

Piranesi's view of *The Villa d'Este at Tivoli* was published in the *Vedute di Roma*. Since the sheet exhibited here appears to have been cut down, it may have come from a bound set. Hind accepted the date of 1773 given by Piranesi's sons in 1792 in the printed catalogue of his works. Because of the many mistakes in this posthumous catalogue, it seems more prudent to assign a date of 1766 to 1775 for the execution of this etching (Robison 1983, pp. 13–14). A *terminus ante quem* can be established in 1775 when this *veduta* appears for the first time in the twenty-first state of the *catalogo inciso* published in that year in the Museo Civico in Bassano del Grappa (Mayer-Haunton in Bettagno 1978, p. 10, no. 5, repr. no. 5). A *terminus post quem* is indicated by the fact that this etching is inscribed by Piranesi with a *C.* for the title of *Cavalier*, which he was awarded in 1766, the same year he produced the etching of *The Large Waterfall at Tivoli*, the only plate of the *Vedute* that was printed with a date (Robison in Bettagno 1983, pp. 11–12; Hind 1922, p. 59, no. 75; Wilton-Ely 1978 [1988], pl. 75).

Most scholars place the initial idea for the etchings of Tivoli in the *Vedute di Roma* around the 1760s

when, according to J.-G. Legrand, Piranesi stayed regularly at the summer home of his patron, Pope Clement XIII in Castel Gandolfo (1758–69). At that time, Piranesi published a series of volumes on the antiquities around Lake Albano and the Town of Cori: *Le Rovine del Castello dell'Acqua Giulia* (1761); *Descrizione e disegno dell'Emissario del Lago Albano* (1762); *Antichità di Albano e di Castel Gandolfo* (1764); and *Antichità di Cora* (1764) (Coffin 1960, pp. 132–33; Focillon 1963, pp. 111–12; Wilton-Ely 1978 [1988], p. 39, 41, 71; Erouart and Mosser in Brunel 1978, p. 234, note 72).

Piranesi devoted twenty-three plates of the *Vedute di Roma* to the sites and monuments of Tivoli: *The Temple of the Sibyl* (Hind 1922, pp. 56–57, nos. 61–63); *The Temple of Coughs* (Hind 1922, p. 58, nos. 69, 70); *The Ponte Lucano and The Tomb of the Plautii* (Hind 1922, p. 58, no. 68, p. 61, no. 83); *The Villa of Maecenas* (Hind 1922, p. 57, no. 65, p. 59, no. 73, p. 62, no. 84); *The Villa of Hadrian* (Hind 1922, p. 62, no. 85, p. 63, no. 90, p. 64, nos. 93, 94, p. 68, nos. 112, 113, p. 72, nos. 131–33, p. 73, no. 134); and *The Small and Large Waterfalls at Tivoli and the Villa d'Este* (Hind 1922, p. 64, no. 92, p. 59, no. 75; Scott 1975, pp. 175–

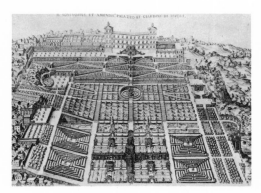

FIGURE 1 Etienne Dupérac, *Engraving of the Villa d'Este*, published in David R. Coffin, *The Villa d'Este at Tivoli*, 1960, fig. 1.

77). The first plate to be issued was one of the three etchings of *The Temple of the Sibyl at Tivoli*. It is listed as a handwritten addition to the fifth state of the *catalogo inciso* of 1762–63, now in the Gabinetto delle Stampe in Rome (Mayer-Haunton in Bettagno 1978, no. 3, p. 10, repr. no. 3; Hind 1922, p. 56, nos. 61–63; Wilton-Ely 1978 [1988], pls. 61–63).

The ten views of *The Villa of Hadrian at Tivoli* were the last issued; the first four appear in the twenty-first state of the 1775 *catalogo inciso*, and the remaining six appear by the publication of the twenty-sixth state of the *catalogo inciso*, which was issued in November 1778 at the time of Piranesi's death (Mayer-Haunton in Bettagno 1978, no. 6, p. 10, repr. no. 6). Piranesi, however, had visited the Villa of Hadrian much earlier. According to Wilton-Ely, Piranesi went to the villa several times between 1755 and 1757, in the company of Robert Adam, Clérisseau, Hubert Robert, and Allan Ramsay (Wilton-Ely 1978 [1988], p. 41, note 28, p. 129; Fleming 1962, pp. 204, 212, 217, figs. 58, 59).

It has been suggested that Piranesi's etching of the Villa d'Este is similar stylistically to the plates of the *Vedute di Roma* issued in the 1770s (CCA Research Files, David Booth report, 26 April 1991). Among these are the views of *The Villa of Hadrian* mentioned above (Wilton-Ely 1978 [1988], pls. 85, 90, 93, 94, 112, 113, 131–34), that of *The Villa Albani*, issued in 1775 (Hind 1922, p. 63, no. 89; Wilton-Ely 1978 [1988], pl. 89; Mayer-Haunton in Bettagno 1978, *catalogo inciso*, 1775, p. 10, no. 5, fig. 5), and *The View of the Villa Pamphili* issued in 1778 (Hind 1922, p. 71, no. 124; Wilton-Ely 1978 [1988], p. 42–43, fig. 61, p. 43, pl. 124; Mayer-Haunton in Bettagno 1978, *catalogo inciso*, 1778, p. 10, no. 6, fig. 6).

Piranesi's view of *The Villa d'Este*, however, does not display the characteristics of the above-mentioned etchings: sharp contrasts of light and shade, a composition based on diagonals, discontinuity in spatial recession, or large forms that loom close to the viewer. Rather, in the etching of *The Villa d'Este*, the gaze of the viewer is directed along a central axis through the gardens to the villa, which is placed at a focal point in the center of a high horizon line.

The Villa d'Este and its gardens were designed by the architect and antiquarian Pirro Ligorio (1513/14–83) for Cardinal Ippolito d'Este (1509–72) after he had been appointed governor of Tivoli in 1549. The villa itself was a remodeled Franciscan monastery attached to the Church of Santa Maria Maggiore. It stood atop a hill that had terraced fountains and gardens, designed by Ligorio between 1565 and 1572. Not all of the garden structures planned by Ligorio were completed at the cardinal's death in 1572 (Coffin 1960, pp. 3–21), but his original plan is known through a 1573 engraving by Etienne Dupérac, which was based on a lost drawing by Ligorio and published in the *Speculum Romanae* (fig. 1) (Coffin 1960, p. 15, fig. 1, pp. 15–16, note 63).

The Villa d'Este remained in the possession of the Este family throughout the middle of the eighteenth century. By the middle of the century, the Este family was renting out the villa to travelers (Coffin 1960, pp. 120–30). Both Charles-Nicolas Cochin, in the second 1758 edition of his *Voyage d'Italie* (Cat. no. 121), and the Abbé de Saint-Non, in the recently discovered diary of the trip he took to Italy between 1759 and 1761 (Rosenberg 1986, p. 159), described the gardens of the villa as being neglected, fountains in disrepair, and overgrown with vegetation, when they visited it, Cochin in 1749, Saint-Non in 1760 (Coffin 1960, p. 130; Cochin 1758 [Michel 1991], vol. I, pp. 132–34, folios 109–12). The Villa d'Este was not considered worthy to be included in the volume (X) on the villas and gardens of Rome, in Giuseppe Vasi's *Delle Magnificenze di Roma Antica e Moderna* (Rome, Niccolò e Marco Pagliarini, 1761, CCA Library, w7358:10 CAGE; Scalabroni 1981, pp. 86–89). The villa was, however, particularly appreciated by the members of the French colony in Rome. The owner of the Villa d'Este at the time, Francesco III d'Este (1698–1780), duke of Modena, was the son-in-law of the duc d'Orléans (Paris and New York 1987–88, p. 94). Charles-François Poerson (1653–1725), director of the French Academy in Rome from 1704 to 1721, called the Villa d'Este one of the marvels of Italy. The next director, Nicolas Vleughels (1668–1737, director, 1725–37), took his students there. Charles-

Joseph Natoire (1700–1777), director of the Academy from 1751 to 1775, visited the villa in 1759. A year later, the Villa d'Este was immortalized by the red chalk drawings Fragonard executed that summer, while he stayed there with the Abbé de Saint-Non (Coffin 1960, pp. 129–131; Cat. no. 91).

David Coffin has noted that Piranesi depicted the Villa d'Este from the same viewpoint as Fragonard had in his red chalk drawing in Besançon, *The Large Cypress Trees at the Villa d'Este* (fig. 2) (Coffin 1960, p. 133, pl. 136; Paris and New York 1987–88, p. 106, no. 30, repr.; Rome 1990–91, pp. 115–16, no. 66, repr. p. 116). Both artists stood behind a circle of cypress trees planted in 1610 to replace a wood pergola located just behind the entrance to the gardens. This circle of cypress trees was depicted by Giovanni Francesco Venturini (1650–1710) in a 1685 engraving (Coffin 1960, p. 107, fig. 115). Since Piranesi spent part of his summers at the pope's residence in Castel Gandolfo, it is quite likely that he visited the Villa d'Este between July and September of 1760, when Fragonard and the Abbé de Saint-Non also were there (Cat. no. 91).

However, when we compare Piranesi's interpretation of the Villa d'Este with Fragonard's (fig. 2), we find a different approach. Fragonard has taken his point of departure from what he could actually see. The large cypress trees enframe the Stairs of the Bubbling Fountains, the Fountain of the Dragon, the Fountain of the Cups by Bernini, the Fountain of Leda, and finally a small part of the center of the garden facade of the villa. Fragonard's red chalk drawing in Besançon corresponds to Cochin's description: "The view of the entrance to the garden is very beautiful because of the geometry of the terraces and the fountains which rise, one above the other, up to the villa which is at the very top on a high hill . . ." (Cochin 1758 [Michel 1991], vol. I, p. 133, folio 111).

Piranesi, on the other hand, depicts a panorama of the gardens and villa. He combines a bird's-eye view with a focused one. According to Cochin's description, the gardens were so overgrown with trees that it was impossible to see the complete facade of the villa. Cochin said, in addition, "all these riches [the fountains] seem to be detached, one from the other, and

do not form a unified whole" (Cochin 1758 [Michel 1991], vol. I, p. 134, folio 112). Piranesi has replaced the circle of cypress trees at the entrance to the Villa d'Este with four statues set in a hemicycle. Coffin believed they represent the liberal arts. Preston Thayer suggested they allude to the Judgment of Paris. Or they may allude to the time of year Piranesi visited the villa. Mercury, the god of travelers, stands to the right of the figure of Ceres, the symbol of the months of August and September. On the other side of the hemicycle, a goddess holds a plaque with the sign of Cancer, the symbol of the months of June and July. In Piranesi's etching, to the left, toward the northeast side of the villa, the viewer's field of vision encompasses the Fountain of Pomona and the wall leading to the two Fountains of Bacchus. To the right, toward the northwest side of the villa, the viewer's field of vision includes the Fountain of Flora, the Grotto of Diana, the Fountain of the Emperors, and the Fountain of Rome. Piranesi presents us with an updated version of Dupérac's 1573 bird's-eye view (fig. 1) (Coffin 1960, fig. 1, nos. 11, 12, 16, 18, 20, 21).

Piranesi's attitude toward nature in the etching of *The Villa d'Este* is quite different from his attitude in *The Large and Small Waterfalls at Tivoli*, *The Temple of the Sibyl at Tivoli*, and *The Villa of Hadrian*. In the latter, his vision of nature is romantic; in the former, his purpose is didactic and archaeological. He has stripped away most of the trees that choked the gardens and fountains in the eighteenth century in order to give the spectator an idea of the original sixteenth-century plan. In much the same way, Piranesi stripped away the later buildings in the *Bird's-Eye View of the Campus Martius* (1762) to show only the Roman monuments (Wilton-Ely 1978 [1988], pp. 74–75; Cat. no. 61). Fragonard's drawings of the Villa d'Este have been characterized as poetic. He was more interested in revealing the beauty of the natural environment than in giving an accurate description of the sculpted fountains or architecture of the villa. However, in comparison to Piranesi's etching, Fragonard's views of the Villa d'Este give us a more accurate idea of what the villa and its gardens looked like in the middle of the eighteenth century.

FIGURE 2 Jean-Honoré Fragonard, *The Large Cypress Trees at the Villa d'Este.* Musée des Beaux-Arts, Besançon, D2842.

Dedication to the People of Rome.   NO. 57

Imaginary Tombs on the Via Appia.

GIOVANNI BATTISTA PIRANESI

Mogliano Veneto 1720–Rome 1778

57. *Le Antichità Romane Opera di Giambattista Piranesi Architetto Veneziano*

Rome [4 vols., published by Bouchard and Gravier, text printed by Angelo Rotili], 1756–[1757]

DATE: printing and compilation of this copy before binding, about 1756–61.

PROVENANCE: C. E. Rappapat, Rare Books, Rome (stamp in upper left corner of all volumes); Ben Weinreb Architectural Books, Ltd., London.

Montréal, Centre Canadien d'Architecture/Canadian Centre for Architecture WM6197:1–4 CAGE

Dedication to the People of Rome

Etching on laid paper (vol. I, pl. I, first frontispiece). Platemark: 18⁷/₁₆ x 27¹/₁₆ inches (468 x 689 mm); page (double): 20¼ x 28⅜ inches (515 x 722 mm). Watermark: none. Inscribed in upper left corner, inside etched border, *I. Tom I*; lower right corner, below etched border, *Piranesi Archit. inv. e. scul.*; inside image, to right of center on monumental tablet, *VRBIS AETERNAE/VESTIGIA/E. RVDERIBVS/TEMPO-RVMQVE. INIVRIIS/VINDICATA/AENEIS. TABVLIS. INCISA/I. B. PIRANESIVS. VENET/ROMAE. DEGENENS/AEVO. SVO./PO-STERIS/ET VTILITATI. PVBLICAE/CVD.*

BIBLIOGRAPHY (for this plate but not for the CCA's version): Focillon (Calvesi/Monferini) 1967, p. 298, third state, first edition; Scott 1975, pp. 113–14, repr. fig. 128; Wilton-Ely 1978 (1988), p. 63, fig. 105, p. 64; Monferini in Bettagno 1978, p. 33, no. 134, fig. 134.

Imaginary Tombs on the Via Appia

Etching on laid paper (vol. II, pl. II, second frontispiece). Platemark: 15⁹/₁₆ x 24¾ inches (396 x 630 mm); page (double): 20¼ x 28¼ inches (515 x 720 mm). Watermark: none. Inscribed at upper right corner, inside etched border, *II. Tom II*; lower right, below etched border, *Gio. Batta. Piranesi inv. dis. e incise.*

BIBLIOGRAPHY (for this plate but not for the CCA's version): Focillon 1964, p. 24, no. 225; Focillon (Calvesi/Monferini) 1967, pp. 298–99, no. 225, p. 304, first edition; Scott 1975, p. 110, fig. 123, p. 109; Wilton-Ely in Brunel 1978, pp. 533–34, figs. 12, 13, p. 547; Wilton-Ely 1978 (1988), pp. 54, 62, fig. 82, p. 54; Monferini in Bettagno 1978, pp. 35–36, no. 165, p. 38, fig. 165.

Bricks from the Entrance to a Crematorium at the End of the Via Appia

Etching (image); engraving (inscriptions outside of etched border) (vol. III, pl. V). Platemark: 13⁷/₁₆ x 9¼ inches (346 x 235 mm); page (single): 20¼ x 14⅜ inches (514 x 366 mm) (excluding hinge). Watermark: none visible. Inscribed at upper right corner, inside etched border, *Tom III. V*; lower right corner, below description, below etched border, *Piranesi Archit. dis. et inc.*

BIBLIOGRAPHY (for this plate but not for the CCA's version): Focillon 1964, p. 27, no. 290; Focillon (Calvesi/Monferini) 1967, pp. 299–300, no. 290, p. 306, first edition; Monferini in Bettagno 1978, p. 38, no. 181, fig. 181; Wilton-Ely 1978 (1988), p. 55, fig. 86.

Cross-section of the Ponte Fabrizio, Rome

Etching (image) and engraving (text outside etched border) (vol. IV, pl. XVIII). Platemark: 15⁹/₁₆ x 23⅜ inches (397 x 594 mm); page (double): 20⅛ x 29³/₁₆ inches (511 x 741 mm). Watermark: left of center, fleur-de-lis in a double circle with a *B* above and a *V* below (Robison 1986, p. 221, no. 32).

Inscribed upper left corner, inside etched border, *Tom IV*, and upper right corner, *XVIII*; lower right, scale in *palmi romani, 70 palmi to 125 mm*; lower right corner, below etched border and below text, *Piranesi Archit. dis. ed inc.*

BIBLIOGRAPHY (for this plate but not for the CCA's version): Focillon 1964, p. 30, no. 353; Focillon (Calvesi/Monferini) 1967, pp. 299–300, no. 353, p. 309, first edition; Monferini in Bettagno 1978, p. 39, no. 200, fig. 200.

Piranesi spent ten years in the preparation and production of the *Antichità Romane*. Monferini noted that plate XV in volume I, *The View of the Interior of the Pantheon*, was based on a drawing made before 1747 when the pediments were added above the niches of the attic (Focillon [Calvesi/Monferini] 1967, p. 299; Focillon 1964, p. 22, no. 172; Scott 1975, p. 121, fig. 139). Furthermore, plate XVIII, also in volume I, shows a tomb that was destroyed in 1746 (Focillon 1964, p. 22, no. 178; Scott 1975, p. 210; Monferini in Bettagno 1978, p. 38, no. 153, fig. 153).

Piranesi originally intended the *Antichità Romane* as an expanded version of the series of etchings he had published in 1750 on Roman tombs, *Camere sepolcrali degli Antichi Romani*. The illustrations of the tombs in volumes II and III of the *Antichità Romane* were probably completed first. The last ones, most likely, were Rome's main public monuments and the *Master Plan of Ancient Rome*, both in volume I, and the plates of the bridges in volume IV (Hind 1922, pp. 81–82; Focillon 1963, pp. 63–66; Focillon [Calvesi/Monferini] 1967, p. 299). The papal *imprimatur* was granted on 25 January 1756. According to a letter of 26 May 1756, written by Bouchard and Gravier to the marquis de Marigny, the four volumes of the first edition were ready for sale by 11 May of that year (Focillon 1963, p. 71; Focillon [Calvesi/Monferini] 1967, p. 299). The publication of the *Antichità Romane* took such a long time because of Piranesi's difficulty in finding a patron for his costly and monumental work. During that time, Piranesi broadened his circle of acquaintances to include several important members of the English community in Rome.

James Caulfield, first earl of Charlemont, Dublin, had established an Academy in Rome for British artists in 1749, under the direction of the painter John Parker. In early 1753, Piranesi approached Parker to see if Lord Charlemont would support his publication of *Antichità Romane*. For a year, Parker made promises to Piranesi on Charlemont's behalf, while doing nothing about Piranesi's request. Before returning to Ireland in March 1754, Charlemont met with Piranesi but did not commit himself to supporting the publication of the *Antichità Romane*. But Piranesi persevered and early in 1755 he wrote Charlemont in Dublin asking for a contribution of 200 *scudi*. He was sent half of that sum with a promise of the remainder after receipt by Charlemont of four copies of the book. Piranesi subsequently designed the frontispieces of the four volumes of the *Antichità Romane* with dedications to Lord Charlemont (Monferini in Bettagno 1978, fig. 132). By the time Piranesi had published the *Antichità Romane* in May 1756, he still had not received the balance of Lord Charlemont's money, although he had delivered two of the four copies ordered to Parker. On 25 August 1756, Piranesi wrote again to Lord Charlemont in Dublin asking for the rest of the money. After issuing seventy copies of the work, Piranesi held up production in hope of a resolution. In January 1757, when Parker went to Bouchard's shop to pick up the last two copies Lord Charlemont had ordered, Piranesi refused to give them to him, and threatened to sue Lord Charlemont for nonpayment. It was then that Piranesi removed Lord Charlemont's name not only from the first frontispiece of volume I (Monferini in Bettagno 1978, fig. 133) but also from the second frontispieces of volumes III and IV. In February of 1757, Piranesi wrote again to Charlemont threatening to dedicate the four volumes of the *Antichità Romane* to the Roman public, and to publish his letters to Charlemont. After a further letter to Charlemont in June of 1757, Piranesi began to include his first two letters in the first volume of each set of the *Antichità Romane*. He also etched in the frontispieces of volumes I, III, and IV, dedications to the people of the city of Rome (Scott 1975, pp. 105–16; Wilton-Ely 1972, pp. v–vi; Wilton-Ely 1978 [1988], pp. 46–48). A further addition to the *Antichità Romane* was made in

Bricks from the Entrance to a Crematorium at the End of the Via Appia.

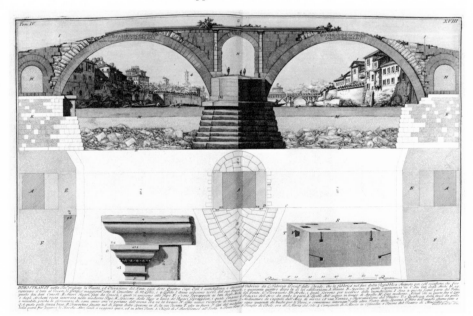

Cross-section of the Ponte Fabrizio, Rome.

1757 when plate LVII, *Avanzi di un Collegio di Silvano Aureliano*, was added to volume IV (Scott 1975, p. 125, note 5, p. 309; Monferini in Bettagno 1978, p. 39, no. 205, fig. 205; Focillon 1964, p. 32, no. 395). Piranesi published three of his letters to Charlemont in 1757 (Cat. no. 58).

A second edition of the *Antichità Romane* was issued in 1784, after Piranesi's death, with a portrait of Piranesi by Joseph Cades and a dedication to Gustavus III of Sweden (Monferini in Bettagno 1978, fig. 135). The text pages were produced by the Salomoni firm. Two unnumbered plates were added by Francesco Piranesi; one plate, in the fourth volume, was given the number XLIVbis (Focillon 1963, p. 132; Focillon 1964, p. 31, nos. 369, 380, 382; Focillon [Calvesi/Monferini] 1967, pp. 297–300, and p. 309, no. 369, p. 310, nos. 380, 382).

The bindings of the four volumes of the CCA's *Antichità Romane* appear to have been made in the latter part of the nineteenth or early twentieth century. The red morocco leather spines are embossed in gold *PIRANESI/ANTICHITA/ROMANAE/TOM [I–IV]/ ROMA 1756*. The covers are faced with red morocco leather and red buckram, and have red morocco leather corners. The endpapers are made of nineteenth- or twentieth-century marbled paper. The hinges affixing most of the plates to the binding, as well as the title page, letters to Charlemont, and preface in volume I, are made of nineteenth-century paper.

The CCA's edition of *Antichità Romane* corresponds in most part to the third version of the first edition mentioned by Focillon and later described in detail by Monferini. Volume I has forty-four plates numbered with roman numerals and sixty-eight pages of text, which includes the preface, *imprimatur*, list of works for sale by Bouchard and Gravier in 1753, two letters to Charlemont dated 25 August 1756 and February 1757, six decorated initials, and two vignettes. Volume II has sixty-three plates; volume III, fifty-four; and volume IV, fifty-seven plates with plate III, the index (CCA Library Archives, Jan Johnson report, 8 August 1988). In volume III, like the one Focillon examined, only three of the four

plates etched by Girolamo Rossi are inscribed with his name. The initial forty pages of text in the CCA's volume I are also numbered in arabic and roman numerals as in the copy examined by Monferini (Focillon [Calvesi/Monferini] 1967, pp. 297–300, no. 308, p. 307, and pp. 300–10, nos. 144–395). The CCA's *Antichità Romane* has the title page of the first edition, the third state of the first frontispiece of volume I and the third state of the second frontispieces of volumes III and IV (with the dedications to the people of Rome), and plate LVII of volume IV, which was added to the first edition in 1757 (Focillon [Calvesi/Monferini] 1967, pp. 298–300). Only the second frontispiece to volume II was left unchanged by Piranesi in the different versions of the first edition. In the CCA's copy, as in a copy in the Vatican Library, the etched inscription on the imaginary tomb of Lord Charlemont (on the right side of the Via Appia)—*JACOPO CARFIE/VICE COMMI/Charle/Regni H.P.A.*— has been partially rubbed out by hand (Focillon [Calvesi/Monferini] 1967, p. 298, St. Barb. X.I.20–23). In addition, on page 1r of the preface, *Agli studiosi delle Antichità Romane*, line 9, the name Charlemont following the title *MiLord* has been rubbed out and replaced with several ink dots. An inscription on plate XXVIII of volume III, *this urn is at Withington Hall, Cheshire—brought from Rome by J.B. Glegg. . .* , is in a nineteenth-century hand.

The watermarks on the plates tend to support the identification of the CCA's copy of the *Antichità Romane* as the third version of the first edition printed between 1756 and 1761. Whether it is a complete or composite edition is not possible to determine because of the date of the binding and the date of the paper hinges. The two different types of paper used for the text pages and for the plates are extremely consistent. The watermarks in the text pages are not clearly visible, nor were watermarks found in the frontispieces to volumes I and II. The paper used for almost all the plates, both single and double, has a watermark of a fleur-de-lis in a double circle with the letters *B* above and *V* below. The watermark has the same measurements as those in other works: various copies of the first edition of the *Antichità Romane* published in 1756 (with the original dedication to Lord Charlemont), found in both the Biblioteca Corsiniana and the Biblioteca Nacional in Madrid; and several copies of the first issue of the second edition of the *Carceri*, published in 1761 (Robison 1986, p. 221, no. 32).

The publication of the *Antichità Romane* secured a place for Piranesi as an important historian of classical archaeology (see Wilton-Ely in *Piranesi* 1979, pp. 317–39). His intention in producing these volumes was not only to record a past that he felt was quickly vanishing but also to show how antiquity could be used as a source of inspiration for the present. Characteristically, Piranesi blended a taste for speculative inquiry with the practical considerations of engineering and architecture in a visually interesting way. He felt that a monument could only be fully understood by studying plans, sections, elevations, and internal views. This in turn must be combined with an understanding of techniques used in construction as well as a survey of the types of materials used, an interest that appears in plates such as the *Bricks from the Entrance to a Crematorium at the End of the Via Appia*. Piranesi also addressed the need to reconstruct incomplete or missing works, which were to be based on a close study of the site and materials. He carefully pointed out, however, that one must use existing antique fragments as models to make the most accurate reconstruction.

Piranesi's creative imagination is exhibited in capricci such as his *Imaginary Tombs on the Via Appia*. This, the second frontispiece to volume II, depicts in a fanciful way the contents of the subsequent two volumes, which are devoted to funerary architecture. Volume IV is dedicated to bridges, theaters, and porticos, and emphasizes the Romans' remarkable engineering feats. The Ponte Fabrizio, depicted in plate XVIII of volume IV, actually the Pons Fabricius, was built in 62 B.C., between the left bank of the Tiber and the Tiber Island. Wilton-Ely has observed that Piranesi's admiration of Roman technology was a reaction to the claims made by the Hellenists in the Graeco-Roman debate that Greek architecture was superior to that of Roman.

Primo Frontespizio dell' Opera delle Antichità Romane. Stemma gentilizio di Milord Charlemont, formato sulla maniera dell' Originale datone dagli Agenti di detto Signore, e che si finge in una tavola di marmo incastrata fra i trofei antichi che accompagnano l'Iscrizione.

NO. 58

GIOVANNI BATTISTA PIRANESI

Mogliano Veneto 1720–Rome 1778

58. *Lettere di giustificazione*

scritti a Milord Charlemont e a' di lui agenti di Roma dal Signor Piranesi Socio della real Società degli Antiquari di Londra intorno la dedica della sua opera delle antichità Rom. Fatta allo stresso Signor ed ultimamente soppressa, *Rome, 1757*

Watermarks: letters *AG* above a *C* (Robinson 1986, no. 55); on page tipped in, *Prima Iscrizione di Milord Charlemont*, fleur-de-lis in a double circle.

EXHIBITION: New York 1989.

Giannalisa Feltrinelli Collection, on deposit at The Pierpont Morgan Library (4274)

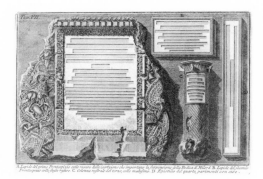

FIGURE 1 Giovanni Battista Piranesi, *Tablets with the Deletions from the Frontispiece.* The Pierpont Morgan Library, New York.

Around 1750, Piranesi published the *Camere sepolcrali degli Antichi Romani le quali esistono dentro e fuori di Roma*, a small-scale publication consisting of eleven plates. He planned to expand the work, and in 1753 he received financial support from the Irish nobleman James Caulfield, first earl of Charlemont. Eventually the project developed into a four-volume work, the *Antichità Romane*, for which the artist was promised patronage from Charlemont. The *Antichità* was published in 1756, but Piranesi never received further payment. After sending several letters to Charlemont and receiving no response, he deleted the citation to the earl and defaced the heraldic achievements in the unsold copies. Some of the confusion regarding payment may have been caused by jealousy on the part of the earl's agent, the English artist John Parker, who may not have forwarded Piranesi's letters to Charlemont (see Scott 1975, pp. 105ff. and Wilton-Ely in London 1978, pp. 58–59). Forty copies of the book were sold before the artist suppressed the original frontispiece.

In 1757, Piranesi issued the *Lettere di giustificazione* as a means of justifying his actions and distributed it to various influential figures. A copy of the pamphlet in a private collection contains a manuscript list which may indicate to whom he planned to send copies. The names on the list are mentioned by surname but these seem to include Andrea Rossi, a Venetian active in Rome; the sculptor, restorer, and dealer in antiquities, Bartolomeo Cavaceppi; the neoclassical painter Anton Raphael Mengs; and the British envoy in Naples, Sir William Hamilton (Northampton 1961, pp. 65–66).

In addition to publishing three of his original letters in the *Lettere di giustificazione*, Piranesi reproduced in miniature all four frontispieces prepared for the *Antichità Romane* with their original inscription to his erstwhile patron Charlemont intact. The miniature frontispieces are followed by reproductions of the manuscript dedications drawn up by the patron. Piranesi also assembled on one plate the tablets that contained inscriptions to the earl of Charlemont, which he had effaced (fig. 1).

GIOVANNI BATTISTA PIRANESI
Veneto Mogliano 1720–Rome 1778

59. *Archaeologists Investigating the Drainage Outlet of Lake Albano*

in IOANNIS.BAPTISTAE/PIRANESII/ ANTIQVARIORVM/REGIAE.SOCIETATIS. LONDINENSIS/SOCII/DE ROMANORVM/ MAGNIFICENTIA/ET.ARCITECTVRA/DELLA MAGNIFICENZA/ED.ARCHITETTVRA/DE' ROMANI/OPERA/DI.GIO.BATTISTA.PIRANESI/ SOCIO.DELLA REALE/ACCADEMIA/DEGLI ANTIQVARI/DI LONDRA *Rome, [The Author], 1761*

Etching (image) and engraving (inscriptions) on laid paper (pl. XXX). Platemark: 15^{15}/$_{16}$ x 44^3/$_{16}$ inches (405 x 1123 mm); page (double): 21^3/$_{16}$ x 59^1/$_8$ inches (538 x 1502 mm). Watermark: right of center, fleur-de-lis in a double circle surmounted by the letters *CB* (Robison 1986, p. 222, no. 35).

Inscribed at lower left, inside etched border, *Piranesi F*; upper edge in center in a ribbon, *Schemata Emissarii Lacus Albani*; upper right corner, inside etched border, *Tab.XXX*.

DATE: printing and compilation of this volume, before binding, 1760s to 1780s.

PROVENANCE: possibly Dr. Richard Robinson, archbishop of Armagh, first baron Rokeby (1709–94), his coat of arms on a bookplate affixed to the back of the front cover; E. P. Goldschmidt & Co., London.

BIBLIOGRAPHY (for this plate but not for the CCA's version): Wittkower 1982, p. 236; Focillon (Calvesi/Monferini) 1967, p. 360; Robison 1970 "Prolegomena," pp. 193, 204; Wilton-Ely 1972 (facsimile), p. vii (introduction), pl. XXX; Scott 1975, p. 169; Wilton-Ely in Brunel 1978, p. 537; Wilton-Ely 1978 (1988), p. 67.

Montréal, Centre Canadien d'Architecture/Canadian Centre for Architecture M7593 CAGE

The CCA's copy of Piranesi's *Della Magnificenza ed architettura de' Romani* is bound together with *Osservazioni di Gio. Battista Piranesi sopra la lettre de M. Mariette aux auteurs de la Gazette littéraire de l'Europe*, *Parere su l'architettura*, and *Della Introduzione e del progresso delle belle arti in Europa ne' tempi an-*

tichi, the latter three published in Rome in 1765. This later edition of *Della Magnificenza* contains all the elements found in the first edition: the Latin title page; the first frontispiece with the Italian title; the frontispiece with the portrait by Domenico Cunego of Pope Clement XIII (1758–69); the one folio dedication to the pope with the *imprimatur* and *approbatio* of 27 May 1760; 212 pages of text, including an index numbered in roman numerals I through CXCIX and CCI through CCXXII, with three vignettes; two decorated letters; and thirty-eight plates including the four missed by Focillon–plates XVII, XVIII, XIX, and XX (Focillon 1964, p. 63, nos. 927–66, pp. 63–65; Focillon [Calvesi/Monferini] 1967, p. 306, nos. 927–66, pp. 360–62; Hind 1922, pp. 84–85; Robison 1970 "Prolegomena," p. 204). The *Osservazioni*, the *Parere*, and the *Della Introduzione* all have their pages numbered consecutively in arabic numerals after the title page of the *Osservazioni* (1–8, 9–16 in the *Parere*, and 17–23 in the *Della Introduzione*). Together, these three works have five vignettes and a colophon on page 23 listing Generoso Salomoni as the printer of the text pages, and a publication date of 1765. There are three single-page plates at the end of *Della Introduzione. Parere su l'architettura* lacks the six plates mentioned by Hind and erroneously thought by Focillon to be at the end of the *Introduzione* (Hind 1922, p. 86; Focillon 1964, p. 65, nos. 967–82, pp. 65–66; Focillon [Calvesi/Monferini] 1967, p. 362, nos. 967–82, pp. 362–63).

Hind, Focillon, and Robison all have found combined editions of the *Della Magnificenza* with the three later works. There is a similar combined edition in the Princeton University Library, which, like the CCA's edition, lacks the six plates of the *Parere* added by Piranesi after 1767, when he began using the title *Cavaliere* with his name, as well as a copy of Piranesi's first *catalogo inciso* of 1761, often added to the first edition of *Della Magnificenza* (CCA Library Research Files, Jan Johnson report, 27 September 1988; Hind 1922, p. 86; Focillon 1964, p. 63; Robison 1970 "Prolegomena," p. 193: Princeton University Library, Marquand:NA 310.P65 e [SA]; Wilton-Ely 1978 [1988], p. 78). Monferini discovered that some

editions of *Della Magnificenza* have a plate like the one exhibited here, the *Archaeologists Investigating the Drainage Outlet of Lake Albano*, plate XXX of *Della Magnificenza*, which is actually the same as plate III, published between April and May 1762 in *Descrizione e disegno dell'Emissario del Lago Albano* (Focillon [Calvesi/Monferini] 1967, p. 360, no. 485, p. 316; Focillon 1964, p. 37, no. 485).

This volume is bound in a late nineteenth-century or early twentieth-century binding. It has a brown leather spine stamped in gold *PIRANESI/MAGNIFI-CENTIA/ROMANORUM* with a crest inscribed, *Royal Institution*; brown leather corners, and reddish-orange buckram covers. The endpapers are green wove paper. A coat of arms, which has been cut down, is affixed inside the front cover (fig. 1). According to David S. Howard, it is the coat of arms of the noted book collector Dr. Richard Robinson (1709–94), fourth son of William Robinson of Rokeby. Dr. Richard Robinson went to Ireland in 1751 as chaplain to the lord lieutenant, the duke of Dorset, and became in 1765 archbishop of Armagh and primate of all Ireland. He was created first baron of Rokeby in 1777. Dr. Richard Robinson was depicted by Sir Joshua Reynolds in two portraits, one now at Rokeby Hall and the other at Christ Church College, Oxford, both of which were engraved by S. W. Reynolds (CCA Library). Because this binding dates from after Dr. Richard Robinson's death, we cannot be sure that the bookplate was on the original binding. It could have been transferred from the original binding, however, when the book was rebound.

Through the watermarks, the compilation and printing of this combined edition can be dated between the mid-1760s and the 1780s. The paper used for both the single-page plates and text pages is of a heavy weight and extremely consistent. The single-page plates of the four works all have a fleur-de-lis in a double circle surmounted by the letters *CB*. This has the same measurements as a watermark in the paper used in several editions of the *Opere varie*, in both the Princeton University Library and in Rotterdam, and in single-page plates printed between 1761 and the 1780s (Robison 1986, p. 222, no. 38). Paper

FIGURE 1 Coat of arms of Dr. Richard Robinson, archbishop of Armagh, inside front cover of *Della Magnificenza ed architettura de' Romani.* Canadian Centre for Architecture, Montréal, M7593 CAGE.

used for all the double-page plates of the *Della Magnificenza*, except for plates VI and XXX, has a fleur-de-lis in a double circle surmounted by the letters *CB* – the same measurements as a watermark in paper used in double-page plates printed throughout the 1760s, 1770s, and 1780s (Robison 1986, p. 222, no. 36bis). The double-page plates VI and XXX of the *Della Magnificenza* were printed on a different paper of lighter weight with a watermark of the same measurements as found in two copies of the *Opere varie* in the British Library printed between 1761 and the mid-1760s (Robison 1986, p. 222, no. 35).

Piranesi's first theoretical work, *Della Magnificenza ed architettura de' Romani*, is closely related to the *Antichità Romane*. In both works, Piranesi proclaims the superiority of Roman over Greek architecture, in particular because of their great achievements in engineering. The drainage outlet at Lake Albano chosen by Piranesi for plate XXX of *Della Magnificenza* was constructed by the Etruscans in the fourth century B.C. and restored by the Julio-Claudian emperors between A.D. 14 and 68. Wilton-Ely, following up on Wittkower, has suggested that the conception of *Della Magnificenza* goes back to at least 1755. Both authors felt that *Della Magnificenza* was conceived as a refutation of Allan Ramsay's (1713–84) *A Dialogue in Taste* – a declaration of the superiority of Greek art – published anonymously in *The Investigator* in 1755. Ramsay's defense of Greek art echoed the theoretical views of not only the artists attached to the French Academy, but of the English colony in Rome as well. Lord Charlemont in particular had been to Greece and Turkey in 1749 before he came to Rome. Between 1750 and 1762, a series of books had been published in Europe proclaiming the superiority of Greek art, including Johann Joachim Winckelmann (1717–68), *Gedanken uber die Nachahmung der griechischen Werke in der Malerey und Bildhauer-Kunst* (Dresden, 1755); the comte de Caylus (1692–1765), *Recueil d'antiquités égyptiennes, étrusques, grecques et romaines* (Paris, 1752–67); and James Stuart (1713–88) and Nicholas Revett (1720–1804), *The Antiquities of Athens*, first published in 1762. Of the English colony in Rome, only William

Chambers (1723–96) clung to the same views as Piranesi (Wittkower 1982, pp. 236–40; Wilton-Ely 1972, pp.v–ix; Wilton-Ely in Brunel 1978, p. 534; Wilton-Ely 1978 [1988], pp. 65–66; Bertelli in Bettagno 1978, pp. 40–41).

In a letter to Robert Mylne (1734–1811) dated 11 November 1760, Piranesi briefly mentioned that *Della Magnificenza* had been under way before 1758, but that the publication in Paris that year of Julien David Le Roy's (1724–1803) *Les Ruines des plus beaux monuments de la Grèce* caused him to hasten its completion (Wilton-Ely 1972, pp. v–vi; Wilton-Ely in Brunel 1978, p. 536; Wilton-Ely 1978 [1988], p. 67, note 15, p. 131). The *approbatio* for the *Della Magnificenza* was granted on 27 May 1760, but the work was not published until 1761, delayed by the completion of the portrait of Clement XIII, who had contributed 1,000 Roman *scudi* to its publication (Scott 1975, p. 154; Bertelli in Bettagno 1978, pp. 40–41). This chronology suggests that Piranesi could have done the preparatory drawings for the *Descrizione e disegno dell'Emissario del Lago Albano* during the summer of 1760. According to J.-G. Legrand, Piranesi often spent time at Pope Clement XIII's summer residence in Castel Gandolfo (Focillon 1963, pp. 111–12; Wilton-Ely 1978 [1988], pp. 41, 71; Erouart and Mosser in Brunel 1978, p. 234, note 72; Scott 1975, pp. 169, 172). Thus Piranesi could have printed plate XXX and added it to the first edition of the *Della Magnificenza* between the summer of 1760 and the date in 1761 when *Della Magnificenza* was finally printed, but before the *Descrizione e disegno dell' Emissario del Lago Albano* was published in 1762. The *Emissario* received its *approbatio* in April 1762 and may have been published as early as May 1762 (Focillon [Calvesi/Monferini] 1967, p. 315; Erouart and Mosser in Brunel 1978, p. 234, note 72). With the growing influence of the ideas of Winckelmann, the comte de Caylus, and Laugier in the 1760s and 1770s, Piranesi must have desired to reissue his *Della Magnificenza* as a combined edition with his other theoretical works.

Pierre-Jean Mariette (1694–1774) wrote to Giovanni Gaetano Bottari (1689–1775) on 31 December

1762 that he had received a copy of Piranesi's *Della Magnificenza*. Mariette waited until 4 November 1764 to publish his critique of Piranesi's espousal of the superiority of Roman art in the *Gazette littéraire de l'Europe*. Piranesi's rejoinder was subsequently printed the following year (Wittkower 1982, pp. 235–47; Focillon 1963, pp. 83–84; Wilton-Ely 1978 [1988], pp. 77–80). A second edition of *Della Magnificenza*, combined with the letter to Mariette, first appears in the 1768 *catalogo inciso* and continues to be mentioned until the one published in November 1778, the year of Piranesi's death (Mayer-Haunton in Bettagno 1978, p. 10, nos. 4–6, figs. 4–6).

This plate, showing three different views of the drainage outlet of Lake Albano, illustrates Piranesi's contribution to the field of architectural illustration. In the upper left corner, in a *trompe-l'œil* etching, he depicts a *veduta* of the drainage outlet from a distance. In the upper right corner, there is another illusionistic etching of a view of a specific area of the drainage outlet. This detail is then shown in section in the center of the plate. Here, Piranesi has stripped away the exterior of the monument to reveal its structure. John Wilton-Ely has observed that the use

of successive multiple images of a monument in one plate was an innovation of Piranesi, first displayed in the plates of the *Antichità Romane* (1756). Although P. Santi Bartoli had employed sections and *vedute* of monuments in his earlier *Antichi sepolcri overo Mausolei Romani ed Etruschi* (Rome, 1727), he had not used such a logical succession of images in one plate. Piranesi wished to impart to his readers a comprehensive knowledge of the inside and outside of the building. His interest in hydraulic engineering is a witness to his early training in the workshop of his uncle, Matteo Lucchesi, an engineer for the *Maestri delle Acque* in Venice (Wilton-Ely 1983, pp. 317–21). In addition, Barbara Stafford has brilliantly suggested that Piranesi's cutting away of the exterior fabric of buildings to reveal their structural components shows the influence of the anatomical illustrations of Vesalius, who removed the skin of the body to expose the bones, muscles, veins, and organs. She suggested that Piranesi may have seen eighteenth-century editions of Vesalius's treatise on the human anatomy, *De Humani Corporis Fabrica*, such as the one published in Leiden in 1725 (Stafford 1991, pp. 58–59).

GIOVANNI BATTISTA PIRANESI

Mogliano Veneto 1720–Rome 1778

60. *Letter, dated Rome, 16 February 1762, to the Marquis de Marigny*

Watermark: coat of arms (cf. Heawood 803; Subiaco, Italy 1761–63).

NO. 60 First page of two-page letter.

PROVENANCE: Alfred Morrison; sale, London, Sotheby's, 12 March 1974, lot 298.

BIBLIOGRAPHY: Morrison, vol. 5, p. 161.

EXHIBITIONS: London 1978, no. 146; New York 1989.

The Pierpont Morgan Library. Gift of Mr. P. Angus Morgan in honor of the Fiftieth Anniversary of the Morgan Library, 1974 (MA 2870)

Abel-François Poisson, marquis de Marigny (1727–81), was the brother of Mme de Pompadour. He served as director of royal buildings between 1751 and 1773, a position selected for him by his famous sister. In preparation for the post, Marigny was sent to Italy in 1749, making the Grand Tour in the company of three carefully selected mentors, the architect François Soufflot, the artist-engraver Charles-Nicolas Cochin, and the Abbé le Blanc.

Piranesi's letter, which may or may not be autograph, recalls that during his visit to Rome twelve years earlier the marquis had acquired etchings of his works in the form of *vedute*. Piranesi now sends him a catalogue of the five volumes of antiquities produced since that time in the hope that he will order them. Piranesi explains that he was compelled to produce *Della Magnificenza* as a defense of Roman architecture but that it is also a history of architecture in general. Piranesi goes on to give the titles of the other works, including *Le Rovine del Castello dell'Acqua Giulia* (1761), *Lapides Capitolini* (1762), the *Descrizione e disegno dell'Emissario del Lago Albano* (1762), and *Il Campo Marzio dell'Antica Roma* (1762). In some cases Piranesi provides the number of plates as well.

The marquis de Marigny was closely involved with the leading French protagonists in the debate on Graeco-Roman art. At the top of the first page of Piranesi's letter, Marigny has added a note on the artist's championing of the Romans, observing that Piranesi could hardly persuade him that the Romans had not borrowed anything from Greek architecture. He also writes that Piranesi is to be informed through Natoire, director of the French Academy in Rome, that four of his volumes will be purchased.

GIOVANNI BATTISTA PIRANESI

Mogliano Veneto 1720–Rome 1778

61. *Bird's-Eye View of the Campus Martius*

in IOANNIS/BAPTISTAE/PIRANESI/
ANTIQVARIORVM/REGIAE.SOCIETATIS/
LONDINENSIS SOCII/CAMPVS.MARTIVS/
ANTIQVAE/VRBIS/IL.CAMPO/MARZIO/
DELL'ANTICA.ROMA/OPERA/DI.G.B..PIRANESI/
SOCIO.DELLA.REAL.SOCIETA/DEGLI.
ANTIQVARI.DI.LONRRA, *Rome, [The Author], 1762*

Etching on laid paper with engraved inscriptions (pl. II). Platemarks: central portion (bird's-eye view), 19⅛ x 28⁹⁄₁₆ inches (486 x 726 mm); each side section (lists of monuments and sculptural fragments), 19⅜ x 4¾ inches (493 x 122 mm); page (formed of three sections): 22³⁄₁₆ x 44¼ inches (563 x 1124 mm). Watermark: right of center, fleur-de-lis in a double circle surmounted by the letters *CB* (Robison 1986, p. 222, no. 35).

Inscribed central section (bird's-eye view) illustrated here: upper left corner, inside etched border, *Tab.II* and in a cartouche, *SCENOGRAPHIA/CAMPI MARTII*/Veterum aedificiorum reliquias/ostendens/e ruderibus nostrique aevi aedificijs/exemptas/cum ejusdem Campi celebriorum/monumentor.congerie; lower left, on the frieze of an entablature, *.ROBERTO.ADAM.ARCH*; lower left corner, outside etched border, *Piranesi F.*; side sections, inscribed inside etched borders at top above a list of monuments and sculptural fragments preceded by arabic numerals (not illustrated), right, *INDEX. RELIQVIARVM/VETER. AEDIFICIOR/CAMPI. MARTII*; left, *INDEX MONVMENTOR/CAMPI. MARTI/QVOR.ECTYPOSIS/EXHIBETVR/IN.CONGERIE.*

DATE: printing and original compilation of this volume before binding, 1760s–80s.

PROVENANCE: Henry Arundell, eighth baron of Wardour (1740–1803), after 1765, his coat of arms on a bookplate inside the front cover; Ben Weinreb Architectural Books, Ltd., London.

BIBLIOGRAPHY (for this plate but not for the CCA's version): Focillon 1964, p. 34, no. 437; Focillon (Calvesi/Monferini) 1967, p. 313, no. 437; Scott 1975, p. 168; Zamboni in Bettagno 1978, p. 46, no. 238, fig. 238; Wilton-Ely 1978 (1988), p. 74, fig. 123, p. 74.

Montréal, Centre Canadien d'Architecture/Canadian Centre for Architecture POM13570 CAGE

This edition of the *Campus Martius* is bound with one of the *Lapides Capitolini sive Fasti consulares triumphalesque Romanorum*. Piranesi first published both works in Rome in 1762. These two books must have been printed as a combined edition since a folio of identical paper falls between the two editions. The title, in roman capitals, reads: *LAPIDES/CAPITOLINI/ SIVE/FASTI/CONSULARES TRIUMPHALESQUE/RO- MANORUM*; the dedication to Pope Clement XIII (1758–69) follows. The paper used for the illustrations and text of the two editions is extremely consistent and is of the same density and weight. The watermarks indicate that this combined edition was printed between 1762 and the 1780s. In the *Campus Martius*, the single plates have a fleur-de-lis in a double circle surmounted by the letters *CB* of the same size as Robison no. 36 (Robison 1986, p. 222). This same watermark is found in paper used for single- and double-page plates in the presentation volumes of the *Antichità Romane* (1756) at the Accademia di San Luca, Rome, and in double-page plates printed throughout the 1760s, 1770s, and 1780s. The paper in all the multiple-plate sheets has, like the *Bird's-Eye View of the Campus Martius* exhibited here, a similar watermark (fig. 1) but of different dimensions (Robison 1986, p. 222, no. 35). This watermark is found in paper used between 1761 and the mid-1760s. It occurs in two versions of the *Opere varie* (1750): in the British Library and in the Beinecke Library of Yale University, both printed in the early 1760s. In the *Lapides Capitolini*, the paper used for the only plate, a double sheet with the *Depiction of the Capitoline Stones* (Focillon 1964, p. 34, no. 427), also has the same watermark (fig. 1) as the *Bird's-Eye View of the Campus Martius* (Robison 1986, p. 222, no. 35). The paper used for the first frontispiece of the *Lapides Capitolini* (Focillon 1964, p. 33, no. 42) has a fleur-de-lis in a double circle surmounted by the letters *CB* of the same measurements as a watermark found

FIGURE 1 Watermark in paper used for the plates of the *Campus Martius*, plate II. Canadian Centre for Architecture, Montréal, POM13570 CAGE.

FIGURE 2 Bookplate bearing coat of arms of Henry Arundell, inside front cover of *Campus Martius*. Canadian Centre for Architecture, Montréal, POM13570 CAGE.

in versions of the *Opere varie* (1750) in the Princeton University Library, in Rotterdam, and in other single-page plates printed between 1761 and the 1780s (Robison 1986, p. 222, no. 38).

The original eighteenth-century binding of the CCA's edition has been restored in the twentieth century. The red leather spine is embossed in gold with a floral pattern above and below the title, which reads: *PIRANESI/CAMPO/MARZO/FASTI/SIMULACRES/ROMANORUM*. Two strips of brown leather have been added alongside the spine on both sides of the covers; the same brown leather was used to reinforce the corners of the two pulp covers faced with blue-gray paper. Although no watermarks were found, the double endpapers appear to date from the eighteenth century. On the back of the front cover, a cut-down bookplate (fig. 2) has been pasted over another bookplate (which is not visible). The inside of the front cover appears to have been left intact during the restoration of the binding. According to David S. Howard, this bookplate has the coat of arms of Henry Arundell, eighth baron of Wardour (1740–1803), of Wardour Castle in Wiltshire. The bookplate shows the coat of arms, quarterly of eight, engraved by Pranker in about 1765 (his signature is cut off here). Henry Arundell became the eighth baron of Wardour in 1756 at the death of his father. Another coat of arms, quarterly of sixteen, engraved by Pranker in 1767, was published in Joseph Edmonson's *Baronageum Genealogicum* (London, 1767). John Wilton-Ely has found correspondence between the Jesuit John Thorpe and Henry Arundell from the 1770s in which Arundell asked Thorpe to buy items from Piranesi to adorn Wardour Castle. Thorpe was a member of the English community in Rome and had close contacts with Piranesi (Wilton-Ely 1978 [1988], p. 111, note 6, p. 134).

Both versions of the *Campus Martius* and the *Lapides Capitolini* have the same elements found in the first editions of these works (CCA Library Archives, Jan Johnson report, January 1988). The *Campus Martius* has the two frontispieces, one in Latin and one in Italian; the four folios containing the dedication to Robert Adam in Latin and Italian with two vignettes; the papal *approbatio* of 16 June 1761 on the recto of the first page of the main text; sixty-nine pages of text numbered in arabic numerals in Latin and Italian with two illustrated letters and four vignettes; twenty-nine pages of indexes in Latin and Italian numbered I to XII and I to XVII in roman numerals; forty-two illustrations by Piranesi, two composed of three plates, two of two plates and one of six plates (pls. I–V, XI–XXX, XXXII–XLVIII); and one illustration (pl. XXXI) etched by Arnold van Westerhout after a drawing by Francesco Fontana. The *Lapides Capitolini* likewise includes all the elements of the first edition: the second frontispiece with the dedication to Pope Clement XIII; the first frontispiece with the title (here reversed); a Latin preface of two folios with the *approbatio* of 16 June 1761; sixty-one pages of Latin text including an index in arabic numerals with four vignettes; and one plate. The colophon on page 61 with the date of publication of the first edition (1762) has a quotation from Virgil's *Georgics* printed inside images of a snake and drawing instruments etched by Piranesi. Since the colophon lists the printer of the text pages as Generoso Salomoni, this firm must have printed the text pages of the *Campus Martius* as well. An entry for the combined edition was not found in the printed broadsheets of Piranesi's works for sale, nor was it mentioned by either Hind or Focillon. The first Latin frontispiece of the *Campus Martius* has Piranesi's address as the Strada Felice in the Palazzo Tomati, where he had moved in 1761 (*Campus Martius*: Hind 1922, p. 85; Focillon 1964, pp. 34–36, nos. 428–79; Focillon [Calvesi/Monferini] 1967, pp. 312–15, nos. 428–79; *Lapides Capitolini*: Hind 1922, p. 85; Focillon 1964, pp. 33–34, nos. 421–27; Focillon [Calvesi/Monferini] 1967, p. 312, nos. 421–27).

Henri Focillon suggested that the conception of the *Campus Martius* went back to the years 1753 to 1756 when Piranesi was preparing his *Antichità Romane* (1756) for publication. Focillon considered the *Campus Martius* as volume V of the *Antichità Romane* (Focillon 1963, p. 107). Piranesi's investigation of the *Campus Martius* grew out of his research for the *Master Plan of Ancient Rome*, plate II in volume I

of the *Antichità Romane.* In the explanation of this plate, Piranesi wrote that another map of Rome was ready for publication (Wilton-Ely 1978 [1988], pp. 62–63, 73, note 42, p. 131, fig. 72, p. 49). Volume I was the last volume of the *Antichità Romane* to be completed. In 1755, through the intermediary of Clérisseau, Piranesi had met Robert Adam and they went about Rome investigating the ancient monuments. According to a letter written in July of 1755 by Robert Adam to his brother James, Piranesi offered to dedicate to Adam a map of the *Campus Martius* that was to be included in the *Antichità Romane.* Adam declined Piranesi's offer because the *Antichità Romane* was to be dedicated to the Irish peer, James Caulfield, the first earl of Charlemont (Scott 1975, p. 111; Wilton-Ely in Brunel 1978, p. 538, note 31; Wilton-Ely 1978 [1988], p. 62; see Cat. no. 57). Later, in the dedication to Robert Adam in a cartouche at the upper left corner of the *Map of the Campus Martius* (which is included in the book on the *Campus Martius* exhibited here, pl. V), a date of 1757 appears in one of the three medallions, and thus establishes a *terminus ante quem* for the completion of this map (*Campus Martius* 1762, pl. V; Scott 1975, p. 165, fig. 194; Wilton-

Ely in Brunel 1978, p. 549, pl. 18). We also know that Adam saw the plates for the *Campus Martius* in Piranesi's studio before Adam's departure from Rome in April of 1757. Piranesi received the papal *approbatio* for the book on 16 June 1761 (Wilton-Ely 1978 [1988], pp. 62, 73; Zamboni in Bettagno 1978, pp. 44–48; Scott 1975, pp. 165–69). The work was finally ready for distribution by 7 April 1762 when Charles-Joseph Natoire (1700–1777), director of the French Academy in Rome, wrote to the marquis de Marigny (1727–81): "This industrious artist [Piranesi] who was very flattered by your kind letter which he received from you, Monseigneur, has asked me to send you his *Campo Marzio* which he has just put up for sale to the public." After Marigny decided to buy a copy of the *Campus Martius*, it was Hubert Robert who went to Piranesi's studio on the Strada Felice to pick up the book (Focillon 1963, pp. 109–11). The first listing of the *Campus Martius* and the *Lapides Capitolini* occurs as a gloss to a version of Piranesi's 1761 broadsheet of works for sale that was sent to consul Joseph Smith (Mayer-Haunton in Bettagno 1978, p. 10, no. 2, as collection of Andrew Robison, fig. 2). They also appear in a printed broadsheet of works for sale published by Piranesi in 1762 to 1763 (Mayer-Haunton in Bettagno 1978, p. 10, no. 3, fig. 3).

The *Campus Martius* is essentially a description of the buildings surviving from classical times in the Field of Mars – the large part of the ancient city between the residential area and the Tiber. Originally used as a parade ground and for elections, the Campus Martius was subsequently covered by theaters, temples, and other public buildings. The history of this development is traced in Piranesi's maps, beginning with a topographical map, followed by the *Scenographia*, an aerial panorama of the entire area. The *Ichnographia* is Piranesi's attempt to reconstruct what he considered to be the culmination of the Roman creative genius for civic planning. The map depicting a bird's-eye view of the Campus Martius isolates the original structures from their medieval surroundings so that antique monuments such as the Pantheon and the theater of Marcellus are seen as freestanding. This technique is followed throughout the book, with the artist consistently depicting the ruins as if they had never been combined with other, later structures. As Wilton-Ely has observed, this was imitated by Adam in his book *Ruins of the Palace of the Emperor Diocletian at Spalatro in Dalmatia* (London 1978, p. 58; see Cat. no 77). Piranesi's maps are followed by plates depicting monuments and antique fragments that glorify the grandeur and magnificence of ancient Rome. In many regards, the *Campus Martius* can be viewed as a response by Piranesi to the work of Johann Joachim Winckelmann, an avid exponent of the superiority of Greek over Roman art (see Cat. no. 62).

Many of Piranesi's maps are hypothetical reconstructions of the area. Although Piranesi carefully justified his reconstruction in the dedication, the element of invention prompted comments by his contemporaries. Charles-Joseph Natoire, director of the French Academy in Rome at the time, wrote to the marquis de Marigny that although the recontructions were partially the product of Piranesi's imagination, "one can gain some insights from them, and this method of execution is always a pleasure to the eye" (Scott 1978, p. 169).

JOHANN JOACHIM WINCKELMANN
Stendal 1717–1768 Trieste

62. *Monumenti antichi*

inediti spiegati ed illustrati da
Giovanni Winckelmann

Roma: A spese del'autore, [1767] 2 vols. A third volume (PML 78761), bound to match the Winckelmann, contains five essays on antique reliefs in the Villa Albani by a Jesuit priest, Stefano Raffei (1712–88).

PROVENANCE: Malden [Massachusetts] Public Library; New York, Phillips, 11 October 1986 (sale 634), lot 56.

BIBLIOGRAPHY: Cicognara 1821, no. 2506; Morgan Library *FR* XXI, 1989, p. 193.

EXHIBITION: New York 1989.

The Pierpont Morgan Library. Purchased on the H.S. Morgan Fund, 1986 (PML 78759–60)

Winckelmann's renown as a scholar and teacher of classical archaeology was firmly established with the publication of his two most influential works: *Die Gedanken über die Nachahmung der Griechischen Werke*, which appeared in Dresden in 1755 before his departure for Rome, and *Geschichte der Kunst des Alterthums*, which was published in Dresden in 1764. He greatly promoted the understanding of antique art, primarily Greek sculpture, and influenced the taste of his contemporaries, among them Goethe and Lessing. Both these fundamental treatises were almost immediately translated into Italian, French, and English.

The son of a poor shoemaker, Johann Joachim Winckelmann was born in 1717 in Stendal, a small town in Prussian Saxony. His education was inadequate, and he was forced to accept various teaching posts in order to earn a livelihood. However, he became librarian and assistant to Count Heinrich von Bünau at Nöthnitz, near Dresden, and later, in 1754, served as librarian to Cardinal Passionei. In Dresden he made the acquaintance of the painter Adam Friedrich Oeser (1717–99), who studied antique sculpture with him in the royal collection.

Winckelmann's position as librarian allowed him to acquire a thorough knowledge of ancient literature (which later formed the basis of his interpretation of Greek art) and inspired him with an ardent desire to visit Rome. To realize this goal, he converted to Catholicism, and with the financial help of Cardinal Archinto and Augustus III, king of Poland and elector of Saxony (1696–1763), he arrived in Rome in November 1755. In 1758, he became librarian to Cardinal Alessandro Albani, the famous collector of classical antiquities, which made it possible for him to study and catalogue the antique monuments. In 1763 he was appointed prefect of the papal antiquities. In 1768, Winckelmann traveled to Vienna where he was honored by the Empress Maria Theresa and given gold and silver medallions.

Winckelmann's *Monumenti*, his last important work, published one year before his untimely death in 1768, represents the culmination and summation of all his previous studies and writings on antique monuments over a span of more than thirteen years. This work is appropriately dedicated to his patron, Cardinal Alessandro Albani, who generously provided his librarian with the leisure to study and write about the antiquities in his collection and elsewhere in Rome. The cardinal also had an important part in the *Monumenti*–the dedication includes the statement: "It is as much your work as mine."

The *Monumenti* differs from Winckelmann's earlier publications, *Die Gedanken über die Nachahmung der Griechischen Werke* and the *Geschichte der Kunst des Alterthums*, in that it is written in Italian and illustrated with 200 engravings by Giovanni Battista Casanova (1728–95) and others. The illustrations made the project very expensive for Winckelmann, who also financed the publication. The book was to be a token of gratitude to the country and, above all, to the city whose antiquities had inspired his research and teaching during the past twelve years. It was truly, more than the other works, "a fruit of the Italian soil" (Justi 1956, p. 381).

The *Monumenti* consists essentially of two parts. The first and smaller part, incorporated later, is a revised version of Winckelmann's history of art. The

NO. 62

second and most important part contains, as the title indicates, unpublished monuments and his exegesis on the "Erklärung schwerer Punkte in der Mythologie, den Gebräuchen und der alten Geschichte, alles aus unbekannten Denkmälern des Altertums" (the explanation of difficult points in mythology, customs and antique history, all from unknown, antique monuments; letter of 8 December 1762). In the preface to volume I, Winckelmann clearly states his motives in undertaking this work: 1) *il vedere* (observing); 2) correcting the mistakes of writers of the past; and 3) discussing the customs of ancient peoples and unexplained or unknown subjects.

Except for a few short chapters on the *arte del disegno* of the Egyptians and Etruscans and a treatise on *bellezza*, the major part of the book is devoted to the Greek monuments. A discussion of mythology and deity in general is followed by chapters on individual deities (such as Cibele or Giove) and Greek and Roman history. Four different indices at the back of volume I give books cited, authors corrected and explained, and additional information on the an-

FIGURE 1 *Apollo Sauroktonos* (the *Lizard-Slayer*), in Winckelmann, *Monumenti antichi*. The Pierpont Morgan Library, New York.

tique monuments. Volume II of the *Monumenti* contains the 208 engravings, mostly full-page reproductions of antique sculpture, some with details, and examples of Egyptian sculpture. The opening shown here is the *Apollo Sauroktonos* (the *Lizard-Slayer*), a statue that was at the Villa Borghese in Rome in 1760 (fig. 1). It was purchased by Napoleon in 1807 and is today in the Louvre. Winckelmann described the *Sauroktonos*: "Among the most beautiful statues of Apollo was the famous one in marble by Praxiteles, surnamed Sauroktonos, meaning lizard-slayer, an idea which is also recorded in a gem" (Winckelmann 1760, p. xix). He calls a copy in the Villa Albani "one

of the most beautiful figures in bronze and one of the most precious jewels of the Villa Albani." There are two further references to the *Apollo Sauroktonos* in the *Trattato preliminare* to volume I, pages xliii and lxxv.

The *Monumenti*, which has been called "a pioneering work in the field of archaeological methodology" (Leppmann 1970, p. 229), reveals Winckelmann in a new role. Instead of the easily explained and the aesthetically pleasing examples considered in his earlier writings, the author is attempting here to throw new light on difficult subjects and to decipher their hidden meanings.

NO. 63 First page of two-page letter.

SIR WILLIAM HAMILTON
Henley 1730–London 1803

63. *Autograph letter signed, Naples, 3 October 1767, to Giovanni Battista Piranesi*

BIBLIOGRAPHY: Wilton-Ely in Brunel 1978, p. 543, note 50; Scott in Bettagno 1983, p. 51.

EXHIBITIONS: Northampton 1961, p. 36; London 1978, no. 243; New York 1989.

The Pierpont Morgan Library

In this letter to Piranesi, the British envoy extraordinary and plenipotentiary at the court of Naples, Sir William Hamilton, writes that he has long been an admirer of the artist's work and thanks him for sending some prints from the *Diverse maniere*. Hamilton further comments: "I am delighted that you have done this work for it will be very useful in my country where we make much use of fireplaces." Hamilton also writes that he hopes to meet Piranesi in Rome in March. As John Wilton-Ely has observed, the date of the letter demonstrates that loose plates for Piranesi's book were in circulation before the work was published in 1769. Piranesi was very much aware of an expanding British market for his works, reflected by the fact that his preface to the *Diverse maniere* appeared in English as well as Italian and French.

GIOVANNI BATTISTA PIRANESI

Mogliano Veneto 1720–Rome 1778

64. *Console Table, Two Sconces, a Clock and Two Vases for the Apartment of Cardinal Giambattista Rezzonico in the Quirinal Palace, Rome*

in DIVERSE MANIERE/D'ADORNARE I CAMMINI/ED OGNI ALTRA PARTE DEGLI EDIFIZJ/DESUNTE DALL'ARCHITETTURA EGIZIA, ETRUSCA, E GRECA/CON UN/RAGIONAMENTO APOLOGETICO/IN DIFESA DELL'ARCHITETTURA EGIZIA, E TOSCANA/OPERA/DEL CAVALIERE GIAMBATTISTA PIRANESI ARCHITETTO./DIVERS MANNERS/OF ORNAMENTING CHIMNEYS/AND ALL OTHER PARTS OF HOUSES/TAKEN FROM THE EGYPTIAN, TUSCAN AND GRECIAN ARCHITECTURE/WITH AN/APOLOGETICAL ESSAY/IN DEFENSE OF THE EGYPTIAN AND TUSCAN ARCHITECTURE/BY JOHN BAPTIST PIRANESI KNIGHT AND ARCHITECT./DIFFERENTES MANIERES/D'ORNER LES CHEMINÉES/ET TOUTE AUTRE PARTIE DES EDIFICES/TIRÈES DE L'ARCHITECTURE EGYPTIENNE, ETRUSQUE, ET GREQUE/AVEC UN/DISCOURS APOLOGETIQUE/EN FAVEUR DE L'ARCHITECTURE EGYPTIENNE, ET TOSCANE/PAR LE CHEVALIER JEAN BAPTISTE PIRANESI ARCHITECT., *Rome, Generoso Salomoni, 1769*

Etching on laid paper (folio 63). Platemark: image, 15¹¹⁄₁₆ x 10 inches (389 x 254 mm); inscription, 2 x 10 inches (51 x 254 mm); page: 23 x 17⅛ inches (586 x 435 mm). Watermark: none.

Inscribed in separate panel below image, *Questo tavolino ed alcuni altri ornamenti che sono sparsi in quest'opera, si/vedono nell'appartamento di Sua Eccᶻa Monsigʳ D. Gio. Batt'a Rezzonico/Nipote e Maggiorduomo di N. SPP. Clemente XIII.*; lower right corner, *Cavalier Piranesi inv. e inc.*

DATE: printing and binding of the etchings in this volume, 1769 to mid-1770s.

Questo tavolino ed alcuni altri ornamenti che sono sparsi in quest'opera, si vedono nell' appartamento di Sua Eccᶻa Monsigʳ D. Gio. Batt'a Rezzonico Nipote e Maggiorduomo di N. S. PP. Clemente XIII.

Cavalier Piranesi inv. e inc.

NO. 64

PROVENANCE: Hugh Pagan, Ltd., Richmond, England (Catalogue no. 14, 1992).

BIBLIOGRAPHY (for this plate but not for the CCA's copy): Focillon 1964, p. 61, no. 923; Watson 1965, p. 25, pl. 2, p. 23; Focillon (Calvesi/Monferini) 1967, p. 357, no. 923, p. 354; Honour 1969, p. 147, repr. p. 50; Rieder 1973, p. 313, note 20; Scott 1975, p. 226, fig. 272, p. 232; Gonzales-Palacios in Bettagno 1978, pp. 59–60; Wilton-Ely 1978 (1988), pp. 102–3, fig. 183, p. 103; Wilton-Ely 1990, p. 192, fig. 2, p. 195.
Montréal, Centre Canadien d'Architecture/Canadian Centre for Architecture IDM92-B2594 CAGE

This copy of Piranesi's *Diverse maniere* is in an eighteenth-century binding. The pulp boards are covered with beige paper. The spine has a now illegible inscription in brown ink. The endpapers are of eighteenth-century paper. Both sheets reveal a watermark showing a hammer and an anvil, with the letter *C* on each side, in a double circle surmounted by a crown and a cross; the name of the town, Fabriano, appears below in a ribbon. This watermark, as well as the coat of arms of Pope Clement XIV (1769–74), is also in the endpapers of a copy of the *Antichità di Albano* in the Harvard College Library. According to Robison, this type of paper was often used as endpaper in the bindings of Piranesi's works from the 1770s (Robison 1986, p. 226, no. 56). The watermarks in the paper of the full-page illustrations also indicate a printing date for the plates between 1769 and the mid-1770s. The double frontispiece and most of the illustrations have the watermark of a fleur-de-lis inside a double circle surmounted by the letters *CB*; the dimensions of this watermark are the same as that in a copy of the *Opere varie* (1750–60) formerly in the collection of the duke of Leeds. Robison has dated this paper from the late 1760s to the early 1790s (Robison 1986, p. 223, no. 39bis). The illustration on folio 58 (Focillon 1964, p. 61, no. 918) was printed on paper with the watermark of a fleur-de-lis in a double circle surmounted by the letters *CB*, of the same dimensions as the watermark in the sheets of the *Opere varie* in the Sir John Soane's Museum, and in a presentation copy of the *Antichità Romane* (1756) in the Accademia di San Luca in Rome. Robison has

dated this paper from the late 1760s to the early 1770s (Robison 1986, p. 222, no. 37).

This version of the *Diverse maniere* contains all the elements described by Hind and Focillon in the first edition of this work (Hind 1922, p. 86; Focillon 1964, pp. 58–62, nos. 854–926; Focillon [Calvesi/Monferini] 1967, pp. 353–57, nos. 854–926). However, because of the differences in plate size and numbering, as well as in the order of the text pages and illustrations, this copy appears to be a variant of the first edition. This copy contains the printed title page; the double-page frontispiece (Focillon 1964, p. 58, no. 854); the dedication (one unnumbered folio) to Cardinal Giambattista Rezzonico, nephew of Pope Clement XIII, signed by Piranesi on 7 January 1769 on the verso; and thirty-five pages of text numbered in arabic numerals containing Piranesi's *Apologetical Essay in Defense of the Egyptian and Tuscan Architecture* in Italian, French, and English. There are two vignettes, the first, an Etruscan capital on page 1, and the second, the ruins of the Villa of Horace on page 35 (Focillon 1964, p. 58, nos. 855, 856). The *Apologetical Essay* in this copy is divided into three sections: the first section extends from pages 1 to 20 and ends with two plates illustrating different types of shells and vases, inscribed *pag. 21* and *pag. 22* in the upper right corners, and *Tavola I* and *Tavola II* in the upper left corners (Focillon 1964, p. 58, nos. 858, 859); the second section includes pages 21 to 30 of the *Apologetical Essay*, with an index on an unnumbered folio (recto and verso) followed by another illustration of different types of Etruscan buildings and ornament, inscribed in the upper right corner, *Tavola I, pag. 31* (Focillon 1964, p. 58, no. 860); the third and final part of the text of the *Apologetical Essay* extends from pages 31 to 35. On the verso of page 35 is the papal *imprimatur*. Another vignette – a small illustration of a commode, sedan chair, vase, and shell – is found on the recto of an unnumbered folio (Focillon 1964, p. 58, no. 857). On the verso of this folio is the *Avviso al Publico*.

The sixty-six full-page illustrations follow the *Apologetical Essay*. Their order differs quite substantially from that noted by Focillon (Focillon 1964, pp.

58–62, nos. 861–926). In this copy, the order of the full-page plates is as follows: Focillon nos. 861–65, 911, 867, 868, 898, 870–910, 869, 912, 866, 913–26. According to Marie Trottier, book conservator at the CCA, this copy is in its original binding and has not been rebound since the eighteenth century. Thus the plates must have been placed in this order when the album left Piranesi's studio. The arabic numerals in the lower right corners are irregular; only rarely do they conform to those noted by Focillon. Furthermore, some plates here have no arabic numerals, such as folios 45 and 46 (Focillon 1964, p. 61, nos. 906, 907). Others, such as folios 14 and 16, repeat the same arabic numeral, 14, in the lower righthand corner (Focillon 1964, p. 59, nos. 874, 876). The sizes of the etched plates differ slightly from those Focillon noted. Some are five millimeters to ten millimeters larger; others are smaller. For instance, folio 1 in this copy measures 383 x 250 millimeters, larger than Focillon's measurements of 340 x 240 millimeters (Focillon 1964, p. 58, no. 861). For the plate exhibited here, Focillon gave almost the same measurements: 390 x 255 millimeters.

Andrew Robison has found several copies of the *Diverse maniere* that have similar discrepancies with the first edition as described by Focillon. One such variant is an early copy in the Princeton University Library (Robison 1970 "Prolegomena," pp. 194–95). Robison has suggested that the frequent occurrence of irregularity in the numbering and order of plates in these early copies of the *Diverse maniere* may have occurred because Piranesi circulated some plates independently, before the work was completed. In fact, in a letter of 3 October 1767 (Cat. no. 63), Sir William Hamilton, British consul in Naples, thanked Piranesi for sending him a selection of etchings of fireplaces. The *Diverse maniere* was one of Piranesi's most popular books and had a wide European distribution. That it was bound quickly to meet the demand may explain why no two bound copies are alike. This rapid production might also account for the difference in the ink tones of various copies, as well as in the etchings themselves: in this copy, the tone varies from sepia to black.

William Rieder has situated the conception and execution of the *Diverse maniere* between 1764 and 1769 (Rieder 1973, p. 316). The earliest indications of the inception of Piranesi's designs for the *Diverse maniere* are the preparatory drawings on the verso of some etchings done in 1764 for, or in connection with, the *Antichità di Albano e di Castel Gandolfo*, the *Raccolta di alcuni disegni del Barbieri da Cento detto Il Guercino*, and the *Antichità di Cora* (Cat. no. 37) (Stampfle 1978, p. xxvi, nos. 59, 61, 62, 65, 67, repr. pp. 62, 64–66). Piranesi must have executed most of the etched plates of the *Diverse maniere* by the end of 1767, when he began to issue them individually. As we have seen, Sir William Hamilton received some loose plates in 1767. A letter that accompanied a proof copy of fifty-seven plates of the *Diverse maniere*, dated 18 November 1767, from Piranesi to Thomas Hollis, indicates that most of the plates were executed by that date.

Rudolf Wittkower was the first historian to note Piranesi's change in attitude toward decorative ornament, as evinced in *Parere su l'architettura* (1765) and in the *Diverse maniere*. Earlier, in *Della Magnificenza ed architettura de' Romani* (1761), Piranesi had proclaimed that the architecture of the Egyptians, Etruscans, and Romans was superior to that of the Greeks. Piranesi noted in particular the qualities of sobriety of ornament and solidity of construction. In his *Parere su l'architettura*, he designed a complex combination of ornate Egyptian, Etruscan, and Greek motifs for exterior decorations, and in his *Diverse maniere*, for interior decorations. In the *Apologetical Essay in Defense of the Egyptian and Tuscan Architecture* of the latter work, Piranesi explained that he wished to create a new *modern* aesthetic of design. In choosing to devote his book mainly to fireplaces, an element that had not existed in ancient times, Piranesi proclaimed the freedom of the architect from the canons of classical decorum. For Wittkower, Piranesi's belief in the importance of the architect's creativity was a direct outgrowth of his earlier works, the *Prima parte* (1743) and the *Carceri* (1749–50, 1761), in which he presented views of imaginary buildings based on the conventions of theatrical design (Witt-

FIGURE 1 *Wall Decoration for the Caffè degli Inglesi, Rome,* in *Diverse maniere,* fol. 46. Canadian Centre for Architecture, Montréal, IDM92–B2594 CAGE.

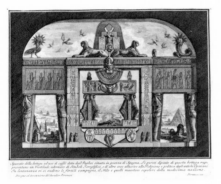

FIGURE 2 *Wall Decoration for the Caffè degli Inglesi, Rome,* in *Diverse maniere,* fol. 45. Canadian Centre for Architecture, Montréal, IDM92–B2594 CAGE.

FIGURE 3 Designed by G. B. Piranesi, *Side Table for Cardinal Giambattista Rezzonico.* Minneapolis Institute of Arts.

kower 1982, pp. 244–46, notes 33–43, pp. 268, 299; Rieder 1973, pp. 309–15; Wilton-Ely 1978 [1988], pp. 107–9).

The influence of this new design aesthetic can be found in the decoration of the priory church and Villa of the Knights of Malta on the Aventine Hill (1764–66), renovated by Piranesi at the request of Cardinal Giambattista Rezzonico (Wittkower 1982, pp. 248–58, notes 1–5, p. 299; Wilton-Ely 1978 [1988], pp. 95–99; see Cat. no. 33). Piranesi believed that certain decorative motifs – lyres, cornucopias, serpents, and bird's wings – were Etruscan in origin. These elements appear in the third plate (Focillon 1964, p. 58, no. 860) accompanying the *Apologetical Essay* in the *Diverse maniere* as well as throughout the priory church, and on the wall in front of the forecourt of the Villa of the Knights of Malta (Focillon 1964, p. 58, no. 860). Wilton-Ely has suggested that these motifs refer to Etruscan cults believed to have been established on the Aventine Hill (Wilton-Ely 1978 [1988], p. 95).

Several designs illustrated in the *Diverse maniere* were actually carried out before publication. At least three chimneypieces were executed before 1769: one, for Senator Abbondio Rezzonico, the brother of Cardinal Giambattista Rezzonico, in the Palazzo Senatorio has never been located; another, for the earl of Exeter at Burghley House, is still in existence; and the third, for the Dutch businessman John Hope, is now in the Rijksmuseum (Focillon 1964, p. 61, no. 924, pp. 58–59, nos. 861, 862; Rieder 1973, p. 313, note 20; Wilton-Ely 1978 [1988], pp. 104, 106, fig. 184, p. 103, figs. 190–93, p. 105). Another work executed before the publication of the *Diverse maniere* was the Caffè degli Inglesi on the Piazza di Spagna. The illusionistic wall paintings of the Caffè degli Inglesi, now destroyed, were the first examples of interior decoration influenced by Egyptian art and architecture in the eighteenth century. Wittkower dated them to around 1760 (figs. 1 and 2, folios 46 and 45 in this copy; Focillon 1964, p. 61, nos. 906, 907; Wilton-Ely 1978 [1988], pp. 107–8, fig. 200, p. 108; Wittkower 1982, pp. 271–72, fig. 353, p. 271).

The plate of the *Diverse maniere* exhibited here illustrates one of Piranesi's most spectacular designs. It shows a side table, one of a pair made for Cardinal Giambattista Rezzonico's apartment in the Quirinal Palace. Both tables, made of gilded oak and lime-wood with a marble top, have survived. One is in the Minneapolis Institute of the Arts (fig. 3), the other is in the Rijksmuseum in Amsterdam (Watson 1965, p. 25, pl. 3; Wilton-Ely 1978 [1988]), p. 102, figs. 181, 182; Wilton-Ely 1990, p. 197, fig. 8, p. 196, fig. 4). According to F. J. B. Watson, the tables illustrate Piranesi's desire to adapt decorative details from ancient architecture to contemporary taste (Watson 1965, p. 20). The classically inspired goat legs support chimera fashioned in an S-shape, which is found in other rococo-style console tables. Rieder has suggested that Piranesi, in making the classically inspired elements of his tables extremely light, particularly the laurel swags, may have been influenced by several console table designs published by Charles De Wailly in 1760 (Rieder 1973, p. 315, fig. 67). Piranesi was influenced also by examples of classical bronze furniture discovered at Pompeii and Herculaneum (Wilton-Ely 1978 [1988], p. 103). Robert Little has suggested that a bronze tripod with claw feet and a circular top supported by winged sphinxes, discovered in 1765 at the Temple of Isis at Pompeii in the eighteenth century, may also have been a source of inspiration for the two console tables of Cardinal Rezzonico (Hayward 1965 [1970], p. 18, fig. 34). It was illustrated by Piranesi in plate 44 of his *Vasi, candelabri, cippi,* published in 1778 (Wilton-Ely 1990, p. 193).

The *Diverse maniere* had a particular influence on two architects, Robert Adam and Charles Cameron (1740–1820): Adam, in the Etruscan Room at Osterley Park (1775–77) and in numerous chimneypiece designs; Charles Cameron, in the interior design of the Palaces of Tsarskoe Selo (1780–96) and Pavlovsk (1782–85) near St. Petersburg (Stillman in Wittkower 1967, pp. 201–4, figs. 5, 7, 9, 12, 14, 15; Scott 1975, p. 225, note 19, p. 315).

GIOVANNI BATTISTA PIRANESI
Mogliano Veneto 1720–Rome 1778

65. *Autograph letter with a drawing of the Warwick Vase*

signed, Rome, 3 August 1772, to Charles Townley, Naples. Accompanied by an autograph draft of Townley's reply, dated Naples, 14 August 1772

Watermark: coat of arms (cf. Heawood 803).

PROVENANCE: Townley papers and archive sale, London, Sotheby's, 22–23 July 1985, lot 557, repr.

BIBLIOGRAPHY: Morgan Library *FR* XXI, 1989, pp. 261–62, 291.

EXHIBITION: New York 1989.

The Pierpont Morgan Library. Purchased as the gift of Mr. John P. Morgan II, Miss Julia P. Wightman, and Mrs. Charles Wrightsman, in memory of Mrs. J. P. Morgan, 1985 (MA 4220)

The celebrated Warwick Vase, which dates from the second century A.D., was found, in pieces, at Patanello near Hadrian's Villa in 1771 by the Scottish painter and excavator Gavin Hamilton (1723–98). It was purchased by Sir William Hamilton, the British minister plenipotentiary at Naples, who had the vase restored probably by Bartolomeo Cavaceppi, the pope's chief restorer. The autograph draft of Townley's reply to Piranesi, written in French (from Naples on 14 August 1772), is preserved with this letter. Townley's response indicates that Piranesi also played a role in the restoration of the vase. He praises Piranesi's drawing of the vase and writes that "it has been given a new and perfect existence in the marvelous hands of the admirable Piranesi. Only he was capable of resuscitating such a phoenix!" ("il recoit une nouvelle existence et parfaite entre les mains merveillieuses de l'admirable Piranesi. lui seul à etè capable de resusciter un tel Phenix!"). Less than one third of the vase is Roman in origin; the rest was restored in the eighteenth century from Carrara marble (fig. 1). The decoration on each side shows four classical heads set against a lion's skin. On the front, Bacchus and Silenus are on a small plinth flanked by

NO. 65

FIGURE 2 G. B. Piranesi, *The Warwick Vase,* in *Vasi, candelabri, cippi.* The Pierpont Morgan Library, New York.

a bearded follower on either side. The arrangement is repeated on the rear side: Bacchus and possibly Ariadne his wife and a bearded head as before. The large intertwined handles on each side are depicted as thick vine stems. On the front of the pedestal an inscription in Latin relates the discovery and restoration dated 1774.

Hamilton tried to sell the Warwick Vase to the British Museum but unable to agree on a price, sold it to his nephew George Greville, earl of Warwick. The vase, which is included in Piranesi's *Vasi, candelabri, cippi* of 1778 (fig. 2), remained in the greenhouse of Warwick Castle until 1978, when it was acquired by the trustees of the Burrell Collection. It is now in the courtyard of the Burrell Collection Gallery of the Glasgow Museum. Piranesi's measurements on the drawing show that the vase measured *palmi* 11:6 in width and *palmi* 7:6 in height. W. Tyrrell of the Burrell Collection kindly provided the following information: from the rim to bottom of pedestal the vase measures 2.94 meters and the maximum width over the handles is 2.6 meters. It weighs 8¼ tons, and is made up of six sections – the bowl, stem, base, and pedestal (the latter in three parts).

Curiously, Piranesi's letter makes no mention of the Warwick Vase drawn at the top, but inquires after Townley's health and introduces a French architect working for the court of Saxony, Etienne Giraud, who is visiting Naples. Townley had embarked on his Grand Tour in 1767. He lived in Rome until 1772 when he left for Naples. An avid collector of antique sculpture, he went into partnership with Thomas Jenkins and supported the excavations undertaken by Gavin Hamilton at Patanello and other locations. Townley's collection of antique sculpture was considerable, including the so-called *Townley Venus* and a marble copy of the *Discus-Thrower* after the bronze original by Myron. The bust mentioned by Piranesi in this letter may be a Roman lady whom Townley named Clytie, in reference to the fable in Ovid's *Metamorphoses* (Book IV.264). The somewhat larger than life-size bust of Italian marble is placed on a base decorated with flower petals. It was bought by Townley from the Laurenzano family in Naples in 1772.

66. *Visitors Examining the Temple of Neptune at Paestum*

in Giovanni Battista Piranesi DIFFERENTES VUES. DE QVELQVES/RESTES. DE. TROIS. GRANDS EDIFICES/QVI SUBSISTENT ENCORE. DANS. LE MILIEV. DE/L'ANCIENNE.VILLE. DE . PESTO AVTREMENT.POS/SIDONIA. QVI EST. SITVEE DANS. LA LVGANIE, *Rome [Francesco Piranesi], 1778–1779*

Etching (image) and engraving (inscription) on laid paper (pl. XVI). Platemark: 19½ x 25⅝ inches (497 x 675 mm); sheet: 21¾ x 30½ inches (533 x 775 mm). Watermark: lower right, fleur-de-lis in a double circle surmounted by the letters *CB* (Robison 1986, p. 222, no. 36).

Inscribed inside etched border upper left corner, *Planche XVI*; lower edge of image inside etched border, center, in a ribbon, *A B Vue des deux restes de rangs de Colonnes qui étoient au Temple de Neptune qui lateralement formoient les/Portiques dans la Celle, et soutenoient le Comble de l'édifice. Cette Vue ci ne presente pas les Murailles de la Celle/qui sont ruinées. C D Colonnes de promenoirs du Temple. E Creux qui recevoient les Solives du toit*; lower right corner of the same ribbon, *Cav. Piranesi F.*

DATE: printing and binding of this volume, about 1778–80.

PROVENANCE: Charles Agar (1736–1809), archbishop of Dublin, and earl of Normanton (his coat of arms on a bookplate inside the front cover) after 1806; William H. Schab Gallery, New York.

BIBLIOGRAPHY (for this plate but not for the CCA's version): Focillon 1964, p. 43, no. 597; Focillon (Calvesi/Monferini) 1967, p. 324, no. 597; Scott 1975, p. 254, fig. 304; Pane 1980, p. 124, pp. 161–62, pls. 96–97; for the CCA's version, New York 1983, pp. 22–23, no. 13; New York 1986, p. 84, fig. 34y.

Montréal, Centre Canadien d'Architecture/Canadian Centre for Architecture DR1984:1458:017

This series of etchings of the *Temples at Paestum* is in an eighteenth-century binding made of pulp boards; four sheets of Italian stamped paper are glued over the covers; the spine and edges are vellum. The paper (fig. 1) is stamped with red boxes on a gray background (originally white) in imitation of a fabric pattern. The edges of the pages are marbled in red. Stamped papers were first used in France and Germany in the fifteenth century, and were widely manufactured in Italy, as well as in France and Germany, during the eighteenth century. In Italy, stamped paper of this type was manufactured in Florence and Venice (Doizy and Ipert 1985, p. 72). Inside the front cover in the upper left corner is an inscription in brown ink, *Normanton*, and in the center is a bookplate with the coat of arms of the earls of Normanton—the lion rampant with a crown above (fig. 2). The inscription on the bookplate, *Earl of Normanton*, has been scratched out. According to David S. Howard, this volume belonged to Charles Agar (1736–1809), third son of Henry Agar, MP, Gowran Castle, Kilkenny County, Ireland, who was created viscount and earl of Normanton on 4 February 1806. He had been appointed archbishop of Dublin in 1801, after having become a baron in 1795 (G.E.C. 1936, pp. 641–43). David S. Howard has also noted that the crest and coronet on the bookplate were taken by the earl of Normanton in 1806 from the head of an engraving by Pranker of the coat of arms of another family whose coat of arms had been published in Joseph Edmondson's *Baronageum Genealogicum* (London, 1766). Charles Agar is portrayed in a painting by George Dance in 1795, which was later engraved by William Daniel in 1809 (CCA Library).

The frontispiece and the two final *vedute*, plates XIX and XX, of this series of etchings were executed by Francesco Piranesi, and are inscribed *Franciscus Piranesi Fecit*. In the 1792 sales catalogue of Piranesi's works, this series was given a publication date of 15 September 1778, accepted by Hind and Focillon (Hind 1922, pp. 19, 87; Focillon 1964, p. 42). Monferini and Pane have pointed out that this is only the *terminus post quem*, since it is the date on which Giovanni Battista Piranesi received the papal *imprimatur*. According to both authors, the series on Paestum must have been published during the year 1778 to 1779, in part after Piranesi's death (Focillon [Calvesi/Monferini] 1967, pp. 322–23; Pane 1980, pp.

FIGURE 1 Stamped paper, on recto cover of G. B. Piranesi, *Différentes vues . . . de l'ancienne ville de Pesto*. Canadian Centre for Architecture, Montréal, DR1984:1458:001–021.

FIGURE 2 Bookplate with the coat of arms of Charles Agar, archbishop of Dublin, first earl of Normanton, inside front cover of *Différentes vues . . . de l'ancienne ville de Pesto*. Canadian Centre for Architecture. Montréal, DR1984:1458:001–021.

121–28). Mention of the series first appeared in one of the posthumous states of the *catalogo inciso* printed after Piranesi's death on 9 November 1778 and now in the Sir John Soane's Museum (Mayer-Haunton in Bettagno 1978, p. 10, no. 6, fig. 6). On the basis of the watermarks in the etched sheets and endpapers, the CCA's copy appears to be an early one, printed between 1778 and 1780, and bound soon after (CCA Research Files, reports of Richard Hemphill, 25 November 1987, and Jan Johnson, 8 August 1988). The endpapers have a fleur-de-lis inside a single circle with the letters *G F S* below. The watermark is similar to one in the endpapers of the copy of the *Descrizione e disegno dell'Emissario del Lago Albano* in the Princeton University Library, which was printed, according to Robison, in the 1770s (Robison 1970 "Prolegomena," p. 189; Robison 1986, p. 219, no. 23). The watermark that appears on the paper used for the etched sheets is found in other large-format etched sheets produced in the 1760s, 1770s, and 1780s.

There are seventeen preparatory drawings in black and sepia ink and gray wash for the series of views of Paestum: one drawing for plate I in the Bibliothèque Nationale, another in the Rijksmusem in Amsterdam for plate XIX, and fifteen drawings for plates II to XVII in the Sir John Soane's Museum in London. The latter once belonged to Robert Adam (Pane 1980, p. 124, pp. 151–83, fig. 54, figs. 57, 60, 63, 66, 69, 72, 75, 78, 81, 84, 87, 90, 93, 95, 98; Venice 1978, pp. 70–71, no. 84, repr. fig. 84). In addition there are several preparatory drawings for the figures and animals in two small sketchbooks in the Biblioteca Estense in Modena (Pane 1980, pp. 125–26, note 4, p. 125, figs. 74, 89, 92, 104–6). These preparatory drawings for the *vedute* of Paestum are much more finished than most of the other preparatory drawings for Piranesi's publications. Giovanni Battista Piranesi probably needed more detailed drawings than usual, since Paestum was a considerable distance from Rome (Wilton-Ely 1978 [1988], p. 117).

There has not been agreement about the authorship of the preparatory drawings for the etchings of Paestum by Giovanni Battista and Francesco Pira-

nesi. Some authors, such as Hind, have attributed only the figures to Francesco. Others, such as Gieseke, have assigned the entire drawing to Francesco, including the architecture. I agree with Thomas that it is difficult to see two hands in the preparatory drawings. Furthermore, it is difficult to make a distinction between Giovanni Battista and Francesco's style, since as Thomas has pointed out, there are very few secure drawings by Francesco Piranesi (Thomas 1954, p. 56). A closer analysis is needed of the drawings in the two sketchbooks in the Biblioteca Estense in Modena where one finds the hands of Giovanni Battista and other members of his family including Francesco (Cavicchi and Zamboni in Bettagno 1983, pp. 111–217). Roberto Pane has attributed the preparatory drawing in the Sir John Soane's Museum for the plate exhibited here, plate XVI, to Francesco (Pane 1980, p. 124, fig. 95).

According to Legrand, Giovanni and his son Francesco went to Paestum with the architect Benedetto Mori for the first time during the last year of Giovanni's life, between 1777 and 1778 (Erouart and Mosser in Bettagno 1978, p. 247). Giovanni Battista Piranesi had been to Naples to see the excavations at Herculaneum before, perhaps as early as 1743 (Robison 1986, p. 10). Dora Wiebenson has suggested that Giovanni Battista Piranesi decided to publish the *vedute* of Paestum in French because he knew that its subject would appeal particularly to the French, since they had adopted the Greek style in all its manifestations (Wiebenson 1969, p. 44). Piranesi's trip to Paestum occurred almost forty years after the temples were rediscovered in 1733 by the English traveler Robert Smith and by the Italian architect Ferdinando Sanfelice. In 1740, Sanfelice wanted to use some of the columns from the temples to adorn the Royal Palace at Capodimonte. Soon after, between 1745 and 1750, count Felice Gazzola, a member of King Carlo III of Bourbon's court at Naples, commissioned Giovanni Battista Natali III, Gaetano Magri, and Antonio Magri to execute drawings of the temples at Paestum. These drawings attracted the attention of Jacques-Germain Soufflot and Gabriel-Pierre-Martin Dumont, both of whom went to Paestum in 1750. Souf-

flot's drawings were the basis for a series of etchings published by Dumont in a first edition in Paris in 1764, and in a second edition in London in French and English in 1769 (Choisi, Mascotti, and Vallet in New York 1986, pp. 41–45, figs. 7a, 7c, p. 71, fig. 7b, p. 72; Paris 1980–81, p. 50, no. 89, repr. p. 50). Du-

mont's *Les plans, coupes, profils, élévations . . . de trois temples antiques dans la Bourgarde de Pesto* was the first illustrated publication on Paestum in the eighteenth century. The drawings commissioned by Gazzola were finally published in 1784 in Rome in *Rovine della Città di Pesto detto Ancora Posidonia* which had etchings by Giovanni Volpato and text by Paolo Antonio Paoli (Bassano del Grappa and Rome 1988, pp. 111–16, nos. 145–63, repr. pp. 114–16).

The English artist Thomas Major (1720–99) had obtained copies of Soufflot's drawings with corrections by Robert Mylne, and published a suite of engravings in French and in English in London in 1768, *The Ruins of Paestum* (*Les Ruines de Paestum*). Major's book replaced Dumont's as the most reliable reference on the Greek temples at Paestum. Soufflot himself owned a copy (McCarthy in New York 1986, pp. 47–50, fig. 11, p. 74).

In *Della Magnificenza ed architettura de' Romani*, published in 1761, Piranesi proclaimed the superiority of Roman over Greek architecture because of the Roman's expertise in engineering (Cat. no. 59). In both plate XXII of the *Della Magnificenza*, which shows the Greek Doric Temple of Concord at Agrigento in Sicily, and in plates IX and X of the *Antichità di Cora* (1764), which depicts the elevation and details of the orders of the Etruscan Doric Temple of Hercules at Cora, Piranesi criticized the proportions of the Greek Doric order. Although both plates were designed in the style of the illustrations in Julien David Le Roy's *Les Ruines des plus beaux monuments de la Grèce* (Paris, 1758), Piranesi also criticized Le Roy's measurements of the Doric order (Focillon 1964, p. 64, no. 951, p. 40, nos. 549, 550; Pane 1980, p. 143). Rudolf Wittkower has noted that Piranesi had begun to develop a more positive attitude toward Greek architecture, which manifested itself in the *Diverse maniere* (1769) (Cat. no. 64). Robert Pane discovered a letter written by Piranesi on 10 February 1762 to Tanucci, the minister of the king of Naples, which indicates that by that date, Piranesi was becoming more open-minded with regard to Greek architecture. Piranesi stated that since the conquering Romans had destroyed much of the Greek architecture in Italy and had used Greek spoils in their buildings, more excavations were necessary in order to better understand the true character of Greek archi-

tecture (Pane 1980, pp. 131–33). The suite of etchings, *Différentes vues de quelques restes de trois grands édifices . . . de Pesto*, reveals, like *Diverse maniere*, a change in Piranesi's attitude toward Greek architecture. Now he was able to appreciate the great beauty of the majestic Greek Doric temples at Paestum. He rationalized his acceptance of Greek architecture by stating that the temples were built on Italian soil (Wilton-Ely 1978 [1988], p. 118; Scott 1975, p. 251). The temple illustrated here, called the Temple of Neptune in the eighteenth century, was actually the Temple of Hera, built in 460 B.C.

Michael McCarthy has suggested that Piranesi's interest in Paestum at the end of his career was due also to a response to the demands of the English art market, for which he was a major supplier of classical antiquities and publications. McCarthy discovered that Piranesi also had taken Augusto Rosa, a maker of cork architectural models, along with him to Paestum. A cork model of *The Temple of Neptune at Paestum* that Rosa executed for Piranesi in 1777 to 1778 was acquired by Sir John Soane and is now in the Sir John Soane's Museum in London (McCarthy 1972, p. 766, figs. 39, 40). It is ironic that Piranesi, in spite of his nationalism, modeled the composition of *Visitors Examining the Temple of Neptune* on a plate from Thomas Major's publication, *The Ruins of Paestum* (Major 1768 [1969], pl. IX). However, Piranesi, through his mastery of the medium of etching, has surpassed Major in evoking the monumentality of the Temple of Neptune. By placing the temple closer to the viewer and by decreasing the amount of sky above the temple, Piranesi has created a more vivid image than Thomas Major. The CCA's version of plate XVI is an early, particularly brilliant impression. The sepia ink, masterfully applied to the copper plate, conveys an impression of the intensity of the southern Italian sunlight and the hot, humid atmosphere. Piranesi remained true to his Venetian training until the end of his career in the painterly quality he imparted to this etching.

NO. 67

RICHARD WILSON

Penegoes, Montgomeryshire 1713?–Mold, Flintshire 1782

67. *View of the Palatine Hill*

Black chalk and stump, lightly heightened with white, on green-gray paper. 9⅝ x 14⁵⁄₁₆ inches (244 x 364 mm). Watermark: none.

Numbered on verso in pen and black ink, *No 39.*

PROVENANCE: P. H. (Lugt 2084); W. B. Tiffin (no mark; see Lugt 2609); his sale, London, Sotheby's, 29 February 1860, lot 1080; R. P. Roupell (Lugt 2234); his sale, London, Christie's, 14 July 1887, lot 1356; Charles Fairfax Murray; J. Pierpont Morgan (no mark; see Lugt 1509).

BIBLIOGRAPHY: Ford 1951a, p. 60, under no. 56.

EXHIBITIONS: Minneapolis 1961, no. 96; New York 1989.

The Pierpont Morgan Library. Purchased by J. Pierpont Morgan, 1910, Acc. no. III, 42a

After studying in London under the little-known portrait painter Thomas Wright, Richard Wilson went to Italy in 1750, arriving in Venice in November of that year. He then traveled to Rome with William Lock of Norbury and possibly also with Thomas Jenkins (Cat. no. 68), arriving in Rome at the end of 1751 or the beginning of 1752. Wilson's presence in Rome by 13 January 1752 is documented by a receipt for advance payment of four pictures (Ford 1951a, p. 158). His exposure to the Venetian settecento landscape painters as well as his study of seventeenth-century painters such as Claude, Poussin, and Gaspard Dughet had a powerful influence on his decision to specialize in landscape, but it was only after his arrival in Rome that he turned away from portraiture and began focusing his attention on landscape art.

In Rome, Wilson became extremely active as a draughtsman, and from this point on he worked almost exclusively in black and white chalk and stump on a gray-green or gray-blue paper, a practice that sets his drawings apart from the majority of English landscape drawings of the period. His sensitive use of this media may have been influenced in part by artists working at the French Academy in Rome in the 1750s, for instance, Louis-Gabriel Blanchet

(1705–72), who frequently employed this technique to great effect (Cat no. 81). Wilson felt that black and white chalk was the most effective means of capturing the essence of a view, and from this time on he seldom varied his approach. His pupil Thomas Jones sums up Wilson's method in his *Memoirs*, writing:

> The first year I was to be confined entirely to making Drawings with black and White Chalks on paper of a Middle Tint, either from his [Wilson's] Studies and Pictures or from Nature – This, he said, was to ground me in the principles of Light & Shade, without being dazzled and misled by the flutter of Colours – He did not approve of *tinted* Drawings and consequently did not encourage his Pupils in the practise – which he s'd hurt the Eye for fine Colouring– (Jones, p. 9).

Wilson drew the Palatine a number of times from various angles. The two most finished examples – both depicting the Palatine Mount – belong to the Dartmouth series and are now in the Cecil Higgins Art Gallery, Bedford, and the Whitworth Art Gallery, Manchester. In 1754 and 1755, Wilson produced about sixty-eight highly finished drawings for William Legge, second earl of Dartmouth (1731–1801). Of the twenty-five that are known today, nineteen were originally part of a group of twenty views of Rome and its environs. David Solkin has proposed that many of Wilson's highly finished drawings were executed in two stages, beginning as topographical views drawn on the spot and then completed in the studio with the addition of stock framing devices (Solkin 1978, pp. 404–14). Although a much less finished work, the Library's *View of the Palatine Hill* shares similar physical characteristics with such drawings. Here Wilson apparently drew in the view across the middle of the sheet first, carefully distinguishing between the middle ground and distance. Probably at some later time he added the atmospheric stumping across the foreground and middle ground, and lastly the classical framing device of the tree on the left. That the tree was added subsequently can be seen by the traces of the buildings visible beneath it, showing that the drawing originally extended to the left edge of the paper. The figures in the right foreground were probably also added later. The

pentimenti clearly visible to the right show Wilson working out the size of the figures; he ultimately decided to reduce their scale and place them in the immediate foreground, presumably to emphasize the grandeur of the ruins.

RICHARD WILSON

Penegoes, Montgomeryshire 1713?–Mold, Flintshire 1782

68. *Portrait of Thomas Jenkins*
(1722–1798)

Black chalk, heightened with white, on green-gray paper. 10¾ x 7¹³⁄₁₆ inches (272 x 198 mm). Watermark: none. Inscribed on verso in pen and brown ink, *Jenkings.*; numbered in pencil, *387/6* and inscribed below that, *Locks sale 1821* and *Wilson del.*

PROVENANCE: William Lock; his sale, London, Sotheby's, 3 May 1821, probably part of lot 387; James (according to Charles Fairfax Murray); A. W. Thibaudeau; his sale, London, Sotheby Wilkinson & Hodge, 9 December 1889, lot 1142; Charles Fairfax Murray; J. Pierpont Morgan (no mark; see Lugt 1509).

BIBLIOGRAPHY: Fairfax Murray, III, no. 42, repr.; Ford 1948, p. 337; Ford 1951a, no. 20; Constable 1953, p. 156, pl. 11a; Grigson 1955, p. 173, no. 25; Sutton and Clements 1968, p. 5, fig. 5, repr.; Ford 1974, p. 419; Brown 1983, p. 290.

EXHIBITIONS: Detroit and Philadelphia 1968, pp. 32–33, no. 1; Cardiff, Wales 1969, no. 55; London and elsewhere 1982–83, no. 24, repr.; New York 1989.

The Pierpont Morgan Library. Purchased by J. Pierpont Morgan, 1910, Acc. no. III, 42

Thomas Jenkins, who was born in Rome, is said to have begun his artistic career studying painting in London under Thomas Hudson (1701-79). By 1753, he was back in Rome, and in that year Wilson and Jenkins were listed in the parish registers of San Lorenzo in Lucina as living together in a house near the north end of the Piazza di Spagna between the Via della Croce and the Via delle Carrozze (Ashby 1913, p. 488). The Library's drawing, with its informal yet elegant portrayal of Jenkins seated, was probably executed during this time. The traditional identification of the sitter as Jenkins is based on the inscription found on the verso.

Brinsley Ford has studied Jenkins's activities in Rome, showing that his accomplishments as a banker, dealer, and agent rapidly overshadowed his work as an artist. Nevertheless, he points out that Jenkins continued to paint and was always recorded as a painter. In 1757 Jenkins was elected a fellow of the Society of Antiquaries in London where he was described as a student of painting in Rome (Pierce 1965, pp. 200–29). He was elected a member of the Accademia di San Luca in 1761, and that same year became a member of the Florentine Academy. Ironically, Wilson himself had aspired to membership in the Accademia di San Luca but was never elected. In Rome, Jenkins was closely associated with Clement XIV, and his knowledge of antique sculpture, coins, and gems was said to be respected by Cardinal Albani, Winckelmann, and the German neoclassical portraitist Anton Raphael Mengs. Jenkins also became an important supplier of antiquities for many English collectors, including the second earl of Dartmouth and Charles Townley. Jenkins's reputation as an entrepreneur is undermined by accounts of his duplicity in restoring marble statues and supplying foreign visitors with fake intaglios and cameos.

Apparently Jenkins also used his influence to manipulate commissions awarded to other British artists. It was probably through him, for example, that Wilson received his commission from Lord Dartmouth to paint two landscapes and produce a series of finished drawings of Rome and its environs (Ford 1974, p. 418). It is interesting to note that the present drawing was in the collection of William Lock, for whom Jenkins is known to have purchased art. Jenkins was also accused of attempting to take patronage away from certain artists. One John Parker, a history painter, wrote to his patron Lord Charlemont on 4 October 1758 that "Piranesi, Russel, Jenkins, and their crew ruined me last winter," claiming they had circulated rumors that lost him the patronage of certain English travelers (Ford 1974, p. 418). By the 1780s Jenkins's connections with English artists had dete-

NO. 68

riorated. In April of 1780, Thomas Jones remarked that attendance at Jenkins's annual Christmas dinner had sharply declined: "Mr Jenkins sat down to a Sumptuous Entertainment attended only by one Person – when he declared it sh'd be the last he should ever provide on the like Occasion –" (Jones, p. 98).

RICHARD WILSON

Penegoes, Montgomeryshire 1713?–Mold, Flintshire 1782

69. *The Roman Campagna with Peasants Dancing*

Black chalk and stump, lightly heightened with white, on gray paper. 11⅞ x 16¼ inches (289 x 412 mm). Watermark: fleur-de-lis within a circle.
Inscribed by Esdaile at lower left in pen and black ink, *1bx* and at lower right, *WE*; on verso at lower left, *1833 WE 1bx Dr Monro's sale* and at center, *Wilson*.

PROVENANCE: Dr. Thomas Monro; his sale, London, Christie's, 1 July 1833, possibly part of lot 140; William Es-

NO. 69

daile (Lugt 2617); Charles Fairfax Murray; J. Pierpont Morgan (no mark; see Lugt 1509).

BIBLIOGRAPHY: Fairfax Murray, III, no. 40, repr.; Constable 1953, p. 217.

EXHIBITION: New York 1989.

The Pierpont Morgan Library. Purchased by J. Pierpont Morgan, 1910, Acc. no. III, 40

While the left side of the drawing is somewhat rubbed and difficult to read, the delicately sketched mountains and the lively handling of the figures add considerably to the charm of the sheet. The figures are quite similar to those in the series of drawings made between 1754 and 1755 for the second earl of Dartmouth. The lithe treatment of the dancing woman, shown leaning back with her left hand on her hip, is similar to a reclining woman who appears in Wilson's Italian sketchbook of 1754 (London 1978, p. 244). The manner in which the torso of each of these figures is drawn is particularly comparable. Other graphic mannerisms, such as the delineation of the grass and plants in the foreground and the shorthand method of sketching in the details in the middle ground, are also characteristic of Wilson's drawings made in Italy during the mid-1750s.

Long after his return to England, Wilson depicted peasants dancing at a river mouth in several paintings, including one in the Victoria and Albert Museum, London, and another in the Bayerische Staatsgemäldesammlungen, Munich. These two pictures have been dated to the early 1770s, and as David Solkin points out, they constitute one of Wilson's "last major articulations of a subject that had preoccupied him since he visited Italy" (London and elsewhere 1982–83, p. 244). W. G. Constable refers to the Library's drawing under his discussion of Wilson's various paintings of river landscapes with peasants dancing. Although the figures are reminiscent of those in the drawing, as are, in a general way, the outlines of the mountains in the background and the configuration of trees framing the composition, the similarities largely end there.

ROBERT ADAM
Edinburgh 1728–London 1792

70. *Album of Landscape Compositions*

79 leaves with drawings on 39 of them; 16 leaves cut out. Pen and black and brown ink, gray wash, occasionally pencil and chalk and white heightening, on gray prepared paper. Bound in contemporary vellum; three ties no longer present. Binding: 17 x 11½ inches (430 x 292 mm); leaves: 16¹¹⁄₁₆ x 11 inches (424 x 280 mm). Watermark: fleur-de-lis in a double circle.

Inscribed on the spine (partially effaced), *Design[s]/on/ [ti]nted /[P]aper by/R ADA[M]*; inscribed in pen and brown ink on verso of front free endpaper by the artist's youngest brother William Adam, *Contents of this Volume/39 Designs on Tinted papers/by R Adam*.

PROVENANCE: possibly Sir Walter Gilbey; B. T. Batsford, Ltd., Booksellers & Publishers, London; purchased in 1916 by Mrs. J. P. Morgan.

BIBLIOGRAPHY: Morgan Library *FR* VI, 1955, pp. 74–75; Fleming 1960, p. 190, note 11; p. 187, fig. 2 (album p. 9); pp. 191, 194; McCormick and Fleming 1962, p. 243, fig. 9 (album p. 24); Fleming 1962, pls. 72, 73 (album pp. 18, 22); Morgan Library *Review* 1969, p. 129; Harris 1971, p. 10, pl. 9 (album p. 18); Edinburgh 1972, p. 1, under Cat. no. 15; Tait 1978a, p. 56, pl. 39 (album p. 22); McCormick 1990, p. 43, note 63.

EXHIBITIONS: Philadelphia and Detroit 1960, no. 1; New York 1989.

The Pierpont Morgan Library. Gift of Junius S. and Henry S. Morgan, Acc. no. 1954.14

The drawings in the album range from relatively finished works to sketches that are very summarily indicated, usually in white or black chalk. Of the album's seventy-nine leaves, only thirty-nine bear drawings. At some point seventeen leaves were cut out of the album, indicating there were originally ninety-six leaves. A. A. Tait has pointed out that the title inscribed in the front of the album was written by Robert's youngest brother, William Adam, who han-

dled the Adam estate for the sales of 1818 and 1822. Between 1816 and 1818, Adam organized his brother's drawings for sale, and it may have been during this time that the sixteen leaves were removed (see Tait 1978 for a discussion of the organization of these sales). With two exceptions, the album contains a series of imaginative designs, including picturesque ruins, rustic bridges, parasol pines, cypresses, and waterfalls. On page 2, there is a black chalk figure copied from the procession on the north side of the Ara Pacis, and on page 34, a black chalk sketch for an ornamental design. Both the subject matter and the Italian watermark of the paper suggest that the drawings were made sometime after Adam's arrival in Italy.

In October of 1754, Adam left Edinburgh to go abroad, traveling with the Hon. Charles Hope who undertook most of the expense. In January of 1755, Adam reached Florence where he was introduced to the French architect and draughtsman Charles-Louis Clérisseau. He was greatly impressed by Clérisseau, and shortly thereafter wrote to his brother James that he planned to retain the French artist as his teacher, remarking: "I wish above all things to learn his manner, to have him with me at Rome, to study close with him and to purchase of his works. What I wished for I obtained. He took a liking to me" (19 February 1754; Fleming 1962, p. 135). Adam arrived in Rome in February; he was introduced to Piranesi, probably through Clérisseau. In his letters to his family, Adam discussed the friendship that developed between them. He described expeditions made in the company of Piranesi, Clérisseau, and Laurent Pécheux (who instructed Adam in figure drawing), referring to them as his "three friends cronys and Instructors." Adam also wrote his family of Piranesi's intention to dedicate to him a map of ancient Rome (see Cat. no. 61). The archaeological expeditions that Adam made with Clérisseau and Piranesi not only had an immediate impact on his work but ultimately inspired him to become the leader of the neoclassical style in England.

Clérisseau, who had been a student at the French Academy in Rome, initially set his pupil to copying

NO. 70   fol. 5

fol. 6

fol. 18

works of art. Adam wrote to James that Clérisseau had instructed him to "forbear inventing or composing either plans or elevations till I have a greater fund" (4 July 1755; McCormick 1990, pp. 25ff., no. 13). Referring to an earlier suggestion by his brother to publish his designs for gardens with ruins, Adam commented:

> I wrote my mother that I had fully considered your proposal of publishing some views in the taste of gardens and gave my reasons against it, which I am convinced you will think reasonable. . . . I have nevertheless been applying myself to these kind of sketches and have already made out a dozen of different views as unlike one another as I could and I hope [they] will prove of use to one, as it will show that I can carry that affair to a greater length than Kent and his disciples have yet brought it, as I have a greater ease in drawing and disposing of trees and buildings and ruins picturesquely which Kent was not quite master of as all his trees are perpendicular and stiff and his ruins good for nothing (26 November 1756; Fleming 1960, p. 362).

John Fleming has pointed out that Adam's description of his picturesque inventions comes very close to the kind of drawings found in the Library's album; other drawings of this type are in the collections of Sir John Clerk of Penicuik, the Sir John Soane's Museum, the Victoria and Albert Museum, and the Metropolitan Museum of Art (Fleming 1960, p. 194). In fact, the vaulted room of a ruin represented on page 6 of the Library's album is identical to one of the Clerk drawings by Adam, *Design for a Park with Artificial Ruins*, although the Library's drawing has a rotunda-like structure attached. The sheet is also less finished and smaller than the Clerk drawing. The general disposition of the composition, with a central ruin and a distant view of a bridge (or in the case of the Clerk drawing, a round temple), is extremely similar. Most of the compositions in the Library's album, in their careful drawing and description of ruins set in idyllic landscapes, reveal Clérisseau's influence. The scene on page 5, however, much more energetic and grand in conception with water rushing through a maze of vaulted ruins, suggests a Piranesian influence.

ROBERT ADAM

Edinburgh 1728–London 1792

71. *Imaginary Landscape with Classical Ruins*

Pen and black and brown ink, gray wash on gray-prepared paper. 10³⁄₁₆ x 16¹¹⁄₁₆ inches (257 x 424 mm). Watermark: none.

Numbered at upper left in pen and brown ink, *67*.

PROVENANCE: Bernard Houthakker, Amsterdam.

BIBLIOGRAPHY: Morgan Library *Review* 1969, p. 129; Harris 1971, p. 10.

EXHIBITIONS: St. Louis 1984, no. 5; New York 1989.

The Pierpont Morgan Library. Purchased as the gift of the Fellows, Acc. no. 1961.39

The size of this sheet and the similarity of the paper, especially the manner in which it was prepared with a gray wash, suggests that it may have been removed either from the Library's Adam album, which is missing sixteen leaves (Cat no. 70), or from another comparable album. Although executed in the same technique, the present drawing is somewhat more finished than those in the Library's album. As A. A. Tait has noted, William Adam and Susanna Clerk (daughter of John Clerk of Eldin, Robert Adam's brother-in-law) dismembered many of Adam's albums and sketchbooks in preparation for sale, often numbering the drawings in the process (Tait 1978, p. 453). This might explain the presence of the number 67 on this sheet.

NO. 72

THOMAS JONES

Aberedw (Radnorshire, Wales) 1742–Penkerrig, Radnorshire 1803

72. *View of the Villa of Maecenas and the Villa d'Este at Tivoli*

Watercolor and some gouache over graphite. 11¼ x 16¹⁵⁄₁₆ inches (286 x 429 mm). Watermark: none.

Signed, inscribed, and dated in sky, *Ruins of Mecenas's Villa & the Villa d'Este at Tivoli. T. Jones 1777*; variously inscribed with color notes.

PROVENANCE: possibly Mrs. Bethea Adams; her sale, London, Sotheby's, 26 July 1961, lot 61; Thos. Agnew & Sons Ltd., London.

BIBLIOGRAPHY: London 1990, no. 9, repr.

EXHIBITION: New York 1989.

The Pierpont Morgan Library. Purchased on the Martha Crawford von Bulow Fund, Acc. no. 1990.15

In November of 1798, Thomas Jones completed his *Memoirs*, which were largely based on a diary he had kept for many years. Although primarily accounts of his life and travels in Italy, the *Memoirs* also provide a lively picture of Jones's relations with other English artists. He discusses the formal training he received in London from Richard Wilson between 1763 and 1765. As Wilson's pupil, he spent the first year copying his master's work (see Cat. no. 67), and it is likely that he came to know his views of Tivoli. Wilson depicted the subject a number of times in his paintings and drawings; indeed, two pictures, *The Cascatelli Grandi and the Villa of Maecenas*, and *The Temple of the Sibyl and the Campagna*, painted on commission in 1752, are Wilson's earliest-known paintings of actual Italian scenery (London and elsewhere 1982–83, pp. 181–83). Through his study of Wilson's work, Jones would have been well acquainted with Italian landscape before traveling to Italy, and it may be that once there, he looked at the landscape through Wilson's eyes. Jones describes the impact—both conscious and unconscious—that Wilson's Italian subjects had on him, remarking:

> In fact I had copied so many Studies of that great Man, & my Old Master, Richard Wilson, which he had made here as in Other parts of Italy, that I insensibly became familiarized with Italian scenes, and enamoured of Ital-

ian forms, and, I suppose, injoyed pleasures unfelt by my Companions (Jones, p. 55).

Although this particular drawing was not executed until 1777, about twelve years after Jones had studied with Wilson, the composition, style, and restrained tonalities are reminiscent of Wilson's landscape drawings. Using pencil, Jones first carefully drew the architectural details across the middle of the sheet, finishing the composition by adding the classical framing device of a tree on the left. Both these formal qualities and to an extent the treatment of the foliage show Wilson's influence. The calculated addition of a tree is suggested by Jones's comment regarding the waterfalls: "But here is wanting the large Umbrageous Tree–to deck the foreground" (Jones, p. 55). Although Jones's use of watercolor departs from Wilson's standard black chalk technique, his almost monochromatic palette of blue-gray watercolor evokes the subdued tonalities of his master's chalk drawings. Jones's careful notes about color suggest he may have intended to make a painting of the subject.

Jones arrived in Tivoli on 9 November 1777 and remained there making sketches for about seven days. His own description of Tivoli and its landscape corresponds closely to what is depicted in this view:

> At Tivoli–the foaming Torrents rush down the Precipices into the deep Abyss with a fearful Noise and horrid Grandeur–The immense Masses of Stone rise abrupt–luxuriantly fringed with Shrubs, and crowned with antique towers and Temples–where the perpendicular & hanging Sides admit of no vegetation, & you discover the naked Rock–the Eye is charmed with the most beautiful variegated Tints–White, Grey, Red & Yellow–opposing, or blending their different Dyes together–(Jones, pp. 66–67).

Other watercolors by Jones of the same subject, all of a similar size, are in the Fitzwilliam Museum, Cambridge; the Yale Center for British Art, New Haven; and the National Museum of Wales, Cardiff (see Manchester, England 1988, nos. 50 and 51). Another watercolor, with a view taken from almost the same spot as the Library's drawing, is owned by Colnaghi.

JOHN BROWN
Edinburgh 1749–Edinburgh 1787

73. *The Cave of Dionysius, Syracuse*

Pen and brown ink and pencil. 18⅛ x 10¾ inches (460 x 273 mm). Watermark: fragment of a Strassburg bend and lily. Signed, dated, and inscribed on the mount, *The cave of Dionysius Syracuse July ye 10th 1772–John Brown Fecit p^r. W Young E-.*

PROVENANCE: sale, London, Christie's, 8 July 1986, lot 7, repr.

BIBLIOGRAPHY: Powell 1952, p. 42.

EXHIBITIONS: London, Royal Academy 1774, no. 18; New York 1989.

Collection of Eugene Victor and Clare Thaw

In October of 1769, John Brown left London for Italy, traveling with his friend and fellow-artist David Erskine. During Brown's stay in Italy he became part of a circle of artists closely connected with Henry Fuseli. Among them was Alexander Runciman, who had left Edinburgh for Rome in March of 1767 and whom Brown presumably had known in Edinburgh in the 1760s. It was probably through Runciman that Brown first met Fuseli. A number of portraits that testify to the friendship between Brown and Runciman survive, including a pencil drawing by Brown showing Runciman resting his head on his crossed hands (National Gallery of Scotland, Edinburgh). One of Runciman's last paintings was a double portrait of himself with John Brown made for the earl of Buchan in 1784.

The only works by Brown known today are drawings. According to Brown's friend and supporter James Burnett, Lord Monboddo, who was assisted by the artist in producing *The Origin and Progress of Language*, Brown considered drawing to be the only important part of visual art. His drawings of genre scenes and depictions of Roman women are the best-known works from his Roman period, although it is clear from *The Cave of Dionysius* and other recorded drawings that landscape was also an important part of his oeuvre. Apparently he also made pencil portraits while in Rome, one said to be the head of Pira-

NO. 73

year MDCCLXXII, ten copies of which were privately printed sometime before March of 1774. The manuscript of the journal, which includes Young's sketches, survives in a private collection (see Sir Brinsley Ford's Grand Tour Archive at the Paul Mellon Centre for Studies in British Art, London). It opens on 17 April 1772, and by June the travelers had crossed to Sicily. Toward the end of July they were continuing their travels to Malta and Gozo. The drawing exhibited here was made on 10 July 1772. Two views of the Temple of Agrigentum by Brown, now in the British Museum, were also executed on this trip. One view was dated 3 August 1772 (Acc. nos. 1983–1–27–2,3).

Brown exhibited *The Cave of Dionysius* at the Royal Academy in 1774 along with a *View of the Colosseum, Rome.* In style and technique, the Thaw sheet is very similar to Brown's drawing *The Basilica of Maxentius and Constantine* in the National Gallery of Scotland. Both are highly finished, with very dense, precise penwork quite different from Brown's other works. The existence of these landscape drawings suggests that at the outset of his career Brown had a strong interest in landscape. This is further confirmed in a letter written to his father from London in 1769, where he mentions that he owned a camera obscura which he described as "useful and even necessary to a landscape painter" (New Haven 1979, p. 55). The Thaw drawing is a vivid interpretation of a romantic subject made all the more intriguing by the addition of a brooding figure who sits on a stone to the left of the cave, and a small cloaked figure shown standing inside the mouth of the cave dramatically gesturing with his arms. The vertical format of the sheet diminishes the size of the figures while emphasizing the opening of the cave. Although the scene has an imaginary quality to it, the rock formations are quite close to the actual appearance of the cave, which since Caravaggio's time has been referred to as "l'Orecchio di Dionigi." The careful penwork, particularly evident in the parallel hatching used to suggest gradations of light and shade, is similar to effects obtained in etchings. Indeed, the handling of the vines and trees that frame the scene is reminiscent of Piranesi's prints, which Brown must have seen.

nesi (Gray 1889, p. 311). After Brown's return to Edinburgh by May of 1781, he began drawing both life-size and miniature portraits. Later that year he received a commission from Lord Buchan, founder of the Society of Antiquaries in Scotland, to make pencil portraits of many of its members. In 1786, Brown went to London, where he drew portraits of members of the royal family and where Charles Townley commissioned him to record his collection of marbles.

This commission was not the first time that Brown had worked for him. Earlier he had accompanied Townley and Sir William Young on their antiquarian tour of Italy. Sir William kept a journal during the tour, *A Journal of a Summer's Excursion, by the road of Montecasino to Naples, and from thence over all the southern parts of Italy, Sicily, and Malta in the*

JOHN BROWN

Edinburgh 1749–Edinburgh 1787

74. *The Dagger Merchant*

Brush and black wash, some pen and black ink, graphite. Verso: Faint sketches of a lizard and the back of a woman, in graphite. 10³⁄₁₆ x 12½ inches (258 x 319 mm). Watermark: none.

Signed at lower left in pen and brown ink, *John Brown Romae.* Numbered on verso at upper right corner in graphite, *56* and at right center, *37*.

PROVENANCE: William Young Ottley; his sale, London, T. Philipe, 11 April 1804, lot 46; Léon Suzor, Paris; sale, Paris, Hôtel Drouot, 16 March 1966, lot 3; Mr. and Mrs. Eugene Victor Thaw, New York.

BIBLIOGRAPHY: Powell 1952, p. 47; Morgan Library *FR* XVI, 1973, p. 110; MacMillan 1986, p. 62; Andersen 1989, p. 33, repr.

EXHIBITIONS: New York and elsewhere 1975–76, no. 69, repr.; New Haven 1979, no. 57, repr.; New York 1989.

The Pierpont Morgan Library. Gift of Mr. and Mrs. Eugene Victor Thaw, Acc. no. 1971.9

This drawing, probably executed after Brown's return from Sicily, has a sinister atmosphere characteristic of the artist's Roman genre scenes. The figures are silhouetted against a dark background, and the lack of setting enhances the mystery surrounding the transaction. By using the white of the paper to highlight the face of the dagger merchant and his gestures, Brown emphasizes the dramatic center of action in the composition. The faces of the figures are carefully and distinctly defined with the pen, while the figures themselves are rendered with broad, boldly applied wash, which tends to simplify and flatten the drapery and forms. Many such characteristics, including the simplification of forms and the use of dramatic gestures to convey the emotional character of the subject, were traits common to artists associated with the style evolved by the Fuseli circle in Rome.

Brown's care in defining the faces of each of the figures demonstrates another connection to Fuseli. These heads can scarcely be described as portrait

NO. 74

studies. Rather, they are typical of Brown's fascination with drawing character heads at which he was supposed to be particularly adept, "frequently following a remarkable character day after day until he completely succeeded in obtaining his resemblance and character" (New Haven 1979, p. 56). It has been pointed out that Brown's interest in physiognomy may have been encouraged by his association with Fuseli who had made many drawings for Lavater's *Essays on Physiognomy*.

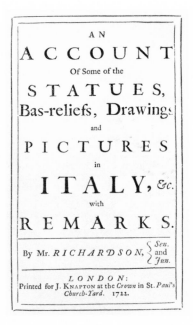

JONATHAN RICHARDSON, SR.
London 1665–London 1745

JONATHAN RICHARDSON, JR.
London 1694–London 1771

75. *An Account of Some of the Statues, Bas-reliefs, Drawings and Pictures in Italy, etc. with Remarks*

London: Printed for J. Knapton at the Crown in St. Paul's Churchyard, 1722.

PROVENANCE: Lord Derby (inscribed on flyleaf).

EXHIBITION: New York 1989.

Giannalisa Feltrinelli Collection, on deposit at The Pierpont Morgan Library (862)

Jonathan Richardson, Jr., son of the portrait painter, visited Italy in 1721. His account describing the art of Italy was written in collaboration with his father and was first published in 1722. In the preface, Richardson's father notes that the book was compiled from the frequent letters that his son had written to him while abroad. Richardson further comments that he expanded on his son's remarks by comparing his observations with other published accounts of Italy,

drawing attention to the fact that in some cases he is describing objects that he has never even seen:

> That I should write upon what I never saw, may appear strange to some; such may please only to observe that My Remarks are Chiefly upon the way of Thinking; which is seen in a Print, or a Drawing, as well as in the Thing itself; These I am well furnish'd with, particularly for those famous Works of the *Vatican* just now mention'd: *Bellori* has moreover describ'd 'em very minutely, and exactly; I mean as to the Figures of each Picture. I remark then on what I have Seen; for the Little that remains on which my Remarks are made, Evidence has been to me instead of Eyes, as it must be in Matters of the greatest Importance.

His introductory remarks are followed by lists of works of art, artists, and antiques. In addition to describing the splendors of Rome, Jonathan Richardson, Jr. also spent a great deal of time in the Tribuna in Florence where he was busy "considering the beauties of the Statues there, and continually found something new to admire" (Haskell and Penny 1981, p. 61).

As Francis Haskell and Nicholas Penny point out, the Richardsons' account of Italy was translated into French six years later and published in Amsterdam. The two authors acknowledge the help they received from the translator, A. Rutgers the Younger, and from the Dutch connoisseur L. H. ten Kate. The additions made to the book would ultimately be of primary importance to the reinterpretation of antique sculpture. The Richardsons emphasized the significance of antique sculpture that had been lost, and discussed the problems of authenticity raised by the survival of numerous antique versions of the same sculpture, such as the *Farnese Hercules.* They concluded that all surviving versions were probably copies of lost originals, comparing the surviving statues to a few volumes washed ashore after a great library had perished at sea. The volumes that survived, they said, were damaged and imperfect editions of earlier texts (Haskell and Penny 1981, pp. 99–100). The Richardsons' conclusions about antique sculpture were only accepted toward the end of the eighteenth century, chiefly in the work of Johann Joachim Winckelmann.

ROBERT ADAM

Edinburgh 1728–London 1792

76. *Autograph letter signed, Augsburg, 18 November 1757, to Messrs. Innes & Clerk*

EXHIBITION: New York 1989.

The Pierpont Morgan Library

By the time this letter, addressed to his London agents, Innes and Clerk, was written, Robert Adam had essentially completed his Grand Tour and was on his way home. He wrote from Augsburg where he planned to "repose for a day or two & then set out for Franckfort." Adam writes of a purchase he hoped to make while in Venice. "I think I mention'd to you in one of my Letters from Vicenza that my Female Venetian Bankeressa had intention to draw on you for £108 or 10 Sterl[ing] which was on account of a Bargain I had made with a Venetian noble, But alas they repented of their Resolution to Sell, entirely changed their minds & even refused more money which I had agreed to give them." Adam continues that he has not lost hope that the purchase may still take place, and that Innes and Clerk should be prepared for this possibility.

Adam first began collecting works of art when he was in Florence, and it was probably under the guidance of the painter and *marchand amateur* Ignazio Hugford (1703-78) that he made his first purchases. At this point he primarily bought drawings by the old masters and several small pictures, but when he arrived in Rome, he began collecting antiquities as well. On 26 January 1756, Adam commented: "[I am] augmenting every day my collection of antique cornices, friezes, figures, bas-reliefs, vases, altars, so that I have now a room as full as it can stick from the roof to the floor" (Fleming 1962, p. 362). Many of his purchases in Italy were clearly speculative, and he often considered the profit to be made on their future sale. A number of years later in London, for example, Adam held a sale at Prestage, 14–16 February 1765, and at Christie's, 25–27 February and 1–2 March 1773,

where he sold paintings, sculpture, and drawings that he had purchased in Italy (see Lugt 1426 and 2123).

NO. 76 First and last pages of four-page letter.

DOMENICO CUNEGO, engraver

Verona 1726–Rome 1803

77. *The Interior of the Temple of Jupiter*

in Robert Adam, Ruins of the Palace of the Emperor Diocletian at Spalatro in Dalmatia *[London], printed for The Author, 1764*

Etching and engraving (pl. XXXIII). Platemark: 18½ x 14³⁄₁₆ inches (470 x 360 mm); page: 21⅝ x 14⅜ inches (549 x 366 mm).

Signed at lower right, *Dom.ᵉ Cunego Sculp.*; inscribed with title, *View of the Inside of the Temple of Jupiter* and at upper right corner, *Plate XXXIII.*

BINDING: late nineteenth or early twentieth century, with modern endpapers; boards of the cover are faced with brown, blue and orange marbled paper with brown leather corners. Spine: brown leather stamped in gold *RUINS/OF/ SPALAT.*

WATERMARKS: fleur-de-lis in a double circle with letter *C* above and letter *M* below (title page); fleur-de-lis in a circle with flower bud above (pls. XLIII, XXXVIII, XXXIX); fleur-de-lis in a circle (pl. XXXVIII).

PROVENANCE: William Russell Mogg, Easton Park, England; Ben Weinreb Architectural Books, Ltd., London.

Montréal, Centre Canadien d'Architecture/Canadian Centre for Architecture, WM792 CAGE

Binding designed by Robert Adam

for Ruins of the Palace of the Emperor Diocletian at Spalatro in Dalmatia

Red goatskin, gold tooled with an outer border of palmettes surrounding a large dentelle of acanthus foliage enclosing conches, military trophies, male and female herms, tridents, and neoclassical palmettes; center: oval medallion enclosing arms of George III. Spine: seven raised bands, gold tooled, with title in second compartment, stamped in gold *RUINS/OF/SPALATRO.* Gilt edges. Marbled endpapers.

BINDING: 21⅛ x 15¼ inches (536 x 388 mm).

PROVENANCE: J. Pearson & Co., London.

BIBLIOGRAPHY: (Morgan) Pearson, English Royal Bindings, pl. [42]; Nixon 1978, under no. 70

EXHIBITIONS: Baltimore 1957–58, no. 499; New York 1989.

The Pierpont Morgan Library. Purchased by J. Pierpont Morgan, 1905, PML 125602

Robert Adam regarded archaeological publications such as this one to be the means of establishing his reputation as an architect in England (see Fleming 1958, pp. 103ff.; McCormick 1990; Edinburgh 1992). The *Ruins of the Palace of the Emperor Diocletian at Spalatro* was not the first publication that the artist undertook, but it was the first that he completed. In 1755, Adam had planned to revise Antoine Desgodetz's *Les edifices antiques de Rome;* although drawings were made and Piranesi was hired to prepare the plates, the project was all but abandoned the following year. After considering several other projects, Adam decided to publish views of Diocletian's palace at Spalato. It is interesting that in 1748, in his *Alcune vedute di archi Trionfali ed altri monumenti,* Piranesi had included a view of the Temple of Clitumnus at Spalato, plate 26 (London 1978, p. 31).

The Emperor Diocletian's palace is located in Spalato (Split), today part of Croatia, on the Dalmatian coast of the Adriatic Sea. Adam, Clérisseau, and two other draughtsmen, Agostino Brunias (active 1752–1810) and Laurent-Benoît Dewez (1731–1812), spent five weeks there drawing and measuring the ruins. They arrived in Spalato on 22 July 1757 and left on 28 August. After the group returned to Venice, Adam set out for Germany (on his way back to England), leaving Clérisseau in Venice to complete the drawings for the plates and to supervise the engraving.

In the summer of 1760, Robert Adam's brother James traveled to Italy to oversee work on the Spalato project and to study with Clérisseau, as his brother Robert had done before him. The correspondence between the Adam brothers during this time makes it clear that they considered Clérisseau simply to be in their employ, and, accordingly, they chose to play down his role as artist in the project. Much to the dismay of Robert, however, Clérisseau told certain Eng-

View of the Inside of the Temple of Jupiter

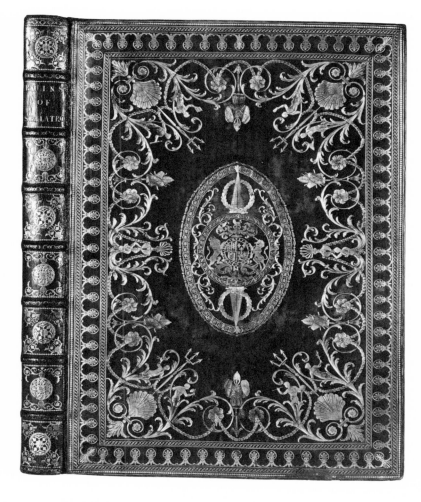

NO. 77

lishmen about the drawings he had prepared for the book. On 24 July 1760, Robert wrote to James from London about a letter he had received from Mr. Smith (Consul Smith), who "pays the highest flummery you can imagine first of me then of Clerisseau and then of your great character and how he longs for you. I am sorry at several of his impressions which shows how little precaution your messmate has taken to conceal his having drawn the view of Spalatro. As Smith terms them those very fine drawings done by Mr. C– under your eye. This he I mean C– has out of vanity I find told to all the English he could lay his hands on . . . and all of them may and I dont doubt but do give it out that all the drawings are Cl–'s and how can it be otherwise when he wishes it should be known. This only leads me to ask you a question, how can I put R.A. delint. at the bottom of the plates when

Cl– has told the contrary" (McCormick 1990, p. 65). There is much correspondence between the brothers about this problem, and in the end a decision was made to include only the engravers' names below the plates, the implication being that they were drawn by Adam.

It is clear from the correspondence and from a group of surviving drawings by Clérisseau (which range from sketches made on the spot to finished drawings probably intended for the engravings) that he played a major role in the production of the book. A drawing by Clérisseau of the interior of the Mausoleum is a typical example of his drawings executed at the site (McCormick 1990, fig. 73). McCormick has pointed out that Clérisseau altered a number of details, but that in general the drawing is very close to how the building appeared in 1757. The engraving depicting the *Temple of Jupiter* (Interior, Mausoleum), which is taken from a different point of view from this drawing, may have been based on a similar sketch by Clérisseau.

It is interesting that Clérisseau's name appears only three times in the book: in the introduction Adam acknowledges that Clérisseau had accompanied him on the expedition, and Clérisseau's name is listed as one of the foreign subscribers to the book. However, Clérisseau—perhaps in an ironic gesture— managed to include his own name once more: IQED IACET CORPUS CLERISSI PICTOR appears in an engraved inscription on a sarcophagus outside the entry to the Temple of Jupiter (plate XXVIII). The first letters of the inscription, *IQED*, seem to be nonsense, and similarly, the inscription on the sarcophagus to the right is indecipherable. Perhaps Clérisseau intentionally added these nonsensical inscriptions in order to mask his self-reference. The inclusion of the word "corpus" may allude both to a human body and a body of works, lending a certain wry humor to the inscription.

The *Ruins of Spalatro* was completed by early 1762, but was not published until 1764. We know that the design of the title page was not decided upon until 6 December 1763. As W. H. Bond has observed, Thomas Hollis, who was an early subscriber to Adam's book, recorded in his diary a consultation by the printer, William Strahan, Jr., on 6 December to design "the Title of a book . . . after the manner of an antient inscription, which was settled accordingly." Strahan returned a day later to show the final proof, and the book was published with a Hollis title page (Bond 1990, pp. 103 and 107).

The careful planning and presentation of the book was also expressed in its outward appearance, which was integral to Adam's conception of the book as a whole. As Howard Nixon and Iain Gordon Brown point out, the bindings that Adam produced for the book appear in four colors and in varying states of elaboration. The system of color coding and graded ornamentation seems to fall into the following categories: the red morocco copies appear to have been intended for members of the royal family or institu-

tions enjoying royal patronage; the existence of one copy in blue and one in green may refer to the Knights of the Garter and Knights of the Thistle respectively, who received copies bound in the colors of their orders. All of these have a central panel, oval or hexagonal, enclosing the arms of King George III. The brown mottled-calf bindings, which have a simple palmette border only, were presumably intended for friends and patrons of a lesser rank (Brown 1993, p. 10).

The Morgan Library's copy of the book, which displays one of the most elaborate decorative patterns, is bound in red morocco with border, dentelle, and an oval center ornament carrying the royal coat of arms. Underneath the oval, scorings for the hexagon and erased gilding can be seen on the leather (Baltimore 1957–58, p. 199). The provenance of the Library's copy before Pearson is unknown, and it is therefore difficult to establish for which royal patron or institution it may have been intended. The only clue appears to be the unidentified shelf marks, *B VI / N.º 13*, inscribed in red ink on the verso of the first free front endpaper. The same binding design with the oval surround appears in another copy, bound in green morocco, that may have belonged to the third earl of Bute and is now in the collection of J. Paul Getty, Jr. The dedication copy to George III and the almost identical Cracherode copy, both in the British Library, have a hexagonal center ornament with the royal arms. Another red copy, with the royal arms in an oval, and with the palmette border, but no dentelle, was presented by Adam to the Royal Academy in 1769 (Nixon 1978, under no. 70). The central ornaments were probably derived from the Roman trophies of Marius found on the balustrade of the Campidoglio on the Capitol; they were published by Piranesi in his *I Trofei di Ottaviano Augusto* of 1753 (Brown 1993, p. 10). The design of the binding as a whole resembles Adam's neoclassical ceiling designs, and as Brown observes, it is easy to imagine when studying the binding that one is looking up at a ceiling. The most elaborate of these bindings share similar characteristics with Adam's dining room ceiling of Hatchlands circa 1759 (Brown 1993, p. 11).

78. *Collection of Etruscan, Greek, and Roman Antiquities*

from the Cabinet of the Honble. Wm. Hamilton his Britannick Majesty's Envoy Extraordinary at the Court of Naples. *4 vols., Naples: F. Morelli, 1766–67 Giannalisa Feltrinelli Collection, on deposit at The Pierpont Morgan Library* (4406)

Sir William Hamilton was appointed the British envoy extraordinary and plenipotentiary at the court of Naples in 1764. In addition to his official duties, Hamilton was an acknowledged authority on the observation of volcanoes and the excavation of archaeological sites as well as a connoisseur and important collector of Greek vases (see Fothergill 1969 for an extensive study on Hamilton). He played an active role as a patron of contemporary artists and also collected old master pictures. In 1766 Hamilton was elected a fellow of the Royal Society, and in 1777 became a member of the Society of Dilettanti. He was also a fellow of the Society of Antiquaries. An astute observer of volcanic phenomena, Hamilton witnessed and described the eruptions of 1776 and 1777 at Vesuvius. His most important publication in this field was the *Campi Phlegraei*, subtitled *Observations on the Volcanoes of the Two Sicilies* (1776). Hamilton's collection of volcanic earths and materials was presented to the British Museum in 1767.

In 1766 Hamilton purchased a collection of Greek vases belonging to the Porcinari family. This eventually developed into a museum that by 1772 included more than seven hundred vases as well as terracottas, ancient glass, bronzes, ivories, antique gems, and coins. That same year Hamilton sold his collection to the trustees of the British Museum where it became the basis of the present department of Greek and Roman antiquities. Although Hamilton would afterward form another collection of Greek vases, most of which was purchased in 1801 by Thomas Hope, it

was this first collection that he published in 1766 and 1767. The text was written by the French author Pierre François Hugues, who wrote under the *nom de plume* D'Hancarville. In the first volume, the text was printed in both French and English (the English text being in italic and the French in roman, on facing pages) whereas in the three subsequent volumes only French was used. The plate section as a rule fol-

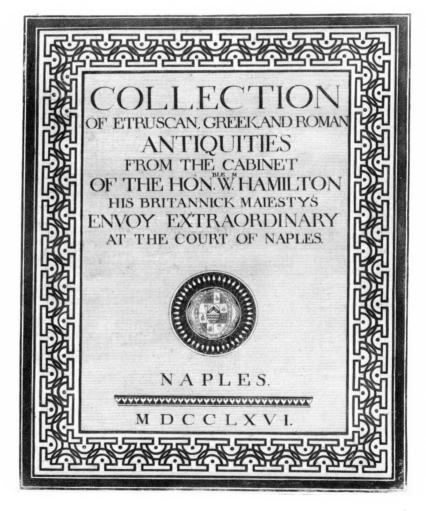

lowed the same layout – an etching of the vase in perspective, its elevation with measurements in *palmi romani*, interleaved with hand-colored antique figural scenes etched in two plates. The cost of printing and illustrating the first edition was undertaken by Hamilton.

Hamilton dedicated these volumes to King George III. The preface to the book makes it clear that Hamilton was committed to describing and reproducing the vases in as much detail as possible so that artists would be able to copy them exactly. It was this careful and accurate presentation that he felt would distinguish his publication from other earlier works and ultimately make the book most useful to contemporary artists:

> It is in this respect that the nature of our work may be considered as absolutely new, for no one has yet undertaken to search out what system the Ancients followed to give their Vases, that elegance which all the World acknowledges to be in them, to discover rules the observation of which conduct infallibly to their imitation, and in short to assign exact measures for fixing their proportions, in order, that the artist who would invent in the same stile, or only copy the Monuments which appeared to him worthy of being copied, may do so with as much truth and precision, as if he had the Originals themselves in his possession. It is by this means, that the present work may contribute to the advancement of the Arts, and make the master-pieces of Antiquity that are worthy of imitation understood as they deserve to be; for we believe it will be readily acknowledged that it is not sufficient to have a general idea of the vases of the Ancients, as they are given us in the Books of the Count de Caylus and Father Montfaulcon. These works at the utmost only shew what members the Ancients employed in the composition of their Vases, but do not indicate their relative proportions, and one should succeed as ill in copying them after these vague notions, as one should in attempting to imitate Greek Architecture with success, without having first studied its proportions (p. vi).

The idea that works of art should not only be admired and thoroughly understood, but must also be useful, was central to Hamilton's aesthetic theory. The preface ends:

> In every Art good models give birth to ideas by exciting the imagination, theory furnishes the means of expressing those ideas, practice puts these means in execution, and this last part which is always the most common is also the easiest. If we complete our design, we shall have done what is insisted upon by Longinus, who thinks with reason, that when one treats of an Art, the principal point consists in shewing how, and by what means, what we teach may be acquired.

While Hamilton clearly intended the book to serve as a practical inspiration to artists, he also recognized its potential to influence contemporary taste and design. The Greek themes and emphasis on purity of line had a direct influence on neoclassical painters. Hamilton also discussed the effect the book would have on the applied arts: "We think also, that we make an agreable present to our Manufacturers of earthen ware and China, and to those who make vases in silver, copper, glass, marble &c . . . they may draw ideas which their ability and taste will know how to improve to their advantage, and to that of the Public" (p. xviii). Even before the books were published, proofs of some of the plates were sent to Josiah Wedgwood at the time he was building his new factory; these proofs have been described as one of the earliest influences in forming Wedgwood's neoclassical style. In 1773, some seven years after the first volume was published, Hamilton sent Wedgwood and Bently some drawings of vases in the collection of the grand duke of Tuscany. He wrote: "As the originals are simply black, with the ornaments in relief, your own ware is capable of imitating them exactly" (8 June 1773) (Morrison 1885, vol. 2, pp. 229–30). He also refers to the expense of his earlier publication, remarking: "If it was not for the comfort I reap from seeing the proper use you have made of it, I should repent ever having meddled with it." Other recipients of Hamilton's volumes, one of whom was Sir Joshua Reynolds, the newly elected president of the Royal Academy, picked up on Hamilton's intentions, commenting on the usefulness of the book to antiquarians and the contribution it made to the advancement of the arts in general.

EDME BOUCHARDON

Chaumont 1698–Paris 1762

79. *Vade Mecum at Rome*

Sketchbook in two volumes and one small unbound gathering, comprising 147 drawings and sketches from ancient statues and paintings. Various media: chiefly red chalk, with some drawings in pen and brown ink, black chalk, or graphite. Binding, limp vellum: vol. I, 8⅛ x 5⁷⁄₁₆ inches (204 x 140 mm); vol. II, 7⅜ x 5⅛ inches (187 x 131 mm). Leaf: vol. I, approx. 7¾ x 5⁷⁄₁₆ inches (198 x 135 mm); vol. II, approx. 7¹⁄₁₆ x 5 inches (182 x 125 mm). Watermark: three hills within circle (cf. Heawood 2611).

PROVENANCE: P. J. Mariette; his sale, 1775, no. 1152 ("Un Portefeuille, contenante 90 dessins, faits à Rome, d'après différents Figures & Monuments antiques, à la sanguine, de petit in-fol."); purchased by Earl Gower (who inscribed in volume I, *Vade mecum de Bouchardon à Rome &c / acheté a* [sic] *la Vente de Mr Mariette*); De Bure, Paris; purchased in 1836 by the Duke of Sutherland (inscribed and signed by him in pen and brown ink on fly leaf *B: n.1698. élève de Coustou le jeune./étudia à Rome - mort à Paris 1762./ce livre fut acheté* [sic] *chez De Bure/à Paris 1836./Sutherland*; purchased from the Sutherland Library by Francis Harvey, London; from whom purchased in 1907 by J. Pierpont Morgan for £125 (no mark; see Lugt 1509).

EXHIBITIONS: New York 1984, no. 111; New York 1989; Paris and New York 1993, no. 45, repr.

The Pierpont Morgan Library. Purchased in 1907

The sculptor Bouchardon won the *prix de Rome* in 1722, becoming a *pensionnaire* at the French Academy in Rome in 1723. He remained there for some nine years before returning to France at the request of Louis XV. Advised and encouraged by Vleughels to go around the city and draw what Rome had to offer, Bouchardon made many careful sketches of statues and monuments in Rome. This sketchbook, his *Vade Mecum*, is executed primarily in red chalk (the artist's preferred medium) and includes sketches after many Renaissance and baroque monuments, including the Jonah in the Chigi chapel in Santa Maria del Popolo (which Raphael designed and Lorenzetti carried out), Maderno's statues of saints ornamenting San Andrea della Valle, and the Turtle Fountain in the Piazza Mattei, which dates to the sixteenth century. As might be expected, Bouchardon did not confine his study to Rome's earlier monuments, but also drew some of its newest monuments, including the sculpture for the tomb of Gregory XIII in St. Peter's which Camillo Rusconi had completed only in 1723.

Bouchardon began the second volume with a pencil sketch of a fountain by Giambattista Bologna and continued in red chalk with a number of studies of Roman portrait busts, many of which, today, are in the Vatican Museum but during the first half of the eighteenth century were still in the Palazzo Belvedere. This volume also includes some sketches of the Trevi Fountain. (Bouchardon actually entered the competition to complete the fountain.) The second volume also contains a striking portrait of a man resting his head in his hands. Although the eyes are closed, it is possible to recognize Bouchardon's face with its full-lipped mouth and aquiline nose.

There are no invented compositions in the *Vade Mecum*. Unlike the *pensionnaires* of the next generation, Bouchardon drew only what he saw. Since he was a sculptor he did not concern himself with pictorial composition. It should also be noted that the small size of these volumes does not really accommodate compositional drawing.

Although Bouchardon was considered one of the finest draughtsmen of his day by contemporaries, he never lost sight of his vocation as a sculptor. It was probably not in his nature to give free play to his imaginative bent and create compositions that mixed real and imaginary elements. While copies of paintings appear to some degree in the *Vade Mecum*, Bouchardon made only a few quick sketches of these in black chalk.

He is the only French sculptor of the eighteenth century for whom a considerable body of drawings exists: over thirteen hundred drawings by him are preserved in the Louvre. He drew constantly and his drawings were greatly prized by knowledgeable contemporaries such as P. J. Mariette and the comte de Caylus. Caylus, who was Bouchardon's friend for many years, commented on his draughtsmanship, recalling that Bouchardon acquired this facility in childhood and never allowed a day to pass without drawing. He noted that so great was Bouchardon's ability that he could draw an entire figure from head to toe without lifting his chalk. There is something in the accomplished manner and clean unbroken line of his drawings which is innovative for its time and looks ahead to the neoclassicism of the end of the century, even anticipating artists like Ingres.

CHARLES-JOSEPH NATOIRE
Nîmes 1700–Castel Gandolfo 1777

80. *A View of the Top of the Cascade at the Villa Aldobrandini, Frascati*

Pen and brown ink, brown wash, black and red chalk, heightened with white on blue paper; partial ruled border, in black chalk. 12¼ x 19⅞ inches (311 x 500 mm). Watermark: none visible through lining.
Signed and dated at lower right, in pen and brown ink, *C. Natoire/1762*; inscribed by the artist at lower center, *il didietro de la Cascata*. On the verso is a mutilated inscription in the artist's hand, *pour monsieur le marquis. . . .*

PROVENANCE: marquis de Marigny (Abel-François Poisson); his sale (as marquis de Menars), Paris, February 1782 (remise au mars 18, Lugt), lot 320, "Six differents veues de Jardins de Rome, a la plume, au bistre, & rehaussé de blanc au pinceau, sur papier bleu," Vestris; P. & D. Colnaghi and Co., London; private collection.

BIBLIOGRAPHY: Morgan Library *FR* XIV, 1967, pp. 125ff.; Duclaux 1975, under no. 55; New York 1981, under no. 101; Duclaux 1991, pp. 10, 11, no. 44.

EXHIBITIONS: London 1965, no. 20; New York 1984, no. 49; New York 1989.
Private collection, promised gift to The Pierpont Morgan Library

Natoire won the *prix de Rome* in 1721 and studied at the French Academy in Rome under the guidance of Nicolas Vleughels, director there from 1724 to 1737. It was under Vleughels, who encouraged drawing *en plein air*, that Natoire began to draw views of Rome. Much later, when Natoire himself became director (1751–75), he encouraged the study of landscape draughtsmanship among his students by practicing it himself. He continued to make these remarkable views of Rome and its environs throughout his life, probably under Pannini's influence. A Pannini-like sensibility is discernable in these lightly colored yet detailed landscapes. In June 1752, at the residence of the duc de Nivernois at Frascati, Natoire drew "quelques points de veue," remarking in a letter to the marquis de Marigny that he hoped to add to these works from time to time. Since the marquis, brother

of the marquise de Pompadour, was director of royal buildings, it was Natoire's obligation to make regular reports to him regarding academy affairs.

Again at Frascati ten years later, Natoire wrote to Marigny on 21 July 1762 that he was sending P. J. Mariette four drawings by Pannini, eight by Robert, and four sketches by Durameau. He added that he was also sending Marigny two drawings which he himself had made during his visit to Frascati—views of the cascade taken from two different aspects.

This drawing and one that the Morgan Library acquired at the same time in 1965 are the pair of drawings to which Natoire referred (fig. 1). Both views are worked in his distinctive mixture of pen and wash, colored chalks, and white heightening. Each is dated 1762 and the artist has inscribed the verso of this drawing, *pour monsieur le marquis. . . .* To make the drawing Natoire must have stood to the right of the Ionic columns marking the head of the cascade.

Two of the five views of this type preserved in the Louvre, namely *La Terrasse de Jardins Farnese sur le Mont Palatin avec a la Arrière-Plan la Ville de Rome* (Inv. 313382) and *Le Palais des Césars dans les Jardins Farnese sur le Mont Palatin a Rome* (Inv. 313883) must belong to the group mentioned in Natoire's letter to Marigny (30 May 1759) in which he mentions that he is sending four drawings of his own, two of which he wishes Marigny to choose for himself and to give the other two to Mariette (*Correspondance des directeurs*, XI, pp. 279, 282).

The most important holdings of drawings of this type by Natoire are at the Musée Atget, Montpellier; the Albertina, Vienna; and the Kunstbibliothek, Berlin.

FIGURE 1 Charles-Joseph Natoire, *The Cascade at the Villa Aldobrandini.* The Pierpont Morgan Library, New York. Purchased as the gift of the Fellows, 1965.

LOUIS-GABRIEL BLANCHET

Paris 1705–Rome 1772

81. *The Arch of Septimius Severus with the Church of SS. Luca and Martina Beyond*

Black chalk, heightened with white, on light brown paper. 15⅛ x 10⅜ inches (384 x 263 mm). Watermark: none visible through lining.

PROVENANCE: Sir John and Lady Witt; Shaunagh Fitzgerald Ltd., London.

EXHIBITIONS: London 1987, no. 27, repr.; New York 1989. *The Pierpont Morgan Library. Purchased as the gift of Countess Elsie Lee Gozzi*, Acc. no. 1988.12

Blanchet was awarded the *prix de Rome* in 1727, mar-

ried, and remained in Rome for the rest of his life. Although chiefly occupied with portraits and religious subjects, he also drew a number of landscapes of the city and its environs, using a soft black and white chalk on gray-green or light brown paper. Blanchet's chalk manner influenced the British artist Richard Wilson, who came to Rome in 1750 as the protégé of William Lock. In this drawing, the attribution to Blanchet is confirmed not only by the style of the work but also by the presence of the artist's signature and inscription on a drawing of this type in the Witt Collection. This drawing is of a Roman ruin and is signed and inscribed at the lower right, *L. G. Blanchet/d'après nature* (London 1968a, no. 28).

There is a curious problem that involves these drawings. Two hundred and seven views of Rome, by far the largest group of related drawings, have been preserved at Eton College since 1945 and identified by the eighteenth-century collector John Peachey (1749–1816) as the work of Etienne Parrocel, one of a well-known family of artists. Peachey attended Eton College (1759–61) and went to Rome before 1779, the year that he became a member of the Society of Dilettanti. According to Cust, he "had been captivated by the remains of classic antiquity, and had formed a small collection of marbles under the auspices of Thomas Jenkins and Gavin Hamilton." He must also have been in contact with Piranesi, who dedicated a plate in *Vasi, candelabri, cippi* (1778) to him. Since Peachey bought the drawings from Lock in 1777 after his return from the Grand Tour, the misidentification of the artist as Parrocel may have come from Lock. That this identification is wrong is confirmed by experts on Blanchet and Etienne Parrocel alike. Scholars working on both artists think that the drawing is certainly by Blanchet and not at all typical of Parrocel. All the drawings involved, namely those at Eton as well as the Morgan Library's drawing and others, formerly in the collection of Sir John and Lady Witt, are by the same artist. One of the drawings in the Witt collection, *Landscape with Trees* (London 1968a, no. 22, fig. 260), carries the numerical inscription, *No undici*, in the same hand as those found on the Eton series. It may be assumed that the group forms a series made by the artist for himself or for an early collector.

In 1577, the then recently founded Accademia di San Luca was given the ancient church of San Martina in the Forum on the site of the Secretarium Senatus near the Arch of Septimius Severus, which was renamed San Luca, after the patron saint of painters. An additional piece of land was purchased and plans for a new church were made, although nothing happened until the seventeenth century when Pietro Cortona, at the invitation of Cardinal Francesco Barberini, protector of the academy, was elected *principe*. With some interruptions construction began in 1635 and the church was completed by 1669 when Pietro da Cortona died.

JEAN-LAURENT LEGEAY

Paris about 1710–Rome after 1788

82. *Arch with Chinese Figures and Ruins*

Pen, black ink, gray wash over graphite underdrawing on laid paper glued down on a mount of blue-green tinted paper with three borders in black ink, gray wash, and gold watercolor. Drawing: 5⅝ x 8¾ inches (143 x 223 mm) at the first border; mount: 7¹⁄₁₆ x 10¼ inches (180 x 260 mm). Watermark: none visible through backing.
Signed on the mount, lower left, under the gold border, *J.L. Le Geay invenit et Delineavit.*

DATE: about 1765–66.

NO. 82

83. *Figures Embarking and Disembarking from the Prow of a Ship in Front of a Tomb*

Pen, black ink, gray wash over graphite underdrawing on laid paper glued down on a mount of blue-green tinted paper with three borders in black and gray wash and gold watercolor. Drawing: 5⅝ x 8¾ inches (144 x 223 mm) at the first border; mount: 1¹/₁₆ x 10⅛ inches (180 x 258 mm). Watermark: none visible through backing.
Signed on the mount, lower left, under the gold border, *J.L. Le Geay invenit et Delineavit.*

DATE: about 1765–66.

PROVENANCE: Alan Irvine, London.

EXHIBITION: Montréal 1989–90, no. 9.

Montréal, Centre Canadien d'Architecture/Canadian Centre for Architecture DR1984:1787; DR1984:1788

These two drawings were discovered by John Harris in 1984 in a private collection in England. Legeay received the *grand prix* of the Académie Royale d'Architecture in 1732. He left Paris five years later to take up his residency at the French Academy in Rome, where he remained until 1742. Legeay, along with Piranesi, contributed etched *vedute* to *Roma antica distinta per Regioni* and *Roma moderna distinta per Rioni*, first published by Giovanni Lorenzo Barbiellini in 1741 (Cat. no. 49). Legeay also etched several plates for the fifth volume of *Novo teatro delle Fabriche et edifici fatte-fare in Roma e fuori di Roma dalla Santità di nostro Signore Papa Clemente XII*, published in 1739 under the auspices of the *Calcografia Camerale Apostolica*. Giuseppe Vasi, Alessandro Specchi, and Philothée-François Duflos also collaborated on this work (Erouart 1982, pp. 22–32, and p. 222, nos. 87–91, p. 23, fig. 14, p. 169, fig. 172). Emil Kaufmann and John Harris suggested that during his years in Rome, Legeay had a definitive influence on Piranesi, Le Lorrain, and Dumont (Kaufmann 1955, p. 106; Harris in Wittkower 1967, pp. 189–96, figs.

1–39). However, Jean-Marie Pérouse de Montclos and Gilbert Erouart have convincingly shown that it was not until much later in his career, in the 1750s and 1760s, during his stay in Germany and England, that Legeay produced etchings and drawings of ruins in the same spirit as Piranesi's early works (Pérouse de Montclos 1969, pp. 42–44; Erouart 1982, pp. 63–64, 73, 149).

Like Clérisseau, Legeay had an unbalanced personality that made it difficult for him to find and keep patrons (Erouart 1982, pp. 70, 74, 78). After he returned to Paris in 1742, Legeay taught architects such as Charles De Wailly (1730–98) and Etienne-Louis Boullée (1728–99), who later had distinguished careers of their own. Because he could not find patronage, Legeay went to Germany in either 1747 or 1748. There he served as court architect, first from 1748 to 1756, to Christian-Louis II, duke of Mecklenburg-Schwerin, and then from 1756 to 1763, to the duke's son King Frederick II of Prussia (Pérouse de Montclos 1969, pp. 39–42; Erouart 1982, pp. 52–69). Legeay designed the Hedwigskirche in Berlin (1747–73), the commons building and colonnade for Frederick II's Palace of Sanssouci, Potsdam (1755–56, 1763), and a park for the castle at Schwerin (1749–55) (Erouart 1982, pp. 95–148). After an argument with Frederick II in 1763, Legeay abruptly left Berlin for London. He was never able to find steady employment again. He wrote to the marquis de Marigny from London on 2 May 1768, asking for his patronage, but was turned down (Paris, Archives Nationales, 01 1911, 1768, 4, published in Erouart 1982, p. 74, note 23, pp. 46–47). In 1770, Legeay applied, without success, to be in charge of the gardens at Versailles. He spent the rest of his life moving from place to place. He was in Paris in 1770, and in Toulouse in 1774 and 1777, where he exhibited at the Salons of the Académie Royale de Peinture. He may have gone to Rome twice at the end of his life, once in 1786 and again in 1788. The last documented evidence of his existence is a letter written in 1788 from Rome to the Royal Building Administration in Potsdam asking for work. It was probably during this last trip to Rome that the sons of Giovanni Battista Piranesi acquired Legeay's drawings, which they left in Rome in 1800 (Erouart 1982, pp. 77–85).

The two drawings exhibited here are characteristic of a type designed to create the effect of an etching or engraving. Legeay signed all of his drawings as a draughtsman would a preparatory drawing for a print – with the words *invenit* and *delineavit*. The tradition for this type of drawing goes back to the sixteenth century. One of the most spectacular examples is the allegory *Without Ceres and Bacchus, Venus Would Freeze* (1599–1602) by Hendrick Goltzius (1558–1617), recently acquired by the Philadelphia Museum of Art. Goltzius executed this drawing in both pen and ink, and brush and oil paint on canvas in order to make it look like a colored engraving

(Nicholas 1992, pp. 4–57, repr. p. 5). One of the earliest drawings of this type by Legeay himself is *City Gate* (Ecole des Beaux-Arts, Paris), executed in Rome in 1739 (Erouart 1982, p. 208, no. 4, p. 27, fig. 20; Rome and elsewhere 1976, pp. 181–82, no. 89, repr. p. 180). It has the same kind of hatching and heavy shadows in the foreground that we find in the two CCA drawings by Legeay, and it is also very close in style to the topographical views Legeay etched while in Rome (Cat. nos. 49, 50).

The *Arch with Chinese Figures and Ruins* and the *Figures Embarking and Disembarking from the Prow of a Ship in Front of a Tomb* were drawn by Legeay during his stay in England. They are mentioned in a letter he wrote from London on 18 August 1766 to

NO. 83

FIGURE 1 G. B. Piranesi, *Ponte Magnifico*, in *Prima parte*, pl. 5, first edition, first issue. National Gallery of Art, Washington, 1976.2.1.

baron de Driberg in Schwerin asking to be reinstated as court architect to the duke of Mecklenburg-Schwerin. He offers the baron "twelve [drawings] . . . with borders in gold ink . . . under glass . . ." (Schwerin, State Archives, Cabinetsablieferung, vol. 389, published in Erouart 1982, pp. 70, 72–73, note 17, p. 92). Later in the letter, Legeay states that six of these drawings were executed in watercolor and six in ink (Erouart 1982, p. 73). Erouart has identified one other ink drawing of this group that is still on its original mount, *The Architectural Fantasy*, now in the Kupferstichkabinett in Berlin. The size of the Berlin drawing is almost identical (165 x 220 mm) to the two drawings in Montréal. However, the mount is larger (270 x 300 mm). Thus the two mounts in Montréal must have been cut down (Berlin, Kupferstichkabinett, Inv. no. 14865, published in Erouart in Brunel 1978, p. 205, note 20, fig. 13; Erouart 1982, p. 219, no. 60, p. 71, fig. 63). The *Arch with Chinese Figures and Ruins* in the CCA is very similar in composition to *The Architectural Fantasy* in Berlin. In both drawings, an arch extends in front of a vista with a building in the distance. The CCA's drawing, like the one in Berlin, was inspired by the etching, *Ponte Magnifico* (fig. 1), from Giovanni Battista Piranesi's *Prima parte* (1743) (Erouart in Brunel 1978, p. 205; Robison 1986, pp. 78–79, no. 6, repr. p. 78). As in the *Ara Antica* of the *Prima parte* and the *Triumphal Arch* of Piranesi's *Grotteschi* (1747–49), fragments of columns, entablatures, statues, and a sphinx are all placed in the foreground of the *Arch with Chinese Figures and Ruins* (Robison 1986, pp. 106–7, no. 18, repr. p. 106, pp. 118–19, no. 22, repr. p. 118). The figure that stands just above the keystone of the arch in the CCA's drawing (fig. 2) was inspired by an etching by François Boucher, *The Bastelleuse Chinoise* (fig. 3), published by Gabriel Huquier between 1738 and 1745 in *Recueil de divers figures chinoises du Cabinet de François Boucher Peintre du Roy . . .* (Paris 1971, p. 39, under no. 4; Jean-Richard 1978, p. 29, no. 18, repr. p. 28). The sphinx at the left side of the arch has an animated, almost playful quality similar to the ones in plate XIV of Book I of Fischer von Erlach's treatise, *Entwurff einer historischen Architectur* (1721). The

curved colonnade behind the obelisk may also have been inspired by Fischer von Erlach's illustration *The Temple of Nineveh* in Book I (Cat. no. 48).

In his letter to the marquis de Marigny (London, 2 May 1768), Legeay offered him a ". . . print executed under a sky where the sun is seen only in profile . . ." (Erouart 1982, p. 46, note 23).

Erouart has identified this print as one from the series of etchings—*Fontane* (1767), *Rovine* (1768), *Tombeaux* (1768), and *Vasi* (n.d.)—each series with the Italian title on its frontispiece and executed by Legeay in London between 1767 and 1768 (Rome and elsewhere 1976, pp. 194–98, nos. 99–101, repr. pp. 196–98; Erouart 1982, pp. 228–31, nos. 127–52, repr. pp. 72–73, 154–55, 251–54). The composition of the CCA's *Figures Embarking and Disembarking from the Prow of a Ship in Front of a Tomb* is very similar to *Landscape with Entrance to a Tomb* (fig. 4), one of the etchings from the series of the *Vasi* in the Cooper-Hewitt Museum, New York (Erouart 1982, p. 231, no. 152, p. 205, fig. 211). In the CCA's drawing, the sarcophagus at the left, with two female caryatids and a segmental pediment, is a variant of one in another etching from the series of the *Vasi* in the Cooper-Hewitt Museum, *Landscape with Ruins Under an Arch* (Erouart 1982, p. 231, no. 151, p. 202, fig. 206).

Erouart has noted a sense of foreboding and doom in the aforementioned series of etchings that Legeay executed in England. The autumnal landscapes, tombs, and wandering female figures allude to an association of love with death (Erouart 1982, pp. 74, 168). The theme of the CCA's drawing, *Figures Embarking and Disembarking from the Prow of a Ship in Front of a Tomb*, is similar to the great painting by Watteau, *Embarquement pour l'Ile de Cythère* (1718–19), once owned by Frederick II of Prussia and now in the Schloss Charlottenburg in Berlin. Like Watteau's painting, Legeay's drawing has the same ambiguous sense of time and place: are figures leaving or arriving at the mythical island of love, in the case of Watteau, and likewise, departing or coming to the tomb, in the case of Legeay? It is possible that in 1763 Legeay saw Watteau's painting, just before he left Berlin for London. The *Embarquement pour l'Ile de*

Cythère was acquired by Frederick II in The Hague some time between 1752 and 1765 (Rosenberg in Washington and elsewhere 1984–85, pp. 406–11, no. 62, repr. pp. 409–10).

In the two CCA drawings, Legeay placed Chinese figures next to Roman and Egyptian ruins, alongside human figures derived from sixteenth-century mannerist sculptures. This juxtaposition of diverse elements adds further to an atmosphere of ambiguity. Such a wide variety of design motifs also implies a renewed contact by Legeay with Piranesi's works in England, in particular the *Parere su l'architettura* (1765) and the *Antichità Romane* (1756) (Erouart 1982, pp. 189, 194). Several Egyptian motifs in the CCA's drawings are derived from the illustrations in the *Parere su l'architettura*. In addition, the triumphal arch on the title page of Legeay's *Vasi* reproduces the image from the first frontispiece of the *Antichità Romane* (1756) (Wunder in Brunel 1978, pp. 558–59, figs. 1, 2; Cat. no. 57). While he was in England, Legeay made a drawing of the Casino that William Chambers designed at Marino near Dublin for Lord Charlemont, the patron Piranesi long sought for the *Antichità Romane* (Erouart 1982, p. 74, no. 59, pp. 218–19, fig. 69, p. 79, private collection, London).

There is a sense of irony expressed by the caricature-like faces of the human figures in these two drawings, a reflection perhaps of Legeay's personality (Erouart 1982, pp. 74, 158). Long considered a marginal figure, Legeay merits the characterization given to him by Cochin in his *Mémoires* as one of the instigators, along with Louis-Joseph Le Lorrain, of the *retour d'un meilleur goust* in the second half of the eighteenth century (Ericksen 1974, p. 30; Erouart 1982, p. 32). His transformation of the theme of Watteau's *Embarquement pour l'Ile de Cythère* clearly marks the passage from rococo to neoclassicism.

The two drawings in the CCA illustrate Legeay's part in the creation of a new role for the architect, that of the *architecte-peintre* (Erouart 1982, p. 184). Many architects of his generation had to turn to selling paintings and drawings when they could not find patrons.

FIGURE 2 Jean-Laurent Legeay, Detail, *Arch with Chinese Figures and Ruins.* Canadian Centre for Architecture, Montréal, DR1984:1787.

FIGURE 3 François Boucher, *Bastelleuse Chinoise* from Huquier's *Recueil de divers figures chinoises du Cabinet de François Boucher.* Cooper-Hewitt Museum, Smithsonian Institution's National Museum of Design, New York.

FIGURE 4 Jean-Laurent Legeay, *Landscape with Entrance to a Tomb*, in *Vasi.* Cooper-Hewitt Museum, Smithsonian Institution's National Museum of Design, New York.

LOUIS-JOSEPH LE LORRAIN
Paris 1715–St. Petersburg 1759

84. *Imaginary Buildings along the Seine, Paris*

Pen, black ink, gray wash, graphite underdrawing with black ink border on laid paper. 17¼ x 33⅛ inches (438 x 842 mm). Watermark: none visible through backing.

DATE: about 1756.

PROVENANCE: Sidney Kaufman Collection, London; sale, London, Christie's, 14 December 1982, lot 64; sale, London, Christie's, 30 November 1983, lot 135, Good Golly Products, Ltd; Clarendon Gallery, London; William H. Schab Gallery, New York.

BIBLIOGRAPHY: Knox and Kaufman 1969, under no. 105.
Montréal, Centre Canadien d'Architecture/Canadian Centre for Architecture DR1986:0270

Charles-Nicolas Cochin in his *Mémoires*, written between 1780 and 1790, called Le Lorrain one of the instigators of the new style, the *goût grec*, which replaced the rococo in art, architecture, the decorative arts, and interior design during the 1750s. Cochin cited in particular Le Lorrain's suite of furniture designed in the antique style for Lalive de Jully (1756–57). In 1754, Le Lorrain used illusionistic Doric columns for the interior decoration of the castle at Åkearö near Stockholm, which he had designed for Count Tessin (Eriksen 1974, pp. 37, 45–46, 49–50, 68–69, 211–12, 267–68, pls. 15, 85–89).

Le Lorrain received the *grand prix* from the Académie Royale de Peinture in 1739. On the recommendation of the architect Ange-Jacques Gabriel (1698–1782), he received permission to leave for the French Academy in Rome in 1740. He stayed in Rome from 30 December 1740 until 12 March 1749. In 1752, he was *agréé* as a historical painter at the Académie Royale. Finally in 1756, he was admitted as a full-fledged member. Le Lorrain also had very close links with the comte de Caylus who recommended that he execute the preparatory drawings for the illustrations in Julien David Le Roy's *Les Ruines des plus beaux monuments de la Grèce* (Paris, 1758). In spite of his many achievements in Paris, Le Lorrain's paintings did not have the same success as those by Joseph-Marie Vien (1716–1809), who had been his colleague at the French Academy in Rome. In 1758, Le Lorrain decided to move to St. Petersburg where he was appointed director of the Imperial Academy of Painting and Sculpture by Empress Elisabeth. He died a year later (Rosenberg 1978, pp. 174–96).

When this drawing was acquired by the CCA, it was identified by George Knox as the work of the Italian artist Simone Pomardi (1760–1830). I have changed its attribution to Le Lorrain because of its similarity in style and theme to three other drawings (fig. 1) in a private Parisian collection, all depicting buildings along a river. These three drawings were exhibited in 1976 in *Piranèse et les Français*, where they were attributed by Gilbert Erouart to Le Lorrain. One of these drawings is inscribed *Le Lorrain* (Rome and elsewhere 1976, pp. 214–15, nos. 113a–c, repr. pp. 216–17). All four drawings are similar in theme to an etching entitled *Projet d'une place pour le Roy*, executed by Le Canu after a drawing by Le Lorrain. This etching can be dated sometime around 1756. It is dedicated to Ange-Laurent de Lalive de Jully, and has the title, *introducteur des ambassadeurs*, next to his name. Lalive de Jully was given that title by Louis XV in 1756 (Rome and elsewhere 1976, pp. 214–15, no. 112, repr. p. 216). This etching, *Projet d'une place pour le Roy*, depicts a grandiose palace placed behind four columns on bases supported by fountains that enframe an equestrian monument along a river.

Pierre Rosenberg suggests that it is possible to attribute the three drawings in the private Parisian collection to Charles Michel-Ange Challe (1718–78), a *pensionnaire* at the French Academy in Rome between 1742 and 1749, the same time as Le Lorrain (letter of 24 January 1992). However, if we compare them with the three *Architectural Fantasies* executed by Challe during his stay in Rome–one in the Metropolitan Museum of Art (New York 1991–92, pp. 40–41, no. 24, repr. p. 40), one formerly in the collection of Phyllis Lambert (Harris in Wittkower 1967, p. 194, fig. 26), and one in the Morgan Library (Cat. no. 85)–

we find that Challe uses much more ornament on his buildings, and does not employ such strong contrasts of light and shadow. He also does not place the obelisks and the columns in the foreground, as the artist of these four drawings does. Rather, Challe puts the columns and obelisks in the middle and in the background. The drawing in the CCA–with its very strong contrasts of light and shade, obelisks in the foreground, and very smooth finished surface–is very similar in style to the painting *An Architectural Fantasy* (fig. 2) in the Louvre. It is signed by Le Lorrain, and was probably executed during his stay in Rome in the 1740s (Roland Michel in Brunel 1978, pp. 571–72, repr. fig. 1; Rosenberg 1978, pp. 180–82, fig. 30, p. 180, fig. 29, p. 181). The painting in the Louvre depicts a circular temple (erected in 1745) in front of the Palazzo Farnese. This temporary decoration was designed by Giovanni Paolo Pannini for the festivities organized by the Abbé de Canillac on the occasion of the first marriage of the dauphin of France (Paris and elsewhere 1992–93, p. 89, fig. 86 [Pannini], p. 92, and no. 52 [Le Lorrain], p. 160, repr. p. 160).

FIGURE 1 Louis-Joseph Le Lorrain, *Imaginary Architectural Landscape*. Private collection, Paris.

FIGURE 2 Louis-Joseph Le Lorrain, *An Architectural Fantasy*. Musée du Louvre, Paris.

NO. 84

FIGURE 3 Louis-Joseph Le Lorrain, title page from G. B. Piranesi, *Opere varie*. New York Public Library.

FIGURE 4 G. B. Piranesi, *Campidoglio antico*, in *Prima parte*, pl. 7, first edition, first issue. National Gallery of Art, Washington, 1976.2.1.

Many of the same decorative motifs found in the CCA's drawing also appear in Le Lorrain's designs for the *Chinea*, executed in Rome between 1745 and 1748 (Rome and elsewhere 1976, pp. 201–3, 206, 210, nos. 103–7, repr. pp. 204–5).

Since the drawing by Le Lorrain in the CCA and the three others in the private Parisian collection are more finished than the sketches by Le Lorrain in the Cooper-Hewitt Museum (Rosenberg 1978, p. 177, figs. 24–27, p. 180), one can conclude they were presentation drawings and were executed probably at the same time as the initial drawing for the etching *Projet d'une place pour le Roy*. They could have been part of a series presented to Lalive de Jully, Le Lorrain's main patron at the time.

Gilbert Erouart has suggested that the three architectural fantasies in the private Parisian collection were executed in St. Petersburg by Le Lorrain with the assistance of Jean-Michel Moreau le Jeune (1741–1814) (Rome and elsewhere 1976, pp. 214–15, nos. 113a–c). However, if we examine the CCA's drawing carefully, we see that there are references to Paris. Behind the first obelisk, to the left and in the background, is not only a bridge resembling the Pont Neuf but also a gothic church resembling Notre Dame. The imaginary buildings in the foreground appear to be placed on the left bank of the Seine facing the Ile de la Cité. The buildings in the background allude to the 1748 competition for the Place Louis XV. In 1748, at the end of the War of Austrian Succession, the *Bureau de la Ville de Paris* approved a proposal to commission an equestrian monument to Louis XV. Edme Bouchardon (1698–1762) was chosen as sculptor. In the CCA's drawing, the equestrian monument to the right and just in front of the U-shaped building is reminiscent of Bouchardon's designs. The marquis de Tournehem proposed on 27 June 1748 a competition for the design of a square, the Place Louis XV, to surround Bouchardon's equestrian monument. Many architects took part, including Juste-Aurèle Meissonnier, Germain Boffrand, Jacques-François Blondel, Cartaud, Mansart de Lévy, and Ange-Jacques Gabriel. The architects could choose any site; most chose the Place Dau-

phine on the Ile de la Cité. No decision was reached by the king in 1748 (Garms 1967, pp. 102–13). Another competition was organized in 1753 by the marquis de Marigny. This time the site chosen by the king was located between the Seine and the Tuileries gardens. Ange-Jacques Gabriel's project won the competition in January 1753, and work was begun on Place Louis XV (Place de la Concorde) in 1755 (Tadgell 1978, pp. 174–79). The building at the left in the CCA's drawing, with its one-quarter rusticated basement and three-quarter-length applied Corinthian columns, bears a general resemblance to Gabriel's design for the two buildings (1755–86) along the north side of the Place Louis XV facing the Seine (Tadgell 1978, figs. 152–55). Since it was Gabriel who, according to Rosenberg, gave Le Lorrain permission to leave for Rome in 1740, the two men may have remained in contact. Thus, Le Lorrain may have been aware of Gabriel's plans for the Place Louis XV before he left for Russia.

Le Lorrain worked, like Legeay, with Piranesi. He etched the vignette on the first version of the title page of Piranesi's *Opere varie* (1750) (fig. 3), and another for that of *Le Magnificenze di Roma* (1751) (Robison 1986, p. 137, fig. 65, repr. p. 137 and p. 154, no. 28, repr.). According to John Harris, of all the *pensionnaires* at the French Academy in Rome during the 1740s, Le Lorrain was the one most deeply influenced by Piranesi (Harris in Wittkower 1967, p. 194–95). Not only does the composition of the CCA's drawing reflect Le Lorrain's vignette for the first version of the title page of Piranesi's *Opere varie*, but the conception of the imaginary urban space recalls the *Campidoglio antico* of Piranesi's *Prima parte* (1743) (fig. 4) (Robison 1986, p. 82, no. 8, repr. p. 82). The fountain, just below the first obelisk in the foreground of Le Lorrain's drawing in the CCA, bears a resemblance to the rococo inventions of Jacques de Lajoüe. However, the U-shaped building to the right, with its restrained sobriety and Doric order, reflects the new style of such later neoclassical buildings as De Wailly's Comédie Française (Théâtre de l'Odéon, 1769–71, 1774–78) and Jean-François Chalgrin's (1739–1811) Church of Saint-Philippe-du-Roule (1755) in Paris.

CHARLES MICHEL-ANGE CHALLE
Paris 1718–Paris 1778

85. *Architectural Fantasy*

Pen and brown ink with gray and black washes. 15¹³⁄₁₆ x 26⅜ inches (402 x 672 mm). Watermark: fleur-de-lis in circle with *V* above.

Signed and dated at lower right, *MAC Challes a rome 1747*.

PROVENANCE: Dr. Edgar Wind; Durlacher Brothers, New York.

BIBLIOGRAPHY: Morgan Library *FR* IV, 1953, p. 64; Wunder 1968, pp. 28, 31, fig. 9; Morgan Library *Review* 1969, pp. 137ff.; Oechslin 1972, fig. 73; Roland Michel 1987, p. 143, fig. 157.

EXHIBITIONS: Kansas City 1956, no. 132; Philadelphia 1961, no. 18; London 1968, no. 121, fig. 261; London 1972, no. 1046, repr.; Rome and elsewhere 1976, no. 23, repr.; New York 1984, no. 61; New York 1989.

The Pierpont Morgan Library. Purchased as the gift of Mrs. W. Murray Crane, Acc. no. 1952.31

NO. 85

Challe, the pupil of Boucher and Lemoyne, was *pensionnaire* at the French Academy in Rome between 1742 and 1749. This boldly conceived composition, dated 1747, shows the artist very much influenced by Piranesi both as to subject and treatment. As Gilbert Erouart noted, this composition was directly inspired by Fischer von Erlach's design for *Les deux Pyramides de la hauteur d'un Stade, que Moeris Roi d'Egÿpte fit dresser pour Soi et pour Sa Reine près de son Mausolée* in his *Entwurff einer historischen Architectur*, Book I, pl. XI (Rome and elsewhere 1976, no. 23). While keeping von Erlach's idea of the circular tomb placed between pyramids, Challe changed the setting from a lake to a Roman forum with architecture and triumphal columns.

It is most probable that Challe knew some of Piranesi's preparations for *Antichità Romane* (1756) or the *Opere varie*, although the prints were not published until 1750, some three years after Challe dated

this composition. The nucleus of the *Antichità*, the *Camere sepolcrali*, was published in 1750. The artist's imagination was to serve him well in his later career as designer of fêtes and funeral pomps for the French court. The drawing is stylistically very similar to another large fantasy drawing by him, *Imaginary Composition with Triumphal Bridge*, dated 1746, formerly in Phyllis Lambert's collection when John Wilton-Ely published both drawings in 1972. In 1753, Challe exhibited *Diverses idées d'Architecture faites sur les descriptions & les anciens vestiges des Monumens publics de la Grèce & de Rome* in the salon, the same year that he was elected to the Académie Royale. He became professor of perspective there in 1758. He is principally known for his drawings of imaginary architectural subjects. It is interesting that Challe spent the last years of his life translating the works of Piranesi, a project that never got beyond the manuscript stage.

CLAUDE-HENRI WATELET

Paris 1718–Paris 1786

86. *Temple of Neptune, Paestum*

Pen and black ink, gray wash and watercolor, over traces of black chalk; framing line in pen and black ink. 12³⁄₁₆ x 10⁷⁄₁₆ inches (310 x 265 mm). Watermark: fleur-de-lis within a coat of arms surmounted by a crown (cf. Heawood 1819). Inscribed on verso by modern hand in pencil: *Very fine view drawn by Hubert Robert XVIIIcy. auction Sotheby 19 may 1899 #96*, and *View of the interior of the temple of Neptune/seen in front.*

PROVENANCE: unidentified collector, *HL* within a heart (in red on recto); sale, London, Sotheby's, 19 May 1899, lot 96; Ivan Phillips, Montréal.

The Phillips Family Collection

In 1764, when Watelet visited Italy, Paestum was a recent archaeological discovery; it is not surprising that the writer and amateur artist was interested in the site. Discovered in 1746, the complex at Paestum intrigued many artists and critics in the 1750s and 1760s, including the architect Soufflot and Winckelmann, both of whom were surprised that so little notice had previously been taken of Paestum. Soufflot wrote in 1750: "Bien des curieux en allant en Grèce et en Egypte pour y voir et y dessiner des monuments antiques ont traversé le golphe de Salerne et passé peut être a la vue de ceux cy, sans les appercevoir" (Mondain-Monval 1914, p. 104).

Watelet probably did not make the journey southward to visit the site himself. It was, afterall, a relatively short visit to Italy, and he was accompanied by his close friend, Marguerite Lecomte. It is clear that this carefully finished watercolor view inside the hexastyle of the Temple was not produced until much later. Watelet knew Hubert Robert well and probably saw the series of red chalk views of Paestum, which the latter drew when he visited Paestum in late spring of 1760 with the Abbé de Saint-Non (see Cat. no. 102). Although at least one of Robert's views represents the same interior view (sale, Mlle L, Paris, Galerie J. Charpentier, 22 June 1933, lot 30, repr.), it is different from Watelet's watercolor. The English artist Thomas Major printed a similar view in the 1760s, *Internal View of the Hexastyle Ipetral Temple taken from the South* (Major 1768; Arnold 1992, fig. 4, repr.) but Watelet's view so closely resembles Paolantonio Paoli's, published in *Le Rovine di Pesto*, 1784 (Arnold 1992, fig. 1) under the patronage of Count Gazola, that it seems likely Watelet based his watercolor on it. A comparison of Paoli's print with Watelet's watercolor reveals the same steeply rising perspective view. Both compositions feature almost identical rocky outcroppings and shrubbery in a foreground populated with a similar arrangement of picturesque local types.

CHARLES-LOUIS CLÉRISSEAU

Paris 1721–Paris 1820

87. *Travelers in the Interior of the "Temple of Mercury" at Baia*

Gouache. 10½ x 18½ inches (268 x 471 mm). Watermark: none visible through lining.

PROVENANCE: sale, London, Christie's, 9 December 1982, lot 230, repr.; Jonathan Scott, London; Richard Day, Ltd., London.

BIBLIOGRAPHY: Morgan Library *FR* XXI, 1989, p. 329; McCormick 1990, p. 245, note 62.

EXHIBITION: New York 1989.

The Pierpont Morgan Library. Purchased as the gift of Mrs. Julius Fleischmann, Mr. and Mrs. Walter Klein, and Mrs. Richard Rodgers, Acc. no. 1985.62

Clérisseau arrived in Rome in 1749 and spent the next twenty years of his life there. The two greatest influences on him were Pannini whose views of Roman ruins attracted the young artist, and Piranesi whose studio was just across the street from the French Academy. He was also a good friend of Winckel-mann who recommended him to Cardinal Albani in connection with some decorations at the Villa Albani. Although attracted to Piranesi, with whom he was strongly allied, he owes perhaps more to Pannini whose subject matter and manner he adopted. Clérisseau attracted the interest of the English architect and designer Robert Adam, who engaged him as his artistic instructor and to make drawings of the palace of Diocletian at Spalato (see Cat. no. 77). He was later employed by Catherine II of Russia, and almost the whole of his oeuvre is now in Russia.

The same subject is found in a pen and wash drawing at the Hermitage. That drawing is larger than the Library's and does not include the figure of the artist at the right. The Hermitage sheet was probably executed in 1761 when Clérisseau accompanied James Adam to Naples (McCormick 1990, fig. 58). Hubert Robert and the Abbé de Saint-Non anticipated Clérisseau and Adam in this journey by a year. Quite possibly Clérisseau knew the suite of drawings Robert made on this trip, for a similar subject is depicted in the drawings of both Clérisseau and Robert. Here Clérisseau has added more figures, including that of another artist, perhaps James Adam, seated at the right.

CHARLES-LOUIS CLÉRISSEAU
Paris 1721–Paris 1820

88. *The Triumphal Arch and Mausoleum of the Julii at Saint-Rémy, Provence*

Graphite and black chalk underdrawing, blue, brown, green, red, and white gouache with a black ink border on lined laid paper. 16½ x 23⅛ inches (420 x 588 mm). Watermarks: none visible.
Signed lower right in brown ink, *Clérisseau*.

DATE: about 1769.

PROVENANCE: James Knapp-Fisher, London; sale, London, Christie's, 30 March 1976, lot 145; P. & D. Colnaghi and Co., Ltd., London; William H. Schab Gallery, New York 1986, cat. no. 68, no. 8.

EXHIBITION: Montréal 1989–90, no. 10.

BIBLIOGRAPHY: McCormick in Washington 1976, p. 86, under no. 138; McCormick 1990, p. 259, note 18.

Montréal, Centre Canadien d'Architecture/Canadian Centre for Architecture DR1986:0004

An essay on Clérisseau's life could have as its title, *On Mischance and Mischief*. What a mischance, for an architect, not to have left a building bearing the mark of his talent. Indeed, even the Château Borély near Marseille–the *bastide* Clérisseau designed for the merchant Louis Borély–was built between 1768 and 1778 by a local architect, Louis Esprit Brun, for Borély's son Louis-Joseph, although Clérisseau had executed at least one preparatory drawing dated 1 September 1767, a short time after his return from Rome (for Clérisseau's life and career, see McCormick 1990, *passim*). If Catherine the Great, empress of Russia, did indeed appoint him *premier architecte* and *membre honoraire de l'Académie Impériale des Arts* in 1778, and then in 1781, *premier architecte de Sa Majesté Impériale*, a title he boasted about, she nonetheless rejected, in 1779, his too grandiose project for a Roman inspired palace whose program had been devised by Cochin and Falconet. The empress only wanted a small house in the antique style for the

park of Tsarskoe Selo. In spite of the drawings and plaster models that Clérisseau sent to St. Petersburg for a monumental triumphal arch, Catherine replaced him, in a similar manner, with "imperial" ingratitude, by a Scot, Charles Cameron (1750–1811), who did not have what we would call *la folie des grandeurs* of the French.

It was not the first time that Clérisseau was overly ambitious in his projects. Without dwelling on the coffeehouse that he had decorated for Winckelmann's patron Cardinal Albani, we should examine his relationship with another great Roman *amateur*, Abbé Filippo Farsetti, whom he had met in 1760. According to Winckelmann, Farsetti wanted his garden at Sala near Venice to represent the ruins of a Roman emperor's residence in the manner of Hadrian's Villa at Tivoli. But in the first letter Winckelmann sent to Clérisseau in 1767, he informed Clérisseau that he was afraid Clérisseau might abandon this magnificent project Farsetti had entrusted to him (McCormick 1990, pp. 113–14, note 55, p. 254; Winckelmann 1781, vol. II, p. 205, with a long note from the translator giving the details of the project that looks ahead to that submitted to Empress Catherine of Russia). Pierre Jean Mariette agreed. "Abbé Farsetti," he wrote, "gave Clérisseau building projects whose execution was beyond the capabilities of one person" (Mariette 1851–60, vol. II, p. 379). The list of patrons who rejected Clérisseau's projects includes Thomas Jefferson, who did not entrust him with building the capitol of Richmond in spite of the praise he gave him in 1785. We must recognize that Clérisseau was largely responsible for his own failures and tribulations because he was not only easily offended but also conceited.

Clérisseau had begun his term at the French Academy in Rome as a *pensionnaire du Roi* in 1749; his stay was extended in 1751. In July 1753, however, he was expelled, in spite of the fact that on 15 May of the previous year, the director, Charles-Joseph Natoire (1700–1777), had written: "He indeed works arduously, he carries out compositions effortlessly on the theme of the ruin." But Clérisseau had become the head of a rebellious group of students who refused to

NO. 88

present their communion tickets to the director (Montaiglon and Guiffrey 1887–1912, vol. X, pp. 117, 184, 188, 411, 418, 423, 431, 436, 451). Clérisseau made his final departure from the Palazzo Mancini, home of the French Academy, around 15 May 1754. According to Natoire's last letter of 29 May, "he left the Academy without a word to me, filled with discontent . . . for he has an unsettled mind; we are finally rid of him" (Montaiglon and Guiffrey 1887–1912, vol. X, p. 464).

Reading the *Correspondance des directeurs de l'Académie de France à Rome* from which this quotation is taken, one has the impression that Clérisseau left immediately for Paris. In fact, he did not, but stayed in Rome for another twelve years. Actually, what he was most criticized for was not simply his absence at the Easter communion. The problem was that the *pensionnaires* did not have the right to make money with their talent. Although this practice was sometimes ignored, it was held against Clérisseau because of his connections with the English in Rome.

According to the English traveler Hayward, James Adam (brother of the architect) had established a company under "Director Mons.ʳ Clérisseau" where painters, engravers, and architects were employed to manufacture objects of quality (McCormick 1990, p. 69, note 56, p. 245).

Clérisseau was in contact with William Chambers even before the Adam brothers. He had met Robert Adam in Florence in 1755, traveled with him, and collaborated on *The Ruins of the Palace of the Emperor Diocletian at Spalatro*, published in London in 1764 (Cat. no. 77). Clérisseau's involvement with Robert Adam in Italy ended with this book. If there were mutual faults in their relationship, they should not be passed over, since they would confirm what we know already about Clérisseau's difficult personality.

Clérisseau's greatest contribution was not in architecture but in interior design. His collaboration, between 1773 and 1774 and 1775 and 1782, on the interior decoration of the two destroyed Parisian residences of Laurent-Grimod de la Reynière was his most important work, along with the extraordinary Ruin Room that he painted himself in *trompe-l'œil* for Père Lesueur at the Monastery of Santa Trinità dei Monti just before his departure from Rome in 1766. Miraculously, this room has been preserved and has been transformed into a dormitory for monks. Its importance is confirmed by eight preparatory drawings in the collection of the Hermitage in St. Petersburg, as well as by the *Lettres familières* Winckelmann wrote in 1767 to Clérisseau while the artist was researching Roman antiquities in the south of France.

The Triumphal Arch at Saint-Rémy, known as Glanum in Roman times, was erected in honor of Julius Caesar, and is the oldest of the ancient monuments preserved in the Roman province of Narbonnaise. The three-tiered Mausoleum of the Julii was erected in honor of the grandsons of Emperor Augustus–Caius Caesar and Lucius–the children of his daughter Julia and son-in-law Agrippa. Caius Caesar died in a military mission in Armenia when he was twenty-three-years old, and Lucius was killed en route to Spain at an ambush at Cartagena (Carthago Nova) when he was eighteen-years old. These two young men had been made "Princes of Youth." Caius was the patron of the city of Nîmes, whose citizens dedicated the Maison Carrée to him (McCormick 1990, p. 138, fig. 116). The great historical importance of the Arch and the Mausoleum, in addition to their exceptional architectural quality, is alluded to by the presence of the two princes in the foreground. A gouache of the same subject in the Victoria and Albert Museum in London is signed, dated, and inscribed: *Arc de Triomphe à Saint-Remy en Provence Clérisseau 1769* (fig. 1, 425 x 500 mm) (McCormick in Washington 1976, p. 86, no. 138, repr.; McCormick 1990, p. 136, fig. 115, p. 138). The general composition is the same but a number of differences eliminate any speculation that the Montréal version is a simple repetition or copy. The trees in the background, in between the two monuments, are different. In the Montréal gouache, the trees are set in front of a village on a hill with houses placed against a view of a mountain in the distance. In the London gouache, there is a sculpted tree trunk, between the two figures

on the left side of the Triumphal Arch, which does not appear in the Montréal version. There are also variations in the stone blocks at the base of the Triumphal Arch. Finally, the right arm of the kneeling man, seen from the back, is bent at a greater angle in the London gouache than in the one in Montréal.

It is clear that Clérisseau's gouaches depicting these monuments were destined to illustrate the albums on *Les Antiquités de la France*, which he planned to publish and for which he received Winckelmann's encouragement. Not only did the latter write to Clérisseau in 1767: "I will examine with great pleasure the drawings you have made of the Pont du Gard, of the Triumphal Arch and of the Mausoleum at Saint-Rémy. Since these three monuments are so different in character, it was essential for you to investigate them before going any further. . . . I would never have thought that France had so many monuments . . ." (Winckelmann 1781, vol. II, p. 209). He also offered "to have a discussion about these beautiful antiquities so that I can possibly help you with this project which you have conceived in order to bring forth your research to the general public" (Winckelmann 1781, vol. II, p. 212).

Thus from 1767 on, Clérisseau's correspondents, who included the comte de Caylus, were aware of the reasons for his departure from Rome during the summer. In September of the next year, according to Abbé Barthélémy's letter of 1768, he was back in Paris and looking for a patron. But "where could he find one?" (McCormick 1990, p. 145, note 37, p. 261). Clérisseau would not be certified by the Académie Royale de Peinture until one year later, when on 2 September 1769 he became *agréé* as a painter of architectural subjects; but even though the simple *agrément* would permit him to show at the Salon, he would never become a full-fledged member of the Académie (Montaiglon 1888, vol. VIII, p. 26). Mariette was aware of Clérisseau's ambitious undertakings, and wrote in his *Abecedario* in 1774 that he also "feared very much that they would amount to nothing because of the enormous expenses that such undertakings require" (Mariette 1851–60, vol. II, p. 380).

In spite of the dedication to comte d'Angiviller, *di-*

FIGURE 1 Charles-Louis Clérisseau, *The Triumphal Arch and Mausoleum of the Julii at St. Rémy*. Courtesy of the Board of Trustees of the Victoria and Albert Museum, London.

recteur des bâtiments du Roi, only the first part of *Les Antiquités de la France—Les Monuments de Nismes—* was published in 1778 (CCA Library, WM450). Baron Grimm also thought that Clérisseau should abandon his great project because of a lack of funds. But what we know of its author can only suggest that he was not a man who knew how to make generous friends. Moreover, Mariette implies in a similar vein that when Clérisseau left to go to England, "he could not have made a better decision, since he will not remain, as in Paris, with nothing to do" (Mariette 1851–60, vol. II, p. 380).

This same *amateur*, with regard to two architectural drawings that Clérisseau had sent him from Italy, indicated that "the figures are drawn by a Venetian called Zucchi, who is now in England" (Mariette 1851–60, vol. II, p. 380, cited by McCormick 1990, p. 145). Antonio Zucchi (1726–95) was one of the associates of the Adam brothers between 1750 and 1760. He was at Abbé Farsetti's at Sala with Clérisseau and Robert Adam, and continued to collaborate with Robert Adam on the decoration of his great English country houses. Zucchi was mentioned directly by James Adam in a letter to his brother that concerned the company they had established to supply "objects of quality" to English noblemen passing through Rome. Other than "Clerisseau segretario al cavaliere," it included five draughtsmen: George Richardson, Domenico Cunego, Antonio Zucchi, Giuseppe Saccho, and Agostino Scarra (McCormick 1990, p. 69, note 57, p. 245).

It is not surprising, given the above, that the two views of the Triumphal Arch and Mausoleum of the Julii at Saint-Rémy in London and Montréal were, until recently, in English collections. In addition, one must not forget that Clerisseau was not the only artist who, in the sixth decade of the eighteenth century, was interested in the antiquities of Provence, in particular those at Saint-Rémy. In 1761, the comte de Caylus made known to an antiquarian from Aix—Esprit Calvet (1728–1810)—his intention to "resume the publication of *Les Antiquités de la France* following the example of Desgodetz" (Perez 1989, p. 1017).

Clérisseau was already in London when Abbé Na-

toire, brother of the director of the French Academy in Rome, wrote to Marigny on 28 July 1772 proposing to illustrate a publication on the antiquities of Provence (Montaiglon and Guiffrey 1887–1912, vol. XI, p. 391) and offering to send to the *directeur des bâtiments* a sample of his talent: a drawing of the ruins at Saint-Rémy (Montaiglon and Guiffrey 1887–1912, vol. XI, p. 389). The *surintendant des bâtiments*, the comte d'Angiviller, in thanking him for his letter, responded on 15 August, "that he would strongly encourage his proposal, but a decision to undertake a new project would have to depend on the actual circumstances even if it were of great utility and of little cost" (Montaiglon and Guiffrey 1887–1912, vol. XI, p. 392).

It is quite probable that at that very moment Marigny was in fact thinking of another artist, one who had already been to Provence in the company of Abbé Barthélémy as early as 1755. This artist was Hubert Robert, who had painted the interior of the Temple of Diana at Nîmes in 1771 (737 x 1019 mm, Phillips Collection, New York). He could have gone to Provence some time between October 1770 and the end of May 1771, if one takes into account his absences at the semi-monthly meetings at the Académie Royale de Peinture (Cayeux 1991, ms., p. 8). It was Robert who was entrusted in 1782 with the task of painting four large views of *The Principal Monuments of France* for the king's bedroom at Fontainebleau. These paintings were shown at the Salon of 1787 and are now in the Louvre. In the third painting of this series, the *Triumphal Arch and the Amphitheater of the City of Orange* (fig. 2), one can see the Mausoleum and the small Triumphal Arch at Saint-Rémy in the background (Washington 1976, p. 92, no. 147, repr.; Salon of 1787, no. 48).

Just before he received the commission for Fontainebleau, Hubert Robert had also painted *The Most Famous Antiquities of France* (1782) for the comte du Nord, Prince Paul of Russia. This painting is still in the Pavlovsk Palace near St. Petersburg (Salon of 1785, no. 209). Included in this painting are the Triumphal Arch and Mausoleum at Saint-Rémy; both monuments are found also in a large watercolor by

FIGURE 2 Hubert Robert, *Triumphal Arch and the Amphitheater of the City of Orange*. Musée du Louvre, Paris.

the artist in the Phoenix Museum of Art. In the center of the painting, toward the back, Robert depicted the Mausoleum at Saint-Rémy projecting in front of the Pont du Gard; slightly to the right, behind it, is the Triumphal Arch. In the large painting in the Louvre (fig. 2), the Triumphal Arch of Orange in the foreground separates the Mausoleum, slightly to the left, from the Triumphal Arch at Saint-Rémy on the right. The background is taken up by the wall of an ancient theater. When Robert had returned to Provence in 1783 to prepare for the Fontainebleau commission, he had drawn in sepia wash over graphite underdrawing the Triumphal Arch at Saint-Rémy and the Mausoleum of the Julii (which he called that "of Marius") from the same angle that Clérisseau had done fourteen years earlier (330 x 425 mm; present location unknown).

The great success achieved by Hubert Robert in this royal commission contrasts with Clérisseau's failure to publish his ambitious project, *Les Antiquités de la France*. It must be stated that the difference in the fates of these two painters of architectural subjects did not prevent them from having what is believed to be a cordial relationship. They worked together on the transformation of the Grande Galerie of the Louvre. At the Salon of 1785, Clérisseau presented *A Painting of an Architectural Subject Belonging to M. Robert* (Salon of 1785, no. 122). Hubert Robert kept this painting until his death. It was listed in the posthumous sale of his belongings on 5 April 1809: "A gouache painting. A very beautiful work on the theme of ruins by Clérisseau" (Gabillot 1895, p. 327).

One should not forget that the two artists were neighbors in the village of Auteuil where Robert was buried and where Clérisseau died twelve years later. Meanwhile, Hubert Robert had without a doubt paid the price for his success among his noble patrons: he was imprisoned during the Reign of Terror. Clérisseau, on the other hand, took the side of the Revolution when he approved, in a letter of 8 December 1794 (18 frimaire an III) the transfer to Paris of paintings by Rubens seized in Antwerp. He then had no reason to worry (Pommier 1991, pp. 240–42).

CHARLES DE WAILLY
Paris 1730–Paris 1798

89. *The Piazza del Popolo, Rome*

Graphite underdrawing, pen, brown ink, gray and brown wash, orange watercolor, white gouache, brown ink border on laid paper glued along the edges on a mount. 8 x 12¾ inches (202 x 326 mm). Watermark: part of a watermark in center, initials *D* and *C* (not identified), perhaps, Heawood 1950 (1981), p. 418, nos. 3267–68, pl. 137.
Inscribed on recto, in brown ink, an interlaced *DW* on the base of the obelisk; signed and dated in brown ink over black chalk along the lower edge, to the right of center, *De Wailly/1759;* stamped on lower right corner of the mount, *ARD* (Lugt 1921, p. 29, no. 172, nonidentified eighteenth-century French matmaker); head of a horse drawn in iron gall ink on the verso showing through recto.

DATE: 1759.

PROVENANCE: John, Lord Northwick, sale, London, Sotheby's, 5 July 1925, lot 45; The Harewood Charitable Trust, sale, London, Christie's, 2 July 1985, lot 106; private collection, Paris; Didier Aaron, Inc., Paris.

EXHIBITIONS: Possibly Paris, Salon of 1771, under no. 161; Montréal 1989–90, no. 8.

Montréal, Centre Canadien d'Architecture/Canadian Centre for Architecture DR1987:0033

Charles De Wailly, who was both an architect and a painter, obtained the *grand prix* of the Académie Royale d'Architecture in 1752 after studies with Jean-Laurent Legeay, Giovanni Niccolò Servandoni (1695–1766), and Jacques-François Blondel (1705–94). He became a *pensionnaire* at the French Academy in Rome in 1754 and stayed until 1757. In 1771, he was received into the Académie Royale de Peinture in Paris and began to exhibit regularly at the Salons. He returned to Italy two more times: a second time in 1771–72, when he went to Genoa to design the interior of the Palazzo Spinola's salone, and took a third short trip with Jacques-Denis Antoine, in 1777. During his first trip to Rome, De Wailly undertook excavations at the Baths of Diocletian with two of his fellow *pensionnaires*, Marie-Joseph Peyre (1730–85) and Pierre-Louis Moreau-Desproux (1727–93). The

three *pensionnaires* were influenced by Piranesi's contemporary archaeological research. At the time, Piranesi was preparing a reconstruction of the Baths of Diocletian (for the *Antichità Romane*) based on his own excavations (Focillon 1964, p. 23, no. 198, p. 24, no. 221; Mosser and Rabreau in Paris 1979, pp. 20, 82–83, 122–23).

A slightly larger version of the CCA's drawing of the Piazza del Popolo is in the Musée de Rouen (fig. 1; 240 x 358 mm). It is enframed by a pen-and-ink border with a numbered list of monuments below the border. This border was based on a 1692 engraving by the Dutch artist Gomar Wouters (1649–96) (Ciucci 1974, p. 75, repr.). It cannot be ascertained, however, whether De Wailly was responsible for this border. His monogram, an interlaced *DW*, is also found at the bottom of the Egyptian obelisk in the Rouen drawing. Rosenberg and Bergot have dated

the Rouen drawing to 1760 because that date appears under De Wailly's monogram on the base of the Column of Trajan in the center of its pendant, *The Piazza Colonna*, also in Rouen (Washington and elsewhere 1981–82, pp. 28–29, no. 34, pl. 72, and p. 29, no. 35, pl. 71). The CCA's and the Musée de Rouen's drawings of the Piazza del Popolo are most likely versions of an earlier drawing executed by De Wailly during his first trip to Rome. There are only about twenty known drawings of ancient and modern monuments that De Wailly actually executed during his first trip to Rome (Mosser and Rabreau in Paris 1979, pp. 20–21, nos. 33–38, 40, 44–49, and pp. 114–15, no. 51). The use of a stylus and graphite underdrawing, particularly in the delineation of the diagonal lines defining the three radial streets, as well as the careful and controlled application of ink, washes, and gouache, all indicate that the CCA's drawing is a replica of an earlier one and was not executed on the site. In the Christie's sales catalogue of 1985, Eileen Harris read the date on the CCA's drawing as 1754 and ascribed the drawing to De Wailly's first Roman sojourn. Closer examination under a microscope revealed a different date: 1759. Rosenberg and Bergot suggested that the Rouen drawing may have been exhibited in 1760 at a special showing of his own drawings that De Wailly organized at the Jardin de l'Infant. He could not as yet exhibit at the Salons since he had not yet been received into the Académie Royale de Peinture (Washington and elsewhere 1981–82, p. 28). Either the Musée de Rouen's drawing, the CCA's drawing, or yet another version was exhibited at the Salon of 1771, where "six small views of Rome: The Piazza del Popolo, the Piazza Colonna, the Piazza of Saint Peter's, the Piazza Navona, the Piazza in front of the Pantheon, and the Piazza in front of Santa Maria Maggiore" are listed among De Wailly's contributions (*Livret du Salon*, p. 30, no. 161). The CCA's and the Musée de Rouen's drawings of the Piazza del Popolo are almost identical. Besides lacking the annotated border, the CCA's drawing has sharper contrasts of light and shade, and a darker tonality; it also has less highlighting with white gouache.

The Piazza del Popolo had a great significance for the artists of De Wailly's generation who came to study in Rome. The Piazza was the major ceremonial entrance to the city, at the northwestern extremity of Rome. Since the Middle Ages, it had been used for festivals and triumphal entries of distinguished visitors. The Via del Corso, in the center, led from the Porta del Popolo, along the course of a former Roman street, the Via Flaminia, to the Capitoline Hill and the site of the Campus Martius. Until the beginning of the sixteenth century, the area in front of the Porta del Popolo was irregular. In 1518, during the pontificate of Leo X, the first street at the right, the Via Leonina (later called the Via Ripetta), was created; it led to the Mausoleum of Augustus. In 1525, Pope Clement VII created the third street to the left, the Via Clementina (later called the Via del Babuino), which led to the Villa Medici. In 1573, a fountain was placed in front of the Porta del Popolo (1543–

1607); and in 1589, Sixtus V entrusted Domenico Fontana with the task of erecting in the Piazza del Popolo an Egyptian obelisk from the Circus Maximus. The Piazza was finally given a focal point in 1658, when Pope Alexander VII commissioned Carlo Rainaldi (1611–91) to construct two churches, Santa Maria di Montesanto (1661–75) at the left, and the Church of Santa Maria dei Miracoli (1662–79) to the right. The two churches were completed after 1671 by Rainaldi's successor, Carlo Fontana (1638–1714). The inner dome of the Church of Santa Maria di Montesanto was finished by Bernini (Ciucci 1974, pp. 5–86; Blunt 1982, pp. 97–98).

In the drawing in the CCA, Charles De Wailly shows the Piazza del Popolo as it appeared in the middle of the eighteenth century – before the curved walls and the terraces on the Pincio were added by Giuseppe Valadier, between 1811 and 1824. De Wailly has chosen a high viewpoint just to the left and close to the obelisk. This bird's-eye view emphasizes the three radial streets leading away from the Piazza. There are two lateral as well as a central perspective point along the horizon. To the left of the Piazza, the viewer sees a small part of the wall in front of the Augustinian monastery (which is adjacent to the Church of Santa Maria del Popolo) as well as an apartment house built during the first half of the seventeenth century. At the right, there are small domestic buildings constructed at the same time (Ciucci 1974, pp. 51–71).

Richard Hemphill had suggested that De Wailly's drawing of the Piazza del Popolo was based on a painting of the Piazza del Popolo by Giovanni Paolo Pannini. It is signed and dated 1741 and is now in the Nelson–Atkins Museum of Art in Kansas City (fig. 2) (CCA, Research Files; Bowron 1981, p. 38, fig. 1, p. 39, fig. 2, p. 40; Arisi 1986, p. 385, no. 307, repr.). At the time that Charles De Wailly was a *pensionnaire* at the French Academy in Rome, Pannini was a professor of perspective. He had close connections with the French community in Rome, having married in 1724 the sister-in-law of Nicolas Vleughels (1668–1737), then the director of the French Academy. Pannini also had French clients, such as the duc de Choiseul,

French ambassador to Pope Benedict XIV (Bowron 1981, p. 42; Arisi 1986, p. 207). De Wailly's original drawing of the Piazza del Popolo may have been done while he was studying under Pannini. The drawing in the CCA exhibits several differences from Pannini's painting. De Wailly has chosen a viewpoint closer to the obelisk and to the churches of Santa Maria di Montesanto and Santa Maria dei Miracoli; consequently he depicts less of the Piazza. This viewpoint has also forced De Wailly to show much less detail of the buildings along the horizon than does Pannini. To the left, only the Palazzo del Quirinale is visible, and to the right, only the dome of the Gesù. In his painting, Pannini depicted the Villa Medici and the Church of Santa Trinità dei Monti to the left, and a series of palaces to the right.

Both De Wailly's and Pannini's views of the Piazza del Popolo are dependent on the tradition of seventeenth-century topographical painting. Bowron has noted that Pannini's view is very close to a 1680 painting by the Dutch artist Gaspar Van Wittel (1652–1736) and to the aforementioned engraving by Gomar Wouters (Bowron 1981, p. 49, fig. 10, p. 50; Ciucci 1974, p. 75, repr.). Piranesi made a radical break with this tradition when he depicted the Piazza del Popolo in one of the first etchings of the *Vedute di Roma* (1745/48–1778) from a low point of view, close to the obelisk (fig. 3). Piranesi was thus able to concentrate the viewer's attention on the facades of the churches of Santa Maria di Montesanto and Santa Maria dei Miracoli and the obelisk, rather than on the distant view along the horizon (Robison in Bettagno 1983, pp. 18–19; Hind 1922, p. 41, no. 14; Focillon 1964, p. 54, no. 794; Scott 1975, p. 321, fig. 23, p. 22).

The principles of radial city planning that De Wailly observed at the Piazza del Popolo had an influence on his unexecuted project for a new opera house and surrounding allées in the Jardin des Tuileries (1781 and 1798) and on the new harbor at Port-Vendres, built between 1779 and 1783 (Mosser and Rabreau in Paris 1979, pp. 68–69, no. 268, repr. p. 68, and pp. 72–73, nos. 281, 283, repr. pp. 80–81).

FIGURE 1 Charles De Wailly, *Rome: The Piazza del Popolo*. Musée de Rouen.

FIGURE 2 G. P. Pannini, *A View of the Piazza del Popolo, Rome*. The William Rockhill Nelson Trust, Nelson-Atkins Museum of Art, Kansas City, Kansas, F79–3.

FIGURE 3 G. B. Piranesi, *Piazza del Popolo, Rome*, in *Vedute di Roma*, vol. 1, folio 21. Canadian Centre for Architecture, Montréal, IDM85–B15668 CAGE.

NO. 90

JEAN-HONORÉ FRAGONARD

Grasse 1732–Paris 1806

90. *View of the Hermit's Courtyard in the Colosseum*

Red chalk. 14½ x 10⁹⁄₁₆ inches (368 x 267 mm). Watermark: not available.

Inscribed in brown ink at lower left: *fragonard Rome 1758*; inscribed in graphite on old mount: *Vue de la Cour de l'Hermite du Colisée.*

PROVENANCE: Janos Scholz, New York; Schaeffer Galleries, New York; private collection, New York

BIBLIOGRAPHY: Ananoff 1961–70, I, no. 385

EXHIBITIONS: New York 1978 [not numbered]; Washington and elsewhere 1978–79, no. 2, repr.; Rome 1990–91, no. 7, repr.

Collection of Alice Steiner

This rather early drawing dated 1758 is unusual in that it predates by two years the series of red chalk drawings Fragonard produced during the summer of 1760, which he spent at Tivoli as the guest of the Abbé de Saint-Non. It is evident from Hubert Robert's drawing of the same subject that both artists were together on the day Fragonard made his drawing. Robert's drawing (now in Besançon) is a little larger, and is taken from a slightly different angle but includes the same details as Fragonard's, such as the coat draped over the ladder (Inv. D. 2987; Cornillot 1957, no. 131, repr.). As Eunice Williams has noted, the inscription at the lower left, *Fragonard*, which is not Fragonard's autograph, may be Natoire's. The second letter has clearly been changed from an *l* to an *r*, and it was Natoire who routinely misspelled Fragonard's name, making it read instead, *Flagonard.*

91. *The Fountain of Pomona at the Villa d'Este, Tivoli*

Red chalk with some faint traces of black chalk on laid paper. 18¾ x 13¾ inches (476 x 349 mm). Watermark: none visible.

DATE: about 1760.

PROVENANCE: George Guy, earl of Warwick (1818–93), Warwick Castle, his mark, lower right corner (Lugt 1921, no. 2600); Gaston Le Breton, Rouen, his sale, Paris, 8 December 1921, no. 136, repr. (as H. Robert); Maurice Feuillet, Paris, his mark, lower right corner (Lugt 1921, supplement, 1956, no. 1864); Marcel Bernheim (ca. 1926–54), Paris, his mark, lower left corner; Charles E. Slatkin Galleries, New York.

BIBLIOGRAPHY: Feuillet 1926, p. 3, under no. 34 (Collection of Marcel Bernheim); Fosca 1954, p. 55, under no. 13 (Collection of Marcel Bernheim); Ananoff 1961–71, p. 383, under no. 908 (as Hubert Robert); Rosenberg in Paris and New York 1987–88, p. 109, under no. 32, fig. 2; Rosenberg and Cuzin in Rome 1990–91, p. 116, under no. 67.

EXHIBITIONS: Ottawa 1976, p. 62, no. 23, repr. p. 63.

Toronto, Private Collection

According to a letter of 27 August 1760 written to the marquis de Marigny by Charles-Joseph Natoire, director of the French Academy in Rome, Fragonard and the Abbé de Saint-Non spent the months of July and August and part of September 1760 at the Villa d'Este. Fragonard was then at the end of his stay (1756–61) as a *pensionnaire* at the French Academy (Paris and New York 1987–88, pp. 67–68).

Fragonard produced several red chalk drawings of known sites and monuments in and around Tivoli while he was at the Villa d'Este in 1760: the Waterfalls, the Temple of the Sibyl, the villas of Hadrian and Maecenas, and the Grotto of Neptune (Paris and New York 1987–88, pp. 97–100, 102–5, 114–15, nos. 24, 25, 27–29, 36, all repr. p. 95, figs. 6, 7; Rome 1990–91, pp. 130–31, no. 75, repr. p. 131). These were the same sites and monuments that Piranesi had depicted

NO. 91

FIGURE 1 Jean-Honoré Fragonard, *The Fountain of Pomona at the Villa d'Este*. Musée des Beaux-Arts et d'Archéologie, Besançon.

(Cat. no. 56). Ten of Fragonard's red chalk drawings of Tivoli were executed for the Abbé de Saint-Non, and are now in the Musée de Besançon. Five of these drawings depict the Villa d'Este: *The Large Cypress Trees, The Fountain of Pomona, The Oval Staircase of the Fountain of the Dragon*, and two views of *The Fountain of the Organ* (Paris and New York 1987–88, pp. 106–7, 109–14, nos. 30, 32–35, all repr.). In addition, Marianne Roland Michel has recently discovered a sixth red chalk drawing of *The Belvedere and the Fountain of Flora*, now with Cailleux, Paris (Paris 1991, no. 59, repr.).

Fragonard made counterproofs in Tivoli of almost all his drawings at Besançon before giving the ten original red chalk drawings to the Abbé de Saint-Non in Tivoli. Later, in Paris, Fragonard continued to make versions of the original Tivoli drawings. Saint-Non engraved in aquatint in Paris between 1761 and 1764 three of the red chalk drawings he had received from Fragonard (Paris and New York 1987–88, p. 95, fig. 4, p. 111, fig. 4, and p. 111, fig. 1; Valence 1985, pp. 312–14). Fragonard executed several etchings himself of the gardens of the Villa d'Este (Paris 1987, nos. 39, 40). According to drawings made by Gabriel de Saint-Aubin in the margin of a 1765 *livret* of the Salon, at least two of the red chalk drawings of the Villa d'Este belonging to the Abbé de Saint-Non were exhibited at the Salon – *The Large Cypress Trees* and *The*

Fountain of Pomona (Paris and New York 1987–88, p. 107, fig. 6, p. 109, fig. 1). In 1765, Saint-Non gave the ten red chalk drawings back to Fragonard who subsequently sold them to Pierre-Adrien Pâris. Pâris donated them to the city of Besançon in 1819 (Paris and New York, 1987–88, p. 95). Pierre Rosenberg has suggested that while the red chalk counterproofs of the Tivoli drawings were made in Tivoli, those counterproofs that were heightened with sepia wash, as well as those versions done in wash over black chalk drawing, were executed later in Paris, perhaps after 1765, when Fragonard received the original red chalk drawings back from Saint-Non (Paris and New York 1987–88, p. 107, fig. 2, pp. 107–8, no. 31, repr. p. 108; Rome 1990–91, pp. 129–30, no. 73, pl. XX).

The drawing by Fragonard exhibited here depicts the Fountain of Pomona, part of the wall of the Alley of One Hundred Fountains, and the entrance to the two Fountains of Bacchus at the northeastern side of the gardens of the Villa d'Este (Coffin 1960, p. 34, nos. 11, 13, 16 assigned in fig. 1; fig. 29). This drawing is a version in reverse of the red chalk drawing of the same subject in Besançon (fig. 1) (Paris and New York 1987–88, pp. 109–10, no. 30, repr. p. 109). Fragonard depicted the Fountain of Pomona, which is in the center of the Besançon drawing, from an oblique viewpoint. The entrance to the two Fountains of Bacchus is at the left, and part of the wall of the Alley of One Hundred Fountains is at the right. One corner of the Villa d'Este is visible in the Besançon drawing, in the background to the right.

The Toronto drawing of the Fountain of Pomona is slightly smaller than the red chalk drawing in Besançon, which measures 488 x 361 millimeters. The Toronto drawing is not a counterproof of the Besançon drawing, as suggested by Rosenberg, because it does not have the hatching lines going in the opposite direction. It has other small differences as well. The top of the wall leading to the entrance to the two Fountains of Bacchus at the right is slightly curved. The clouds in the sky are depicted with many more cursive lines added to the horizontal hatching. The branches of the tree, behind the wall to the right, hang down closer to the volute above the archway in front of the Fountain of Pomona. Fragonard made less use of hatching lines and did more rubbing with the stump to produce the shadows in the Toronto drawing. He may have begun the Toronto drawing by tracing the main outlines of the architectural elements and trees from a counterproof of the Besançon drawing (identified by Ananoff), formerly in the collection of Vivant Denon. Its dimensions of 490 x 360 millimeters are closer to those of the Besançon drawing (Ananoff 1961–71, p. 94, no. 2159, not repr.; sale, London, Sotheby's, 23 March 1960, p. 7, no. 17, not repr.). The Toronto drawing exhibits very slight, barely perceptible traces of black chalk underdrawing. Eunice Williams noted that this type of underdrawing is found in several of the Besançon red chalk drawings (Williams in Washington and elsewhere 1978–79, p. 42, no. 8, repr. p. 43).

When the Toronto drawing was sold in Paris in 1921 and published by Ananoff in 1961, it was attributed to Hubert Robert. It was correctly attributed to Fragonard by Feuillet, Fosca, and Rosenberg. Hubert Robert was not mentioned in Natoire's letter as being at the Villa d'Este with Fragonard and the Abbé de Saint-Non in 1760 (Valence 1985, p. 86). There is a red chalk drawing by Robert of *The Fountain of the Organ* (fig. 2) that was based on a lost red chalk drawing by Fragonard; unfortunately, it is not evidence in itself that Robert visited the Villa d'Este while Fragonard and the Abbé de Saint-Non were there in 1760, since Robert could have copied the Fragonard drawing later (Washington 1978a, no. 6, Robert, pp. 38–39, repr. p. 39; Rosenberg and Cuzin in Rome 1990–91, pp. 27–28, notes 15–18, p. 30, fig. 4, Fragonard, p. 22). However, the two artists were close friends while in Rome, and did have so much mutual influence on each other during the years 1750 to 1761 that it is often difficult to tell their drawings apart.

The drawing of *The Belvedere and the Fountain of Flora of the Villa d'Este*, recently discovered by Marianne Roland Michel (fig. 3), was originally attributed to Hubert Robert because of the inscription *Robert* on the mount with his signature on the reverse. By comparison with other drawings by Hubert Robert at the recent exhibition *J. H. Fragonard e Hubert*

Robert a Roma it was definitely established as one of the first drawings Fragonard executed at the Villa d'Este (Rosenberg and Cuzin in Rome 1990–91, p. 133, no. 79, repr.). Eunice Williams had noted earlier that it is particularly in the treatment of the trees and the foliage where one distinguishes the styles of Fragonard and Hubert Robert. For the trunks and branches of the trees, Fragonard starts with loosely drawn outlines. He then adds parallel diagonal hatchings placed close together, sharply drawn sawtooth motifs, and staccato dots to build up the mass of the foliage (Williams in Washington and elsewhere 1978–79, p. 40, no. 7, repr. p. 41). In his Roman drawings (fig. 2), Hubert Robert depicts much less luxuriant, dense foliage, with less hatching. He often adds supplementary outlines to reinforce the forms of the branches of the trees (Williams in Washington and elsewhere 1978–79, p. 170, no. 70, repr. p. 171). Like the view of *The Belvedere and the Fountain of Flora* (fig. 3), the Toronto version of *The Fountain of Pomona* exhibits the rich and dense foliage created by the graphic conventions that differentiate Fragonard's drawings from Robert's. The brilliant quality of the light and the precision of detail indicate that Fragonard most likely executed the Toronto drawing while he was still at the Villa d'Este in Tivoli in the summer of 1760.

As we have shown with regard to the drawings of *The Fountain of Pomona*, Fragonard also made two versions of the original red chalk drawing of *The Large Cypress Trees* in Besançon (Cat. no. 56). One red chalk counterproof, formerly in the collection of Ian Woodner, was heightened with sepia wash; a version in the same direction as the original drawing in the Albertina was executed in black graphite underdrawing heightened with sepia wash (Roland Michel 1987, p. 38, and p. 32, fig. 23, p. 33, fig. 24).

It is difficult to assign a precise purpose to Fragonard's versions of the original red chalk drawings of the Villa d'Este at Besançon. Obviously, he made the initial red chalk counterproofs as a record for himself of what he gave to the Abbé de Saint-Non. The later versions are a testimony to the importance he attached to the Villa d'Este as a source of inspiration.

FIGURE 2 Hubert Robert, *The Fountain of the Organ of the Villa d'Este, Tivoli*. National Gallery of Art, Washington, 1990.129.1.

FIGURE 3 Jean-Honoré Fragonard, *The Belvedere and the Fountain of Flora of the Villa d'Este*. Paris, Cailleux.

JEAN-HONORÉ FRAGONARD

Grasse 1732–Paris 1806

92. *The Eruption of Monte Nuovo*

Pen and brush and brown ink, over black chalk. 8¹¹⁄₁₆ x 6½ inches (221 x 165 mm). Watermark: probably Vanderley; letter *V* and shield enclosing fleur-de-lis [cut off]. Inscribed at lower center below dolphin, *Monte novo*; at lower left, *Dy*.

PROVENANCE: probably M. de Bourguignon de Fabregoules, Aix-en-Provence; M. Charles-Joseph-Barthélemi Giraud, Perne; Flury-Hérard, Paris (Lugt 1015, numbered in pen and black ink, *268*); probably his sale, Paris, Blaisot, 13–15 May 1861; H. M. Calmann, Ltd., London.

BIBLIOGRAPHY: Morgan Library *FR* VII, 1955, pp. 76f.; Morgan Library *Review* 1969, pp. 144f.

EXHIBITIONS: New York 1984, no. 117; New York 1989.

The Pierpont Morgan Library. Purchased as the gift of Rowland Burdon-Muller, Acc. no. 1955.2

FIGURE 1 Jean-Honoré Fragonard, *The Eruption of Monte Nuovo*, in Abbé de Saint-Non, *Voyage pittoresque*. The Pierpont Morgan Library, New York.

Although this drawing is not Fragonard's final design, it is preparatory for the tailpiece for chapter eleven, engraved by Charles Guttenberg, in the Abbé de Saint-Non's *Voyage pittoresque ou description des royaumes de Naples et de Sicile* (fig. 1) (Paris 1781–86, I, part 2, p. 22). This chapter is devoted to a description of the Phlegraean Fields, the volcanic district west of Naples. Saint-Non notes in his commentary on the illustrations that the representation of "l'effet de la terrible explosion du volcan qui a donné naissance à Monte Nuovo," because it was the most recent and at the same time most extraordinary volcanic phenomenon of the region, had been selected as an appropriate conclusion to this chapter. The eruption, which occurred in September 1538, destroyed an entire town and its inhabitants, creating a new mountain, *Monte Nuovo*. There is some change between Fragonard's design and the final engraving in the book, but most of the basic elements remain the same. In the engraving, Fragonard's sea gods and dolphins are replaced by a more realistic knot of rocks and rushes. The view of Vesuvius erupting remains as does the vertical orientation of both works, but the knob-like ornament at the base of the design area disappears in the engraving. The drawing also has something in common with the horizontally oriented title-page vignette which Fragonard also designed. Here, the city of Naples is personified by a crowned woman, with frightened sea nymphs fleeing into the rushes from an erupting Vesuvius, seen in the background. The sea nymphs' tails resemble twisted dolphins' tails, and the rushes they flee into have very much the same sort of drooping pointed leaves, very similar to those in the Morgan drawing.

Felice Stampfle discovered some years ago that Fragonard freely adapted part of Stefano della Bella's etching (*Raccolta di varii cappricii et nove inventioni di cartelle et ornamenti*, pl. 9 [de Vesme 1035]; de Vesme/Massar 1971, I, pp. 156f.; II, p. 226, repr.). Here, the fantastic sea creatures (with human forms and leafy scrolls instead of feet) above the rush-enclosed roundel with the view of the mountain are taken from Stefano's print, as is the coiled dolphin at the base of the roundel.

JEAN-HONORÉ FRAGONARD
Grasse 1732–Paris 1806

93. *An Imaginary Italian Garden*

Brush and brown wash over black chalk. 11¾ x 16⅝ inches (298 x 422 mm). Watermark: not available.

PROVENANCE: K. E. Maison, London; Otto Wertheimer, Paris; Knoedler, New York; T. Edward Hanley, Bradford, Pennsylvania; Mr. and Mrs. Eugene Victor Thaw, New York.

BIBLIOGRAPHY: Ananoff 1961–70, I, no. 364, fig. 133.

EXHIBITIONS: Buffalo 1960, no. 75; New York 1961, no. 63; New York 1967, p. 63; Columbus, Ohio 1968, p. 72; New York and elsewhere 1975–76, no. 36, repr.; Washington and elsewhere 1978–79, no. 40, repr.; Richmond, Virginia 1981, no. 14, repr.

Collection of Eugene Victor and Clare Thaw

This free and boldly conceived capriccio of an Italian garden is very different from Fragonard's work of the late 1750s and 1760s, when he was a student in Rome. Indeed this sketch, as Eunice Williams points out, owes something to Piranesi in inspiration. While the relationship between Robert and Piranesi is well known, that between Fragonard and Piranesi has not been sufficiently explored. It seems likely, however, if not documented, that Fragonard, like other *pensionnaires*, would have been quite aware of Piranesi and probably knew him personally. Fragonard accompanied his friend Bergeret to Rome in the 1770s, the most likely date of this work, and Piranesi was a frequent visitor to Bergeret's weekly salon. The subject of this drawing, while imaginary, may be loosely based on the artist's recollections of the gardens of the Villa Madama, and most likely was made after he returned to Paris. Stylistically it is similar to three other drawings, *Entrance of the Villa Hadriana in Tivoli* (Ananoff 1445), *Park Scene with Antiques* (Ananoff 1598), and *The Imprisoned Giant* (Ananoff 1918).

HUBERT ROBERT
Paris 1733–Paris 1808

94. *Draughtsman in an Italian Church*

Red chalk. 12 15/16 x 17 5/8 inches (329 x 448 mm). Watermark: none visible through lining.
Dated in lower left corner, *1763*.

PROVENANCE: M. le Vicomte Beuret; his sale, Paris, Georges Petit, 25 November 1924, lot 19; Charles Férault (Lugt S. 2793a); Mrs. W. H. Crocker; Frank Perls Gallery, Beverly Hills; Mr. Eugene Victor Thaw, New York.

BIBLIOGRAPHY: *Le Gaulois artistique*, 12 May 1928, p. 189, repr. in advertisement of Charles Férault; Morgan Library *FR* XX, 1984, p. 294; Roland Michel 1987, p. 76, no. 65.

EXHIBITIONS: New York and elsewhere 1975–76, no. 37, repr.; Washington 1978, no. 13, repr.; New York 1984a, no. 7; New York 1989; Rome 1990–91, no. 117, repr.

The Pierpont Morgan Library. Gift of Mr. and Mrs. Eugene Victor Thaw, Acc. no. 1981.74

Robert went to Rome in 1754 under the sponsorship of his patron, the duc de Choiseul, then the comte de Stainville, the French ambassador. In Italy until 1765, he became friendly with Fragonard and the Abbé de Saint-Non in whose company he visited Naples. Robert was influenced by Pannini and the Italian *prospettivisti*, and by his passion for classical antiquity. Here the artist is sketching Domenichino's fresco *The Flagellation of St. Andrew* in the Oratory of St. Andrew (adjacent to San Gregorio al Celio, Rome). As is recorded in Natoire's reports to Marigny, Domenichino and above all Raphael were the artists considered most important for the *pensionnaires* to study. In another view of the Oratory, Robert depicted three artists at work (Rome 1990–91, no. 117a). Victor Carlson (Washington 1978a, p. 52) noted that these drawings must have been made at the same time because the artist's easel, propped up against the holy water font, appears in both.

HUBERT ROBERT

Paris 1733–Paris 1808

95. *Draughtsman Sketching at the Villa Madama*

Red chalk. 18½ x 13½ inches (470 x 343 mm). Watermark: none visible through lining.
Signed and inscribed in pen and black ink at lower right, *villa madama Robert 56?*

PROVENANCE: possibly the artist's family, perhaps one of the many drawings sold in lots in his sale, 5 April 1809; possibly Destailleur; art market Paris (as indicated by presence of customs stamp on verso of mount which indicates that it passed through Paris, probably in the 1930s); private collection, Florida; sale, William Doyle Galleries, New York, 25 January 1989, lot 86.

EXHIBITION: New York 1989.

Collection of Eugene Victor and Clare Thaw

Robert must have visited the Villa Madama in the company of another young artist, who is shown sketching in one of the picturesque arched grottos of the garden, perched on an overturned basket. To judge from the old mount, this drawing was in the same collection with another of Robert's drawings of the same approximate size and technique, *View of the Stables at the Villa Giulia* (Paris and New York 1993, no. 74, repr.). The two mounts are identical. Mr. Thaw purchased both at the same auction in 1989. It seems very probable that both drawings came from one of Robert's *albums factices* and that the blue mount which surrounds both drawings was made by the artist himself. It was Robert's custom to remove drawings from his sketchbooks when he used the drawing as a study for a painting, later placing them in an album.

NO. 95

ROBERT 173

HUBERT ROBERT
Paris 1733–Paris 1808

96. *The Oval Staircase at the Villa d'Este*

NO. 96

Watercolor, brown wash, over black chalk. 18⅞ x 19½ inches (480 x 495 mm). Watermark: none visible through lining.

PROVENANCE: P. J. Mariette; marquis de Lagoy; Pierre Crozat; Duke Ludwig I of Hesse-Darmstadt, in 1812; H.-J. von Dalberg, 1773–1833; Hessischen Landesmuseum, Darmstadt; Wildenstein & Co., Ltd., London.

EXHIBITIONS: London 1934, no. 34, pl. X; New York 1984, no. 76; New York 1989.

Private collection, promised gift to The Pierpont Morgan Library

In this attractively finished view, Robert's handling of watercolor is extremely similar to Pannini's, who was one of the greatest influences on the young French artist. Mariette, who found Robert's paintings less interesting generally than his drawings (into which he felt Robert put a good deal of spirit), especially liked the drawings which the artist had lightly colored, commenting later in his biographical sketch that Robert made some of these colored drawings for him. *The Oval Staircase* was one of a group of important eighteenth-century French and Italian drawings that came on the market in 1933 when the Hessischen Landesmuseum exchanged them for a collection of Rhenish art (see Lugt S. 1257 c–e).

Though the view depicted here was identified as the entrance to the Villa Aldobrandini at Frascati, it is really an imaginary view at the Villa d'Este, based on one of the oval staircases at either side of the Fountain of the Dragon, which can be seen in other eighteenth-century drawings, including one by Fragonard, now in a private collection in Minneapolis (Rome 1990–91, no. 69, repr.). Although no freestanding sculptural figures at the foot and head of the staircases exist now, they were part of the original decorative scheme, as can be seen in a seventeenth-century engraving by Venturini (Coffin 1960, fig. 16). The figures were probably still in place during the eighteenth century, since they were included in views by Fragonard and other contemporary artists.

NO. 97

HUBERT ROBERT

Paris 1733–Paris 1808

97. *The South Façade of the Palazzo Poli with the Trevi Fountain under Construction*

Red chalk. 12¹¹⁄₁₆ x 17⁹⁄₁₆ inches (323 x 447 mm). Watermark: none.

PROVENANCE: Mme A.; her sale, Paris, Hôtel Drouot, 6 November 1922, lot 16; Mrs. Charles Mitchell; her daughter, Mrs. Allerton Cushman.

BIBLIOGRAPHY: Morgan Library *FR* XVII, 1976, p. 178.

EXHIBITIONS: Washington 1978a, no. 10, repr.; New York 1981, no. 107, repr.; New York 1984, no. 75; New York 1989.

The Pierpont Morgan Library. Gift of Mrs. Allerton Cushman in honor of Janos Scholz, Acc. no. 1973.51

This view must have been drawn during the latter half of Robert's eleven-year stay in Rome, probably around 1760 or 1761, for the Trevi Fountain was completed in May of 1762, some 122 years after Pope Urban VIII commissioned Bernini to redesign it in 1640. Not until the time of Clement XII was the project realized; the final design was the work of Nicolas Salvi. The fountain dates to Roman times and is the terminal for the Acqua Vergine aqueduct (still in use today), whose flow begins in the village of Salone, nine miles east of Rome, and courses part of the way through the original stone channels made by Agrippa's engineers.

Palazzo Poli, seen in the background of this drawing, was the Roman residence of the counts of Conti, who later became the dukes of Poli. A counterproof of Robert's drawing in the Bibliothèque de Besançon is reproduced as plate 42 in *La Rome d'Hubert Robert,* by G. K. Loukomski and Pierre de Nolhac (Paris, 1930). Robert's inscription along the lower center of the counterproof, *Fontana di Trevi coperta di legnani e tele*, was mistakenly identified in this publication as that of Pierre-Adrien Pâris, the architect friend of both Robert and Fragonard. At his death in 1819 Pâris left his entire collection to Besançon. These included some 330 drawings, some of which, like the inscribed view of the Trevi Fountain, are counterproofs.

HUBERT ROBERT

Paris 1733–Paris 1808

98. *Sketchbook, Rome, 1760–63*

39 leaves including manuscript title page lettered, *Croquis Faits à Rome par hubert Robert en 1760. Rome 1760.* Mostly pen and brown ink, brown wash, over slight indications in black chalk; some sketches in black chalk, also in graphite, a few in red chalk, and several watercolors. Binding: red paper board sides with calf back and corners. 9³⁄₁₆ x 5¼ inches (233 x 134 mm). Leaf: 9 x 4⁷⁄₁₆ inches (228 x 113 mm). Watermark: *[H]ONIG* and fragment of shield.

PROVENANCE: presumably part of the sale of the artist's estate, Paris, Paillet et Olivier, 5 April 1809; Adrien Fauchier-Magnan, Neuilly (not in his sale, London, Sotheby's, 4 December 1935); David David-Weill, Neuilly.

BIBLIOGRAPHY: Mongan and Sachs 1940, p. 338 under no. 635 (mentioned as formerly in the Fauchier-Magnan collection); Morgan Library *FR* IX, 1958–59, pp. 104f.; Baltimore and elsewhere 1985, under no. 54; Roland Michel 1987, p. 86, pl. 51, figs. 84, 85; Rome 1990–91, under no. 107.

EXHIBITIONS: Paris 1933, p. 49, no. 37 (as in David-Weill Collection); Washington 1978a, no. 15, 3 figures, p. 57; New York 1984, no. 118; New York 1989.

The Pierpont Morgan Library. Purchased as the gift of the Fellows with the assistance of an anonymous contribution from a foundation, Acc. no. 1958.5

More than fifty sketchbooks or *albums factices* were included in the sale after Robert's death (sale, Paris, Paillet et Olivier, 5 April 1809, lots 342, 343, 346, 353). Since 1958, when the Library acquired the Roman sketchbook, the important *Album de Voyage*, formerly in the collection of the marquis de Ganay, has been dismembered and sold at auction (sale, Mo-

naco, Sotheby's, 1 December 1989, lots 20, 26, 27, 30, 35, 38, 52, 53, 56), leaving the Morgan book as the only true sketchbook by Hubert Robert—true in distinction to the *albums factices*, books made by the artist with sheets he himself removed from his sketchbooks.

Robert began to work in this little book in 1760 and continued to use it for at least three more years, since one opening (folio 14 verso), a study for an etching in *Les Soirées de Rome*, is dated 1763. First the artist ruled borders throughout in pen and gray ink and then began to draw with black chalk. On the initial pages, drawn in a somewhat tentative manner, he sketched ordinary subjects. These include several studies of a laundry shed, a rusticated Renaissance doorway, and sketches of Roman peasant women. Eventually, however, he began to draw more freely and with great assurance in pen and brown ink. Although the sketchbook contains a pleasing variety of subjects, Robert devoted most of its pages to straightforward recordings of Roman monuments as well as many brilliant pen and wash drawings that are imaginative variations on Roman monuments.

Many of these show the artist giving way to a piranesian streak of invention, taking familiar Roman monuments, such as the statues of *Marcus Aurelius* and the *Horse Tamers*, the Pantheon, the colonnade of St. Peter's, and the Pyramid of Cestius, and rearranging them in fantastic combinations, all the more remarkable for their small format. Especially interesting in this connection are folios 14 to 21. On folio 14, for example, the Pantheon is combined with a section of St. Peter's colonnade, and folio 15 shows the colonnade again, this time with the obelisk, thrown into conjunction with three immense pyramids. Folio 16 is a view of a fantastic building with statues and arches while folio 17 shows a fantastic bridge like a porticoed temple. On folio 18, Robert sketched a sparkling capriccio with the Capitoline hill, *Marcus Aurelius*, and the *Horse Tamers*, and on folio 20, he invented a full-blown architectural fantasy with arcaded bridges and the *Horse Tamers*—one bridge even includes a palace built onto it. On folio 21, Robert placed the statue of *Marcus Aurelius* in front of a villa, while on folio 35, he depicted a fantastic view of the Pyramid of Cestius.

In view of how well Robert worked in pen and wash, it is surprising that this technique is relatively uncommon in his oeuvre. For the most part, Robert drew in red chalk, but his technique in pen and wash is equally formidable. His pen and wash drawings in the Roman sketchbook are varied and in some instances parallel Piranesi's. Indeed, Piranesi's first biographer, Legrand, mentioned the two artists' sketching expeditions together: "Piranesi ne faisait point de dessins finis, un gros trait à la sanguine sur lequel il revenait ensuite à la plume et au pinceau, et par parties seulement lui suffisait pour arrêter ses idées . . .". He goes on to say:

> Le peintre Robert, avec lequel il dessinait quelquefois aussi d'après nature et qui était si bien en état d'apprécier son talent, ne concevait pas ce qu'on pouvait faire des croquis aussi peu arrêtés. Piranesi voyant son étonnement lui disant 'Le dessin n'est pas sur mon papier, j'en conviens, mais il est tout entier dans ma tête et le verrez par ma planche' (Legrand, folio 135 and verso).

The Morgan sketchbook also contains a few landscapes, notably the watercolor for *La Balance*, an idealized pastoral subject with some young people playing on an improvised swing (folio 37). There are six studies for *Les Soireés de Rome* in this book (Cat. no. 120). Robert decided to execute the suite of ten etchings in honor of the visit to Rome of the gifted amateur Claude-Henri Watelet (see Cat. no. 86) and Marguerite Lecomte, both of whom arrived in Rome on 18 December 1763. The etched suite first appeared in 1764. Another study, signed and dated 1764, for *Le Poteau*, the last plate in *Les Soirées de Rome*, was in the Ganay sketchbook in which Robert worked between 1762 and 1764.

Since the Morgan sketchbook was not included in Henriot's catalogue of the David-Weill Collection published in 1927, it may be assumed that it was still in the collection of Adrien Fauchier-Magnan. By 1933, however, when the sketchbook was in the Robert exhibition at the Musée de l'Orangerie, it was in the David-Weill Collection from which it was eventually acquired by the Library.

NO. 98   fol. 15

fol. 17

fol. 20

NO. 99

HUBERT ROBERT
Paris 1733–Paris 1808

99. *The "Temple of Mercury" at Pozzuoli*

Red chalk. 12½ x 17⁷⁄₁₆ inches (316 x 443 mm). Watermark: none visible through lining.

Signed and inscribed in red chalk, *Roberti Intrata del tempio di Mercurio Pozzuoli 17.*

PROVENANCE: François Rénaud, Paris (Lugt 1042); H. Shickman Gallery, New York; M. Christian Humann, New York; private collection, New York; P. & D. Colnaghi & Co., New York.

EXHIBITIONS: New York 1985, no. 4, repr.; New York 1989.

Collection of Mr. and Mrs. Henry Tang

FIGURE 1 Hubert Robert, *The Temple of Mercury at Pozzuoli*, in Abbé de Saint-Non, *Voyage pittoresque*, vol. I, part 2, opposite p. 212. The Pierpont Morgan Library, New York.

Although the date has been partially effaced, Robert most probably made this drawing (which actually represents one of the baths at Baia) in 1760 when he visited both Paestum and Pozzuoli with the Abbé de Saint-Non. The pair left Rome for Naples on 17 April 1760. In this connection the abbé speaks of Robert in his journal, ". . . un des Elèves de notre accadémie à Rome, jeune Peintre de la plus grande Espérance et du premier Talent dans le genre de l'Architecture et des Ruînes, j'ai pris mon essor pour aller voir ces Temples fameux de Pestum dont j'avois depuis longtems entendu parler, mais que l'éloignement ne m'avoit pas permis d'aller visiter à l'autre voyage." Robert's treatment of the ruins here is similar to other ruins depicted in the *Scuola di Virgilio*, a drawing which must date from the same trip and is now in the Yale University Art Gallery (Washington 1978a, no. 5, repr.). As Victor Carlson notes, the abbé paid Robert's expenses for the journey and in return Robert made the drawings from which the Abbé de Saint-Non would later select subjects to etch for the *Voyage pittoresque* and in fact a plate of this drawing (engraved by Guttenberg) appears opposite page 212 in volume I, part 2 (fig. 1). It is interesting to note that Clérisseau, like Robert, chose to enliven his view of the *Travelers in the Interior of the Temple of Mercury at Baia* (Cat. no. 87) with the same detail – visitors being carried piggyback across the water collected in a Roman bath (which was believed at this time to be a temple). Although he did not mention Pozzuoli and its surroundings in his journal when he returned to the area in the spring of 1760, the Abbé de Saint-Non had a good deal to say about this location on his first visit in December 1759, specifically about the so-called Temple of Mercury: "on doit s'arrêter pour voir les Restes de trois Temples fameux à peu de distance les uns des autres: l'un est celui de Vénus, l'autre de Diane, et le troisième de Mercure, mais dans lequel on ne peut entrer que porté sur les Epaules des Matelots, parce qu'il est actuellement plein d'Eau."

NO. 100

HUBERT ROBERT

Paris 1733–Paris 1808

100. *View of the Campidoglio, Rome*

Red chalk. 13⅛ x 17⅝ inches (334 x 447 mm). Watermark: none visible through lining.
Dated at lower left center, *1762*.

PROVENANCE: Charles Fairfax Murray; J. Pierpont Morgan (no mark; see Lugt S. 1509).

BIBLIOGRAPHY: Fairfax Murray, III, no. 117, repr.; Held 1990, pp. 151ff., repr.

EXHIBITIONS: Dayton 1971, no. 20, repr.; New York 1978 [no. 48]; New York 1989.

The Pierpont Morgan Library. Purchased by J. Pierpont Morgan, 1910, Acc. no. III, 117

One of Robert's favorite places to sketch was the Campidoglio with Michelangelo's architectural masterpiece—the piazza and buildings at the summit of the staircase alongside Santa Maria in Aracoeli. Aside from the site, Robert was attracted to the monuments such as the equestrian statue of *Marcus Aure-* *lius*, the pair of lions, and the *Horse Tamers*, all of which would recur in his drawings and paintings throughout his career. He drew a great series of red chalk drawings of the Capitoline Hill, apparently in 1762 since many are dated; seven of them are at Valence (see Valence 1985, nos. 22–27) and the Louvre. Most of these drawings include the *Marcus Aurelius*, viewed from different angles. Other views including the famous bronze are at Karlsruhe and Berlin (Rome 1990–91, under no. 107, figs. a & b). The Library's drawing, which also shows *Marcus Aurelius*, comprehends a broad view of the Campidoglio with emphasis on the Palazzo dei Conservatori. Since the same compositional details and individuals appear in several drawings, it is likely that many were produced on the same day. Catherine Boulot, who wrote the Robert entries for the recent exhibition at the Villa Medici (Rome 1990–91, no. 106), notes that he put a cupola on the then unfinished church of Santa Rita da Cascia, at the foot of the Aracoeli steps, in order to make a more pleasing composition. Robert included this imaginary dome in the background of the Morgan drawing as well.

HUBERT ROBERT

Paris 1733–Paris 1808

101. *Vaulted Passageway with a View of the Pyramid of Cestius through a Doric Portico*

Pen, black ink, sepia wash and blue and orange watercolor over black chalk underdrawing on laid paper with a double border in black ink. 10½ x 8⅝ inches (267 x 220 mm). Watermark: none.

Inscribed or signed on the verso, *Robert fecit*, in brown ink.

DATE· about 1760–65.

PROVENANCE: Cailleux, Paris.

BIBLIOGRAPHY: Paris 1992, no. 11, repr.

NO. 101

EXHIBITION: Paris 1992, no. 11.

Montréal, Centre Canadien d'Architecture/Canadian Centre for Architecture. Acquired with a gift from Mrs. Marjorie Bronfman, DR1993:0001

This drawing illustrates the importance of both Giovanni Battista Piranesi and Giovanni Paolo Pannini for Hubert Robert's development during his eleven years of study in Rome from 1754 to 1765 (Roland Michel in Paris 1992, no. 1). The *Vaulted Passageway* is similar in style to several other pen, ink, and watercolor drawings executed by Robert in oval formats in the early part of his career: one, the *Statue of Marcus Aurelius in a Gallery with a Ruined Barrel Vault*, dated 1759, in a private collection, and the other, the *Statue of Marcus Aurelius in an Oval Colonnade*, dated by Carlson to 1767, in the Robert Lehman Collection at the Metropolitan Museum of Art (Paris 1979, pp. 21–22, fig. 37, p. 21; Washington 1978a, p. 30, no. 2, repr. p. 31). That the CCA's drawing was reproduced in an aquatint executed by the Abbé de Saint-Non in 1767 and published in his *Recueil de griffonis* (fig. 1) indicates that Hubert Robert carried out this drawing in Rome (Cayeux 1963, p. 340, no. 102). Hubert Robert may have given the Abbé de Saint-Non this drawing in 1760. Robert went to Naples and Paestum with the abbé in April and June of 1760; he may also have spent part of the summer, between July and September of the same year, with the Abbé de Saint-Non and Fragonard at the Villa d'Este in Tivoli, although there is no documentary evidence for Robert's presence (Cayeux 1989, pp. 62–63).

Giovanni Paolo Pannini was professor of perspective at the French Academy in Rome during Robert's stay there. The composition of this drawing is close to two versions of a painting by Pannini, *Alexander Visiting the Tomb of Achilles*, the first dated 1719, his presentation piece to the Accademia di San Luca, and a second later version, in which the Pyramid of Cestius is seen through a vaulted portico with fluted Ionic columns (Arisi 1986, p. 278, no. 114, repr. p. 278, Rome, Accademia di San Luca, and p. 361, no. 259, repr. p. 361, Musée des Beaux-Arts de Narbonne; Kiene in Paris and elsewhere 1992–93, p. 130, no. 30).

Hubert Robert also made a painted version of the theme of Pannini's painting but used a different composition (Kiene in Paris and elsewhere 1992–93, no. 53, Musée du Louvre, p. 161, repr. p. 161). Robert owned several paintings by Pannini, among them a version of the *Exit of the duc de Choiseul from the Piazza of St. Peter's*, which Pannini probably gave the young artist in Rome (Cayeux 1989, pp. 38–40, note 6, p. 359; Arisi 1986, no. 445, 1754, Gemäldegalerie, Berlin, pp. 450–51, repr. p. 451, pls. 174, 175, p. 166, and no. 472, National Gallery of Scotland, p. 466, repr. p. 466).

In addition, there are references to Piranesi's works. The double portico with Doric columns is derived from the *Atrio Dorico* (fig. 2) of Piranesi's *Prima parte* (1743) (Robison 1986, p. 94, no. 13, repr. p. 94). The Pyramid of Cestius in the background was represented by Piranesi throughout his career, first in the *Varie Vedute* (1745; Cat. no. 50). Piranesi depicted it twice in the *Vedute di Roma*, once in 1745 to 1746, and a second time in 1761 (Hind 1922, p. 48, nos. 35–36; Focillon 1964, p. 53, no. 810, p. 52, no. 745; Robison in Bettagno 1983, pp. 18, 32; Wilton-Ely 1978 [1988] pls. 13, 57]. Finally, it reappears in the *Antichità Romane* (1756, vol. III, pl. XL; Focillon 1964, p. 29, no. 322; Wilton-Ely 1978 [1988], p. 35, fig. 46).

Hubert Robert was in close contact with Piranesi during the 1760s. According to Legrand, the two artists often drew together outdoors (Erouart and Mosser in Brunel 1978, p. 231). In 1762, Hubert Robert went to Piranesi's studio on the Strada Felice to pick up the copy of Piranesi's *Campus Martius* that was ordered by the marquis de Marigny (Focillon 1963, pp. 110–11). Robert used Piranesi's *Antichità di Cora* (1764) as a source of inspiration in 1765, his last year in Rome. The Temple of Hercules at Cora is depicted on a sheet dated 1765 from a sketchbook formerly in the collection of the marquis de Ganay (Roland Michel in Rome and elsewhere 1976, p. 304; Cayeux 1989, p. 74; sale, Monaco, Sotheby's, 1 December 1989, lot. 61; Focillon 1964, p. 40, no. 548). Hubert Robert had visited the Greek temples at Paestum with the Abbé de Saint-Non in 1760. A drawing of the Temple of Hera, known as "the Temple of Neptune" and the Temple of Argive Hera, known as "the Basilica" at Paestum, executed by Robert in 1760 on that trip, which is in the Morgan Library, is exhibited here (Cat. no. 102). However, Robert's interpretation of the Doric order in this drawing is faithful to Piranesi's. The Doric order of the portico in Robert's drawing is Roman rather than Greek, since the columns have bases. The Doric column without base, like the one used at the temples of Paestum and at the Acropolis in Athens, was to become one of the hallmarks of the neoclassical style of architecture (McCarthy 1972, p. 760).

FIGURE 1 Abbé de Saint-Non, aquatint of Hubert Robert's *Vaulted Passageway with a View of the Pyramid of Cestius through a Doric Portico*, from *Recueil de griffonis*. Paris, Cailleux.

FIGURE 2 G. B. Piranesi, *Atrio Dorico*, in *Prima parte*, pl. 12, first edition, first issue. National Gallery of Art, Washington, 1976.2.1.

FIGURE 1 Hubert Robert, *View of Paestum*, in *Voyage pittoresque*, vol. III, opposite p. 157. The Pierpont Morgan Library, New York.

HUBERT ROBERT
Paris 1733–Paris 1808

102. *View of the Temple of Neptune and the Basilica at Paestum, 1760*

Red chalk. 13⅝₁₆ x 19¹⁄₁₆ inches (340 x 483 mm). Watermark: fleur-de-lis within a circle, surmounted by a crown. Signed at lower left, in red chalk, *Roberti 1760*; inscribed at lower center, possibly by the artist, in pen and brown ink, *vue d'est* (?) *des Temples de* and in a different ink, *a* (superimposed over the *de*) *pestum* and *Roberti f*? (effaced).

PROVENANCE: Adolphe Stein, Paris.

BIBLIOGRAPHY: Morgan Library *FR* XX, 1984, p. 294.

EXHIBITION: New York 1989.

NO. 102

The Pierpont Morgan Library. Purchased on the von Bulow Fund, Acc. no. 1982.103

This drawing is close enough to Robert's view of Paestum in the *Voyage pittoresque* (fig. 1) (Paris 1781–86, III, pl. opposite p. 157) to be counted as one of his preparations for the plate. The figural group in the foreground is different, as is the temple, viewed from an angle showing more side. Saint-Non eventually chose a drawing (now in the Musée des Beaux-Arts, Rouen) with a more frontal view of the temple as the basis for the print in the *Voyage pittoresque* (Rome 1990–91, no. 44, repr.).

Robert made a number of similarly sized drawings of the temple on this trip, for which he was highly praised by Mariette in his *Abecedario*. "M. l'abbé de Saint-Non l'a beaucoup fait travailler dans le temps qu'il étoit à Rome, en 1760 et 1761, et lui a fait faire le voyage de Naples. Il en a profité pour dessiner sur le lieu les fameuses antiquités de Pestum, qu'il a parfaitement rendues." While *View of the Temple at Paestum* was on the art market in 1969 (Paris, Hôtel Drouot, 26 November 1969, no. 17 A, repr., 330 x 440 mm), another view is known today only through its counterproof preserved in the Bibliothèque Municipale, Besançon. The drawing that was sold at the Hôtel Drouot in 1969 is extremely close to the Morgan sheet. Even the reed hut and staffage figures are much the same. The temple itself is seen from a less frontal viewpoint than in the Morgan drawing. The tree, which overarches the temple, and the treatment of the sky, also differ. A larger drawing, in which the artist has completely surrounded the temple with water, is in the Pushkin Museum, Moscow (380 x 550 mm). Since very nearly the same view of the temple and basilica appears in both the Morgan and Rouen drawings, and the sky is much the same in both, especially the darkly mottled clouds which Robert used as accents in a wide expanse of sky, it seems likely that both drawings were made on the same day. In the Abbé de Saint-Non's journal, only Robert is mentioned: "J'avois emmené avec moy Robert jeune Peintre de la plus grande Espérance et du premier Talent dans le genre de l'Architecture et des Ruînes."

HUBERT ROBERT
Paris 1733–Paris 1808

103. *Roman View with Horsemen Passing through the Arch of Titus*

Red chalk. 14¹¹/₁₆ x 19½ inches (371 x 496 mm). Watermark: none visible through lining.

PROVENANCE: private collection, Massachusetts.

EXHIBITION: New York and Richmond 1985–86, no. 18, repr.; New York 1989.

Collection of Eugene Victor and Clare Thaw

The Roman Triumphal Arch was a natural subject for artists, and the Arch of Titus, on the Velia at the top of the Via Sacra looking through to the Forum or the Colosseum, was frequently depicted by them. Although Robert often invented views of ruins, the Arch of Titus actually appeared in the eighteenth century the way that it does in this drawing. This is well documented by the work of other contemporary artists, including Piranesi.

Built by Domitian some time after A.D. 81 to commemorate the victory of Titus and Vespasian in the Judean War in A.D. 70, the arch was severely damaged in the succeeding centuries. Many of its stones were stolen, and in the Middle Ages the arch was built into the structures of other buildings. When these buildings, which acted as a support for the arch, were destroyed, the structure fell into a state of even greater dilapidation. Although near collapse, it was not until 1821 that a restoration was undertaken. Since the Thaw drawing is sketchy, it is not clear which side Robert studied. Only one of the two side-reliefs in the passage is indicated, and it is so summarily sketched that identifying it either with the panel of Titus riding in the triumphal chariot or the procession carrying the spoils of the temple is not possible. The imperial eagle is centered in the coffered vault of the arch, and the pairs of winged victories with wreaths in the spandrels of both facades are visible. There is, moreover, no distant view of the Colosseum or the Forum.

Three other drawings show different aspects of the arch. A view of the west side looking through to the Colosseum is in the Musée des Beaux-Arts in Valence (Beau 1968, no. 5, repr.). Robert sketched a similar view in another drawing, now in the Musée Marmottan, Paris (see also Beau, no. 5d). The third drawing, now in the Wallraf-Richartz Museum, Cologne, shows a detail of the arch by moonlight. As the Thaw drawing corresponds most closely to the painting in the Uffizi, it may properly be considered a preliminary sketch. The two works have many points of comparison, but in the painting the artist has moved the viewpoint sharply to the right.

NO. 103

HUBERT ROBERT

Paris 1733–Paris 1808

104. *A Herdsman and Shepherdess Resting in Classical Ruins*

Pen and black ink, gray and brown wash, and watercolor.
12¹⁄₁₆ x 14¹³⁄₁₆ inches (305 x 375 mm).
Signed and dated at lower left in pen and black ink, *Robert 1772.*

PROVENANCE: Robert von Hirsch, Basel; his sale, London, Sotheby's, 20–21 June 1978, lot 58, repr.; the Phillips Family.

EXHIBITION: Richmond, Virginia 1981, no. 32, repr.

The Phillips Family Collection

Clearly dated 1772, this work was made after Robert's return to France in 1765. It belongs to a genre of capriccio made especially to be framed and hung in the picture galleries of private collectors. Robert made numerous drawings of this character, executed in the same pen and watercolor manner, a number of which are reproduced by Victor Carlson (Washington 1978a). A comparable watercolor, *Figures in Classical Ruins, 1778*, now at the Metropolitan Museum (ibid., no. 47, repr.), is somewhat larger. The temple, which forms a prominent feature of the Phillips drawing, although previously identified as part of Bernini's colonnade, seems much more likely to be based on Robert's recollection of the Temple of Neptune at Paestum than any Roman site. Another drawing of this type, *Four Figures Standing in Antique Ruins*, dated around 1780–85 (ibid., no. 57, repr.), includes a long row of Doric columns reminiscent of the artist's red chalk studies of the ruins at Paestum, which he visited in 1760 (see Cat. no. 102).

HUBERT ROBERT

Paris 1733–Paris 1808

105. *A Vaulted Chamber with the Statue of Menander*

Red chalk on laid paper. 17⁷/₁₆ x 14⅞ inches (443 x 378 mm). Watermark: none visible.

DATE: about 1775–80.

PROVENANCE: Galerie Cailleux, Paris; Charles E. Slatkin Galleries, New York.

BIBLIOGRAPHY: Roland Michel in Brunel 1978, p. 321, under no. 181; Carlson in Washington 1978a, p. 124, under no. 49, William M. Griswold in New York 1992–93, p. 226, under no 80.

EXHIBITIONS: New York 1956–57, no. XVI, repr.; New York 1959a no. 57, repr.; Philadelphia and Detroit 1960, no. 108, not repr.

Toronto, Private Collection

While the date of 1779 inscribed on the mat is quite plausible for this red chalk drawing, it is also possible to demonstrate an earlier date, as indicated by the graphic conventions used to delineate the small figures inside the vaulted chamber.

This drawing, formerly called *The Baths of Diocletian*, can be related to two groups of works by Hubert Robert, both dated around 1780. The first comprises a series of paintings and drawings in which the artist has chosen to represent two rows of columns supporting a collapsed barrel vault. In the second group, Robert has added the statue of Menander. The most famous work in the first group is the *View of the Grande Galerie of the Louvre as a Ruin* (fig. 1), which was exhibited at the Salon of 1796 along with its pendant in which this chamber has been transformed into an imaginary museum gallery (Sahut in Paris 1979a, no. 81, RF 1975–11, pp. 31–33, repr. p. 33, and no. 58, RF 1975–10, pp. 28–30, repr. p. 29).

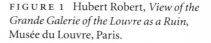
NO. 105

In contrast to what I proposed several years ago, it is possible that these two paintings were executed considerably earlier, in the middle of the 1780s (Cayeux in Geneva 1979, *Dessins et Peintures*, under no. 22). In 1784 Hubert Robert was put in charge of presenting the king's paintings to the public. Robert had already exhibited a painting at the Salon of 1785, *A Long Gallery in Ruins Illuminated from the Vault*, a composition based on the same architectural elements as the *View of the Grande Galerie*. The two paintings of the Louvre galleries reveal the artist as capable of projecting his thoughts into the future as he was in turning them back toward the past–a past that has come to its final end and is in ruins.

FIGURE 1   Hubert Robert, *View of the Grande Galerie of the Louvre as a Ruin*, Musée du Louvre, Paris.

FIGURE 2 Hubert Robert, *Vaulted Chamber* from the Dining Room of Méréville. Art Institute of Chicago, 1900.382.

FIGURE 3 Hubert Robert, *Statue of Menander* published in *Un album de croquis d' Hubert Robert (1733–1808)*, fig. 10. Geneva, Cailleux.

This was not the first time that Robert depicted this theme. In 1766, the Abbé de Saint-Non had made an aquatint of a colonnade in ruins after a watercolor drawing by Robert, which I dated 1759. In the foreground, but seen from the back, is the equestrian statue of *Marcus Aurelius* from the Capitol in Rome (Paris 1979a, no. 37, pp. 21–22, repr. (drawing) p. 21, note 125, p. 60). Among the framed drawings in the Calvière sale, which took place on 5 May 1779, was one (no. 89) entitled *A Perspective View of a Gallery with a Vault in Ruins.* This drawing, executed with pen strokes of great verve washed with watercolor, is known to us through a sketch Gabriel de Saint-Aubin made in the margin of the catalogue of this collection. It seems to have been drawn in a vertical format, while the Toronto version is executed in a horizontal one. The composition of the two drawings is the same, however. A series of columns, placed very close to one another at the left, leads the eye to an opening toward the exterior, which is actually a perspective point. In spite of the presence of numerous figures inspired by the ordinary populace of Rome, the drawing of *A Vaulted Chamber with the Statue of Menander* in Toronto, like that of the gallery in the Calvière collection, expresses the vanity of this grandiose edifice whose barrel vault has not been able to withstand the test of time.

This chamber is a contrived imaginary ruin with no relationship whatsoever to any known building, even to those still in existence and in a ruined state in Rome or in Provence. If one wishes to take a stab at a bit of psychoanalysis, one could say that the author of these constructions, in his flight into the future, reveals his nostalgia for a past grandeur that has completely disappeared. The same composition, executed by Robert between 1787 and 1788 to decorate the dining room of Méréville, the chateau of his protector, the court banker the marquis de la Borde, is also found in one of the large paintings now in the Art Institute of Chicago (fig. 2). Another sketch, in the collection of the marquis de Biron in 1914, was recently sold at auction in London (Sotheby's, 8 July 1981, lot 95).

The above-mentioned sketch of the watercolor in the Calvière sale reveals (left foreground) the presence of an isolated mass in front of the colonnade. We can interpret this rapid notation as an evocation of the statue of the Greek comic poet Menander, also located in the left foreground of the red chalk drawing, *A Vaulted Chamber*, exhibited here. The presence of this ancient statue on its square high pedestal is the second reason to compare the red chalk drawing in Toronto with several other works by Hubert Robert. He had seen the famous statue in the Museo Pio Clementino in the Vatican, and he drew at least three sketches (fig. 3) of it between 1760 and 1763 in the album that was formerly in the collection of Ernest May (Geneva 1979, *Album*, nos. 9, 10, 29, all repr.).

A statue of Menander also appears in a large watercolor drawing in the Musée des Beaux-Arts de Lille, signed and dated by Robert in 1780 (Roland Michel in Brunel 1978, no. 181, pp. 320–21, 800 x 770 mm, repr. p. 319; William M. Griswold in New York 1992–93, no. 80, pp. 266–68, repr. p. 267). This time the statue is in the right foreground. This inversion can be explained by the fact that Hubert Robert quite often applied wash to counterproofs of his own drawings. It is interesting to note that the massive pedestal of the statue is used as a fountain in both the Toronto and Lille drawings. Some of the water flows into a circular basin in which a group of women do their washing. In both works, the statue of Menander is placed in front of an apse; the inclined head of the poet rests on his chest. There is also a young man wearing a hat. He is seated on an antique fragment lying on the ground in the foreground toward the center.

The statue of Menander is found again, but to the left as in the red chalk drawing in Toronto, in two other drawings executed in watercolor over black ink wash. One, formerly in the collection of the marquis de Biron, is now in the Metropolitan Museum of Art in New York. The second is in the Kunsthalle in Karlsruhe. Marianne Roland Michel has dated both around 1773 (Roland Michel in Brunel 1978, p. 321). This is one reason why we might assign a date earlier than the accepted one of 1779 to the red chalk drawing, *A Vaulted Chamber with the Statue of Menander*. The columns in the watercolor in Karlsruhe have Corinthian capitals as in the drawing in Toronto. Those in the watercolor in New York have capitals of the Tuscan order, a variant of the Doric.

This later type of column is found in yet two other watercolors by Robert, both dated 1780. Now the tomb of a young woman who is partially reclining has replaced the statue of Menander; the colonnade is interrupted by a transept; the crossing is surmounted by a cupola, as in Piranesi's *Vestibolo d'antico Tempio* from the *Prima parte* of 1743 (Robison 1986, p. 88, no. 11, repr.). The first watercolor, now in the Albertina in Vienna, has a dedicatory inscription with the names of Chabot and Danville in addition to that of Robert; these refer to Elisabeth-Louise de La Rochefoucauld, daughter of the duchesse d'Anville, and wife of the duc de Chabot. The duchess received drawing lessons from Hubert Robert and presided over a kind of private academy of which he was a member (Valence 1985, p. 80, no. 3). The second watercolor was sold by the artist in 1796 to the architect Trou, and appeared recently at auction in London (Christie's, 13–14 March 1984, no. 141). It has as its pendant another watercolor, also formerly in the Trou Collection, with a statue of Menander practically identical with the one in the Musée des Beaux-Arts de Lille. In these two works, the barrel vault is intact, but debris and rubble are piled halfway to the top of the colonnade.

Thus, for some thirty years, from around 1759 to the end of his career, marked by the paintings of the Grand Galerie of the Louvre, Hubert Robert was fascinated, even haunted, by the theme of a colonnade surmounted by a collapsed barrel vault that recedes into the distance and opens on to a brilliant source of light. The *Vaulted Chamber with the Statue of Menander* is a witness to the influence of the capricci of Giovanni Paolo Pannini and the later *vedute* of Robert's great friend Piranesi. Like Pannini and Piranesi, Hubert Robert evoked the emotive power of ancient ruins. In this drawing as in others, however, Robert's ruins are more provocative because they are entirely imaginary.

JEAN-CHARLES DELAFOSSE
Paris 1734–Paris 1791

106. *Masquerade in a Vauxhall*

Watercolor, pen, and black ink, gray, gold, and brown wash, black chalk with a border in black ink on lined laid paper. 12⅜ x 16 inches (315 x 405 mm). Watermark: none visible through backing.
Signed in brown ink, lower left, *J.C. Delafosse.*

DATE: about 1770–80.

PROVENANCE: Didier Aaron, Inc., New York.

BIBLIOGRAPHY: New York 1984a, no. 12, fig. 22; Rosenfeld in Montréal 1989–90, no. 5, unpublished.

EXHIBITION: Montréal 1989–90, no. 5.

Montréal, Centre Canadien d'Architecture/Canadian Centre for Architecture DR1984:1462

NO. 106

Originally trained as a sculptor, Delafosse was apprenticed to Jean-Baptist Poulet at the Accademia di San Luca in 1747. His first known drawing, *Projet d'un piédestal pour le Roy*, is dated 1763. It may have been executed in conjunction with the inauguration of the equestrian monument of Louis XV by Bouchardon in the Place Louis XV that same year. By 1767, Delafosse was calling himself *architecte et professeur pour le dessin* at the Accademia di San Luca. His major opus, the *Nouvelle Iconologie Historique*, a collection of engravings of designs for vases, trophies, cartouches, medallions, and furniture (issued in segments in 1768, 1773, 1776, and 1785), had a significant influence on the development of the Louis XVI style.

Delafosse may have gone to Italy in 1772 when he traveled to Corsica. Between 1776 and 1783, he was responsible for the construction of two houses–the Hôtel Titon and the Hôtel Goix–on the rue du Faubourg Poissonnière, a district where Ledoux also constructed houses. In 1781, Delafosse was accepted into the Académie Royale de Peinture in Bordeaux; after his acceptance, he returned to Paris. Delafosse took an active part in the French Revolution as a member of the Garde Nationale (Levallet 1929, pp. 158–70; Gallet 1963, pp. 157–201; Eriksen 1974, p. 170; Mosser in Brunel 1978, p. 103).

According to Monique Mosser, between 1770 and 1785 Delafosse produced a large number of suites of drawings made to be engraved. In 1984, Beverly

Schreiber-Jacoby suggested that the CCA's drawing, *Masquerade in a Vauxhall*, was part of a suite that included two other drawings of similar dimensions and subject. These two drawings are now in the Cooper-Hewitt Museum (fig. 1). In the 1770s and 1780s, temporary buildings made of wood for entertainment purposes were erected along the Champs-Elysées in imitation of English practice. They are described by Jean-François Blondel in his *Cours d'architecture* (Paris, 1771, vol. II, p. 189). Richard Wunder believes that the two drawings in the Cooper-Hewitt Museum depict two vauxhalls that were actually built (Wunder 1962, pp. 93–94, fig. 5: 1911.28.38, 401 x 310 mm, and 1911.28.39, 401 x 308 mm).

In contrast to Richard Wunder, I think these drawings show masquerades in imaginary vauxhalls. The hall in the background of the CCA's drawing is based on the *Vestibolo d'antico Tempio* in Piranesi's *Prima parte* (1743) (fig. 2) (Robison 1986, p. 88, no. 11, repr. p. 88). It has a similar basilica-like space in the foreground with a transept in the center and a hemicycle in the background, all articulated by freestanding massive fluted Corinthian columns. Monique Mosser has noted that on other occasions Delafosse was influenced by Piranesi's *Diverse maniere* (1769) and *Parere su l'architettura* (1765), which he could have procured in Paris. Delafosse also adapted one of the etchings from the *Prima parte*–the *Vestiggi d'antichi Edificj*–in his *Landscape with Ruins, a Sphinx and a Pyramid*, now in the Musée des Arts Décoratifs in Paris (Mosser in Brunel 1978, pp. 105, 108, 113, no. 49A, repr. p. 106).

Since the CCA's drawing, as well as the two drawings in the Cooper-Hewitt Museum, have so many details of medallions, vases (fig. 3), trophies, and portals similar to the illustrations in the *Nouvelle Iconologie Historique*, I believe one can assign to them a date between 1770 and 1780. The freestanding fluted Corinthian columns supporting a straight entablature at the corners of the crossing of the vauxhall in the CCA's drawing recall those at the crossing of Soufflot's Church of Sainte-Geneviève (1757–1790) (Kalnein and Levey 1972, pp. 319–21, fig. 279).

JEAN-FRANÇOIS-THÉRESE CHALGRIN

Paris 1739–Paris 1811

107. *Interior of St. Peter's, Rome*

Pen and black ink, gray and brown wash. 16½ x 11⅝ inches
(419 x 294 mm). Watermark: none visible through lining.
Signed and dated at lower left, *chalgrin fecit Rome 1763.*

PROVENANCE: Charles Fairfax Murray; J. Pierpont Morgan (no mark; see Lugt S. 1509).

BIBLIOGRAPHY: Paris 1986, under no. 13.

EXHIBITION: New York 1989.

The Pierpont Morgan Library. Purchased by J. Pierpont Morgan, 1910, Acc. no. III, 112a

This architect, trained by Boullée and Moreau, received the *prix d'architecture* in 1758, enabling him to spend a few years at the French Academy in Rome. Chalgrin executed this atmospheric view of St. Peter's in 1763, while he was still a *pensionnaire.* After his return to Paris, he was named *inspecteur des travaux de la ville de Paris* and embarked on a busy career, building churches such as the severely neoclassic St. Philippe de Roule in Paris (1769–84), which became the prototype for the basilica-style church at the end of the eighteenth century. Chalgrin eventually became *architecte du roi,* and among other accomplishments, finished St. Sulpice and modified the Palais du Luxembourg.

A similar view of St. Peter's by Chalgrin, which was on the art market in Paris a few years ago, was probably made at the same time. It shows the lighting of the cross on Good Friday, a popular subject for artists. In 1782, almost twenty years later, Louis-Jean Desprez drew a view of St. Peter's similar to the Morgan sheet (Brunswick and elsewhere 1985, no. 92), at the same time that he also drew the luminous cross at St. Peter's during Holy Week (Inv. 26219, *Inventaire général des dessins du Musée du Louvre,* V, no. 3642, repr.).

Chalgrin's last and perhaps most famous commission was the Arc de Triomphe at l'Etoile which was completed only after his death in 1811.

NO. 107

LOUIS-JEAN DESPREZ
Auxerre 1743–Stockholm 1804

108. *Fantastic Interior with Torture Scene*

NO. 108

Pen and brown ink with gray-black ink in background, brown and gray washes, heightened with white. 18⅜ x 14⁵⁄₁₆ inches (467 x 363 mm). Watermark: indecipherable through lining.

PROVENANCE: Sir Thomas Lawrence; H. M. Calmann, Ltd., London.

BIBLIOGRAPHY: Morgan Library *FR* I, 1950, p. 54.

EXHIBITIONS: Rome and elsewhere 1976, no. 64, repr.; New York 1984, no. 83; New York 1989.

The Pierpont Morgan Library. Purchased as the gift of the Fellows, Acc. no. 1950.8

Desprez won the *prix d'architecture* in 1776 at the age of thirty-three and went to Rome to study at the French Academy where he may have known Piranesi. He certainly knew the artist's son, Francesco, who executed a series of prints after drawings of Rome and Naples by Desprez. It may have been Francesco, while serving as "commissaire des antiquités à Rome de la Cour de Suède," who introduced Gustavus III to Desprez and thus laid the foundation for a long and close relationship between the French artist and the Swedish king. Desprez became the designer for the Stockholm Opera, whose many productions were written or conceived by Gustavus. The king was so pleased with the work of his collaborator that he was led to remark: "There are only two people with imagination in this country, Desprez and I."

Even in Piranesi's time the impact of his *Carceri*, the famous prison series of etchings, had begun to influence new themes and innovative modes of expression in artists and writers. This drawing certainly represents a romantic variation on Piranesi's *Carceri*.

The attribution of this drawing to Desprez has been questioned in the 1976 catalogue, where a similarity to the works of Petit-Radel, Nicolle's master, has been noted, without really changing the attribution. Monique Mosser has also pointed out certain similarities between this drawing and Challe's *Fantastic Courtyard*, now in the Royal Institute of British Architects, London (Rome and elsewhere 1976, no. 27, repr.).

LOUIS-JEAN DESPREZ
Auxerre 1743–Stockholm 1804

109. *The Triumph of Hannibal*

Pen, black ink, black, beige, gray, green watercolor, heightened with white, red, blue gouache with a border in black ink on four pieces of laid paper glued together with traces of a double lining of paper and linen. 22⁷⁄₁₆ x 36³⁄₁₆ inches (570 x 919 mm). Watermark: none visible.

DATE: about 1780–90.

PROVENANCE: Christopher Mendez, London.

Montréal, Centre Canadien d'Architecture/Canadian Centre for Architecture DR1984:1641

Between 1768 and 1776, Louis-Jean Desprez was a student at the Académie Royale d'Architecture. After obtaining the *grand prix* in 1776, he left to take up residence at the French Academy in Rome. He interrupted his studies between December 1777 and January 1779 to accompany Dominique Vivant Denon and several other artists to Naples and Sicily in order to make drawings for the illustrations of the *Voyage pittoresque ou description des royaumes de Naples et de Sicile*, published by the Abbé de Saint-Non in Paris between 1781 and 1786 (Wollin 1935, pp. 32–109). Desprez made preparatory drawings for 136 etched plates in the *Voyage pittoresque*. A great number of these drawings provided material throughout Desprez's career for a series of engravings dedicated to Italian and Roman history. At the end of his stay in Rome, he became more and more interested in painting, and was encouraged by Louis-Jean François Lagrenée (1724–1805), director of the French Academy in Rome from 1781 to 1787. Gustavus III of Sweden, who had come to Rome at the end of 1783, appointed Desprez to be his stage designer in 1784. Desprez went to Sweden in 1785 and produced stage designs for *Queen Christina* (1785), *Gustave Vasa* (1786), *Armida* (1787), *Frigga* (1787), *Semiramis*, and *Aeneas at Carthage* (1799). In 1788, Desprez was appointed Gustavus III's architect in charge of the royal castles at Haga and Drottningholm. Many of Desprez's architectural designs were never brought to

fruition, such as his plan for a large royal castle at Haga. However, among the buildings constructed were the Botanical Institute at Uppsala, two wings and the main staircase of the castle at Haga, the Temple of Love and Psyche, the copper tents, the stables, and the Chinese Pavilion, also at Haga, all begun in 1788. After the death of Gustavus III in 1792, Desprez's career declined. He tried unsuccessfully to procure commissions from Catherine the Great and Napoleon Bonaparte. He spent the later part of his career as a painter (Magnusson in Paris 1974, pp. 3–23; Mosser in Brunel 1978, pp. 121–22; Ulf Cederlöf and Olle Granath in Stockholm 1992, pp. 145–50).

When this gouache was acquired by the CCA, it was identified as a design for a stage set. It is much larger than most of Desprez's stage designs, which measure on the average approximately 320 x 550 millimeters. The fragments of a linen and paper backing on the verso indicate, according to Thea Burns, that this gouache was mounted originally on a canvas, like a painting. By the end of his life, Desprez was painting mainly battle scenes and historical subjects, such as the watercolor *The Foundation of Alexandria* exhibited at the Académie Royale de Peinture in 1804 (Wollin 1939, p. 267, fig. 233, p. 265; Stockholm 1992, p. 39, fig. 23, 355 x 525 mm). According to Nils Wollin (1939, p. 265), and Per Bjurström (1990), Desprez, while in Sweden, drew inspiration from the prints and drawings he had produced in Italy. An aquatint, *The Taking of Selinunte by Hannibal*, executed by Desprez in Italy, may give us a clue to the subject of the CCA's gouache (Wollin 1933, p. 58, no. 30, repr. p. 145, second state, National Museum; Stockholm 1992, p. 138, fig. 139). It is possible that in the CCA's drawing, the turbaned figure seated on the litter and being carried into the theater is Hannibal. The turban certainly alludes to a non-Roman figure. Behind Hannibal is a theater, and above the theater an imaginary town on a hill whose buildings recall the Sicilian monuments in the *Voyage pittoresque* as well as several buildings Desprez planned in Stockholm.

Ulf Cederlöf has discovered a pen and ink preparatory drawing for the CCA's gouache (fig. 1) in a private Swedish collection. In this preparatory drawing

FIGURE 1 Louis-Jean Desprez, Preparatory Drawing for *The Triumph of Hannibal*. Private collection, Sweden.

FIGURE 2 Claude-Louis Chatelet, *Doric Temple at Segesta*, in Abbé de Saint-Non, *Voyage pittoresque*, vol. IV, fig. 66. Canadian Centre for Architecture, Montréal, IDM85–B7899:4.

FIGURE 4 Louis-Jean Desprez, Detail, Doric Temple in a Grotto, in *The Triumph of Hannibal*. Canadian Centre for Architecture, Montréal, DR1984:1641.

FIGURE 3 Louis-Jean Desprez, *Tomb of Theron*, in Abbé de Saint-Non, *Voyage pittoresque*, vol. IV, fig. 88. Canadian Centre for Architecture, Montréal, IDM85–B7899:4.

we find a similar theater, resembling the Roman theater at Herculaneum, drawn by Pierre-Adrian Pâris (1745–1819) and etched by Pierre-Philippe Choffard in volume II of the *Voyage pittoresque* (Paris, 1782, no. 28). In the CCA's drawing, there are several buildings above the theater on a hill that do not appear in the preparatory drawing in Sweden. The references to Sicily are found in the Doric Greek temple, to the left at the top of the hill, which recalls the Doric temples at Segesta (fig. 2) and Agrigento illustrated in the *Voyage pittoresque* (Paris, 1785, IV, part I, no. 66, drawn by Claude-Louis Chatelet (1753–94), etched by Louis-Joseph Masquelier; nos. 67 and 85, drawn by Desprez, etched by Jean Duplessis-Bertaux and Emmanuelle-Jean Nepomucène Ghendt). In the center, at the top of the hill, is the so-called Tomb of Theron at Agrigento (fig. 3), which was drawn by Desprez for the *Voyage pittoresque* (Paris, 1785, IV, part I, no. 88, etched by Gabriel-Augustin Coiny and Ghendt).

Several buildings in the CCA's gouache allude to Desprez's activities in Sweden. The Doric temple in a grotto just to the left above the theater (fig. 4) is derived from a design Desprez made for Frigga's temple in old Uppsala for the 1787 opera *Frigga* (Wollin 1939, p. 42, fig. 21; Stockholm, 1992, p. 82). It also reflects the mausoleum Desprez planned in 1791 for Gustavus III (Wollin 1939, p. 156, figs. 164, 165, p. 177). The massive medieval castle, with two round fortified towers just below the Doric temple, resembles a design by Desprez for a prison (Wollin 1933, p. 184, fig. 84). The long building to the right of the two fortified towers of the medieval castle is similar to Desprez's project for the stables at Haga (Wollin 1939, p. 105, figs. 89, 90, p. 99). In Sweden, Desprez remained in contact with Francesco Piranesi, who continued to make aquatints after his drawings and provided him with antique sculptures for Gustavus III's collection (Caira Lumetti 1990, pp. 93–125). The two griffins facing each other, on the first level of the two porticos on either side of the theater, are derived from a relief on a fireplace in Piranesi's *Diverse maniere* (Focillon 1964, p. 59, no. 880).

Desprez's eclecticism, however, is quite different

from that shown by Piranesi in his *Diverse maniere*. In addition to Greek and Roman buildings, Desprez introduced the motif of a medieval fortified castle. Bjurström has noted that in his set of designs for the operas *Queen Christina* and *Gustave Vasa*, Desprez turned to Sicilian medieval monuments and folk traditions (Bjurström 1990; Stockholm 1992, p. 69, fig. 58, p. 75, fig. 64). The medieval fortress in the CCA's gouache is derived from the ruined fortress of Frederick II at Lucera of 1233 that Desprez depicted in the *Voyage pittoresque* (Wollin 1935, p. 202, fig. 38, p. 108,

fig. 1; *Voyage pittoresque*, Paris, 1783, III, no. 5, etching by Nicolas Charles Vavin). In fact, Desprez also made a reconstruction of Frederick II's fortress at Lucera (Wollin 1935, p. 203, fig. 40). The imaginary city in the background of the CCA's gouache reveals how Desprez transposed the ancient world from Italy to Sweden. At the same time, by including Sicilian monuments from the Middle Ages, his work creates a bridge between the eighteenth and nineteenth centuries, and shows that the seeds of romanticism can be found in neoclassicism.

NO. 109

FIGURE 1 Louis-Jean Desprez, *View of the Ruins of the Temple of Juno at Metapontum with the Encampment of an Archeological Expedition*, in Abbé de Saint-Non, *Voyage pittoresque,* vol. III, opposite p. 77. The Pierpont Morgan Library, New York.

LOUIS-JEAN DESPREZ

Auxerre 1743–Stockholm 1804

110. *View of the Ruins of the Temple of Juno at Metapontum*

Pen and black ink, and watercolor, with traces of graphite. 8³⁄₁₆ x 13⁷⁄₁₆ inches (208 x 341 mm). Watermark: D & C BLAUW.

PROVENANCE: The Hermitage, Leningrad; sale, Leipzig, Boerner, 29 April 1931, no. 52; Albert Mayer, Paris; Seligmann, Paris, 1936; Winslow and Anna Ames, New London, Connecticut (blind stamp at upper left corner).

BIBLIOGRAPHY: de Ricci 1935, no. 23; Morgan Library *FR* IX, 1959, pp. 109f.; Morgan Library *Review*, 1969, p. 141.

EXHIBITIONS: Paris 1934, no. 425; Dayton 1971, no. 29, repr.; New York 1982, under no. 34, repr.; New York 1984, no. 120; New York 1989.

The Pierpont Morgan Library. Purchased as the gift of the Fellows, Acc. no. 1959.2

This drawing was engraved in the same direction by Jean-Duplessis-Bertaux and Charles Guttenberg as an illustration in the Abbé de Saint-Non's *Voyage pittoresque ou description des royaumes de Naples et de Sicile* (fig. 1) (Paris 1781–86, III, pl. 37, opposite p. 77). The abbé began this project in 1760 with Robert and Fragonard and later involved Desprez and Chatelet, whose eventual share in the work far exceeded that of Robert's and Fragonard's. Desprez, who won the *prix de Rome* in 1776, was almost immediately draughted by the Abbé de Saint-Non upon his arrival in Rome. A preliminary drawing for this design is in the Nationalmuseum in Stockholm, where so much of Desprez's work is preserved. For this illustration the abbé comments:

> Après avoir mesuré les restes de ce Monument vénérable, nous voulûmes en avons plusieurs vues sous différents aspects, un de nos Dessinateurs imagina de représenter dans le Tableau qu'il en fit une Société entière de Voyageurs et d'Amateurs d'Antiquités qui se sont établis au milieu du Temple sous une Tente dressée à la hâte. C'est le moment de la halte et l'instant où l'on fait les apprêts du Repas, tandisque les Architectes, les Dessinateurs prennent des mesures, et travaillent chacun de leur côté. Le mouvement, l'action & l'esprit répandus dans ces différens Grouppes de Figures, nous ont paru ajouter infiniment d'intérêt et de piquant à cette jolie Vue qui est d'ailleurs parfaitement exacte et conforme à la vérité.

The abbé also wrote that the columns at Metapontum measure "seize pieds et une pouce," which means that Desprez's figures are far from scale.

The drawing, which is in the same direction as the print, does not seem to have been traced for transfer. Although executed with a lively touch, it may have been made after the preparatory drawing. It is interesting to note that Desprez and Francesco Piranesi had a successful business in Paris in the early 1780s with Desprez producing line etchings worked up in watercolor, a technique which he may have picked up from Ducros and Paolo-Antonio Paoli. He met the latter in Brindisi while touring with Vivant Denon in 1778 (Griffiths 1988, p. 429).

NO. 110

VICTOR-JEAN NICOLLE

Paris 1754–Paris 1826

111. *The Temple of Vesta, Rome*

Watercolor, pen and brown ink, over preliminary indications in black chalk; ruled border in pen and brown ink. 8 1/16 x 12 1/4 inches (205 x 309 mm).

Signed at middle left, in pen and brown ink, *V.J. Nicolle*; inscribed on back of old mount, by the artist, *Vue du Temple de Vesta, Situé au bord du tibre; prise du Coté de Transtevere* [sic]; *à Rome.*

PROVENANCE: Jean Baptiste de Meryan, marquis de Lagoy (Lugt 1710); Raymond Ferrier (Lugt S. 2207a); his sale, Paris, E. Pape, 24 December 1924 (with its pendant drawing, *Le Temple de la Concorde, Rome*); private collection, southern France; Galerie Cailleux, Paris.

BIBLIOGRAPHY: Morgan Library *FR* XX, 1984, pp. 282–83.
EXHIBITIONS: New York 1984, no. 88; New York 1989.

The Pierpont Morgan Library. Purchased on the von Bulow Fund, Acc. no. 1983.32

NO. 111

Born in Paris, Nicolle was a student at Bachelier's school and worked under the architect Petit-Radel. He spent a good deal of his time in Rome where he became one of the most attractive recorders of the Italian scene. He seems to have gone there first in 1779, again between 1787 and 1799, and again from 1806 to 1810. Since Nicolle signed but did not date this large watercolor, it is not known precisely when it or its pendant, *The Temple of Concord*, was executed. Both were originally in the collection of the marquis de Lagoy (1764–1829), the well-known collector who owned more than three thousand drawings and was deputy for Aix-en-Provence under the restoration. The pair stayed together until 1983 when the Library purchased the view of the *Temple of Vesta*, and the Phillips Family purchased the other. These drawings are very much of a size with another pair of highly finished Roman views in the Louvre, *Le Ponte Rotto à Rome* (204 x 312 mm, RF 14628), and *La Place Trajane à Rome, avec la Colonne et l'Eglise de Sainte-Marie de Lorette à Rome* (202 x 310 mm, RF 14629).

Highly finished and meticulously detailed works such as these were obviously made to be enjoyed as independent works of art. They differ from Nicolle's other work, which is often small and meant for book illustration.

NO. 112

VICTOR-JEAN NICOLLE

Paris 1754–Paris 1826

112. *The Temple of Concord*

Watercolor, pen and brown ink, over preliminary indica-
tions in black chalk; ruled border in pen and brown ink.
Sight measurements: 8¹⁄₁₆ x 12¼ inches (205 x 309 mm).
Watermark: none visible through lining.
Signed and inscribed at right, in pen and brown ink, *V. J.
Nicolle.*

PROVENANCE: Jean Baptiste de Meryan, marquis de Lagoy (Lugt 1710); Raymond Ferrier (Lugt S. 2207a); his sale,
Paris, E. Pape, 24 December 1924 (with its pendant drawing, *Vue du Temple de Vesta, Rome*); private collection,
southern France; Galerie Cailleux, Paris.

EXHIBITION: New York 1989.

The Phillips Family Collection

The pendant to *The Temple of Vesta* (Cat no. 111), this
view also includes the Arch of Septimius Severus.

LOUIS FRANÇOIS CASSAS
Azay-le-Ferron 1756–Versailles 1827

113. *Landscape with the Arch of Drusus*

Pen and brown ink, watercolor, over traces of black chalk. 9⁷⁄₁₆ x 13¾ inches (240 x 348 mm). Watermark: none visible through lining.

Signed, dated, and inscribed by the artist, at lower left, in pen and brown ink, *L F Cassas f. 1778 a Rome.*

PROVENANCE: Charles Fairfax Murray; J. Pierpont Morgan (no mark; see Lugt S. 1509).

EXHIBITIONS: New York 1984, no. 90; New York 1989.

The Pierpont Morgan Library. Purchased by J. Pierpont Morgan, 1910, Acc. no. III, 112b

A student of Vien, Lagrenée le jeune, and Leprince, Cassas is known primarily for his landscapes and illustrations for travel books. Although the *Arch of Drusus* does not relate to the *Voyage pittoresque,* Cassas worked on the Abbé de Saint-Non's project and also drew and etched a series of views of Greece, Sicily, and Rome. Later he traveled through the Holy Land, Syria, and Egypt producing numerous drawings and plans, which were used in such books as *Voyage pittoresque de la Syrie, de la Phénicie, de la Palestine et de la Basse-Egypte,* produced by Didot. Cassas also traveled extensively along the Dalmatian coast and prepared the extensive series of travel drawings for *Voyage pittoresque de l'Istrie et de la Dalmatie, rédigé d'après l'itinéraire de Cassas, par Lavallée* (Paris, Didot, 1800, 14 volumes). His last project took him back to Italy as well as to Greece: *Grandes Vues pittoresques des principaux sites et monuments de la Grèce, de la Sicile, et des septs collines de Rome, dessinées et gravées à l'eau-forte, au trait, par Cassas et Bance, avec un texte par C.-P. Landon* (Paris, Didot, 1813).

NO. 113

JEAN-FRANÇOIS THOMAS,
called THOMAS DE THOMON
Bern 1759–St. Petersburg 1813

114. *Sixteen Sketches of Real and Imaginary Sites in Italy with One Frontispiece*

Pen, black ink, each with a border in black ink, cut out and lined, laid paper; black chalk underdrawing on frontispiece only. Each varying between 2⅛ and 1¾ inches (54 and 45 mm) in height and 3⅛ and 2⅝ inches (81 and 66 mm) in width. Watermark: none.

Inscribed on frontispiece (DR1993:0002:001), *Croquis fait par M. Thomon architecte*; (DR1993:0002:005), *Temple di Minerva, Amedica*; (DR1993:0002:007), *Souvenir d'Italie*; (DR1993:0002:016), *Phiramis de Sextius*; (DR1993:0002: 011), *Roca di papa*.

DATE: about 1785–91.

PROVENANCE: Art Market, London; Cailleux, Paris.

BIBLIOGRAPHY: Paris 1991, no. 86, repr.

EXHIBITION: Paris 1991, no. 86.

Montréal, Centre Canadien d'Architecture/Canadian Centre for Architecture DR1993:0002:001-017

Jean-François Thomas, called Thomas de Thomon, was a very influential French proponent of neoclassicism. He was active mainly in Russia. Two recent articles by Boris Lossky have brought to light new information about Thomas de Thomon's life. Lossky discovered that Thomas de Thomon was born in Bern, in 1759, not in Nancy, in 1754. He has often been called a student of either Ledoux or Boullée because his built works show affinities with both these architects. But Lossky discovered documentation that Thomas de Thomon was actually a student of Julien David Le Roy, author of *Les Ruines des plus beaux monuments de la Grèce* (Paris, 1758) (Lossky 1986 [1988], pp. 81–83), at the Académie Royale d'Architecture between 1777 and 1785. Lossky believes that Thomas de Thomon left for Rome in 1785, soon after he failed, for the last time, to obtain the *grand prix*.

Although he did not win, Thomas de Thomon managed to stay at the French Academy in Rome as an external student. A drawing of the *Colonnade of the Temple of Hadrian* (sold in Paris in 1973) signed *J-F Thomas à Rome ce mois de juillet 1788*, and an *Italian Landscape*, signed *Thomas de Thomon pinx^t 1791* (now in the Kunstbibliothek, Berlin), indicate that Thomas de Thomon was in Italy during those years. From Rome, Thomas de Thomon went to Venice and Vienna in 1791 and then in 1799 to St. Petersburg via Warsaw, Hamburg, and Riga. He was appointed court architect to Emperor Alexander I of Russia in 1802, remaining there until his death in 1813 (Lossky 1985, pp. 591–604; Lossky 1986 [1988], pp. 83–84). All the buildings Thomas de Thoman constructed in St. Petersburg are illustrated in a posthumously published book, *Description accompagnée des plans, coupes, et élévations de plusieurs édifices remarquables construits depuis le commencement de ce siècle à Saint-Petersbourg et dans quelques gouvernements de l'Empire Russe* (Paris, 1819). Depicted are the Imperial Theater, St. Petersburg (1802–5, destroyed); the Theater, Odessa (1804–5); Warehouses, St. Petersburg (1805–8); the Memorial Temple to Paul I, Pavlovsk (1805–11); the Column of Glory, Poltava (1805–16); and the Stock Exchange, St. Petersburg (1805–16).

The drawings in this exhibition were probably done while Thomas de Thomon was in Italy. They are similar in style to his *Italian Landscape*, which is signed and dated 1791 and is now in the Kunstbibliothek (Berckenhagen 1970, p. 412, no. Hdz 4584, repr. p. 413, 108 x 166 mm). These sketches show both real and imaginary views of Rome and its surrounding countryside. Among the ancient and modern monuments of Rome represented in these small *vedute* are the *Basilica of St. Peter's* (DR1993:0002:002), the *Temple of Hercules at Cora* (DR1993:0002:004), the *Temple of Minerva Medica* (DR1993:0002:005), and the *Tomb of Cecilia Maetella* (DR1993:0002:008). The other sketches show imaginary views.

Marianne Roland Michel noted that these sketches reveal the influences of both Giovanni Battista Piranesi and Hubert Robert (Roland Michel in Paris 1991, no. 86). Roland Michel found in Thomas

DR1993:0002:001

DR1993:0002:002

DR1993:0002:006

DR1993:0002:010

DR1993:0002:014

DR1993:0002:003

DR1993:0002:007

DR1993:0002:011

DR1993:0002:015

DR1993:0002:004

DR1993:0002:008

DR1993:0002:012

DR1993:0002:016

DR1993:0002:005

DR1993:0002:009

DR1993:0002:013

DR1993:0002:017

NO. 114

de Thomon's *Traité de peinture précédé de l'origine des arts* (St. Petersburg, 1809) a list of the subjects of his works. One item, *Souvenirs d'Italie et compositions diverses*, may refer to these sketches, which were probably executed as a repertory that Thomas de Thomon kept for further use. He may also have intended to publish them as a suite of etchings, similar to Hubert Robert's *Soirées de Rome* (1765), which are also small in format (Cat. no. 120). Thomas de Thomon, like many architects of his generation, had to earn his living painting and drawing, since architectural commissions were scarce.

The composition of the sketch, *A Palace above the Arch of a Bridge* (DR1993:0002:007), was reused in a larger drawing of the same subject, now in the British Museum (Rome and elsewhere 1976, p. 342, no. 191, repr. p. 344). Marianne Roland Michel points out that Thomas de Thomon's initial sketch was based on a composition represented in both a drawing and a painting by Hubert Robert. The former, a watercolor drawing, was executed in Rome in 1761 and is now in the Albertina in Vienna (Rome 1990–91, pp. 142–43, no. 89, p. 41, fig. 6). The latter, *Bridge with a Monumental Building*, was painted for the duc de Choiseul in Paris toward 1768 and is now in the Bowes Museum at Barnard Castle (Rome and elsewhere 1976, pp. 315–16, no. 178, repr. p. 313). Both Hubert Robert and Thomas de Thomon were influenced in this composition by Piranesi's *Ponte Magnifico* from the *Prima parte* (1743) and his *Fantastic Port Monument* (1747–48) (Roland Michel in Paris 1991, no. 86; Robison 1986, p. 78, no. 6, repr. and p. 132, no. 27, repr. p. 132). Earlier in Paris, just before he left for Rome, Thomas de Thomon had copied another drawing by Hubert Robert. Thomon's oval watercolor (signed and dated 1785 and now in the Musée des Beaux-Arts, Strasbourg), *A Gallery with the Statue of Marcus Aurelius*, is based on another oval watercolor executed by Hubert Robert in 1759 of the same subject (Lossky

1986 [1988], p. 83, fig. 4; Paris 1979, p. 21, fig. 57, pp. 21–22).

The other small sketches are based on compositions by Piranesi. Two sketches (DR1993:0002:017 and DR1993:0002:012) show the so-called Tomb of Nero, actually the tomb of P. Vibius Maranus on the Via Cassia, depicted by Piranesi in several drawings, one in the National Gallery of Art (1747), the source of inspiration for the first, and another in the Louvre (1743), the source for the second (Robison 1986, p, 29, fig. 32; Paris 1990–91, pp. 134–36, no. 142, repr. p. 135). Piranesi illustrated the so-called Tomb of Nero first in the *Ruine di sepolcro antico* in the *Prima parte* (1743) (Robison 1986, p. 103, no. 17, repr.) and later in the *Antichità Romane* (1756; vol. III, pl. XIV; Focillon 1964, p. 28, no. 299). The other composition by Piranesi, represented by Thomas de Thomon in another sketch (DR1993:0002:013), is a plate from the *Carceri*, probably from the second edition published between 1761 and 1778, *Staircase with Trophies* (Robison 1986, p. 164, no. 34, repr. p. 166).

Finally, one sketch (DR1993:0002:016), a pyramid surrounded by four columns, reveals not only the influence of *The Tomb of Arthemisia* in Fischer von Erlach's *Entwurff einer historischen Architectur* (Vienna 1721, pl. VI), but also the close links between Thomas de Thomon's architecture and that of Etienne-Louis Boullée (1728–99). This sketch is similar to a design by Boullée in the Bibliothèque Nationale for the *Cenotaph for Turenne*, which was to be illustrated in his unpublished work, *Architecture, essai sur l'art*, written during the late 1780s and early 1790s (Pérouse de Montclos 1969, pp. 193, 246, figs. 133–34). These drawings reveal that both Boullée and Thomas de Thomon turned to the same sources—Italian architecture, Piranesi, Hubert Robert, and Fischer von Erlach—to create a new revolutionary architecture at the end of the eighteenth century.

JEAN-HENRI-ALEXANDRE PERNET

Paris 1763?–Paris? after 1791

115. *Architectural Capriccio*

Pen and black ink, gray and brown wash and watercolor, over graphite. 15⅞ x 23½ inches (425 x 596 mm). Watermark: none visible through lining.
Signed at lower center, *Pernet.*

PROVENANCE: Galerie de la Scala, Paris; John Cassayd-Smith, Minneapolis; R. M. Light & Co., Inc., Santa Barbara.

EXHIBITION: New York 1989.

The Pierpont Morgan Library. Purchased on the Baker Fund, Acc. no. 1989.38

In this exceptionally complex capriccio, Pernet has combined elements from the Falls at Tivoli, the Arch of Septimius Severus, and the Temple of Castor and Pollux on the Forum. Little is known about the artist who never traveled to Italy but was evidently familiar with the Roman works of Fragonard and Robert. Pernet also knew Piranesi's prints, evident in this un-

usually large and fantastic view organized in diagonal strata like some of the plates in Piranesi's *Vedute di Roma.* He studied with de Machy when he was enrolled as a pupil at the Académie Royale de Peinture in 1783. The large format of this drawing is unusual since most of Pernet's surviving watercolors consist of very small roundels or oval paintings, usually paired or matched with others of the same size and shape. Comparable watercolors to the Morgan sheet are in the British Museum, the Royal Institute of British Architects, and the Louvre, which acquired its first work by the artist in 1982—a large architectural capriccio with Roman ruins (Paris 1984, no. 107, repr.). The Paris drawing is inspired by the water theater at Hadrian's Villa outside Tivoli or the marketplace at Pozzuoli known as the Temple of Serapis in the eighteenth century, which further suggests that the artist either knew Fragonard or Robert's drawings or perhaps the engravings by Saint-Non or Desprez. Pernet also made drawings for ornamental engravings for decoration on boxes and buttons.

ANNE CLAUDE DE TUBIÈRES, COMTE
DE CAYLUS

Paris 1692–Paris 1765

116. *Recueil d'antiquités égyptiennes, étrusques, grecques et romaines*

Paris: chez Desaint & Saillant, 1752–1767. 7 vols.; the last volume published posthumously.

EXHIBITION: New York 1989.

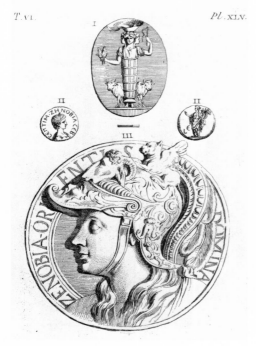

FIGURE 1 Comte de Caylus, *Recueil d'antiquités*, vol. VI, pl. XLV. The Pierpont Morgan Library, New York, PML 76356.

NO. 116

The Pierpont Morgan Library. Gift of Paul Mellon, PML 76351–57

The comte de Caylus, antiquarian, collector, and dilettante etcher, gave up a short military career to devote himself to the study of the antique. After traveling in Italy (*Voyage d'Italie*, 1714–15), and in Greece, Turkey, and the Middle East in search of Troy, Caylus returned to Paris. He corresponded with Mariette, studied drawing with Watteau, and became a patron of such contemporary artists as Greuze, Van Loo, and Bouchardon. Caylus's *Recueil d'antiquités*, published between 1752 and 1767, influenced Parisian taste and earned him wide respect throughout Europe. Piranesi, in his *Diverse maniere* (pp. 17–18), quotes Caylus at length on the elegance and variety of form of Etruscan vases.

The *Recueil d'antiquités*, which Caylus dedicated to the members of the Académie Royale and the Académie des Inscriptions et Belles-Lettres, consists of descriptions and engravings of mostly small antique works of art in the author's own collection, including specimens in glass and terracotta. A circular picture of the comte's cabinet, showing some of his collection exhibited on shelves, decorates the title page of volume 1. The same volume has a frontispiece representing "le fond de mon jardin" after a design by Edme Bouchardon whose biography Caylus wrote in 1762. In the foreword to the first volume, Caylus states that the antique statuettes and reliefs were drawn and described with the greatest precision. Plate XLV in volume VI, for example, shows three works of art on one page (fig. 1): I. a carnelian with a triple figure of the *Diana of Ephesus*, the so-called *Triformis* (since she was worshiped in three different forms); II. two sides of a coin inscribed CEπTIM. ZHNOBIA.CEB; III. a circular marble relief inscribed *Zenobia Orientis Domina*. The last, measuring about 81 centimeters in diameter, was, according to Caylus, in the garden court of the grand master's palace on Malta in 1764. Zenobia, the ambitious "queen of the East," reigned in Palmyra, Syria, a province of the Roman Empire; she was deposed by Emperor Aurelian in A.D. 272. Criticizing antiquarians who consider these art works simply as adjuncts to history, Caylus asserts that the engravings in his book serve a dual purpose: to acquaint readers with the images and foster a taste for the antique, and to record them for posterity should the originals be destroyed. As to the study of fragments, he suggests: "il faut souvent oser ignorer, & ne pas rougir d'aveu qui fait plus d'honneur que l'étalage pompeux d'une érudition inutile: je voudrais qu'on cherchât moins à éblouir qu'instruire."

Caylus recommends comparison as a valid method of connoisseurship. He classifies each work according to country, then chronologically within each geographical area. Each of the seven volumes begins with a chapter on the Egyptians, whose monuments are notable for their grandeur. This is followed by a chapter on the Etruscans, whose works show greater detail at the expense of this grandeur. The Greek works of art, described in the third chapter of each volume, reveal that "knowledge is joined to noble elegance which has led to the greatest perfection." The fourth chapter is devoted to Roman antiques which, according to Caylus, are derivative. Volumes III through VII include chapters on *Antiquités Gauloises*, antique works surviving in France. *Tome sixième & dernier*, as the title reads, was intended by the author as an "adieu au Lecteur," and the seventh, *supplément*, includes as a frontispiece – a portrait of Caylus in the form of a medallion, signed *Littret* (Littret de Montigny, ca. 1735–75) and dated 1766.

The *Recueil* came very close to the basic principles of a history of art (Justi 1956, III, pp. 104ff.). The comte de Caylus was the most important forerunner of Winckelmann, although the latter failed to mention Caylus's name in his discussion of earlier writers on the antique. Caylus regretted that he lacked Winckelmann's thorough knowledge of ancient literature, but he sought the help and opinions of famous antiquarians such as the Abbé Barthélemy, Paciaudi, and others. Caylus's approach was to describe the objects carefully, focusing on their design, beauties, and even shortcomings. It has been said that he started out an amateur and ended up a scholar.

CHARLES-NICOLAS COCHIN
THE YOUNGER
Paris 1715–Paris 1790

JÉRÔME CHARLES BELLICARD
Paris 1726–Paris 1786

117. *Observations sur les antiquités d'Herculanum*

Paris: Chez Ch. Ant. Jombert, 1757.

PROVENANCE: Girolamo Cavatti, Udine (his name and *Ao 1811* inscribed on verso of fly leaf).

EXHIBITION: New York 1989.

Giannalisa Feltrinelli Collection, on deposit at The Pierpont Morgan Library (4174)

NO. 117

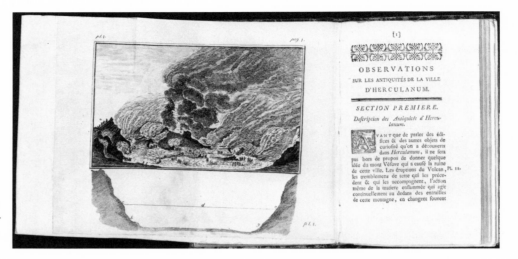

FIGURE 1 Charles-Nicolas Cochin the Younger, and Jérôme Charles Bellicard, *Observations sur les antiquités de la ville d'Herculanum.* Engraving, *An Eruption of Vesuvius* by Jérôme Charles Bellicard, opposite page 1.

Cochin accompanied M. de Vandières, the future marquis de Marigny, on his trip to Italy in order to complete his art education. Joined by the Abbé le Blanc and the architect Soufflot, the group of travelers set out in December 1749 and arrived in Rome, where they met Bellicard, a young architect who had received the *prix de Rome* in 1747 and was a *pensionnaire* at the French Academy. They evidently took him along to Naples and Herculaneum, and it was on this trip that Cochin resolved to write, in collaboration with Bellicard, his *Observations.* Another more detailed account of this journey was published in Cochin's three volume *Voyage d'Italie* of 1758 (Cat. no. 121).

The *Observations* is comprised of three parts: a description of the most important antiquities excavated from the subterranean city, preceded by Bellicard's exposition on the present state of Vesuvius; a dissertation by Cochin on the paintings and sculpture found at Herculaneum; and a description by Bellicard of antiquities located in the vicinity of Naples, i.e. Pozzuoli, Baia, Cuma, and Capua. These three sections are preceded by an essay on the history of Herculaneum "provided by a scholar who wished to remain anonymous." The illustrations, including the eruption of Vesuvius shown here (fig. 1), are primarily engravings by Bellicard; Cochin, however, engraved those of the paintings and sculpture after his drawings which were made from memory.

The number of printings of the *Observations,*

completed within a relatively short period of time, suggests that the work was extremely popular with the French public, who were eager to learn more about the fabulous treasures emerging from under a crust of lava and ashes. When Cochin and Bellicard visited Herculaneum in 1749 to 1751, systematic excavations had already been in progress since 1738. In fact, as early as 1719, a few statues had come to light when Prince d'Elboeuf was building a country house at Portici. The excavations of 1738 were started by Charles III, king of Spain, and continued for more than forty years, until 1780. The excavated works of art were installed at the royal palace in Portici, where they were jealously guarded. Visitors described the difficulties they had in obtaining permission to see them, sketch them, or even take notes (Haskell and Penny 1981, p. 75). Cochin and Bellicard therefore had to make drawings from memory. Winckelmann, who in 1762 accompanied Count Brühl (the German minister at the court of Saxony) to Herculaneum, fared better because he was on friendly terms with the guard of the royal cabinet, Cammillo Paderni, and enjoyed the king's favor. In 1755, Bernardo Tanucci, the secretary of state at the court of Naples, founded the Accademia Ercolanese, which published, in nine volumes, the *Antichità di Ercolano* (1757–96), the first comprehensive, lavishly illustrated work on the antiquities. The projected volume on marble sculpture did not appear (Haskell and Penny 1981, p. 74).

GABRIEL-PIERRE-MARTIN DUMONT,
delineator

Paris 1720–Paris 1791

JEAN-BAPTISTE BICHARD, etcher

Paris 1722–Paris 1769?

118. *The Piazza and Church of St. Peter's, Rome; Second Title Page Dedicated to the Marquis de Marigny*

in Gabriel-Pierre-Martin Dumont
DETAILS/DES/PLUS INTÉRESSANTES PARTIES/D'ARCHITECTURE/DE/LA BASILIQUE DE Sᵀ PIERRE/DE ROME/LEVÉS ET DESSINÉS SUR LE LIEU;/PAR GABRIEL-MARTIN DUMONT,/ PROFESSEUR D'ARCHITECTURE, MEMBRE DES ACADÉMIES/DE ROME, FLORENCE ET BOLOGNE, *Paris, the author, Madame Chereau, and Messrs. Joulain, father and son, 1763*

Etching (image) and engraving (inscription) on laid paper (folio 5 recto). Platemark: 14¾ x 11 inches (375 x 280 mm); page: 21¼ x 15 inches (540 x 380 mm). Watermark: upper edge, center, illegible.

Inscribed above outer border: upper left corner, *N.º 1.*, upper right corner, *1.*; center, *Vue Perspective de la Basilique et de la Colonnade de Sᵗ. Pierre du Vatican*; inside border under image, lower left, *Dumont Delin.*; lower right, *Bichard Sculp.* and center, *LES ÉLEVATIONS, COUPES ET/PROFILS ENTIERS DE LA BASILIQUE DE S.ᵀ/PIERRE DU VATICAN A ROME,/Pour servir de I.ʳᵉ Partie aux Détails cottés, mesurés sur le lieu,/examinés, approuvés par l'Académie Royale d'Architecture./DÉDIÉS A M.LE MARQUIS DE MARIGNY./Le tout mis au jour par le S.ʳ Dumont, Membre des Académies de Rome,/Florence et Bologne*; below border, and at right, around border, *La Colonnade et la Basilique de Sᵗ. Pierre de Rome ont ensemble pres de 1600 Pieds de longeur et environ 4000 de circuit./La hauteur des Colonnes de socle compris est de 43. pieds, celle de l'Entablement de 9. pieds.la Balustrade 6. pieds 9. pouces le tout en semble est de 58. pieds 9. pouces.*

DATE: execution of this etching, 1762–63.

PROVENANCE: Geoffrey Steele, Lumberville, Bucks County, Pennsylvania.

Montréal, Centre Canadien d'Architecture/Canadian Centre for Architecture M39818I

The ninety-two folios of Dumont's illustrated, measured survey of the Church of St. Peter's in Rome, his three printed *Extraits des registres de l'Académie royale d'architecture*, dated 12 December 1763 (folio 94), 22 January 1765 (folio 26), 17 August 1766 (folio 95), and the *Catalogue de l'œuvre complet de M.ʳ Dumont* (folio 96), are bound together in modern brown leather with the spine stamped in gold *OEUVRE/DE/ DUMONT TOME I*. The folios of the survey of St. Peter's are not bound in order. In addition to the second title page exhibited here, the ninety-two folios comprise a sheet with the portrait of Dumont (folio 1 recto); a written dedication to the marquis de Marigny (folio 2 recto); an introduction to Dumont's survey of St. Peter's (folio 3 recto and verso); the history of St. Peter's with a vignette of the church by Israel Sylvestre (folio 4 recto); and fifty-six illustrations of details of St. Peter's. The illustrations that follow the second title page were etched by various engravers, including Jean-Gustave Taraval, Claude-René-Gabriel Poulleau, and N. Henin. On folio 22, there is a comparison of the dimensions of the Church of St. Peter's in Rome and of the Cathedral of Notre Dame in Paris. On folio 23, another comparison of churches in Rome, Paris, Turin, Constantinople, and Vienna is very similar to the two etchings executed by Juste-Aurèle Meissonnier (1695–1750) and published by Gabriel Huquier in 1745, *Parallèle général des édifices considérables depuis les égyptiens, les grecs, jusqu'à nos jours* for which there are preparatory drawings in the CCA (DR1986:0746, 0748).

Gabriel-Pierre-Martin Dumont was awarded the *grand prix* of the Académie Royale d'Architecture in 1737. His stay in Rome as a *pensionnaire* at the French Academy lasted from 1742 to 1746. He was received into the Accademia di San Luca with a project for a *Temple of the Arts* in April of 1746, just before his return to France. In 1750, he returned to Italy and was received into the academies of Bologna and Florence. During his second stay in Italy (1750–55), Dumont visited the temples at Paestum with Jacques-Germain Soufflot, whose drawings he etched for the publication *Suite de plans, coupes, profils, élévations géométrales et perspectives de trois temples antiques . . . dans la Bourgade de Poesto qui est la ville Paestum de Pline* (Paris, 1764, republished London and Paris, 1769). Dumont specialized in publications on archi-

tecture and was appointed a professor at the Académie Royale d'Architecture on his return from Italy in 1755. Besides the one exhibited here, his most important works are *Recueil de plusieurs parties de l'architecture sacrée et profane de différents maîtres tant d'Italie que de France* (Paris, 1767) and *Parallèle de plans des plus belles salles de spectacles d'Italie et de la France* (Paris, 1765–74). He also wrote the article on theaters in the *Encyclopédie* (1774) (Oechslin in Brunel 1978, pp. 143–44).

According to the introduction to the work exhibited here on St. Peter's (folio 3 recto and verso), Dumont began making measured drawings during his first stay in Rome as a *pensionnaire* at the French Academy. When he arrived in Rome in 1742 the restoration of the cupola of St. Peter's was under way. Oechslin has suggested that Dumont's measured drawings of St. Peter's were the equivalent of the other *pensionnaires* copying important fresco paintings in the Vatican palace. Dumont's drawings of St. Peter's are a continuation of the Renaissance and baroque tradition of studying the ancient and modern Roman monuments through measured drawings. Many of Dumont's illustrations of St. Peter's recall Etienne Dupérac's etchings of St. Peter's (1565) or the illustrations published in Antoine Desgodetz's (1653–1728) *Les Edifices antiques de Rome dessinés et mesurés très exactement* (Paris, 1682) (Oechslin in Rome and elsewhere 1976, pp. 143–44).

In the eighteenth century, Desgodetz's book on St. Peter's served as a model for other archaeological investigations, because he presented his own measurements for the building rather than relying on earlier writers such as Serlio (Wiebenson 1969, p. 52). According to the Proceedings of the Royal Academy of Architecture included in the CCA's volume, Dumont first presented his etchings of St. Peter's to the Académie Royale on 9 August 1763. After his work was published in its first edition in 1763, it was reviewed and discussed at several meetings of the Académie, in 1764, 1765, and 1766, in much the same way that Desgodetz's book on Rome had been used earlier at the end of the seventeenth century as the basis of discussions at the Académie. Dumont used the Piazza and

Church of St. Peter's primarily as a source for the study of the orders. In the extract dated 17 August 1766, Dumont's measurements of the orders at St. Peter's were compared favorably to those of Desgodetz.

Dumont's comparison of the Church of St. Peter's to the Cathedral of Notre Dame in Paris (folio 22) and to other churches built in various cities from Constantinople to London (folio 23) is part of a debate on the ideal form for a church–a debate that occurred throughout the eighteenth century, from Abbé de Cordemoy's *Nouveau traité de toute l'architecture* (Paris, 1706) to Abbé Laugier's *Essai sur l'architecture* (Paris, 1753). The debate over Gothic, Roman, or Greek sources for the form of a cathedral was to reach a conclusion in Soufflot's design for the Church of Sainte-Geneviève (1757–1790) (Nyberg in Wittkower 1967, pp. 159–69; Herrmann 1962, pp. 102–30).

It is significant that for the illustration on the second title page of *Détails des plus intéressantes parties d'architecture de la Basilique de Saint-Pierre*, Dumont adapted Piranesi's third view of the Piazza and Church of St. Peter's, executed for the *Vedute di Roma* (Hind 1922, p. 70, no. 120; Focillon 1964, p. 51, no. 720; Wilton-Ely 1978 [1988], pl. 120). Piranesi etched three views of the Piazza of St. Peter's. The first (Hind 1922, p. 38, no. 3; Focillon 1964, p. 54, no. 787; Wilton-Ely 1978 [1988], pl. 3; see Cat. no. 55) has been dated by Robison between 1745–46 and 1748 (Robison in Bettagno 1983, pp. 18–19). The second (Hind 1922, p. 66, no. 101; Focillon 1964, p. 51, no. 721; Wilton-Ely 1978 [1988], pl. 101) is illustrated and listed in the first *catalogo inciso* in the Accademia di San Luca, Rome, 1761 (Mayer-Haunton in Bettagno 1978, p. 10, no. 1, repr. fig. 1). Although Piranesi's third view of St. Peter's was not listed until the *catalogo inciso* of 1775 in Bassano del Grappa (Mayer-Haunton in Bettagno 1978, p. 11, no. 5, repr. fig. 5), Dumont's etching indicates that it must have been done by 1763. Dumont's illustration of the Piazza of St. Peter's shows that Piranesi's works still had a strong attraction for former *pensionnaires* of the French Academy in Rome even after they returned to France.

ENNEMOND-ALEXANDRE PETITOT,
author and delineator
Lyons 1727–Parma 1801

BENIGNO BOSSI, etcher
Como 1727–Parma 1793

119. *Vase Supported by Two Satyrs*

in SUITE DE VASES *[Parma, Benigno Bossi, or Milan, Gioachino Bettalli, 1764]*

Etching on laid paper (no. 13, folio 15). Platemark: 6½ x 8⅝ inches (166 x 219 mm); page: 9¹/₁₆ x 14½ inches (247 x 369 mm). Watermark: none.
Inscribed inside etched border, upper right, *13*; lower left, *Petitot In.*; lower right, *Bossi Sc.*
DATE: execution of the etching, 1763–64.
PROVENANCE: Marlborough Rare Books, Ltd., London.
BIBLIOGRAPHY: Rome and elsewhere 1988, p. 93, no. 92, repr. p. 93.

Montréal, Centre Canadien d'Architecture/Canadian Centre for Architecture ID88–B1157 CAGE

This etching is part of a set of Petitot's *Suite de Vases* bound in a restored eighteenth-century binding of light brown leather and stamped in gold on the spine, *BOSSI SUITE DE VASES* with embossed rosettes. The endpapers are modern. According to Davis S. Howard, the bookplate inside the front cover has the coat of arms of George Thomas Paget (fig. 1), son of Lord Alfred Paget. George Thomas Paget died in 1939. This copy of the *Suite de Vases* has the illustrated frontispiece; the two letters of dedication signed by Petitot and Bossi to Guillaume Du Tillot (1710–74), minister of state to the duke of Parma; and thirty illustrations of vases. Since the title page is missing, it is not possible to ascertain whether this copy is the first edition published in 1764 in Parma by Bossi or the second edition published in Milan that same year by Gioachino Bettalli (Pellegri 1965, p. 83; Brunel 1978, pp. 259–60; Paul Bédarida in Rome and elsewhere 1988, p. 85, note 4).

Petitot received his early training in Lyons, in the

FIGURE 1 Bookplate bearing the coat of arms of George Thomas Paget, glued inside front cover of E-A. Petitot, *Suite de Vases*. Canadian Centre for Architecture, Montréal, ID88–B1157 CAGE.

FIGURE 2 Jean-Laurent Legeay, *Vase Supported by Two Sphinxes*, in *Vasi*. Cooper-Hewitt Museum, Smithsonian Institution's Museum of Design, New York.

workshops of his father, Simon, an architect and engineer, and Jacques-Germain Soufflot. He then went to Paris and received the *grand prix* of the Académie Royale d'Architecture in 1745. From 1746 to 1750 he pursued his studies at the French Academy in Rome where he came into contact with Giovanni Battista Piranesi and Gabriel-Pierre-Martin Dumont (1720–91), Jérôme-Charles Bellicard (1726–86) and Joseph-Marie Vien (1716–1809). There is a sketchbook in the Louvre with drawings from a trip Petitot took with Bellicard and Vien in 1749 to sites around Rome and Naples (Rome and elsewhere 1988, pp. 47–49). Petitot designed the second *Feste della Chinea* in 1749. His temporary decoration was a reconstruction of the recently excavated theater at Herculaneum (Brunel 1978, no. 133, repr. pp. 252, 254–55, 258).

Petitot began his career as an architect when he returned to Paris in 1750. On the recommendation of the comte de Caylus, for whom he had produced several illustrations of the *Recueil d'antiquités* (1752–67), Petitot became architect to Filippo of Bourbon, duke of Parma (1749–65) in 1753. The duke had married Louise-Elisabeth, daughter of Louis XV. Petitot remained in Parma for the rest of his life (Pellegri 1965, *passim*; Erouart in Rome and elsewhere 1976, pp. 250–51). Besides designing many temporary decorations for court festivals, Petitot also constructed several buildings and monuments in Parma. These include the Hunting Lodge at Colorno; and in Parma, the library of the Palazzo della Pilotta, the facade of the Church of San Pietro, the Palazzo di Riserva, the Casino dello Stradone, and the *Ara Amicitiae*, a monument erected in the Piazza Maggiore. In addition to the two suites of etchings exhibited here, Petitot also published *Raisonnement sur la perspective* (Parma, 1758) and *Descrizione delle feste celebrate in Parma l'anno 1769 per le nozze del Reale Infante Duca Ferdinando di Borbone* (Roberto Tassi in Rome and elsewhere 1988, pp. 7–13, and nos. 33–67, pp. 62–83, nos. 124–25, pp. 102–5).

Since the end of the seventeenth century, it had been the practice of artists and architects to design vases and make engravings from their designs. Fischer von Erlach devoted Book V of his 1721 *Entwurff*

einer historischen Architectur to vases, which he depicted in front of imaginary palace designs. This practice was particularly prevalent at the French Academy in Rome during the second half of the eighteenth century. The sculptor Jacques-François Salcy (1717–76) published in Rome in 1746 a series of thirty etchings of vases. Louis-Joseph Le Lorrain, Joseph-Marie Vien, and Charles De Wailly also produced a series of vase etchings between the 1750s and 1760. Piranesi himself published a series of vases in *Vasi, candelabri, cippi* (1770–78). Several of Piranesi's etchings reproduced monumental vases reconstructed from ancient fragments; he then sold these etchings to foreign clients (Wilton-Ely 1978 [1988], pp. 111–13).

According to his dedication to Du Tillot, Petitot decided to publish this suite of vases in order to illustrate three vases he had designed for the gardens at the ducal villa at Colorno; these are represented in plates 1 to 3 (Bédarida in Rome and elsewhere 1988, pp. 91–92, nos. 81–83, pls. 2–4, repr. p. 91). In addition, plate 5 of Petitot's *Suite de Vases* presents a design that was sculpted by Jean-Baptiste Boudard (1710–68) and later placed on the rooftop of the Casino dello Stradone, a building designed by Petitot (Rome and elsewhere 1988, p. 91, no. 84, repr. p. 91). Bédarida believes that the incentive to publish the twenty-six other designs was encouraged by a visit from the French amateur Claude-Henri Watelet (1718–86) in 1763. Watelet had etched the vases of Jean-Baptiste Pierre in 1749 and those of Le Lorrain in 1752, which were dedicated to Madame Geoffrin. Of the thirteen red chalk preparatory drawings for the illustrations of vases that were originally presented by Petitot to Du Tillot and later appeared in the Delteil sale in Paris in 1917, only one has survived (Bédarida in Rome and elsewhere 1988, p. 85, note 3, p. 90, no. 80, repr. p. 90; private collection, Paris). The red chalk drawing for the dedication to Du Tillot, now lost, had a date of 1763 (1988, pp. 84–85).

Petitot's vase designs have been called piranesian in inspiration (Pellegri 1965, p. 83; Pierre Arrizoli in Brunel 1978, pp. 259–60; Bédarida in Rome and elsewhere 1988, p. 84). Petitot's diverse Egyptian, Roman, and Greek decorative motifs can be compared to the many decorative motifs assembled by Piranesi in his *Parere su l'architettura* (1765) and *Diverse maniere* (1764–69). In 1967, John Harris noticed that there was a common "pervasive dissolution of the Vitruvian vocabulary" shared by Piranesi (in the above works) and by a group of *pensionnaires* who were at the French Academy in Rome between 1740 and 1750, among them Louis-Joseph Le Lorrain, Gabriel-Pierre-Martin Dumont, and Jean-Laurent Legeay (Harris in Wittkower 1967, pp. 191–92; Erouart 1982, p. 186). It is quite possible that Petitot, while in Parma, still maintained contact with Piranesi. The *Diverse maniere*, although in the planning stage in 1764, was not published until 1769, five years after Petitot's *Suite de Vases.*

When we examine Petitot's etching, *Vase Supported by Two Satyrs*, it is apparent that he went beyond Piranesi, Le Lorrain, and Salcy in the reaction against Vitruvian norms of harmony. In this design, Petitot has destroyed the integrity of the shape of the vase itself. The top part resembles the lower part of a column. At the base of the vase is a rim decorated with a Greek key fret motif. The flutes of the truncated column-like vase are actually blades of wheat tied with a cord. Petitot's satirical wit is closest to Legeay's. However, even in the *Vase Supported by Two Sphinxes* (fig. 2), the second plate of Legeay's undated suite, *Vasi*, which was executed in England between 1767 and 1768, Legeay did not go as far as Petitot in the transformation of conventional forms (Erouart 1982, p. 230, no. 146, p. 185, fig. 191).

NO. 119

LES
SOIRÉES DE ROME
DÉDIÉES
A M.^{DE} LE COMTE
des Académies
de S Luc de Rome,
des Sciences et Arts
de Bologne, Florence

Suite de Dix Planches dessinées et gravées par M.^r
Robert, Pensionaire du Roi de France à Rome.
A Paris chés Wille Graveur du Roi Quay des Augustins.

NO. 120, Plate 1

NO. 120, Plate 6

NO. 120, Plate 8

FIGURE 1 Hubert Robert, *Sketchbook*,
folio 13 verso. The Pierpont Morgan
Library, New York.

HUBERT ROBERT

Paris 1733–Paris 1808

120. *Les Soirées de Rome*

Paris [1765]. (Baudicour 1861, 2; nos. 1–10, first of three states)

Suite of ten etchings, executed between 1763 and 1764. Various measurements: from 135 x 93 mm to 139 x 95 mm. Watermarks: Auvergne with fragments of chaplets (4193); circle with fleur-de-lis surmounted by another fleur-de-lis (4218); various letters (4218).

Inscribed on title page, *LES/SOIRÉES DE ROME/DÉDIÉES/ A M^DE LE COMTE,/des Académies/de S Luc de Rome des Sciences et Arts/de Bologne, Florence & c.*; below, *Suite de Dix Planches dessinées et gravées par M^r./Robert, Pensionaire du Roi de France à Rome./A Paris chés Wille Graveur du Roi Quay des Augustins.*

EXHIBITION: New York 1989.

Giannalisa Feltrinelli Collection, on deposit at The Pierpont Morgan Library (4193 and 4218)

Robert dedicated these etchings to Marguerite Le Comte who accompanied the noted *amateur* Claude-Henri Watelet (see Cat. no. 86) on his visit to Italy in December 1763. Robert also participated in designing a small printed book which was prepared by some of the students at the French Academy in honor of Watelet and Mme Le Comte's visit. For that project, Robert contributed two designs for borders. Although the plates for *Les Soirées de Rome* were executed in Rome, the suite was printed in Paris, probably in 1765 after Robert's return from Italy. The first edition was published by Wille with *A Paris chés Wille Graveur du Roi Quay des Augustins* added to the title page. In the second edition, Wille's name and address are replaced with the inscription, *A Paris chez Prévost Graveur rue S^t. Thomas porte S^t. Jacques près le Jeu de Paulme,* and in the third edition yet another printer and address replaces that of Prévost, *à Paris, chez Basan freres rue et hotel Serpente.*

Robert originally intended what now is plate 2 to be the title page but he soon expanded the suite of eight etchings into ten, with the additions of plate 1– the title page with the dedication to Mme Le Comte– and plate 10.

FIGURE 2 Hubert Robert, *Sketchbook,* folio 14 verso. The Pierpont Morgan Library, New York.

FIGURE 3 Hubert Robert, *Sketchbook,* folio 21 verso. The Pierpont Morgan Library, New York.

The Morgan sketchbook (Cat. no. 98) contains sketches that are clearly early ideas for four of the etched plates, namely plates 4, 6, and 8. On folio 13v (fig. 1) there is a sketch for plate 3, and on folio 14v (fig. 2) Robert concentrated on the tomb that appears on plate 6. (This is the drawing which bears the date 1763.) Seven pages later, on folio 21v (fig. 3), there are three small sketches, two of which also relate to the *Soirées de Rome*; one of these corresponds to the etched plate 4, while the other develops more fully Robert's idea for plate 6, which he had begun earlier with the drawing of the tomb on folio 14v. Still later, on folio 23, Robert sketched a drawing that stands somewhere between plates 6 and 8 of the etched suite, and made another sketch that is even later and closer to plate 8.

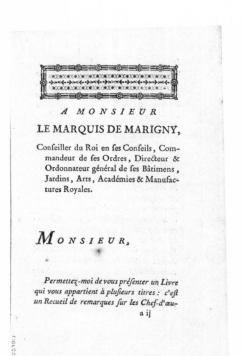

NO. 121

CHARLES-NICOLAS COCHIN
THE YOUNGER

Paris 1715–Paris 1790

121. *Dedication to the Marquis de Marigny*

in Voyage/d'Italie,/ou/Recueil de Notes/Sur les Ouvrages de Peinture & de Sculp-/ture, qu'on voit dans les principales/villes d'Italie. *Paris, Chez Ant.*^{oine} *Jombert, 1758, volume 1*

Letterpress. Folio aij recto: 6⅞ x 4 inches (165 x 101 mm). Watermark: partial one at upper edge center (illegible).

PROVENANCE: Léonce Laget, Paris.

BIBLIOGRAPHY (for the work as a whole): Cochin 1758 (Michel 1991), introduction, pp. 1–69; Eriksen 1974, pp. 34–36, 199, 204–5; Hautecoeur 1952, vol. IV, pp. 1–5; Rabreau 1975, pp. 213–14.

Montréal, Centre Canadien d'Architecture/Canadian Centre for Architecture POY12540:1 CAGE

The CCA's three volumes of Cochin's *Voyage d'Italie* are bound in eighteenth-century brown leather with double endpapers of laid eighteenth-century paper, and red, yellow, and orange marbled paper, also from the eighteenth century. The spine is stamped in gold on red leather *VOYAGE/D'ITALIE/TOME I [II]* above a series of flowers also stamped in gold.

In 1746, Mme de Pompadour arranged for her brother, Abel-François de Vandières, later the marquis de Marigny (1725–81), to succeed her husband's uncle, Le Normant de Tournehem, at his death, as *directeur général des bâtiments, jardins, arts, académies, et manufactures royales.* She then decided that her brother should go to Italy in order to gain the necessary knowledge for his future post. She chose as his traveling companions the writer Jean-Bernard le Blanc (1706–81), known as Abbé le Blanc, the architect Jacques-Germain Soufflot (1713–80), and the draughtsman, illustrator, and engraver Charles-Nicolas Cochin the Younger, who held the title of *dessinateur des menus plaisirs du roi.* Vandières was

only twenty-one-years old at the beginning of the trip. Correspondence to Vandières while he was in Italy is in the Pierpont Morgan Library, the Bibliothèque historique de la ville de Paris, and the Bibliothèque de l'Institut d'art et d'archéologie. The letters in the Library were written by Mme de Pompadour (Cochin 1758 [Michel 1991], pp. 2–3, note 5, p. 2). Vandières and his traveling companions were depicted in a caricature by Pier Leone Ghezzi (1674–1755) that is now in the Metropolitan Museum of Art (fig. 1) (Rogers Fund 1972, 1972.84).

The group's itinerary was published in the first 1756 edition of the *Voyage d'Italie.* They left Paris on 20 December 1749 and arrived in Turin on 24 February 1750. By 25 March 1750 they were in Rome after having traveled to Parma, Modena, Ancona, and Loreto. Soufflot became ill after going to Paestum in May and June of 1750, and therefore returned to France. His place was taken by the young architect Jérôme-Charles Bellicard (1726–86). They stayed in Rome until 3 March 1751 when they began their trip back to Paris via Caprarola, Siena, Florence, Luca, Pisa, Bologna, Venice, Vicenza, Verona, Mantua, Genoa, Brescia, and Milan. They left Genoa for Marseilles on 13 August 1751. Le Normant de Tournehem had died by then and Vandières immediately returned to Paris to take his post as *directeur général des bâtiments,* a post he occupied until 1773 (Cochin 1758 [Michel 1991], p. 11–12).

Ironically, according to Christian Michel, it was Abbé le Blanc who was supposed to write the account of the trip, not Cochin. Soufflot was entrusted with making a survey of theater design in Italy, and Cochin was to make drawings of public squares and fountains. Practically all of Cochin's drawings are lost; he does not describe Rome in the second 1758 edition of the book (Cochin 1758 [Michel 1991], pp. 15–18). Michel has noted that the first edition of Cochin's book, which has survived in only two copies, was an actual account of the trip, intended for only his close friends. Both of the extant copies, one in the Bibliothèque Nationale and one in a Parisian private collection, belonged to the marquis de Marigny. The second 1758 edition was rewritten as an introduction to the art of painting and was intended for the general public (Cochin 1758 [Michel 1991], pp. 18–20). Cochin preferred High Renaissance and baroque paintings of the second half of the seventeenth century; his aim was to teach the public the principles of good painting. After his return from Rome in 1751, a major part of Cochin's activity was devoted to writing: he felt that artists, not writers, should instruct the public in aesthetics. Cochin's attitude represented a reaction to the new *métier* of *critique d'art*, which had developed following the revival of the Salons in 1737 (Cochin 1758 [Michel 1991], pp. 20–34).

Architecture plays a minor role in Cochin's book; he mentions only sixty buildings. According to Michel, Cochin was most attentive to the problems of architectural style during the first part of the trip, when Soufflot was a member of the group (Cochin 1758 [Michel 1991], p. 37). Cochin's few comments on architecture, however, are significant, for example, his condemnation of the interiors of Juvarra's Stupinighi Palace as being in the style of the "folies de Meissonnier" (Cochin 1758, vol. I, p. 93, folio 31 [Michel 1991, p. 37]). In his disdain for the rococo, Cochin was influenced by Abbé le Blanc. Le Blanc, in a letter to the comte de Caylus written in 1737 or 1738 (*Lettres . . . concernant le gouvernement, la politique et les mœurs des Anglais et Français*, Paris 1747), condemned the rococo style in architecture and called for a more simplified style based on Vitruvius, ancient architecture, and the architecture of Louis XIV (Eriksen 1974, appendix, no. I, pp. 226–32).

Curiously, Cochin did not espouse a slavish imitation of Roman and Greek architecture (Cochin 1758 [Michel 1991, p. 37]). He also did not like the Doric order, whose superiority was proclaimed in the treatises of Abbé J. L. de Cordemoy and Abbé Marc-Antoine Laugier (Cochin 1758, vol. III, p. 398, folio 190 [Michel 1991]; Middleton 1962, p. 278–320; Eriksen 1974, pp. 48–51). As in painting, Cochin preferred High Renaissance and baroque architecture, praising Palladio's Teatro Olimpico and Bernini's Church of the Assumption at Ariccia (Cochin 1758 [Michel 1991, p. 37]). He called the seventeenth-century fa-

cade of Milan Cathedral "very beautiful and grecian in style." Cochin equated "grecian" with the classical style (Eriksen 1974, p. 49; Cochin 1758, vol. I, folio 32 [Michel 1991, p. 94]). His moderation with regard to the importance of ancient architecture had an influence on Marigny, since Marigny never totally condemned the rococo style. Nor did Marigny believe that architects should study only ancient architecture; he thought they should study the problems of modern architecture as well (Eriksen 1974, pp. 205–6).

In the dedication of the *Voyage d'Italie* to the marquis de Marigny, Cochin extolled the trip they took to Italy together as a watershed in the evolution of artistic taste in France. Because of his instruction from Abbé le Blanc, Cochin, and Soufflot, Marigny was able to bring about a change in taste, "le triomphe du bon goût," through his patronage of important architectural projects and the encouragement of artists of great talent.

Indeed, Hautecoeur, Eriksen, and Michel all agree that Marigny's choice in 1755 of Jacques-Germain Soufflot to design the Church of Sainte-Geneviève, and of Ange-Jacques Gabriel (1698–1782) to design the Place Louis XV was significant for the future development of neoclassicism. Cochin also played a major role in these developments. In 1755, he was appointed secretary of the Académie Royale de Peinture as well as the intermediary between the Royal Arts Administration and the artists. In his *Mémoires*, written between 1780 and 1790, Cochin characterized the period following Marigny's return from Italy in 1751 as the triumph of *le goust grec*, a style initiated in the 1750s in the decorative arts and interior design by Louis-Joseph Le Lorrain (see Cat. no. 84) and in architecture by Jacques-Germain Soufflot (Eriksen 1974, appendix, no. IX, pp. 269–70). It was against those French proponents of *le oust grec* that Piranesi addressed his polemical works between 1761 and 1765: *Della Magnificenza ed architettura de' Romani; Parere su l'architettura; Osservazioni di Gio. Battista Piranesi sopra la lettre de M. Mariette*; and *Della Introduzione e del progresso delle belle arti* (Cat. no. 59).

FIGURE 1 Pier Leone Ghezzi, *Caricature: The Marquis de Vandières, Abbé le Blanc, the Architect Jacques-Germain Soufflot, and the Engraver Charles-Nicolas Cochin the Younger*. Metropolitan Museum of Art, New York, 1972.84.

ENNEMOND-ALEXANDRE PETITOT,
author and delineator

Lyons 1727–Parma 1801

BENIGNO BOSSI, etcher

Como 1727–Parma 1793

122. *Self-portrait of Ennemond-Alexandre Petitot*

L'Auteur des Figures à la Grecque

NO. 122

in MASCARADE/A LA/GRECQVE/DEDIEE A/MONSIEUR LE MARQVIS DE FELINO /PREMIER MINISTRE DE S.A.R./PAR SON TRES HVMBLE SERVITEVR BENIGNO BOSSI/PARME MDCCLXXI, *Milan, Gioachino Bettalli, 1771*

Etching on laid paper (no. 10, folio 10). Platemark: 10⅝ x 7³⁄₁₆ inches (270 x 183 mm); page: 19⅝ x 12⅝ inches (498 x 322 mm). Watermark: none.
Inscribed outside border, upper right, *10*; lower left, *Chev.ʳ F E.A. Petitot inv.*; lower right, *Gravé par Benigno Bossi*; center, *L'Auteur des Figures à la Grecque*.

DATE: execution of the etching, 1771.

PROVENANCE: Christopher Mendez, London.

BIBLIOGRAPHY (for this plate but not for the CCA's copy): Pellegri 1965, p. 134, repr. pl. 89, p. 145; Rome and elsewhere 1976, p. 258, no. 135B, repr. p. 257; Rome and elsewhere 1988, p. 127, no. 165, p. 128, repr. p. 135.

Montréal, Centre Canadien d'Architecture/Canadian Centre for Architecture POM12425 CAGE

This set of Petitot's *Mascarade à la grecque* is in a nineteenth-century binding covered with orange wove paper. The endpapers of wove paper are also from the nineteenth century. Inside the front cover is the bookplate of Ludovic Halévy (1834–1908), the writer and librettist of operas who was also a friend of the French painter Degas. Halévy's collection of short stories, *La Famille Cardinal*, inspired a series of monotypes by Degas. He, his wife, and his son Daniel (1872–1962), the author of *Mon ami Degas* (1960), were portrayed by Degas in pastels and photographs (Paris, Ottawa, New York 1988–89, pp. 278–84, 535–39; Curtiss in Halévy 1964, pp. 9–17).

The CCA's copy of Petitot's *Mascarade à la grecque* is complete and contains the etched frontispiece and nine plates. The other eight plates show people from diverse strata of society dressed like the author in costumes composed of motifs derived from Greek and Roman art. Represented in the series are a canteen keeper, a grenadier, a monk, a priestess, a shepherd, a shepherdess, a bride, and a groom (Pellegri 1965, pp. 134–35, pls. 89–91, pp. 145–47; Brunel 1978, pp. 258–59; Rome and elsewhere 1988, pp. 126–27, nos. 156–55, repr. pp. 129–35).

Svend Eriksen has traced the development of the style in architecture and the decorative arts known as *le goût grec*. This style originated in the mid-1750s and reached its apogee in the mid-1760s. Eriksen published one of the earliest manifestations of this style—a book on a suite of furniture designed in 1756 by Louis-Joseph Le Lorrain for Ange-Laurent de Lalive de Jully (1725–79), and executed before 1757 by an unknown cabinetmaker. The oak and ebony veneer writing table and cartonnier with ormolu mounts by Philippe Caffieri (1714–74), now in the Musée Condée at Chantilly, exhibits many of the decorative motifs typical of the style: ormolu side rails treated as a frieze and decorated with a band of Vitruvian scrolls, garlands of oak and laurel leaves, an ormolu mount in the form of the mask and hide of the Nemaean Lion, legs in the form of crenellated columns with lion's paws, and an ormolu frieze at the top of the cartonnier with Greek key fret motifs. In an inventory of his art collection made in 1764, Lalive de Jully himself called the desk "dans le goût grec." Le Lorrain himself had executed the preparatory drawings (at the request of the comte de Caylus) in Julien David Le Roy's pioneering book, *Les Ruines des plus beaux monuments de la Grèce* (Paris, 1758) (Eriksen 1961, pp. 340–47, figs. 5–16; Eriksen 1974, pp. 45–46, 49–50, 68, pls. 85–89).

A letter written by Baron Grimm on 1 May 1763 describes two prints after drawings by Louis Carrogis (called Carmontelle, 1717–1806) of people wearing costumes in the Greek style. According to Eriksen, Carmontelle's designs started a craze for balls in which the participants wore costumes in the Greek style. The *goût grec* became such a mania that Nicholas-Thomas Barthe satirized it in his play *L'Amateur* in 1764. Barthe stated: "The style is Greek, our furniture, our jewels, fabric, hairstyles, riding habits, everything is Greek, except our souls" (Eriksen 1974, pp. 50–51). Christian Michel has suggested that Petitot executed the original designs for his *Mascarade à la grecque* in 1763 after a set of etchings by the comte de Caylus sent to the son of the duke of Parma. On 16 May of that year, the comte de Caylus wrote to Padre Paciaudi in Parma telling him that the duke's son would receive a set of etchings showing figures in Greek costumes. According to Michel, these etchings probably resembled the set of anonymous etchings published by Eriksen (Eriksen 1974, pp. 50–51, pls. 351–64; Michel in Rome and elsewhere 1988, p. 126). In the dedication to *Mascarade à la grecque*, Petitot referred to preparatory drawings for the illustrations of the *Mascarade* that he presented to Guillaume Du Tillot. In the catalogue of the sale of Du Tillot's collection in 1777, they were described as being in red chalk. Petitot's original drawings probably represented designs of costumes worn in a court festivity. They are lost; the ten drawings executed in watercolor and white gouache on blue paper, now in a private collection in Parma, were, according to Michel, probably made after Petitot's etchings, following the publication of the suite (Michel in Rome and elsewhere 1988, pp. 126–27, no. 153, pls. XII–XVI). Michel does not believe that Petitot executed the actual preparatory drawings for the etchings published by Bossi in 1771, since only Bossi signed the title page. The *Mascarade à la grecque* was the last work Petitot dedicated to Du Tillot, who fell into disgrace soon after and returned to Paris where he died in 1774.

Pierre Arrizoli has noted that in addition to the elements derived from Greek and Roman architecture, such as the crenellated column, broken Corinthian capitol, and the ribbons decorated with the Greek key fret motif that Petitot wears on his chest, there are also allusions to Egyptian art. Petitot wears an Egyptian headdress and stands in front of a pyramid. Arrizoli has seen in this plate an influence of Piranesi's *Diverse maniere* (Brunel 1978, pp. 258–59). If in fact the original drawings for Petitot's *Mascarade à la grecque* are dated 1763, as Michel has suggested, then the Egyptian influences may have come from Fischer von Erlach's 1721 treatise rather than from Piranesi's *Diverse maniere*, which was only published in 1769. As in the illustrations of the *Suite de Vases* (Cat. no. 119), Petitot imparts to his self-portrait a wonderfully witty quality, especially apparent in the oversized book and the caliper he holds in his hand to measure masonry, a reference perhaps to the pretentious character of many amateur archaeologists.

NO. 123

JEAN-CLAUDE-RICHARD DE SAINT-NON

Paris 1727–Paris 1791

123. *Recueil de griffonis, de vües, paysages, fragments antiques et sujets historiques, gravés tant à l'eau forte qu'au lavis*

Second edition. Paris: chez la veuve Lavoye [c. 1790]

296 etched plates and aquatints. Binding: mottled calf with gilt tooled boards with double palmette border. Spine: gilt banded with stylized fields of rosettes and urns, gilt label on red morocco band, RECUEIL/DE/GRIFFONIS/DE VUES/DE/SAINT NON. Marbled endpapers with bookplate of Paul Mellon, Oak Spring. Binding: 520 x 356 mm. Watermarks: various Auvergne papers, T. Dupuy (MOYEN/T. DUPUY/AUVERGNE) and letters *IHS* between cross and heart with three swords in a circle (cf. Heawood 2993 and 2997); on aquatints, paper of Delafore (Delaforet?) FIN/DE LA FORE/ 1788 (see Cayeux 1964, p. 311).

PROVENANCE: Paul Mellon, Oak Spring.

BIBLIOGRAPHY: Morgan Library *FR* XIX, 1981, p. 24.

EXHIBITION: New York 1989.

The Pierpont Morgan Library. The Paul Mellon Gift, PML 76759

Like many amateurs of his time, Saint-Non learned to etch producing printed suites, such as *Fragments choisis,* from studies that Fragonard and Robert made after classical antiquities and Italian paintings when they were in Italy as students. *Les Griffonis* translates as "scribbles" or "rough sketches" and many of the prints in this book were made intentionally to resemble drawings. *Les Griffonis* was published after Saint-Non's *Voyage pittoresque* but the illustrations were prepared between 1755 and 1778. They include the work of many artists such as Ango, Boucher, Clodion, Doyen, Greuze, and Leprince. While many plates derive from studies by Hubert Robert, 168 – the greatest number of studies by a single artist – are by Fragonard.

The first fifty-nine prints in the book are etchings.

However, by 1768 Saint-Non was using a new technique, aquatint, which imitated wash drawings. Prints produced by the aquatint process had the same effect as the colored washes often used to enhance drawings, and gave the print a different, somewhat softer appearance as well as a greater immediacy. Delafosse and Saint-Non developed their processes at much the same time as Leprince, in whose studio Saint-Non first saw the technique. He was much attracted to it and was excited by its possibilities.

The contents of the book are quite mixed and include what appear to be the abbé's earliest etchings, which he made after landscape drawings by Leprince and Boucher. Saint-Non studied the etching technique with Leprince. A number of the Leprince subjects are Roman antique sites. Next are etchings made after drawings by Robert and Fragonard of villas and gardens seen first hand by the abbé on his visit to Rome in the early 1760s. These are followed by some Neapolitan caricatures and a large series of studies of curious antiquities after drawings by Robert. These are the last etchings in *Les Griffonis*. The abbé then turned to the aquatint method for his oriental heads after the Tiepolos, and other Roman subjects. These last prints replicating Roman paintings and antiquities predominate the work; the remaining plates consist of similar but smaller suites of Bolognese, Neapolitan, and Venetian subjects. Generally, all of these suites are of the same nature and character as the aquatints in the abbé's *Fragments choisis*. Some of the Roman subjects appear also in the *Fragments choisis* while others are executed in the same size and format as the *Fragments choisis*. The two last plates after Fragonard, *The Departure from the Stable* (1776) and *Benjamin Franklin crowned by Liberty* (1778), are quite different in subject matter from the other *Griffonis*.

While most of the drawings the abbé collected for *Les Griffonis* were made in connection with his trip to Italy, the prints were made in France after his return. This is supported by the exclusively French paper used for the prints in this copy as well as in all of the copies studied by Jean de Cayeux.

JEAN-CLAUDE-RICHARD DE SAINT-NON
Paris 1727–Paris 1791

124. *Voyage pittoresque ou description des royaumes de Naples et de Sicile. . . .*

Paris: Clousier, 4 vols., 1781–85. Stroganoff copy.
Contemporary binding blue morocco, decorated with gilt coat of arms of baron Stroganoff surrounded by Greek key motif on boards, spine ornamented with *filets dorés et au pointillé*, lined with marbled paper, plates gilt-edged. Book plate of baron Gregoire de Stroganoff on inner cover. Two hundred and eighty-four plates, and also five title-page vignettes, fifteen heading vignettes, ninety-six cul-de-lampes, six maps, and fourteen plates of medals. Binding: 509 x 334 mm. Watermarks: various Auvergne watermarks. Numbered and inscribed in an old hand in pen and black ink, *2796/5 vols. 285 planch. gr.*

BIBLIOGRAPHY: Morgan Library *FR* XVI, 1973, p. 56.

EXHIBITION: New York 1989.

The Pierpont Morgan Library. Gift of Rowland Burdon-Muller, PML 62641-5

The younger son of a noble, well-to-do family, Saint-Non took great interest in the arts, studying printmaking with Jean-Baptiste Leprince. In October of 1759 he began what was to be a two-year trip to Italy. The abbé's itinerary and his reactions are recounted amusingly in his journal, which was unknown until quite recently when it suddenly appeared. Pierre Rosenberg and Barbara Bréjon-de Lavergnée published it in 1986.

The thirty-two-year-old abbé arrived in Rome in mid-November after a pleasant journey of about six weeks. He traveled by way of Lyon and Geneva where he paid a visit to Voltaire. Other stopovers, pleasant or uninteresting–in the abbé's view–are recorded in his diary. Almost immediately after arriving in Rome, he left for Naples. The abbé also wished to visit the sites of recent archaeological excavations at Pozzuoli and Paestum before the start of the rainy season. Eventually he returned to Rome where, with the exception of a summer at the Villa d'Este at Tivoli, he stayed until April of 1761. Then he and Fragonard commenced a leisurely return to Paris, arriving there at the end of September 1761.

The *Voyage pittoresque*, one of the most beautiful French illustrated books of the eighteenth century, was assembled over two decades. It is not known what kind of publication the abbé had in mind for the impressive assemblage of drawings of Italian sites that he had collected during his two-year trip to Italy. In 1777, however, he was invited by the Abbé de La Borde to prepare the Italian section of a book that, according to the prospectus, was to include views of Switzerland and Italy. Since the project was expensive, the idea of including the Swiss views was dropped in the fear that the book's subscribers would find them monotonous. (These Swiss views were in fact published between 1780 and 1783 as a separate

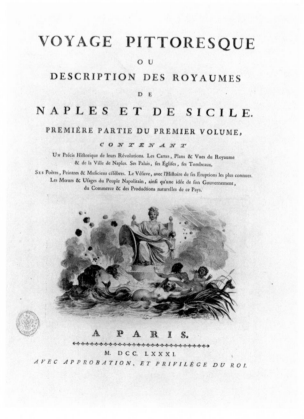

book.) The publishers of the *Voyage pittoresque* decided to concentrate on the Italian section, ultimately limiting the book's scope to Naples and Sicily. In addition to the illustrations provided by Fragonard and Robert, it soon became clear that many more illustrations were needed for this ambitious project, and other artists were invited to supply illustrations. Among them, Desprez and Chatelet were recruited by Baron Vivant Denon, acting for Saint-Non, while Denon was attached to the French embassy in Naples.

Like other French amateur antiquarians, notably the comte de Caylus, the abbé was drawn to southern Italy by the then newly discovered Greek ruins at Herculaneum (excavated in 1738) near Naples, at Paestum (excavated in 1748), and around Pozzuoli. Ultimately he concentrated on this area in the *Voyage pittoresque*. While he would have drawn inspiration from the comte's *Recueil* (Cat. no. 116) as well as from Cochin's and Bellicard's Herculaneum publication of 1754 (Cat. no. 117), he must also have known and admired the sumptuous Hamilton publication of Etruscan, Greek, and Roman antiquities (Cat. no. 78) with its folio format and orange and black illustrations simulating red-figured Greek vase painting. Hamilton's influence becomes apparent in volume II of the *Voyage pittoresque*, which is devoted in large measure to the description of antiquities at Herculaneum and Pompeii. There the abbé himself etched some twenty-four vignettes printed in a two-plate two-color process, first using a terracotta tone and then black ink so that the orange-red figural motives stand out in striking relief. The vignettes are based on motives taken from red-figured vase painting. Although the abbé alludes to Hamilton's prospectus for the work (published in 1766) in the avant-propos for volume II of the *Voyage pittoresque*, he does not specifically mention the complete Hamilton publication.

The text of the book is the collaboration of several authors, including Chamfort, Vivant Denon, Déodat de Dolmieu, Romé de l'Isle, d'Ennery, and Faujas. Saint-Non himself provided a dedicatory letter to Marie Antoinette.

HUBERT ROBERT

Paris 1733–Paris 1808

125. *Autograph letter to M. Le Barbier*

Pen and black ink on pale green writing paper.

Gift of John H. Plummer and William M. Voelkle in honor of Herbert F. Cahoon, 1989

In this letter dated 13 March but with no year indicated, Robert apologizes to the painter Jean-Jacques Le Barbier, secretary-treasurer of the Société des Amis des Arts. He has not been able to locate the paintings that he wishes to present to the society, in part because his affliction of gout has made it difficult to get around. He will send them as soon as he is able. Robert continues with a description of the paintings. Both represent Roman ruins. One shows an antique structure at the end of a great road, and the other must depict a view of the entrance to the Vatican Museum at the time of its construction near the papal apartments. Unlike Fragonard, who returned to Rome in the 1770s with Bergeret de Grancourt (see Cat. no. 93), Robert never found an opportunity to return. He continued, however, to draw on his memories of Rome in his paintings, with the help of the sketches he had made during his long stay there.

Although it is not certain in what year he wrote this letter to Le Barbier, it was most likely written during the early 1790s, the same time that the Société des Amis des Arts was being founded under the initiative of De Wailly. One of the goals of the Société was to gather funds by subscription in order to buy art and thereby make up for the lack of art patrons. Some of Robert's paintings were purchased in 1790, 1791, and 1792. Later, Robert was denounced, and in October 1793 he was imprisoned. Released a year later, he served, along with Fragonard, on the committee for the organization of the new national museum at the Louvre from 1795 until 1802. Robert had some experience in such matters for he had served as advisor to Louis XVI in the 1780s. The idea for a national museum actually originated with this enlightened monarch.

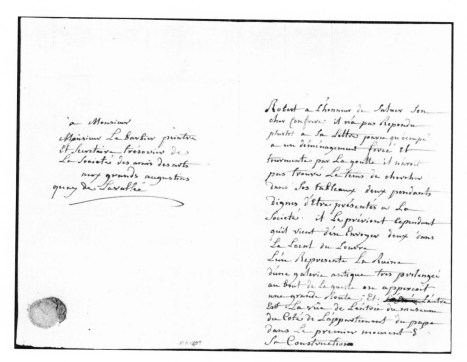

NO. 125

JEAN-CLAUDE-RICHARD DE SAINT-NON

Paris 1727–Paris 1791

126. *Fragments choisis dans les peintures et les tableaux les plus interessants des palais et des eglises de l'Italie*

Paris, 1770–72

100 aquatint plates by Saint-Non after drawings by Hubert Robert, Fragonard, and Ango in three suites (of six published): *Premiere suite* with engraved aquatint title by Hubert Robert and thirty-nine numbered (2–40) aquatint plates in gray; *Seconde suite* with engraved aquatint title by Robert and nineteen numbered (42–60) aquatint plates in gray; *Troisieme suite* with engraved aquatint title by Fragonard and thirty-nine numbered (2–40) aquatint plates in brown. Watermarks: illegible, probably Auvergne; end fly-paper: grapes with indecipherable letters below.

BINDING: Mottled calf, gilt spine, marbled endpapers, edges red.

PROVENANCE: Sir Joshua Reynolds, with signature and stamp (Lugt 2364); Mrs. Mostyn, daughter of Mrs. Thrale and friend of Reynolds, sold 1857 according to pencil note; Leonard B. Schlosser, New York; sale, New York, Sotheby's, 17–18 June 1992, lot 495.

The Pierpont Morgan Library. Purchased on the Gordon N. Ray Fund, PML 127307

Unlike *Les Griffonis, Fragments choisis* is composed entirely of aquatints. As a book, it is straightforward rather than complicated like *Les Griffonis. Les Griffonis* is varied in its techniques and contents while *Fragments* consists simply of three suites of aquatints reproducing paintings: two suites for Rome and one for Bologna, each introduced by a title page. The title pages for both Roman suites are based on designs by Hubert Robert, but the title page for the third or Bolognese suite is after a design by Fragonard, the abbé's companion on his return to France in 1761.

While the aquatints for the Roman suites are based on drawings by both Fragonard and Ango, Fragonard executed all the drawings for the Bolognese aquatints. This accords with what is known about the abbé's return trip to France. It is well established that the abbé had arrived in Rome by mid-November of 1759 and departed in April 1761 for his return to France. While traveling in Italy, he was accompanied by artists, first by Hubert Robert, and later by Fragonard and Ango. Both Fragonard and Ango—at the abbé's request—made copies after notable paintings in Naples and Rome, but since Fragonard was the only artist to make the return to France with the abbé, he alone drew copies of paintings in Bologna and Venice. *Fragments choisis* does not include any of the aquatints made after Venetian paintings; these appear in *Les Griffonis.* Interestingly, a number of the aquatints after paintings in Rome appear in both *Les Griffonis* and *Fragments.* While *Fragments* does not bear a publication date, it could not have been published before 1772, the latest date found on the aquatints; they are all dated between 1770 and 1772. Although the artists made the drawings during 1760 and 1761, they were not translated into prints until after the abbé's return to France in late September 1761. At first he devoted his efforts to making etchings after a number of the drawings (see Cat. no. 123), but he did not begin to work in the aquatint process until 1765.

Additional interest is provided by Sir Joshua Reynolds's early ownership of the Morgan copy. It appears to have been printed early, with rich, clear outlines and inking.

JACQUES-LOUIS DAVID
Paris 1748–Brussels 1825

127. *Warrior and Amazon*

Black chalk and gray wash. 5³⁄₁₆ x 7⁹⁄₁₆ inches (132 x 192 mm). Watermark: none visible through lining.
Inscribed by the artist at lower right, *au Capitole*; monogrammed by the artist's two sons, Jules and Eugène, at the time of the 1826 sale, at lower right, in pen and brown ink, *E.D. / J.D.*

Banquet Scene

Black chalk and gray wash. 6¹⁄₁₆ x 8⁵⁄₁₆ inches (154 x 211 mm). Watermark: none visible through lining.
Inscribed by the artist in black chalk at lower right, *a Venise a la librairie*; monogrammed at the time of the 1826 sale by the artist's two sons, Jules and Eugène, in pen and brown ink at lower left, *E.D./ J.D.*

PROVENANCE: Jules and Eugène David (Lugt 1437 and 839); David sale, Paris, salle Lebrun, 17 April 1826, part of lot 66; 2nd David sale, Paris, 11 March 1835, lot 10; M. Chassegnolle (David's grandson?); marquise de Ludre (David's great-granddaughter); Jacques Seligmann & Co., New York; Felice Stampfle, New York.

BIBLIOGRAPHY: Morgan Library *FR* XIX, 1981, p. 186.

EXHIBITION: New York 1989.

The Pierpont Morgan Library. Gift of Miss Felice Stampfle, Acc no. 1978.42:1–2

David made numerous copies of Roman art and antiquities during his sojourn in Italy. While the drawing of a warrior and amazon was executed in Rome and annotated by the artist, *au Capitole*, David inscribed the banquet scene, *a Venise a la librairie*. The drawing is in fact the artist's copy of the Grimani Altar, which is now in the Museo Archeologico, Venice. These two drawings were on the same page, folio 1 of album 10, along with two other classical studies by the artist—a battle with some gladiators, inscribed by the artist, *au Vatican sur un tombeau*, and a sheet of figure studies with a man alongside a seated woman playing a lyre, as well as a centaur and woman em-

NO. 127

bracing. The latter drawing, like the *Banquet Scene*, was inscribed by the artist, *a Venise a la Librairie*.

David was *agréé* at the *Académie Royale* in 1781 and received as a history painter in 1783, having emerged from Rome as effective leader of the French school.

When the albums are compared, the uniformity of their organization makes it clear that they were compiled by the artist himself. However, after the death of Mme David, her sons Jules and Eugène, anticipating the 1826 sale, marked the drawings with their paraphs to guarantee the authenticity of each sheet. From the evidence of the double numbering system on the album leaves and the guard leaves that describe the contents of the albums, Arlette Sérullaz has concluded that by April 1826 (and the supervening sale) the twelve albums had been slightly modified (Sérullaz 1991, pp. 15ff.).

JACQUES-LOUIS DAVID

Paris 1748–Brussels 1825

128. *The Campidoglio*

Graphite and gray wash. 3⅝ x 7¼ inches (92 x 184 mm).
Watermark: none.
Monogrammed by the artist's two sons, Jules and Eugène,
at the time of the 1826 sale, at lower left, in pen and brown
ink, *E.D. / J.D.*

View of Castel Sant'Angelo

Graphite and gray wash. 3¹/₁₆ x 7⅛ inches (77 x 180 mm).
Watermark: none.
Monogrammed by the artist's two sons, Jules and Eugène,
at the time of the 1826 sale, at lower right, in pen and brown
ink, *E.D. / J.D.*

PROVENANCE: Jules and Eugène David (Lugt 1437 and
839); David sale, Paris, salle Lebrun, 17 April 1826, part of
lot 66; 2nd David sale, Paris, 11 March 1835, lot 10; M. Chassegnolle (David's grandson?); marquise de Ludre (David's
great-granddaughter); Jacques Seligmann & Co., New
York; Helene C. Seiferheld, New York; Mrs. John Colgate
Jessup, New York.

BIBLIOGRAPHY: David 1880, pp. 651, 653: Cantinelli 1930,
p. 120; Holma 1940, p. 113; Dowd 1948, pp. 9ff. and 195;
Hautecoeur 1954, p. 38.

EXHIBITION: New York 1989.

*The Pierpont Morgan Library. Bequest of Mrs. Pauline
Jessup*, Acc. no. 1988.39:1–2

These two small drawings are part of a group of
eleven landscapes in album 10 of David's *albums factices*, which also contains a number of works after
antiquities. There were originally twelve of these *albums factices*. Two of them, albums 7 and 9, went immediately to the Louvre at the time of the second
David sale in 1835, while the heirs and people closest
to David obtained the remaining ten. Album 1 eventually went to the Fogg Art Museum as the bequest of
Grenville L. Winthrop. Both albums 3 and 10 were on
the New York art market in the 1950s. While album 3
was sold more or less intact to the Nationalmuseum,
Stockholm, in 1959, album 10 was dismembered and
the leaves sold separately.

In addition to the drawings of the Campidoglio
and Castel Sant'Angelo, and those after antique subjects (Cat. no. 127), the Library has recently acquired
another landscape, also from album 10, depicting a
carriage passing though an Alpine landscape (Acc.
no. 1991.6). All three of these landscapes were on
folio 17 of the album before it was dismembered.

David made his first trip to Italy in 1774 after he
won the *prix de Rome*. Like many *pensionnaires* before and after him, he sketched the antiquities and
paintings of Rome and other places in Italy. There
is little doubt that these antiquities made a lasting
impression on him, becoming the inspiration for
the neoclassical subject matter of his most famous
paintings.

The Campidoglo

NO. 128

View of Castel Sant'Angelo

Index of Contributors

Contributors

JEAN DE CAYEUX has had a dual career as an art historian and a dealer in paintings and drawings. The author of numerous articles in the *Bulletin de la Société de l'histoire de l'art français*, he is noted for his publications on the works of Hubert Robert. He is presently interested in the history of porcelain in Chantilly, Vincennes, and Sèvres.

CHRISTINE CHALLINGSWORTH has been on the staff of the Center for Advanced Study in the Visual Arts at the National Gallery of Art in Washington since 1977 when she catalogued drawings for the Foundation for Documents of Architecture. She is presently research assistant to the dean of the center.

CARA D. DENISON, curator in the Department of Drawings and Prints at the Pierpont Morgan Library, has written numerous exhibition catalogues and articles in connection with the Library's collections. Most recently, she collaborated on *Sketching at Home and Abroad* and wrote the catalogue for an exhibition of the Library's French drawings at the Louvre.

ELISABETH KIEVEN holds a doctorate degree from the University of Bonn and is on the faculty at the University of Stuttgart. Her area of expertise is Roman architecture and architectural drawings of the seventeenth and eighteenth centuries. She has published catalogues for the Gabinetto Nazionale delle Stampe in Rome. Her book on the architect Alessandro Galilei is soon to be published.

RUTH S. KRAEMER is research assistant at the Pierpont Morgan Library. She is the author of the catalogue *Drawings by Benjamin West*, as well as several articles on French book illustrators, notably Gravelot and, most recently, Charles-Nicolas Cochin.

HENRY MILLON is dean of the Center for Advanced Study in the Visual Arts at the National Gallery of Art, Washington. He was director of the American Academy in Rome from 1974 to 1977. A specialist in architectural history, he has written on Filippo Juvarra as well as Renaissance, baroque, and rococo architecture. He is presently preparing a catalogue raisonné of Juvarra's drawings.

MYRA NAN ROSENFELD is research curator at the Centre Canadien d'Architecture in Montréal. She has a doctorate from Harvard University and has published articles and books on the art and architecture of the Renaissance and eighteenth century. She is the author of *Sebastiano Serlio: On Domestic Architecture* and *Largillière and the Eighteenth-Century Portrait.*

STEPHANIE WILES, associate curator in the Department of Drawings and Prints at the Pierpont Morgan Library, has collaborated on numerous exhibition catalogues based on the Library's collections, most recently *Sketching at Home and Abroad.* In addition, she has written an article on H. Siddons Mowbray, who painted the mural decorations in the Pierpont Morgan Library.

JOHN WILTON-ELY, formerly director of Educational Studies at Sotheby's, London, is professor emeritus of the history of art at the University of Hull. He has written several books on Piranesi, most recently *Piranesi as Architect and Designer,* and lectures widely on the decorative arts.

Bibliography

References Cited
Books and Articles

ACKERMAN 1970

James S. Ackerman, *The Architecture of Michelangelo*, Harmondsworth, England, 1970.

ANANOFF 1961–70

Alexandre Ananoff, *L'oeuvre dessiné de Jean-Honoré Fragonard (1732–1806): Catalogue raisonné*, 4 vols., Paris, 1961–70.

ANDERSEN 1989

Jørgen Andersen, *De år i Rom: Abildgaard, Sergel, Füssli*, Copenhagen, 1989.

ARISI 1986

Ferdinando Arisi, *Gian Paolo Panini e i fasti della Roma del '700*, Rome, 1986.

ARNOLD 1992

Dana Arnold, "Count Gazola and the Temples at Paestum," *Apollo* CXXXVI, August 1992, pp. 95–99.

ASHBY 1913

Thomas Ashby, "Thomas Jenkins in Rome," *Papers of the British School at Rome* VI, 1913, pp. 487–511.

AURENHAMMER 1973

Hans Aurenhammer, *J.B. Fischer von Erlach*, London, 1973.

BACOU 1974

Roseline Bacou, *Piranèse: Gravures et dessins*, Paris, 1974.

BAUDICOR 1861

Prosper de Baudicor, *Le peintre-graveur français continué, ou, Catalogue raisonné des estampes gravées par les peintres et les dessinateurs de l'école française nées dans le XVIIIe siècle*, Tome 2, Paris, 1861.

BEAU 1968

Marguerite Beau, *La Collection des dessins d'Hubert Robert au Musée de Valence*, Lyon, 1968.

BECK AND BOL 1982

Herbert Beck and Peter C. Bol, ed., *Forschungen zur Villa Albani: Antike Kunst und die Epoche der Aufklärung*, Berlin, 1982.

BERCKENHAGEN 1970

Ekhart Berckenhagen, *Die französischen Zeichnungen der Kunstbibliothek Berlin*, Berlin, 1970.

BERLINER 1958–59

Rudolf Berliner, "Die Zeichnungen von Carlo und Filippo Marchionni," *Münchner Jahrbuch der bildenden Kunst* 9/10, 1958–59, pp. 267–396.

BERTELLI AND PIETRANGELI 1985

Le piccole vedute di Roma di Giambattista Piranesi, introduction by Carlo Bertelli, notes by Carlo Pietrangeli, Milan, 1985.

BETTAGNO 1978

Alessandro Bettagno, ed., *Piranesi: Incisioni, rami, legature, architetture*, Vicenza, 1978.

BETTAGNO 1983

Alessandro Bettagno, ed., *Piranesi tra Venezia e l'Europa*, Atti del convegno internazionale di studio promosso dall'Istituto di storia dell'arte della Fond: ne Giorgio Cini, Venice, 1978 (published by Olschki, Florence, 1983).

BEVILACQUA 1989

Mario Bevilacqua, "Casa Giannini a Piazza Capranica e la tipologia del palazzo ed appartamenti nella Roma di metà '700," *Studi sul Settecento Romano* 5, 1989, pp. 205–20.

BIANCHI 1955

Lidia Bianchi, *Disegni di Ferdinando Fuga e di altri architetti del Settecento*, Rome, 1955.

BIANCONI 1802

Giovanni Lodovico Bianconi, "Elogio storico del cavaliere Giambattista Piranesi, celebre antiquario ed incisore di Roma, riportato nell'Antologia Romana l'anno 1779, Lettere al marchese Filippo Hercolani," in *Opere*, Vol. 2, Milan, 1802, pp. 127–40.

BJURSTRÖM 1979

Per Bjurström, *Drawings in Swedish Public Collections: Italian Drawings*, Stockholm, 1979.

BJURSTRÖM 1990

Per Bjurström, "Louis-Jean Desprez and His Sicilian Recollections," synopsis of a talk given at the Center for Advanced Study in the Visual Arts, National Gallery of Art, Washington, October 11, 1990.

BLONDEL 1771–77
Jacques François Blondel, *Cours d'architecture, ou, Traité de la décoration, distribution & construction des bâtiments*, Paris, 1771–77.

BLUNT 1982
Anthony Blunt, *Guide to Baroque Rome*, London, 1982.

BOËTHIUS 1960
Axel Boëthius, *The Golden House of Nero*, Ann Arbor, Michigan, 1960.

BOND 1990
W. H. Bond, *Thomas Hollis of Lincoln's Inn: A Whig and His Books*, Cambridge, 1990.

BORSELLINO 1988
Enzo Borsellino, *Palazzo Corsini alla Lungara: Storia di un cantiere*, Fasano, 1988.

BÖSEL AND GARMS 1981
Richard Bösel amd Jörg Garms, "Die Plansammlung des Collegium Germanicum Hungaricum. 1. Der Gebäudekomplex von S. Apollinare in Rom," *Römische Historische Mitteilungen* 23, 1981, pp. 335–84.

BOTTARI 1754
Giovanni Gaetano Bottari, *Dialoghi sopra le tre arti del disegno*, Lucca, 1754.

BOULLÉE 1968
Etienne-Louis Boullée, *Architecture, essai sur l'art*, introduction by Jean-Marie Pérouse de Montclos, Paris, 1968.

BOWRON 1981
Edgar Peters Bowron, "A View of the Piazza del Popolo, Rome, by Giovanni Paolo Pannini," Nelson-Atkins Museum of Art, *Bulletin* V, January 1981, pp. 37–55.

BROWN 1983
David Brown, review of *Richard Wilson: The Landscape of Reaction*, catalogue by David Solkin, Tate Gallery and elsewhere 1982–83, *Master Drawings* XXI, 1983, pp. 289–92.

BROWN 1993
Iain Gordon Brown, "With an Uncommon Splendour," *Apollo* CXXXVII, January 1993, pp. 6–11.

BRUNEL 1978
Georges Brunel, *Piranèse et les Français, Académie de France à Rome* (colloquy held at the Villa Medici, 1976), Rome, 1978.

BURDA 1967
Hubert Burda, *Die Ruine in den Bildern Hubert Roberts*, Munich, 1967.

BURKE 1884 (1969)
Sir Bernard Burke, *The General Armory of England, Scotland, Ireland, and Wales*, London, 1884, reprint, Baltimore, 1969.

BURKE 1970
Burke's Peerage, London, 1970.

BUSIRI VICI 1976
Andrea Busiri Vici, *Trittico paesistico romano del '700: Paolo Anesi, Paolo Monaldi, Alessio De Marchis*, Rome, 1976.

CAIRA LUMETTI 1990
Rosana Caira Lumetti, *La cultura dei Lumi tra Italia e Svezia: Il ruolo di Francesco Piranesi*, Rome, 1990.

CAMPIGLIA 1739
Gio. Domenico Campiglia, *Il quinto Libro del novo teatro delle fabriche et edifici fatte fare in Roma e fuori di Roma dalla Santità di nostro Signore Papa Clemente XII*, Rome, 1739.

CANTINELLI 1930
Richard Cantinelli, *Jacques-Louis David, 1748–1825*, Paris, 1930.

CARANDENTE 1975
Giovanni Carandente, *Il palazzo Doria Pamphili*, Milan, 1975.

CAYEUX 1963
Jean de Cayeux, "Introduction au catalogue critique des griffonis de Saint-Non," *Bulletin de la Société de l'histoire de l'art français*, 1963, pp. 297–384.

CAYEUX 1989
Jean de Cayeux, *Hubert Robert*, Paris, 1989.

CAYEUX 1991
Jean de Cayeux, *Hubert Robert en Provence*, lecture given at La Fontaine de Vaucluse, 1991, manuscript.

CECCHELLI 1981–82
Marco Cecchelli, *Benedetto XIV (Prospero Lambertini): Convegno internazionale di studi storici*, Cento, 1979 (published Cento, 1981–82).

CHAMBERLAIN 1937
Samuel Chamberlain, "The Triumphal Arches of Piranesi," *Print Collector's Quarterly* 24, no. 1, February 1937, pp. 62–79.

CICOGNARA 1821

Leopoldo Cicognara, *Catalogo ragionato dei libri d'arte e d'antichità*, Pisa, 1821.

CIUCCI 1974

Giorgio Ciucci, *La Piazza del Popolo: Storia, architettura, urbanistica*, Rome, 1974.

COCHIN 1758 (MICHEL 1991)

Charles-Nicolas Cochin, *Le voyage d'Italie de Charles-Nicolas Cochin (1758)*, facsimile edition with introduction and notes by Christian Michel, Rome, 1991.

COFFIN 1960

David R. Coffin, *The Villa d'Este at Tivoli*, Princeton, 1960.

CONSTABLE 1953

W. G. Constable, *Richard Wilson*, Cambridge, Massachusetts, 1953.

CORBOZ 1978

André Corboz, *Peinture militante et architecture révolutionnaire: A propos du thème du tunnel chez Hubert Robert*, Basel, 1978.

CORFIATO 1951

Hector O. Corfiato, ed., *Piranesi Compositions*, London, 1951.

CORNILLOT 1957

Marie Lucie Cornillot, *Collection Pierre-Adrien Pâris, Besançon: Inventaire général des dessins des musées de province*, Paris, 1957.

CURCIO 1989

Giovanna Curcio, "L'area di Montecitorio: La città pubblica e la città privata nella Roma della prima metà del Settecento," *Studi sul Settecento Romano* 5, 1989, pp. 157–204.

DACOS 1969

Nicole Dacos, *La découverte de la Domus Aurea et la formation des grotesques à la Renaissance*, London, 1969.

DAVID 1880

Jacques-Louis Jules David, *Le peintre Louis David, 1748–1825*, Paris, 1880.

DE FINE LICHT 1968

Kjeld De Fine Licht, *The Rotunda in Rome, a Study of Hadrian's Pantheon*, Copenhagen, 1968.

DE FUSCO 1973

Renato De Fusco, *Luigi Vanvitelli*, Naples, 1973.

DE RICCI 1935

Seymour de Ricci, *Dessins du dix-huitième siècle: Collection Albert Meyer*, Paris, 1935.

DEBENEDETTI 1989

Elisa Debenedetti, ed., *L'architettura da Clemente XI a Benedetto XIV: Pluralità di tendenze*, Rome, 1989.

DISTINTA RELAZIONE 1748

Distinta relazione della solenne processione seguita per il trasporto dello standardo di S. Caterina de Ricci . . . Rome, November 1748.

DOIZY AND IPERT 1985

Marie-Ange Doizy and Stephane Ipert, *Le papier marbré, son histoire et sa fabrication*, Paris, 1985.

DOMARUS 1915

Kurt von Domarus, *Pietro Bracci: Beiträge zur römischen Kunstgeschichte des XVIII. Jahrhunderts*, Strassburg, 1915.

DONÒ AND MARINO 1989

A. Donò and A. Marino, "Note su Emanuele Rodriguez Dos Santos, architetto lusitano in Roma," *Studi sul Settecento Romano* 5, 1989, pp. 97–129.

DOWD 1948

David Lloyd Dowd, *Pageant-Master of the Republic, Jacques-Louis David and the French Revolution*, Lincoln, Nebraska, 1948.

DUCLAUX 1975

Lise Duclaux, *Musée du Louvre, Inventaire général des dessins: Ecole française XII*, Paris, 1975.

DUCLAUX 1991

Lise Duclaux, *Les cahiers du dessin français: Charles Natoire, 1700–1777*, Paris, 1991.

EDWARDS 1808

Edward Edwards, *Anecdotes of Painters*, London, 1808.

ELLING 1975

Christian Elling, *Rome: The Biography of Her Architecture from Bernini to Thorvaldsen*, London, 1975.

ERICHSEN 1976

Johannes Erichsen, "Eine Zeichnung zu Piranesis 'Prima Parte,'" *Pantheon* XXXIV, 1976, pp. 212–16.

ERIKSEN 1962

Svend Eriksen, "Marigny and le goût grec," *Burlington Magazine* CIV, March 1962, pp. 96–101.

ERIKSEN 1974

Svend Eriksen, *Early Neo-Classicism in France*, translated by Peter Thornton, London, 1974.

EROUART 1982

Gilbert Erouart, *L'architecture au pinceau: Jean-Laurent*

Legeay, un Piranesién français dans l'Europe des Lumières, Paris, 1982.

FAIRFAX MURRAY
J. Pierpont Morgan Collection of Drawings by the Old Masters Formed by C. Fairfax Murray, London, 1905–12.

FEUILLET 1926
Maurice Feuillet, *Les dessins d'Honoré Fragonard et de Hubert Robert des la Bibliothèque et Musée de Besançon, Collection de P.-A. Pâris, architecte du roi, 1745–1819*, Paris, 1926.

FISCHER 1966
Marianne Fischer, "Piranesis radiertes Oeuvre und die zugehörigen Entwürfe in der Kunstbibliothek," *Berliner Museen* XVI, 1966, pp. 17–24.

FISCHER 1968
Manfred F. Fischer, "Die Umbaupläne des Giovanni Battista Piranesi für den Chor von S. Giovanni in Laterano," *Münchner Jahrbuch der bildenden Kunst* XIX, 1968, pp. 207–28.

FISCHER 1990
Festschrift to Erik Fischer: European Drawings from Six Centuries, Copenhagen, 1990.

FLEMING 1958
John Fleming, "The Journey to Spalatro," *Architectural Review* 123, February 1958, pp. 103–7.

FLEMING 1960
John Fleming, "An Italian Sketchbook by Robert Adam, Clérisseau and Others," *Connoisseur* CXLVI, December 1960, pp. 186–94.

FLEMING 1962
John Fleming, *Robert Adam and His Circle in Edinburgh & Rome*, London, 1962.

FOCILLON 1963
Henri Focillon, *Giovanni Battista Piranesi*, Paris, 1963.

FOCILLON 1964
Henri Focillon, *Giovanni Battista Piranesi: Essai de catalogue raisonné de son oeuvre*, Paris, 1964.

FOCILLON (CALVESI/MONFERINI) 1967
Henri Focillon, *Giovanni Battista Piranesi*, edited by Maurizio Calvesi and Augusta Monferini, translated by Giuseppe Guglielmi, Bologna, 1967.

FORD 1948
Brinsley Ford, "The Dartmouth Collection of Drawings by Richard Wilson," *Burlington Magazine* XC, December 1948, pp. 337–45.

FORD 1951
Brinsley Ford, "Richard Wilson in Rome," *Burlington Magazine* XCIII, May 1951, pp. 157–66.

FORD 1951A
Brinsley Ford, *The Drawings of Richard Wilson*, London, 1951.

FORD 1974
Brinsley Ford, "Thomas Jenkins: Banker, Dealer, and Unofficial English Agent," *Apollo* XCIX, June 1974, pp. 416–25.

FOSCA 1954
François Fosca, *Les dessins de Fragonard*, Paris, 1954.

FOTHERGILL 1969
Brian Fothergill, *Sir William Hamilton, Envoy Extraordinary*, London, 1969.

FREEDLEY 1940
George Freedley, *Theatrical Designs from the Baroque through Neoclassicism*, New York, 1940.

FRUTAZ 1962
Amato Pietro Frutaz, *Le piante di Roma*, Vols. I–III, Rome, 1962.

G.E.C. 1936
G.E.C., *The Complete Peerage of England, Scotland, Ireland, Great Britain, and the United Kingdom*, Vol. IX, revised by H. A. Doubleday and Lord Howard de Walden, London, 1936.

GABILLOT 1895
C. Gabillot, *Hubert Robert et son temps*, Paris, 1895.

GADDI 1736
Giambattista Gaddi, *Roma nobilitata nelle sue fabbriche*, Rome, 1736.

GALLET 1963
Michel Gallet, "Jean-Charles Delafosse, Architecte," *Gazette des beaux-arts* LXI, March 1963, pp. 157–64.

GARMS 1967
Jörg Garms, "Projects for the Pont Neuf and Place Dauphine in the First Half of the Eighteenth Century," *Journal of the Society of Architectural Historians* XXVI, no. 2, May 1967, pp. 102–13.

GARMS 1974
Jörg Garms, "Beiträge zum Leben, Werk und Milieu Van-

vitellis," *Römische Historische Mitteilungen* 16, 1974, pp. 107–90.

GARMS 1974A

Jörg Garms, "Die Briefe des Luigi Vanvitelli an seinen Bruder Urbano in Rom," *Römische Historische Mitteilungen* 16, 1974, pp. 107–90.

GASPARRI 1985

Carlo Gasparri, "Piranesi a Villa Albani," in *Committenze della famiglia Albani, Note sulla Villa Albani Torlonia*, Rome, 1985.

GASPARRI 1985–86

Carlo Gasparri, "Piranesi a Villa Albani," *Studi sul Settecento Romano* 1/2, 1985–86, pp. 211–24.

LE GAULOIS 1928

Le Gaulois artistique, 12 May 1928, p. 189.

GAUS 1967

Joachim Gaus, *Carlo Marchionni: Ein Beitrag zur römischen Architektur des Settecento*, Cologne, 1967.

GIUNTELLA 1971

Vittorio Emanuele Giuntella, *Roma nel Settecento*, Bologna, 1971.

GOWING 1986

Lawrence Gowing, *The Originality of Thomas Jones*, New York, 1986.

GRADARA 1920

Costanza Gradara, *Pietro Bracci, scultore romano, 1700–1773*, Milano, 1920.

GRAY 1889

J. M. Gray, "John Brown, the Draftsman," *Magazine of Art*, July 1889, pp. 310–15.

GRIFFITHS 1988

Antony Griffiths, "Giovanni Volpato," *Print Quarterly* V, December 1988, pp. 427–29.

GRIGSON 1955

Geoffrey Grigson, *English Drawing from Samuel Cooper to Gwen John*, London, 1955.

HANNAH 1987

Robert Hannah, "The Classical Model for a Piranesi Drawing Rediscovered," *Master Drawings* XXV, 1987, pp. 270–72.

HARRIS 1970

John Harris, *Sir William Chambers, Knight of the Polar Star*, University Park, Pennsylvania, 1970.

HARRIS 1971

John Harris, *A Catalogue of British Drawings for Architecture, Decoration, Sculpture, and Landscape Gardening, 1550–1900, in American Collections*, Upper Saddle River, New Jersey, 1971.

HASKELL AND PENNY 1981

Francis Haskell and Nicholas Penny, *Taste and the Antique*, New Haven, 1981.

HAUTECOEUR 1912

Louis Hautecoeur, *L'architecture classique à Saint-Pétersbourg à la fin du XVIIIe siècle*, Paris, 1912.

HAUTECOEUR 1952

Louis Hautecoeur, *Histoire de l'architecture classique en France. Tome IV, La seconde moitié du XVIIIe siècle, le style Louis XVI*, Paris, 1952.

HAUTECOEUR 1954

Louis Hautecoeur, *Louis David*, Paris, 1954.

HAWLEY 1964

Henry Hawley, "Neo-Classicism in Italian Pictures," *Antiques* 86, September 1964, pp. 316–19.

HAYWARD 1965 (1970)

World Furniture, an Illustrated History, edited by Helena Hayward, London, 1965 (reprinted 1970).

HEAWOOD 1950 (1981)

Edward Heawood, *Watermarks, Mainly of the 17th and 18th Centuries*, Hilversum, 1950 (reprinted 1981).

HELD 1990

Jutta Held, *Monument und Volk: Vorrevolutionare Wahrnehmung in den Bildern des ausgehenden Ancien Regime*, Cologne, 1990.

HERRMANN 1962

Wolfgang Herrmann, *Laugier and Eighteenth-Century French Theory*, London, 1962.

HIBBARD 1983

Howard Hibbard, *Caravaggio*, New York, 1983.

HIND 1913–14

Arthur M. Hind, "Giovanni Battista Piranesi, Some Further Notes and a List of His Works," *Burlington Magazine* XXIV, part I, December 1913, pp. 135–38; part II, January 1914, pp. 187–203; part III, February 1914, pp. 262–64.

HIND 1914

Arthur M. Hind, "Giovanni Battista Piranesi, Some Further Notes and a List of His Works," *Burlington Magazine* XXIV, January 1914, pp. 187–203.

HIND 1922
Arthur M. Hind, *Giovanni Battista Piranesi, a Critical Study*, London, 1922.

HOBSON 1982
Marian Hobson, *The Object of Art: The Theory of Illusion in Eighteenth-Century France*, Cambridge, 1982.

HOLMA 1940
Klaus Holma, *David, son évolution et son style*, Paris, 1940.

HONOUR 1961
Hugh Honour, *Chinoiserie, the Vision of Cathay*, London, 1961.

HONOUR 1969
Hugh Honour, *Cabinet Makers and Furniture Designers*, London, 1969.

IVERSEN 1958
Erik Iversen, "Fischer von Erlach as Historian of Architecture," review of G. Kunoth, *Die historische Architektur Fischers von Erlach*, *Burlington Magazine* C, September 1958, pp. 323–25.

JEAN-RICHARD 1978
Pierrette Jean-Richard, *L'oeuvre gravé de François Boucher dans la Collection Edmond de Rothschild*, Paris, 1978.

JESSE 1843–44
John Heneage Jesse, *George Selwyn and His Contemporaries*, London, 1843–44.

JOACHIM AND MCCULLAGH 1979
Harold Joachim and Suzanne Folds McCullagh, *Italian Drawings in the Art Institute of Chicago*, Chicago, 1979.

JOHNSTON 1971
Catherine Johnston, *Il Seicento e il Settecento a Bologna*, Milan, 1971.

JONES
"Memoirs of Thomas Jones," introduction by A. Paul Oppé, *Walpole Society* XXXII, 1946–48, London, 1951.

JUSTI 1956
Carl Justi, *Winckelmann und seine Zeitgenossen*, 3 vols., Cologne, 1956.

KALNEIN AND LEVEY 1972
Wend Graf Kalnein and Michael Levey, *Art and Architec-*
ture of the Eighteenth Century in France, Harmondsworth, England, 1972.

KAUFMANN 1955
Emil Kaufmann, *Architecture in the Age of Reason*, Cambridge, Massachusetts, 1955.

KIEVEN
Elisabeth Kieven, *Alessandro Galilei (1691–1737), Architect in England, Florence, and Rome*, London, in press.

KIEVEN 1989
Elisabeth Kieven, "Überlegungen zu Architektur und Ausstattung der Cappella Corsini," *Studi sul Settecento Romano* 5, 1989, pp. 69–91.

KNOX AND KAUFMAN 1969
George Knox and S. Kaufman, *Fantastic & Ornamental Drawings: A Selection of Drawings from the Kaufman Collection*, Portsmouth, England, 1969.

KUNOTH 1956
George Kunoth, *Die historische Architektur Fischers von Erlach*, Düsseldorf, 1956.

LAMBERT 1988
Phyllis Lambert, *Centre Canadien d'Architecture: Les débuts, 1979–1984/Canadian Centre for Architecture: The First Five Years, 1979–1984*, Montréal, 1988.

LEPPMANN 1970
Wolfgang Leppmann, *Winckelmann*, New York, 1970.

LEVALLET 1929
Geneviève Levallet, "L'ornemantiste Jean-Charles Delafosse," *Gazette des beaux-arts* 1, March 1929, pp. 158–69.

LOSSKY 1985
Boris Lossky, "Un architecte français en Russie à l'aube du XIXe siècle, J.-F. Thomas, dit de Thomon," *Revue d'études slaves* LVII, 1985, pp. 591–604.

LOSSKY 1986 (1988)
Boris Lossky, "Formation artistique et premières étapes de la carrière de l'architecte Jean-François Thomas, dit de Thomon, 1759–1813," *Bulletin de la Société de l'histoire de l'art français*, 1986 (1988), pp. 81–86.

LOUKOMSKI AND NOLHAC 1930
G. K. Loukomski and Pierre de Nolhac, *La Rome d'Hubert Robert*, Paris, 1930.

LUGT 1921
Frits Lugt, *Les marques de collections de dessins & d'estampes*, Amsterdam, 1921; supplement, The Hague, 1956.

LUGT 1938–64

Frits Lugt, *Répertoire des catalogues de ventes publiques*, The Hague, 1938–64.

MCCARTHY 1972

Michael McCarthy, "Documents on the Greek Revival in Architecture," *Burlington Magazine* CXIV, November 1972, pp. 760–69.

MCCORMICK 1990

Thomas J. McCormick, *Charles-Louis Clérisseau and the Genesis of Neo-Classicism*, Cambridge, Massachusetts, 1990.

MCCORMICK AND FLEMING 1962

Thomas J. McCormick and John Fleming, "A Ruin Room by Clérisseau," *Connoisseur* CXLIX, April 1962, pp. 239–43.

MACMILLAN 1986

Duncan Macmillan, *Painting in Scotland, The Golden Age*, Oxford, 1986.

MAJOR 1768

Thomas Major, *The Ruins of Paestum, Otherwise Posidonia, in Magna Graecia*, London, 1768.

MAJOR 1768 (1969)

Thomas Major, *Les ruines de Paestum ou de Posidonie dans la grande Grèce*, London, 1768, facsimile edition, Farnborough, 1969.

MALLORY 1977

Nina A. Mallory, *Roman Rococo Architecture from Clement XI to Benedict XIV (1700–1758)*, New York, 1977.

MANNUCCI 1925–33

Silvio Mannucci, *Nobiliario e blasonario del regno d'Italia*, 5 vols., Rome, 1925–33.

MARIETTE 1851–60

P. J. Mariette, *Abecedario de P. J. Mariette et autres notes inédites de cet amateur sur les arts et les artistes*, edited by P. de Chennevières and A. de Montaiglon, Paris, 1851–60.

MATTHIAE 1952

Guglielmo Matthiae, *Ferdinando Fuga e la sua opera romana*, Rome, 1952.

MATURI 1966

Miscellanea Walter Maturi, Torino, 1966.

MAYOR 1945

A. Hyatt Mayor, *The Bibiena Family*, New York, 1945.

MAYOR 1952

A. Hyatt Mayor, *Giovanni Battista Piranesi*, New York, 1952.

MEISSONNIER 1969

Juste Aurèle Meissonnier, *Oeuvre de Juste Aurèle Meissonnier*, introduction by Dorothea Nyberg, New York, 1969.

METROPOLITAN MUSEUM OF ART 1965

Metropolitan Museum of Art, "Italian Drawings from the Collection of Janos Scholz," *Metropolitan Museum of Art Bulletin*, part II, May 1965, pp. 337–44.

MIDDLETON 1962

R. D. Middleton, "The Abbé de Cordemoy and the Graeco-Gothic Ideal: A Prelude to Romantic Classicism," *Journal of the Warburg and Courtauld Institutes* XXV, 1962, pp. 278–320.

MIDDLETON 1963

R. D. Middleton, "The Abbé de Cordemoy and the Graeco-Gothic Ideal, Part II," *Journal of the Warburg and Courtauld Institutes* XXVI, 1963, pp. 90–123.

MILIZIA 1785

Francesco Milizia, *Memorie degli architetti antichi e moderni*, Bassano, 1785.

MILLON 1984

Henry A. Millon, *Filippo Juvarra, Drawings from the Roman Period, 1704–1714*, Rome, 1984.

MONDAIN-MONVAL 1914

J. Mondain-Monval, *Soufflot: Sa vie, son oeuvre, son esthetique*, Paris, 1914.

MONGAN AND SACHS 1940

Agnes Mongan and Paul J. Sachs, *Drawings in the Fogg Museum of Art*, Vol. I, Cambridge, Massachusetts, 1940.

MONTAIGLON 1888

A. de Montaiglon, ed., *Procès-verbaux de l'Académie royale de peinture et de sculpture, 1648–1793*, 10 vols., Paris, 1875–92.

MONTAIGLON AND GUIFFREY 1887–1912

A. de Montaiglon et J. Guiffrey, *Correspondance des directeurs de l'Académie de France à Rome avec les surintendants des bâtiments*, Paris, 1887–1912.

MORGAN, *ROYAL*

John Pearson & Co., *English Royal Bindings, Henry VIII to Queen Victoria [in the collection of Pierpont Morgan]*, London, [ca. 1900].

MORGAN LIBRARY *FR* I–XX, 1950–86

Pierpont Morgan Library, *First* [and subsequent] *Report to the Fellows of the Pierpont Morgan Library*, New York, 1950–86. (Reports edited by Frederick B. Adams, Jr. through 1968; by Charles Ryskamp 1969 through 1986; entries by members of the staff of Department of Drawings and Prints.)

MORGAN LIBRARY *REVIEW* 1969

The Pierpont Morgan Library, a Review of Acquisitions, 1949–1968, Pierpont Morgan Library, New York, 1969.

MORRISON

Alfred Morrison, *Catalogue of the Collection of Autograph Letters and Historical Documents Formed between 1865 and 1882*, 13 vols., London, 1883–92.

MURRAY 1971

Peter Murray, *Piranesi and the Grandeur of Ancient Rome*, London, 1971.

NICHOLS 1992

Lawrence W. Nichols, "The 'Pen Works' of Hendrick Goltzius," Philadelphia Museum of Art, *Bulletin* 88, Winter 1992, pp. 2–54.

NIXON 1978

Howard M. Nixon, *Five Centuries of English Bookbinding*, London, 1978.

NOACK 1924

Friedrich Noack, "Des Kardinals Albani Beziehungen zu Künstlern," *Cicerone* XVI, May 1924, pp. 451–59.

OECHSLIN 1972

Werner Oechslin, *Bildungsgut und Antikenrezeption im frühen Settecento in Rom: Studien zum römischen Aufenthalt Bernardo Antonio Vittones*, Zurich, 1972.

OENSLAGER 1975

Donald Oenslager, *Stage Design, Four Centuries of Scenic Invention*, New York, 1975.

PANE 1956

Roberto Pane, *Ferdinando Fuga*, Naples, 1956.

PANE 1978

Roberto Pane, "Piranesi disegnatore di figure," *Napoli nobilissima, rivista di arti figurative, archeologia e urbanistica* XVII, September–October 1978, pp. 161–66.

PANE 1980

Roberto Pane, *Paestum nelle acqueforti di Piranesi*, Milan, 1980.

PASQUALI 1991

Susanna Pasquali, "Il Pantheon e la chiesa di S. Maria Maria(?) ad Martyres a Roma: I restauri del 1756–58," *Thema* 1, 1991, no. 1 (in press).

PASTOR 1928–39

Ludwig Pastor, *Geschichte der Päpste seit dem Ausgang des Mittelalters, mit Benutzung des päpstlichen Geheim-Archives und vieler anderer Archive*, Freiburg im Breisgau, 1928–39.

PATELLA 1979

Luca Maria Patella, "Per una lettura tecnologico-strutturale dei due rami della 'Caduta di Fetonte,'" in *Piranesi, nei luoghi di Piranesi*, Part IV, *I rami*, Istituto nazionale per la grafica-calcografia, Rome, 1979, pp. 5–41.

PAUL MELLON GIFT 1981

The Paul Mellon Gift to the Pierpont Morgan Library, New York, 1981.

PELLEGRI 1965

Marco Pellegri, *Ennemondo Alessandro Petitot, 1727–1801: Architetto francese alla real corte dei Borboni di Parma*, Parma, 1965.

PENNY 1978

Nicholas Penny, *Piranesi*, London, 1978.

PEREZ 1989

M.-F. Perez, "A propos de la publication des *Antiquités de la France* par Clérisseau," in *Transactions of the Seventh International Congress of the Enlightenment/Actes du Septième Congrès des Lumières*, Budapest, 1987 (published Oxford, 1989).

PÉROUSE DE MONTCLOS 1969

Jean-Marie Pérouse de Montclos, *Etienne-Louis Boullée, 1728–1799: De l'architecture classique à l'architecture révolutionnaire*, Paris, 1969.

PETRUCCI 1934

Carlo Alberto Petrucci, *Catalogo generale delle stampe tratte dai rami incisi posseduti dalla Regia Calcografia di Roma*, Rome, 1934.

PETRUCCI 1953

Carlo Alberto Petrucci, *Catalogo generale delle stampe tratte dai rami incisi posseduti dalla Calcografia Nazionale*, Rome, 1953.

PEVSNER AND LANG 1968

Nicholas Pevsner and S. Lang, "The Egyptian Revival," in Nicholas Pevsner, *Studies in Italian Art, Architecture, and*

Design. Vol. I: *From Mannerism to Romanticism*, London, 1968, pp. 212–35.

PIERCE 1965
S. Rowland Pierce, "Thomas Jenkins in Rome," *Antiquaries Journal* XLV, 1965, pp. 200–29.

PIETRANGELI 1990
Carlo Pietrangeli, *San Giovanni in Laterano*, Florence, 1990.

PINTO 1986
John A. Pinto, *The Trevi Fountain*, New Haven, 1986.

PIRANESI 1979
Piranesi e la cultura antiquaria: Gli antecedenti e il contesto, atti del convegno 14–17 Novembre 1979, Rome, 1983.

POMMIER 1991
Edmond Pommier, *L'art de la liberté*, Paris, 1991.

POWELL 1952
Nicolas Powell, "Brown and the Women of Rome," *Signature* 14, 1952, pp. 40–50.

QUARENGHI 1988
Giacomo Quarenghi, *Giacomo Quarenghi, architetto a Pietroburgo: Lettere e altri scritti*, edited by Vanni Zanella, Venice, 1988.

RABREAU 1975
Daniel Rabreau, "Autour du *Voyage d'Italie* (1750): Soufflot, Cochin et M. de Marigny, réformateurs de l'architecture theatrale française," *Bollettino del Centro internazionale di studi di architettura Andrea Palladio* 17, 1975, pp. 213–14.

REUDENBACH 1979
Bruno Reudenbach, *G.B. Piranesi, Architektur als Bild: Der Wandel in der Architekturauffassung des achtzehnten Jahrhunderts*, Munich, 1979.

RIEDER 1973
William Rieder, "Piranesi's *Diverse Maniere*," *Burlington Magazine* CXV, May 1973, pp. 309–17.

ROBISON 1970 "PROLEGOMENA"
Andrew Robison, "Giovanni Battista Piranesi: Prolegomena to the Princeton Collections," *Princeton University Library Chronicle* XXXI, Spring 1970, pp. 165–206.

ROBISON 1970 "VEDUTE"
Andrew Robison, "The *Vedute di Roma* of Giovanni Battista Piranesi: Notes Toward a Revision of Hind's Catalogue," *Nouvelles de l'estampe* 4, 1970, pp. 180–98.

ROBISON 1973
Andrew Robison, "Piranesi's Ship on Wheels," *Master Drawings* XI, 1973, pp. 389–92.

ROBISON 1977
Andrew Robison, "Preliminary Drawings for Piranesi's Early Architectural Fantasies," *Master Drawings* XV, 1977, pp. 387–401.

ROBISON 1986
Andrew Robison, *Piranesi, Early Architectural Fantasies: A Catalogue Raisonné of the Etchings*, Washington, 1986.

ROLAND MICHEL 1987
Marianne Roland Michel, *Le dessin français au XVIIIe siècle*, Fribourg, 1987.

ROSA 1966
Mario Rosa, "Benedetto XIV," *Dizionario biografico degli Italiani* 8, Rome, 1966, pp. 393–408.

ROSENBERG 1978
Pierre Rosenberg, "Louis-Joseph Le Lorrain (1715–1759)," *Revue de l'art* 40–41, 1978, pp. 173–202.

ROSENBERG 1986
J.C.R. de Saint-Non and Jean-Honoré Fragonard, *Panopticon italiano: Un diario di viaggio ritrovato, 1759–1761*, edited by Pierre Rosenberg, Rome, 1986.

ROVERE, VIALE, BRINCKMANN 1937
L. Rovere, V. Viale, and A. E. Brinckmann, *Filippo Juvarra*, Milan, 1937.

RUGGIERO 1989
Maria Grazia Pastura Ruggiero, "Fonti per la storia del teatro romano nel Settecento conservate nell'Archivio di Stato di Roma," in *Il Teatro a Roma nel Settecento II*, Rome, 1989, pp. 505–87.

RUVIGNY 1914
Marquis de Ruvigny, *The Titled Nobility of Europe*, London, 1914.

RYKWERT 1980
Joseph Rykwert, *The First Moderns: The Architects of the Eighteenth Century*, Cambridge, Massachusetts, 1980.

SAMOGGIA 1977
L. Samoggia, "Benedetto XIV. e il Portogallo: Su alcuni aspetti delle relazioni diplomatiche e culturali durante il regno di Giovanni V.," *Giornata di studi padani*, 1977.

SARTORI 1990
Claudio Sartori, *I libretti italiani a stampa dalle origini al 1800*, Vol. I, Cuneo, 1990.

SASSOLI 1992

Giuseppe Vasi, *Delle magnificenze di Roma antica e moderna di Giuseppe Vasi, 1747–61*, facsimile ed. by Mario Gori Sassoli, Rome, 1992.

SCALABRONI 1981

Luisa Scalabroni, *Giuseppe Vasi (1710–1782)*, Rome, 1981.

SCHIAVO 1956

Armando Schiavo, *La fontana di Trevi e le altre opere di Nicola Salvi*, Rome, 1956.

SCHOLZ 1962

Janos Scholz, ed., *Baroque and Romantic Stage Design*, intro. by A. Hyatt Mayor, New York, 1950 (reprinted 1962).

SCHOLZ 1976

Janos Scholz, *Italian Master Drawings, 1350–1800, from the Janos Scholz Collection*, New York, 1976.

SCOTT 1975

Jonathan Scott, *Piranesi*, New York, 1975.

SÉRULLAZ 1991

Arlette Sérullaz, *Inventaire général des dessins, Ecole française: Dessins de Jacques-Louis David, 1748–1825*, Paris, 1991.

SOBOTIK 1986

Kent Sobotik, "Two Newly Identified Drawings by Giovanni Battista Piranesi," *Master Drawings* XXIII–XXIV, 1986, pp. 55–60.

SOLKIN 1978

David H. Solkin, "Some New Light on the Drawings of Richard Wilson," *Master Drawings* XVI, 1978, pp. 404–14.

STAFFORD 1991

Barbara Maria Stafford, *Body Criticism: Imaging the Unseen in Enlightenment Art and Medicine*, Cambridge, Massachusetts, 1991.

STAMPFLE 1948

Felice Stampfle, "An Unknown Group of Drawings by Giovanni Battista Piranesi," *Art Bulletin* XXX, no. 2, June 1948, pp. 122–41.

STAMPFLE 1978

Felice Stampfle, *Giovanni Battista Piranesi: Drawings in the Pierpont Morgan Library*, New York, 1978.

STIEGER 1975

Franz Stieger, *Opernlexikon*, Part I, Vol. III, Tutzing, 1975.

SUTTON AND CLEMENTS 1968

Denys Sutton and Ann Clements, *An Italian Sketchbook by Richard Wilson, RA*, London, 1968.

TADGELL 1978

Christopher Tadgell, *Ange-Jacques Gabriel*, London, 1978.

TAFURI 1964

Manfredo Tafuri, "Un 'fuoco' urbano della Roma barocca: Chiesa dei Trinitari, Largo Goldoni, S. Maria Aracoeli, S. Antonio dei Portoghesi-Emmanuel Rodriguez Dos Santos," *Quaderni dell'Istituto di storia d'architettura* 61, 1964, pp. 1–20.

TAFURI 1987

Manfredo Tafuri, *The Sphere and the Labyrinth: Avant-gardes and Architecture from Piranesi to the 1970s*, translated by Pellegrino d'Acierno and Robert Connolly, Cambridge, Massachusetts, 1987.

TAIT 1978

A. A. Tait, "The Sale of Robert Adam's Drawings," *Burlington Magazine* CXX, July 1978, pp. 451–54.

TAIT 1978A

A. A. Tait, "Robert Adam and John Clerk of Eldin," *Master Drawings* XVI, 1978, pp. 53–57.

THOMAS 1952–55

Hylton Thomas, "Piranesi and Pompeii," *Kunstmuseets Årsskrift*, 1952–55, pp. 13–28.

THOMAS 1954

Hylton Thomas, *The Drawings of Giovanni Battista Piranesi*, New York, 1954.

TIETZE 1947

Hans Tietze, *European Master Drawings in the United States*, New York, 1947.

TOLNAY 1943

Charles de Tolnay, *History and Technique of Old Master Drawings*, New York, 1943.

VANVITELLI 1976–77

Luigi Vanvitelli, *Le lettere di Luigi Vanvitelli della Biblioteca palatina di Caserta*, edited by Franco Strazzullo, Galatina, 1976–77.

VANVITELLI 1979

Luigi Vanvitelli e il '700 europeo: Congresso internazionale di studi, Vol. 1, Naples, 1973 (published Naples, 1979).

VARAGNOLI 1988

C. Varagnoli, "Ricerche sull'opera architettonica di Gregorini e Passalcqua," *Architettura, storia e documenti* 1–2 (1988), pp. 21–65.

VENUTI 1763 (1977)

Ridolfino Venuti, *Accuratà, e succinta descrizione topografica delle antichità di Roma*, Rome, 1763.

VESME/MASSAR 1971

Alexandre de Vesme, *Stefano della Bella: Catalogue raisonné*, introduction by Phyllis Dearborn Massar, New York, 1971.

VIALE FERRERO 1968

Mercedes Viale Ferrero, "Disegni di Filippo Juvarra per il Teatro Capranica a Roma," *Antichità viva* VII, March–April 1968, pp. 11–20.

VIALE FERRERO 1970

Mercedes Viale Ferrero, *Filippo Juvarra, scenografo e architetto teatrale*, New York, 1970.

VIALE FERRERO 1981

Mercedes Viale Ferrero, "Scene di Filippo Juvarra per il *Lucio Papirio* di Francesco Gasparini (Roma, Teatro Capranica, 1713–1714)," in *Francesco Gasparini (1661–1727): Atti del primo Convegno internazionale del Comune di Camaiore*, edited by Fabrizio Della Seta and Franco Piperno (conference held 1978) published in Florence, 1981, pp. 245–57.

VIALE FERRERO 1985

Mercedes Viale Ferrero, "Disegni scenici di Filippo Juvarra per 'Giulio Cesare nell'Egitto' di Antonio Ottoboni," in *Studi Juvarriani: Atti del convegno dell'Accademia delle Scienze, Torino, 1979*, published in Rome, 1985, pp. 127–69.

VISENTINI 1771

Antonio Visentini, *Osservazioni di Antonio Visentini, architetto veneto, che servono di continuazione al trattato di Teofilo Gallaccini sopra gli errori degli architetti*, Venezia, 1771.

VOLKMANN 1965

Hans Volkmann, *Giovanni Baptista Piranesi, Architekt und Graphiker*, Berlin, 1965.

WATSON 1965

F.J.B. Watson, "A Side Table by Piranesi: A Masterpiece of Neo-Classic Furniture," *Minneapolis Institute of the Arts Bulletin* LIV, 1965, pp. 19–29.

WIEBENSON 1969

Dora Wiebenson, *Sources of Greek Revival Architecture*, London, 1969.

WILTON-ELY 1972

Giovanni Battista Piranesi, *The Polemical Works, Rome, 1757, 1761, 1765, 1769*, edited and introduced by John Wilton-Ely, Westmead, Farnborough, England, 1972.

WILTON-ELY 1976

John Wilton-Ely, "Piranesian Symbols on the Aventine," *Apollo* CIII, 1976, pp. 214–27.

WILTON-ELY 1978

John Wilton-Ely, *The Mind and Art of Giovanni Battista Piranesi*, London, 1978.

WILTON-ELY 1978 (1988)

John Wilton-Ely, *The Mind and Art of Giovanni Battista Piranesi*, London, 1978, first paperback edition, 1988.

WILTON-ELY 1990

John Wilton-Ely, "Nature and Antiquity: Reflections on Piranesi as a Furniture Designer," *Journal of the Furniture History Society* XXVI, 1990, pp. 191–97.

WINCKELMANN 1760

L'Abbé Winckelmann, *Description des pierres gravées du feu Baron de Stosch*, Florence, 1760.

WINCKELMANN 1781

L'Abbé Winckelmann, *Lettres familières de M. Winckelmann, Deuxième partie*, translated by Hendrik Jansen, Amsterdam, 1781.

WISCH AND MUNSHOWER 1990

Barbara Wisch and Susan Scott Munshower, ed., "All the world's a Stage . . .": *Art and Pageantry in the Renaissance and Baroque*, University Park, Pennsylvania, 1990.

WITTKOWER 1967

Essays in the History of Architecture Presented to Rudolf Wittkower, London, 1967.

WITTKOWER 1973

Rudolf Wittkower, *Art and Architecture in Italy, 1600–1750*, Harmondsworth, England, 1973.

WITTKOWER 1975

Rudolf Wittkower, *Studies in the Italian Baroque*, London, 1975.

WITTKOWER 1982

Rudolf Wittkower, *Studies in the Italian Baroque*, London, 1982 (reprint).

WOLLIN 1933

Nils Wollin, *Gravures originales de Desprez ou executées d'après ses dessins*, Malmö, 1933.

WOLLIN 1935
Nils Wollin, *Desprez en Italie*, Malmö, 1935.

WOLLIN 1939
Nils Wollin, *Desprez en Suède, sa vie et ses travaux en Suède, en Angleterre, et en Russie, 1784–1804*, Stockholm, 1939.

WUNDER 1962
Richard P. Wunder, *Extravagant Drawings of the Eighteenth Century from the Collection of the Cooper Union Museum*, New York, 1962.

WUNDER 1968
Richard P. Wunder, "Charles Michel-Ange Challe: A Study of His Life and Work," *Apollo* LXXXVII, January 1968, pp. 22–33.

Exhibition Catalogues

AMSTERDAM 1989
De verzameling van mr. Carel Vosmaer (1826–1888), catalogue by F. L. Bastet et al., Rijksprentenkabinet, Rijksmuseum, Amsterdam, 1989.

ANN ARBOR 1977
Pompeii as Source and Inspiration: Reflections in Eighteenth- and Nineteenth-Century Art, Museum of Art, University of Michigan, Ann Arbor, 1977.

BALTIMORE 1957–58
The History of Bookbinding, 525–1950 A.D., Baltimore Museum of Art and Walters Art Gallery, Baltimore, 1957–58.

BALTIMORE AND ELSEWHERE 1985
Regency to Empire: French Printmaking, 1715–1814, organized by Victor I. Carlson and John W. Ittmann, Baltimore Museum of Art, Baltimore; Museum of Fine Arts, Boston; Minneapolis Institute of Arts, Minneapolis, 1985.

BASSANO DEL GRAPPA AND ROME 1988
Giovanni Volpato, 1735–1803, catalogue by Giorgio Marini, essays by Grazia Bernini Pezzini, Fabio Fiorani, Maria Elisa Tittoni, introduction by Paola Marini, Museo-Biblioteca-Archivio, Bassano del Grappa, and Istituto nazionale per la grafica, Gabinetto disegni e stampe, Rome, 1988.

BERLIN 1975
Italienische Zeichnungen der Kunstbibliothek, Berlin, Architektur und Dekoration, 16. bis 18. Jahrhundert, catalogue by Sabine Jacob, Kunstbibliothek, Berlin, 1975.

BRUNSWICK, MAINE 1985
Old Master Drawings at Bowdoin College, catalogue by David P. Becker, Bowdoin College Museum of Art, Brunswick, Maine, 1985.

BUFFALO 1960
The T. Edward Hanley Collection: Drawings, Watercolors, Pastels, Albright Art Gallery, Buffalo, 1960.

CARDIFF, WALES 1969
Richard Wilson, Painter, 1713–1782: An Exhibition about the Man, His Life, and His Work, Welsh Arts Council, Cardiff, 1969.

CLEVELAND 1964
Neo-Classicism: Style and Motif, catalogue by Henry Hawley, Cleveland Museum of Art, Cleveland, Ohio, 1964.

COLUMBUS, OHIO 1968
Works from the Hanley Collection, Columbus Gallery of Fine Arts, Columbus, Ohio, 1968.

DALLAS AND HOUSTON 1977–78
Drawings from the Janos Scholz Collection, Dallas Museum of Fine Arts, Dallas, and Museum of Fine Arts, Houston, 1977–78.

DAYTON 1971
French Artists in Italy, 1600–1900, Dayton Art Institute, Dayton, Ohio, 1971.

DETROIT AND CHICAGO 1981
The Golden Age of Naples: Art and Civilization under the Bourbons, 1734–1805, Detroit Institute of Arts, Detroit, and Art Institute of Chicago, Chicago, 1981–82.

DETROIT AND PHILADELPHIA 1968
Romantic Art in Britain: Paintings and Drawings, 1760–1860, catalogue by Frederick Cummings and Allen Staley,

Detroit Institute of Arts, Detroit, and Philadelphia Museum of Art, Philadelphia, 1968.

EDINBURGH 1972
Robert Adam and Scotland: The Picturesque Drawings, catalogue by A. A. Tait, Scottish Arts Council Gallery, Edinburgh, 1972.

EDINBURGH 1992
Iain Gordon Brown, *Monumental Reputation, Robert Adam & the Emperor's Palace*, National Library of Scotland, Edinburgh, 1992.

FLORENCE 1980
Maestri romani del Sei e Settecento, catalogue by Anthony Blunt, Istituto Alinari, Florence, 1980.

GENEVA 1979, *ALBUM*
Un album de croquis d'Hubert Robert (1733–1808), catalogue by Jean Cailleux, Galerie Cailleux, Geneva, 1979.

GENEVA 1979, *DESSINS ET PEINTURES*
Hubert Robert (1733–1808): Dessins et peintures, catalogue by Jean Cailleux, Galerie Cailleux, Geneva, 1979.

HAMBURG AND COLOGNE 1963–64
Italienische Meisterzeichnungen vom 14. bis zum 18. Jahrhundert aus amerikanischem Besitz: Die Sammlung Janos Scholz, New York, Kunsthalle, Hamburg, and Wallraf-Richartz-Museum, Cologne, 1963–64.

KANSAS CITY 1956
"The Century of Mozart," *Bulletin* I, no. 1, Nelson Gallery and Atkins Museum, Kansas City, Kansas, 1956.

LONDON 1934
Exhibition of French Drawings from Clouet to Ingres, Wildenstein and Co., Ltd., London, 1934.

LONDON 1965
Exhibition of Old Master Drawings, June 16th to July 7th, 1965, P. & D. Colnaghi & Co., Ltd., London, 1965.

LONDON 1968
France in the Eighteenth Century, catalogue by Denys Sutton, Royal Academy of Arts, London, 1968.

LONDON 1968A
Italian Drawings from the Collection of Janos Scholz, Arts Council, London, 1968.

LONDON 1972
The Age of Neo-Classicism, Royal Academy and Victoria and Albert Museum, London (Arts Council of Great Britain), 1972.

LONDON 1973–74
Etchings by Giovanni Battista Piranesi, 1720–1778, P. & D. Colnaghi & Co., Ltd., London, 1973–74.

LONDON 1978
Piranesi, catalogue by John Wilton-Ely, Hayward Gallery (Arts Council of Great Britain), London, 1978.

LONDON 1982
Master Prints and Drawings, 15th to 19th Centuries, Artemis Fine Arts, Ltd., London, 1982.

LONDON 1987
Exhibition of Old Master Drawings, Shaunagh Fitzgerald Ltd., London, 1987.

LONDON 1990
English Watercolours and Drawings, Thos. Agnew & Sons Ltd., London, March 12–April 6, 1990.

LONDON 1990A
An Exhibition of Architectural and Decorative Drawings, Harari & Johns Ltd., London, 1990.

LONDON AND ELSEWHERE 1982–83
Richard Wilson: The Landscape of Reaction, catalogue by David H. Solkin, Tate Gallery, London; National Museum of Wales, Cardiff; and Yale Center for British Art, New Haven, Connecticut, 1982–83.

LOS ANGELES 1976
Old Master Drawings from American Collections, catalogue by Ebria Feinblatt, Los Angeles County Museum of Art, Los Angeles, 1976.

MANCHESTER, ENGLAND 1988
Travels in Italy, 1776–1783, Based on the Memoirs of Thomas Jones, catalogue by Francis W. Hawcroft, Whitworth Art Gallery, University of Manchester, Manchester, 1988.

MESSINA 1966
Mostra di Filippo Juvarra, architetto e scenografo, catalogue by Vittorio Viale, Palazzo dell'Università, Messina, 1966.

MIDDLETOWN, CONNECTICUT 1969
Italian Master Drawings from the Collection of Janos Scholz, Wesleyan University, Middletown, Connecticut, 1969.

MINNEAPOLIS 1961
The Eighteenth Century: One Hundred Drawings by One Hundred Artists, University of Minnesota Gallery, Minneapolis, 1961.

MONTGOMERY 1976
Venetian Drawings from the Collection of Janos Scholz, cat-

alogue by Diane J. Gingold, Montgomery Museum of Fine Arts, Montgomery, Alabama, 1976.

MONTRÉAL 1989–90

French Architecture in the Age of Jacques-Germain Soufflot, unpublished catalogue by Myra Nan Rosenfeld, Centre Canadien d'Architecture/Canadian Centre for Architecture, Montréal, 1989–90.

NEW HAVEN 1964

Italian Drawings from the Collection of Janos Scholz: A Loan Exhibition, Yale University Art Gallery, New Haven, Connecticut, 1964.

NEW HAVEN 1979

The Fuseli Circle in Rome, Early Romantic Art of the 1770s, catalogue by Nancy L. Pressly, Yale Center for British Art, New Haven, 1979.

NEW YORK 1949

Drawings by Giovanni Battista Piranesi, catalogue by Felice Stampfle, Pierpont Morgan Library, New York, 1949.

NEW YORK 1956–57

Exhibition of Drawings by Old and Modern Masters, Charles E. Slatkin Galleries, New York, 1956–57.

NEW YORK 1959

French Drawings from American Collections: Clouet to Matisse, Metropolitan Museum of Art, New York, 1959.

NEW YORK 1959A

French Master Drawings, Renaissance to Modern: A Loan Exhibition, Charles E. Slatkin Galleries, New York, 1959.

NEW YORK 1961

Paintings and Drawings from the Hanley Collection, Wildenstein and Co., New York, 1961.

NEW YORK 1965

Italian Drawings from the Collection of Janos Scholz, Metropolitan Museum of Art, New York, 1965.

NEW YORK 1967

Master Drawings, Charles E. Slatkin Galleries, New York, 1967.

NEW YORK 1971

Drawings from New York Collections, III: The Eighteenth Century in Italy, catalogue by Jacob Bean and Felice Stampfle, Metropolitan Museum of Art, New York, 1971.

NEW YORK 1972

Giovanni Battista Piranesi: Drawings and Etchings at Columbia University, catalogue by Dorothea Nyberg et al., Avery Architectural Library, Columbia University, New York, 1972.

NEW YORK 1974

Major Acquisitions of the Pierpont Morgan Library, 1924–1974, Pierpont Morgan Library, New York, 1974.

NEW YORK 1975

Architectural and Ornament Drawings: Juvarra, Vanvitelli, the Bibiena Family, & Other Italian Draughtsmen, catalogue by Mary L. Myers, Metropolitan Museum of Art, New York, 1975.

NEW YORK 1978

Artists in Rome in the 18th Century, Metropolitan Museum of Art, New York, 1978.

NEW YORK 1981

European Drawings, 1375–1825, catalogue by Cara D. Denison and Helen B. Mules, with the assistance of Jane V. Shoaf, Pierpont Morgan Library, New York, 1981.

NEW YORK 1983

Early Architecture, Etchings, and Woodcut Illustrations from the 15th to the 18th Century, William H. Schab Gallery, New York, 1983.

NEW YORK 1984

French Drawings, 1550–1825, checklist by Cara D. Denison, Pierpont Morgan Library, New York, 1984.

NEW YORK 1984A

French Master Drawings, catalogue by Beverly Schreiber-Jacoby, Didier Aaron, Inc., New York, 1984.

NEW YORK 1984B

Master Prints & Drawings of Five Centuries, William H. Schab Gallery, New York, 1984.

NEW YORK 1985

French Drawings, 1760–1880, P. & D. Colnaghi & Co., Ltd., New York, 1985.

NEW YORK 1986

Paestum and the Doric Revival, 1750–1830, edited by Joselita Raspi Serra, New York Academy of Design, New York, 1986.

NEW YORK 1986A

Master Prints & Drawings of Five Centuries, William H. Schab Gallery, New York, 1986.

NEW YORK 1988

Master Drawings, 1550–1850, Kate de Rothschild and Didier Aaron, Inc., New York, 1988.

NEW YORK 1989

Exploring Rome: Piranesi and His Contemporaries, Pierpont Morgan Library, New York, 1989.

NEW YORK 1991–92

French Architectural and Ornament Drawings of the Eighteenth Century, catalogue by Mary Meyers, Metropolitan Museum of Art, New York, 1991–92.

NEW YORK 1992–93

Masterworks from the Musée des Beaux-Arts, Lille, Metropolitan Museum of Art, New York, 1992–93.

NEW YORK AND ELSEWHERE 1957

Treasures from the Pierpont Morgan Library: Fiftieth Anniversary Exhibition, Pierpont Morgan Library, New York; Cleveland Museum of Art, Cleveland; Art Institute of Chicago, Chicago; California Palace of the Legion of Honor, San Francisco; Henry E. Huntington Library and Art Gallery, San Marino; Nelson Gallery and Atkins Museum, Kansas City; Museum of Fine Arts of Houston, Houston; Fogg Art Museum, Harvard University, Cambridge, 1957.

NEW YORK AND ELSEWHERE 1975–76

Drawings from the Collection of Mr. and Mrs. Eugene V. Thaw, catalogue by Felice Stampfle and Cara D. Denison, Pierpont Morgan Library, New York; Cleveland Museum of Art, Cleveland; Art Institute of Chicago, Chicago; National Gallery of Canada, Ottawa, 1975–76.

NEW YORK AND PHILADELPHIA 1967

Selections from the Collection of Dr. and Mrs. T. Edward Hanley, Gallery of Modern Art, New York, and Philadelphia Museum of Art, Philadelphia, 1967.

NEW YORK AND RICHMOND 1985–86

Drawings from the Collection of Mr. & Mrs. Eugene Victor Thaw, Part II, catalogue by Cara D. Denison, William Robinson, Julia Herd, and Stephanie Wiles, Pierpont Morgan Library, New York, and Virginia Museum of Fine Arts, Richmond, 1985–86.

NEWARK 1960

Old Master Drawings, Newark Museum, Newark, New Jersey, 1960.

NORTHAMPTON 1961

Piranesi, catalogue by Philip Hofer, Karl Lehmann, Rudolf Wittkower, Smith College Museum of Art, Northampton, Massachusetts, 1961.

NOTRE DAME 1980

Janos Scholz, Musician and Collector, catalogue by Janos Scholz, Snite Museum of Art, University of Notre Dame, Notre Dame, Indiana, 1980.

OAKLAND 1960

Venetian Drawings, 1600–1800, Mills College Art Gallery, Oakland, California, 1960.

OBERLIN 1951

"Exhibition of Master Drawings of the 18th Century in France and Italy," *Bulletin* VIII, Allen Memorial Art Museum, Oberlin College, Oberlin, Ohio, 1951, pp. 50–79.

OTTAWA 1976

European Drawings from Canadian Collections, 1500–1900/ Dessins européens des collections canadiennes, 1500–1900, catalogue by Mary Cazort Taylor, National Gallery of Canada, Ottawa, 1976.

PARIS 1933

Exposition Hubert Robert, catalogue by Charles Sterling, introduction by Pierre de Nolhac, Musée de l'Orangerie, Paris, 1933.

PARIS 1971

François Boucher: Gravures et dessins provenant du Cabinet des Dessins de la Collection Edmond de Rothschild au Musée du Louvre, catalogue by Pierrette Jean-Richard, Musée du Louvre, Paris, 1971.

PARIS 1974

Louis-Jean Desprez, 1743–1804, catalogue by Börje Magnusson, Centre culturel suédois, Hôtel de Marle, Paris, 1974.

PARIS 1979

Charles De Wailly, peintre, architecte dans l'Europe des Lumières, catalogue by Monique Mosser and Daniel Rabreau, Caisse nationale des monuments historiques et des sites, Hôtel de Sully, Paris, 1979.

PARIS 1979A

Le Louvre d'Hubert Robert, catalogue by Marie-Catherine Sahut, Musée du Louvre, Paris, 1979.

PARIS 1980–81

Soufflot et son temps, 1780–1980, Caisse nationale des monuments historiques et des sites, Paris, 1980–81.

PARIS 1984

Acquisitions du Cabinet des Dessins, 1973–1983, Musée du Louvre, Cabinet des Dessins, Paris, 1984.

PARIS 1986

Artistes en voyage au XVIIIe siècle, Galerie Cailleux, Paris and Geneva, 1986.

PARIS 1987

Aspects de Fragonard: Peintures, dessins, estampes, catalogue by Marianne Roland Michel, Galerie Cailleux, Paris, 1987.

PARIS 1990–91

La Rome baroque de Maratti à Piranèse, catalogue by Catherine Legrand and Domitilla d'Ormesson-Peugeot, Musée du Louvre, Paris, 1990–91.

PARIS 1991

Le rouge et le noir: Cent dessins français de 1700 à 1850, catalogue by Marianne Roland Michel, Galerie Cailleux, Paris, 1991.

PARIS 1992

40 Dessins par Hubert Robert, unpublished catalogue by Marianne Roland Michel, 11e Salon du dessin de Collection Hôtel George V, Cailleux, Paris, 1992.

PARIS AND ELSEWHERE 1992–93

Pannini, catalogue by Michael Kiene, Musée du Louvre, Paris; Museo Civico, Piacenza; Herzog Anton Ulrich Museum, Braunschweig, 1992–93.

PARIS AND NEW YORK 1987–88

Fragonard, catalogue by Pierre Rosenberg, Galeries nationales du Grand Palais, Paris, and Metropolitan Museum of Art, New York, 1987–88.

PARIS AND NEW YORK 1993

French Drawings, catalogue by Cara D. Denison, Musée du Louvre, Paris, and Pierpont Morgan Library, New York, 1993.

PHILADELPHIA 1968

Drawings by the Bibiena Family, catalogue by Diane M. Kelder, Philadelphia Museum of Art, Philadelphia, 1968.

PHILADELPHIA 1989

Piranesi, Rome Recorded: A Complete Edition of Giovanni Battista Piranesi's Vedute di Roma *from the Collection of the Arthur Ross Foundation*, University of Pennsylvania, Arthur Ross Gallery, Furness Building, Philadelphia, 1989.

PHILADELPHIA AND DETROIT 1960

The Ruins of Rome, catalogue by Robert C. Smith, University Museum, University of Pennsylvania, Philadelphia, and Detroit Institute of Arts, Detroit, 1960.

POUGHKEEPSIE 1961

Centennial Loan Exhibition, Drawings and Watercolors from Alumnae & their Families, Vassar College, Poughkeepsie, 1961.

RICHMOND, VIRGINIA 1981

Three Masters of Landscape: Fragonard, Robert, and Boucher, Virginia Museum of Fine Arts, Richmond, 1981.

ROME 1967–68

Giovanni Battista e Francesco Piranesi, Calcografia nazionale, Rome, 1967–68.

ROME 1988

Ferdinando Fuga e l'architettura romana del Settecento: I disegni di architettura dalle collezioni del Gabinetto nazionale delle stampe, il Settecento, catalogue by Elisabeth Kieven, Calcografia nazionale, Rome, 1988.

ROME 1990–91

J. H. Fragonard e H. Robert a Roma, catalogue by Jean-Pierre Cuzin, Pierre Rosenberg, and Catherine Bulot, Villa Medici, Rome, 1990–91.

ROME 1991

In urbe architectus: Modelli, disegni, misure: La professione dell'architetto, Roma, 1680–1750, catalogue by Bruno Contardi and Giovanna Curcio, Museo nazionale di Castel Sant'Angelo, Rome, 1991.

ROME 1991A

Architettura del Settecento a Roma nei disegni della Raccolta grafica comunale, catalogue by Elisabeth Kieven, Gabinetto comunale delle stampe in Palazzo Braschi, Rome, 1991.

ROME 1992

Piranesi architetto, catalogue by John Wilton-Ely, American Academy in Rome, Rome, 1992.

ROME AND CORI 1979

Piranesi nei luoghi di Piranesi, Castel Sant'Angelo, S. Maria del Priorato, Orti Farnesiani, and Istituto nazionale per la grafica-calcografia, Rome; Palazzetto Luciani, Cori, 1979.

ROME AND ELSEWHERE 1976

Piranèse et les Français, 1740–1790, Villa Medici, Rome; Palais des États de Bourgogne, Dijon; Hôtel de Sully, Paris, 1976.

ROME AND ELSEWHERE 1988

Feste, fontane, festoni a Parma nel Settecento: Projetti e decorazioni, disegni e incisioni dell'architetto E. A. Petitot (1727–1801), catalogue by Paul Bédarida, introduction by Roberto Tassi, Centre culturel français, Rome; Museo Fondazione Glauco Lombardi, Parma; Musée des arts décoratifs, Lyons, 1988.

ROME AND MOGLIANO VENETO 1989

Piranesi e la veduta del Settecento a Roma, catalogue by A.

Bettagno, G. Perocco, S. Tozzi, A. Marigotta, F. Fiorani, introduction by L. Cavazzi, Palazzo Braschi, Rome, and Villa la Marignana-Benetton, Mogliano Veneto, 1989.

ST. LOUIS 1984

The Spirit of Antiquity: Giovanni Battista Piranesi, Robert Adam, and Charles-Louis Clérisseau, Washington University Gallery of Art, St. Louis, Missouri, 1984.

SAN FRANCISCO 1966

Cathay Invoked: Chinoiserie, a Celestial Empire in the West, California Palace of the Legion of Honor, San Francisco, 1966.

STOCKHOLM 1970

Pierpont Morgan Library gästar Nationalmuseum, Nationalmuseum, Stockholm, 1970.

STOCKHOLM 1992

Louis-Jean Desprez, tecknare, teaterkonstnär, arkitekt, catalogue by Magnus Olausson and Ulf Cederlöf, introduction by Olle Granath, Nationalmuseum, Stockholm, 1992.

STORRS 1973

The Academy of Europe: Rome in the 18th Century, catalogue by Frederick den Broeder, William Benton Museum of Art, University of Connecticut, Storrs, Connecticut, 1973.

VALENCE 1985

Les Hubert Robert de la Collection Veyrenc au Musée de Valence, catalogue by Jean de Cayeux, Musée de Valence, Valence, 1985.

VANCOUVER AND ELSEWHERE 1989–90

18th-Century Venetian Art in Canadian Collections/L'art vénitien du dix-huitième siècle dans les collections canadiennes, catalogue by George Knox, Vancouver Art Gallery, Vancouver, British Columbia; Musée du Québec, Quebec; Agnes Etherington Art Centre, Kingston, Ontario, 1989–90.

VENICE 1957

Catalogue of the Exhibition of Venetian Drawings from the Collection Janos Scholz, catalogue by Michelangelo Muraro, Fondazione Giorgio Cini, Venice, 1957.

VENICE 1978

Disegni di Giambattista Piranesi, catalogue by Alessandro Bettagno, Fondazione Giorgio Cini, Venice, 1978.

WASHINGTON 1976

The Eye of Thomas Jefferson, catalogue by William Howard Adams, National Galley of Art, Washington, 1976.

WASHINGTON 1978

Giovanni Battista Piranesi: The Early Architectural Fantasies, catalogue by Andrew Robison, National Gallery of Art, Washington, 1978.

WASHINGTON 1978A

Hubert Robert: Drawings & Watercolors, catalogue by Victor Carlson, National Gallery of Art, Washington, 1978–79.

WASHINGTON AND ELSEWHERE 1974–75

Venetian Drawings from American Collections: A Loan Exhibition, catalogue and introduction by Terisio Pignatti, International Exhibitions Foundation, National Gallery of Art, Washington; Kimbell Art Museum, Fort Worth, Texas; St. Louis Art Museum, St. Louis, Missouri, 1974–75.

WASHINGTON AND ELSEWHERE 1978–79

Drawings by Fragonard in North American Collections, catalogue by Eunice Williams, National Gallery of Art, Washington; Fogg Art Museum, Harvard University, Cambridge; Frick Collection, New York, 1978–79.

WASHINGTON AND ELSEWHERE 1981–82

French Master Drawings from the Rouen Museum: From Caron to Delacroix, 1981–1982, catalogue by Pierre Rosenberg and François Bergot, International Exhibitions Foundation, National Gallery of Art, Washington; National Academy of Design, New York; Minneapolis Institute of Arts, Minneapolis; J. Paul Getty Museum, Malibu, 1981–82.

WASHINGTON AND ELSEWHERE 1984–85

Watteau, 1684–1721, catalogue by Margaret Morgan Grasselli and Pierre Rosenberg (French edition), National Gallery of Art, Washington; Galeries nationales du Grand Palais, Paris; Schloss Charlottenburg, Berlin, 1984–85.

WATERVILLE 1956

An Exhibition of Drawings, Colby College, Waterville, Maine, 1956.

WELLESLEY AND NEW YORK 1960

Eighteenth-Century Italian Drawings: A Loan Exhibition, Wellesley College, Wellesley, Massachusetts, and Charles E. Slatkin Galleries, New York, 1960.

EXPLORING ROME: PIRANESI AND HIS CONTEMPORARIES

was typeset, printed, and bound by The Stinehour Press in Lunenburg, Vermont. The types used are Minion designed by Robert Slimbach for Adobe Systems Incorporated and Arrighi italic designed by Frederic Warde for the Monotype Corporation. The paper is Mohawk Superfine with Strathmore Pastelle endleaves. The book was designed by Jerry Kelly.